Analyzing Banking Risk

*A Framework for Assessing
Corporate Governance and
Risk Management*

Analyzing Banking Risk

A Framework for Assessing Corporate Governance and Risk Management

3rd Edition

Hennie van Greuning
Sonja Brajovic Bratanovic

THE WORLD BANK
WASHINGTON, D.C.

Design services by EEI Communications

ISBN 978-0-8213-7728-4
eISBN 978-0-8213-7898-4
DOI: 10.1596/978-0-8213-7728-4

Library of Congress Cataloging-in-Publication Data has been requested.

Contents

Boxes

Figures

Tables

Foreword to the Third Edition

Many models exist for analyzing risk of banks and other corporate entities. This publication aims to complement existing methodologies by establishing a comprehensive framework for the assessment of banks, not only by using financial data but also by considering corporate governance. It takes as axiomatic that each of the key players in the corporate governance process (such as shareholders, directors, executive managers, and internal and external auditors) is responsible for some component of financial and operational risk management.

The book uses basic tools and techniques of financial risk analysis principles to demonstrate how data can be converted into information through graphic highlights of risk trends and thereby alert senior management and boards when action may be required.

The financial sector crisis building up since 2007 has brought into stark relief the necessity of an integrated approach to risk management, highlighting key questions that should have been asked and perhaps were never asked. This book demonstrates the power of basic risk management principles in assisting the nonspecialist director, executive, or analyst to integrate various risk areas and ensures that the interrelationships between different risk categories are clearly portrayed. The proposed framework also accommodates the fact that some risks might be immaterial in less sophisticated environments. A detailed questionnaire assists persons involved in performing due diligence or other investigative work on banks.

This third edition of *Analyzing Banking Risk* remains faithful to the objectives of the original. As such, the publication has been useful as a basis for a graduate banking risk analysis course as well as many risk analysis workshops. It now includes expanded material on management of the treasury function, including market performance and risk measurement as well as operational risk management.

This publication emphasizes risk management *principles*, and aims at being useful to a wide body of readers. The target audience remains those responsible for the analysis of banks and for the senior management or organizations directing their efforts. Since the publication provides an overview of the spectrum of corporate governance and risk management, it is not aimed at the narrow technical specialist who focuses on only one particular risk management area.

Kenneth G. Lay, CFA
Treasurer
The World Bank
Washington, D.C.
January 2009

Acknowledgments

The authors are grateful to Ken Lay, vice president and treasurer of the World Bank. He has supported funding of this publication since its first edition.

Many colleagues from the World Bank Treasury contributed to our understanding of the actual processes followed in treasury environments. We are deeply grateful to them for the time they made available and the sharing of materials developed by them.

Hector Sierra reviewed the material on market risk management and contributed to the enhancements of the material on risk and performance measurement practices.

John Gandolfo influenced the approach taken in the chapter on operational risk, by emphasizing the importance of a coherent strategy and governance structure as a prerequisite for effective operational risk management.

Jennifer Johnson-Calari had provided significant technical input as a reviewer and contributor to the material on portfolio management processes.

Despite the extent and quality of the inputs that we have received, we are solely responsible for the contents of this publication.

Hennie van Greuning
Sonja Brajovic Bratanovic

January 2009

Overview of Banking Risks

Key Messages

- This publication will discuss the assessment, analysis, and management of banking risks.
- Banks are exposed to financial, operational and environmental risks.
- A series of key players are accountable for corporate governance and various dimensions of financial risk management.
- Analytical tools provided in this publication include a risk management questionnaire containing data input tables.
- Ratios and graphs provide high-level management information.

1.1 Introduction: The Changing Bank Environment

This publication provides a comprehensive overview of topics related to the assessment, analysis, and management of banking risks and offers a high-level corporate governance framework (aimed at nonspecialist executives). The framework emphasizes the accountability of key players in the corporate governance process in relation to the management of different dimensions of financial risk.

Since the 1980s, rapid innovations in financial markets and the internationalization of financial flows have changed the face of banking almost beyond recognition. Technological progress and deregulation have both provided new opportunities for and increased competitive pressures among banks and nonbanks alike. In the late 1980s, margins attained from traditional banking business began to diminish and capital adequacy requirements began to increase. Banks have responded to these new challenges with vigor and imagination by entering new business areas focusing on superior information and knowledge management capabilities.

The growth in international financial markets and a greater diversity of financial instruments have allowed banks wider access to funds. At the same time, opportunities to design new products and provide more services have arisen. The pace of these changes does not appear to be slowing as banks are constantly involved in developing new instruments, products, and services. Traditional banking practice—based on the receipt of deposits and the granting of loans—is today only one part of a typical bank's business, and it is often its least profitable.

Information-based activities, such as trading in financial markets and income generation through fees, are now the major sources of a bank's profitability. Financial innovation has also led to the increased market orientation and marketability of bank assets, in particular through the introduction of securitization and more advanced derivative products.

The introduction of prudential capital requirements, which initially led to a variety of new "off-balance-sheet" financial instruments, was originally considered a prime motivator for such innovation. Financial derivatives, such as guarantees and letters of credit, as well as derivative instruments, such as futures and options, were not always shown as assets or liabilities even though they exposed banks to major risks. During the past few years, accounting regulators in major countries and the International Accounting Standards Board (IASB) have rectified some deficiencies in accounting practices by requiring all financial instruments to be shown on the balance sheets of entities trading in them.

The correlation between different types of risk, both within an individual bank and throughout the banking system, has therefore increased and become more complex. Internationalization and deregulation have increased the possibilities for contagion, as evidenced by the spread of financial crises from Thailand to the rest of Southeast Asia, to East Asia, Eastern Europe, and South America in the late 1990s, and by their effect on banking systems in the rest of the world. The financial sector crisis starting in 2007, originated in the United States and spread to the European Union and then to the rest of the world. The evolution of banking systems and markets has also raised important macro-prudential concerns and monetary policy issues.

Some instruments are technically very complicated and are poorly understood—except by a small group of experts who have specialized in their valuation, modeling, and measurement—while many others pose complex problems in terms of technology, accounting, and operational risk management and control.

Although techniques for risk management and measurement have advanced, recent failures in accurate pricing of asset-backed products have shown that banking is still exposed to failures on a global scale. Despite the efforts of accounting regulators, adequate disclosure of the nature and extent of these risks to shareholders and boards of directors is still at an early and somewhat experimental stage.

The more general concern that financial innovation in banking may have the effect of concentrating risk and increasing volatility within the banking system as a whole is as relevant at the end of the first decade of the 21st century as it was in the heady days of the late 1990s, when huge profits were made through the financial engineering efforts of innovative finance experts. Recent developments have increased the need for and complicated the function of risk measurement, risk management, and integrated approaches to internal controls. The quality of corporate governance of banks has become a much-debated topic, and the approach to regulation and supervision is changing dramatically.

For the individual bank, the new banking environment and increased market volatility has necessitated an integrated approach to asset-liability and risk management techniques.

1.2 Bank Exposure to Risk

Banks are subjected to a wide array of risks in the course of their operations, as illustrated in table 1.1. In general, banking risks fall into three categories: financial, operational, and environmental risks.

Financial risks in turn comprise two types of risk. Traditional banking risks—including balance sheet and income statement structure, credit, and solvency risks—can result in loss for a bank if they are not properly managed. Treasury risks, based on financial arbitrage, can result in a profit if the arbitrage is correct or a loss if it is incorrect. The main categories of treasury risk are liquidity, interest rate, currency, and market (including counterparty) risks.

Financial risks are also subject to complex interdependencies that may significantly increase a bank's overall risk profile. For example, a bank engaged in the foreign currency business is normally exposed to currency risk, but it will also be exposed to additional liquidity and interest rate risk if the bank carries open positions or mismatches in its forward book.

Operational risks are related to a bank's overall business processes and the potential impact thereon of compliance with bank policies and procedures, internal systems and technology, information security, measures against mismanagement and fraud, and business continuity concerns. Another aspect of operational risk encompasses the bank's strategic planning, governance and organizational structure, management of staff careers and internal resources, product and knowledge development, and customer acquisition approach.

Environmental risks are associated with a bank's business environment, including macroeconomic and policy concerns, legal and regulatory factors, and the overall financial sector infrastructure and payment systems of the jurisdictions in which it operates. Environmental risks include all types of exogenous risks that, if they were to materialize, could jeopardize a bank's operations or undermine its ability to continue in business.

Table 1.1 The Banking Risk Spectrum

Financial Risks	Operational Risks	Environmental Risks
Balance sheet structure	Internal fraud	Country and political risks
Earnings and income statement structure	External fraud	Macroeconomic policy
Capital adequacy	Employment practices and workplace safety	Financial infrastructure
Credit	Clients, products, and business services	Legal infrastructure
Liquidity	Damage to physical assets	Banking crisis and contagion
Market	Business disruption and system failures (technology risks)	
Interest rate	Execution, delivery, and process management	
Currency		

1.3 Corporate Governance

As discussed, liberalization and the volatility of financial markets, increased competition, and diversification expose banks to new risks and challenges, requiring the continuous innovation of ways to manage business and its associated risks in order to remain competitive. The increasing market orientation of banks has also necessitated changes in the approach to regulation and supervision. The responsibility for maintenance of the banking system and markets is being redefined, in one country after another, as a partnership among a number of key players who manage various dimensions of financial and operational risks. This approach reconfirms that the quality of bank management, and especially the risk management process, are the key concerns in ensuring the safety and stability of both individual banks and the banking system as a whole. Table 1.2 portrays a risk management partnership in which each key player has a clearly defined accountability for a specific dimension of every risk area.

The workings of the risk management partnership may be summarized as follows:

Bank regulators and supervisors cannot prevent bank failures. Their primary role is to act as facilitators in the process of risk management and to enhance and monitor the statutory framework in which risk management is undertaken. By creating a sound enabling environment, regulators and supervisors have a crucial role in influencing the other key players.

Shareholders are in a position to appoint the people in charge of the corporate governance process and should be carefully screened by regulators to ensure that they do not intend to use the bank solely to finance their own or their associates' enterprises.

Ultimate responsibility for the way in which a bank's business is conducted lies with the **board of directors** (sometimes called the **supervisory board**). The board has to set the strategic direction, appoint management, establish operational policies, and, most important, take responsibility for ensuring the soundness of a bank.

Executive management of a bank has to be "fit and proper," meaning not only that managers subscribe to standards of ethical behavior, but also that they have the competence and experience necessary to run the bank. Because the management is responsible for the implementation of the board's policies through its day-to-day running of the bank, it is vital that it has intimate knowledge of the financial risks that are being managed.

The **audit committee** and the **internal auditors** should be regarded as an extension of the board's risk management policy function. The internal auditors traditionally performed an independent appraisal of a bank's *compliance* with its internal control systems, accounting practices, and information systems. However, most modern internal auditors would describe their task as providing assurance regarding the bank's corporate governance, control systems, and

Table 1.2 Partnership in Corporate Governance of Banks

Financial and Other Risk Management Areas / Key Players and Responsibilities	Balance Sheet Structure	Income Statement Structure & Profitability	Solvency Risk & Capital Adequacy	Credit Risk	Liquidity Risk	Market Risk	Interest Rate Risk	Currency Risk	Operational Risk
Systemic (key players):	**Accountability (dimension of risk for which key player is responsible)**								
Legal and Regulatory Authorities	Set regulatory framework, including risk exposure limits and other risk management parameters, which will **optimize** risk management in the banking sector								
Supervisory Authorities	**Monitor** financial viability and effectiveness of risk management. Check compliance with regulations								
Institutional (key players):									
Shareholders	**Appoint** "fit and proper" boards, management, and auditors								
Board of Directors	Set risk management and other bank **policies.** Ultimate responsibility for the entity								
Executive Management	Create systems to **implement** board policies, including risk management, in day-to-day operations								
Audit Committee/ Internal Audit	Test **compliance** with board policies and provide assurance regarding corporate governance, control systems, and risk management processes								
External Auditors	Express **opinion** and **evaluate** risk management policies								
Public/Consumer (key players)									
Should demand transparency and full disclosure:									
Investors/Depositors	Understand **responsibility** and insist on full disclosure. Take responsibility for own decisions								
Rating Agencies and Media	Insist on **transparency and full disclosure.** Inform the public and **emphasize ability to service debt**								
Analysts	Analyze **quantitative and non-quantitative risk-based information** and advise clients								

risk management processes. Assurance can be achieved only through an understanding and analysis of the key risk indicators driving the individual processes making up each business line. Although audit committees play a valuable role in assisting management in identifying and addressing risk areas, the prime responsibility for risk management cannot be abdicated to them, but rather should be integrated into all levels of management.

External auditors have come to play an important *evaluative* role in the risk-based financial information process. Because bank supervisors neither can nor should repeat the work done by external auditors, proper liaison mechanisms are necessary between these two parties, particularly on a trilateral basis that includes bank management. The audit approach should be risk oriented, rather than based on a traditional balance sheet and income statement audit. Overreliance on external auditors would weaken the partnership, especially if it leads to a weakening of the management and supervisory roles.

The **public/consumers** as market participants have to accept responsibility for their own investment decisions. To do so, they require transparent disclosure of financial information and informed financial analyses. The public can be assisted in its role as risk manager if the definition of public is widened to include the financial media, financial analysts such as stockbrokers, and rating agencies. The small or unsophisticated depositor would normally need more protection than simply transparent disclosure.

1.4 Risk-Based Analysis of Banks

Banking supervision, which is based on an ongoing analytical review of banks, continues to be one of the key factors in maintaining stability and confidence in the financial system. Chapter 15 explores bank supervision arrangements, the supervision process, and the role of supervisors in ensuring that banks operate in a safe and sound manner—that banks understand and adequately manage risks associated with their operations and that they hold sufficient capital and reserves to support these risks. The methodology used in an analytical review of banks, during the off-site surveillance and on-site supervision process, is similar to that of private sector analysts (for example, external auditors or a bank's risk managers), except that the ultimate objective of the analysis is somewhat different. The analytical framework for the risk-based bank analysis advocated in this publication is therefore universally applicable.

Bank appraisal in a competitive and volatile market environment is a complex process. In addition to effective management and supervision, other factors necessary to ensure the safety of banking institutions and the stability of financial systems and markets include sound and sustainable macroeconomic policies and well-developed and consistent legal frameworks. Adequate financial sector infrastructure, effective market discipline, and sufficient banking sector safety nets are also crucial. To attain a meaningful assessment and interpretation of particular findings, estimates of future potential, a diagnosis of key issues, and formulation of effective and practical courses of action, a bank analyst must have extensive knowledge of the particular regulatory, market, and economic environment in which a bank operates. In short, to be able to do the job well, an analyst must have a holistic perspective on the financial system, even when considering a specific bank.

The practices of bank supervisors and the appraisal methods practiced by financial analysts continue to evolve. This evolution is necessary in part to meet the challenges of innovation and new developments, and in part to accommodate the broader process of convergence of international supervisory standards and practices, which are themselves continually discussed by the Basel Committee on Banking Supervision. Traditional banking analysis has been based on a range of quantitative supervisory tools to assess a bank's condition, including ratios. Ratios normally relate to liquidity, the adequacy of capital, loan portfolio quality, insider and connected lending, large exposures, and open foreign exchange positions. While these measurements are extremely useful, they are not in themselves an adequate indication of the risk profile of a bank, the stability of its financial condition, or its prospects. The picture reflected by financial ratios also largely depends on the timeliness, completeness, and accuracy of data used to compute them. For this reason, the importance of quality data that is both useful and transparent is discussed in chapter 14. Chapter 14 also attempts to add another dimension to the issue of transparency, that is, accountability, which has become an important topic because of both the increasing importance of corporate governance and risk management for modern financial institutions and bank supervisors (considered in chapters 3 and 15).

The central technique for analyzing financial risk is the detailed review of a bank. Risk-based bank analysis includes important qualitative factors and places financial ratios within a broad framework of risk assessment, risk management, and changes or trends in such risks. Risk-based bank analysis also underscores the relevant institutional aspects. Such aspects include the quality and style of corporate governance and management; the adequacy, completeness, and consistency of a bank's policies and procedures; the effectiveness and completeness of internal controls; and the timeliness and accuracy of management information systems and information support.

It has been said that risk rises exponentially with the pace of change, but that bankers are slow to adjust their perception of risk. In practical terms, this implies that the market's ability to innovate is in most circumstances greater than its ability to understand and properly accommodate the accompanying risk. Traditionally, banks have seen the management of credit risk as their most important task, but as banking has changed and the market environment has become more complex and volatile, the critical need to manage exposure to other operational and financial risks has become apparent. The elements of the risk-based analytical review covered in this publication are summarized in table 1.2. Chapter 4 discusses the overall structure of a bank's balance sheet and focuses on the imbalances and mismatches in balance sheet structure that expose a bank to financial risk. Aspects of profitability, including management of a bank's income and expenses, is elaborated in chapter 5. Chapter 6 considers capital adequacy and the quality of a bank's capital, while chapter 7 covers credit risk management, including aspects of portfolio composition and quality and related policies and procedures. Components of the asset-liability management process (liquidity risk, interest rate risk, and currency risk) are discussed in chapters 8 to 12; management of the liquidity portfolio in chapter 9; and market risk in chapter 10. Operational risk is covered in chapter 13. Numerous graphs and tables facilitate the understanding of these subjects. Although the discussions and information contained in the graphs and tables in chapters 4 through 12 refer mainly to individual institutions, the same type of analysis can be conducted at the industry level.

This publication pays special attention to risk exposures and the quality and effectiveness of a bank's risk management processes. Risk management normally involves several steps for each type of financial risk and for the overall risk profile. These steps include the identification of an objective function, the risk management target, and measure of performance. Also important is the identification and measurement of specific risk exposures in relation to the selected objective function, including assessment of the sensitivity of performance to expected and unexpected changes in underlying factors. Decisions must also be made on the acceptable degree of risk exposure and on the methods and instruments to hedge excessive exposure, as well as on choosing and executing hedging transactions. In addition, the responsibilities for various aspects of risk management must be assigned, the effectiveness of the risk management process assessed, and the competent and diligent execution of responsibilities ensured.

Where appropriate, a bank should be analyzed as both a single entity and on a consolidated basis, taking into account exposures of subsidiaries and other related enterprises at home and abroad. A holistic perspective is necessary when assessing a bank on a consolidated basis, especially in the case of institutions that are spread over a number of jurisdictions and/or foreign markets. A broad view serves to accommodate variations in the features of specific financial risks that are present in different environments.

A risk-based bank analysis should also indicate whether an individual institution's behavior is in line with peer group trends and industry norms, particularly when it comes to significant issues such as profitability, structure of the balance sheet, and capital adequacy. A thorough analysis can indicate the nature of and reasons for any deviations. A material change in risk profile experienced by an individual institution could be the result of unique circumstances that have no impact on the banking sector as a whole, or it could be an early indicator of trends that might be followed by other banks.

1.5 Analytical Tools Provided

Each analysis may be unique, but the overall analytical process has many consistent aspects with regard to off-site surveillance, on-site examination, a bank's own risk management, or evaluation by technical professionals. This publication provides tools to assist with the bank analysis, including a questionnaire and a series of spreadsheet-based data input tables to enable an analyst to collect and manipulate data in a systematic manner (appendix 1). This publication is not a manual on how to use the tools, but a conceptual framework to explain the background to the tools.

Questionnaire to facilitate the risk-based analysis of banks. The questionnaire and data tables should be completed by the bank being evaluated. The questions (see appendix A) are designed to capture management's perspective on and understanding of the bank's risk management process. The background and financial information requested in the questionnaire should provide an overview of the bank to allow for assessment of the quality and comprehensiveness of bank policies, management, and control processes, as well as financial and management information. Questions fall into several categories:

- Institutional development needs

- Overview of the financial sector and regulation

- Overview of the bank (history and group and organizational structure)

- Accounting systems, management information and internal controls, and information technology

- Corporate governance, covering certain key players and accountabilities

- Risk management, including balance sheet structure management, earnings and income statement structure, credit risk, and the other major types of financial and operational risk discussed in chapters 4 through 13

Data input tables. The framework contains a series of input tables for financial data collection. The data can be manipulated into either ratios or graphs. The tables are related to the major financial risk management areas. The balance sheet and income statement serve as anchor schedules, with detail provided by all the other schedules. These tables can be easily modeled using commonly available spreadsheet software to produce ratios, statistical tables, and graphs, which can assist executives in the interpretation and analysis of a bank's financial risk management process and its financial condition.

The use of ratio analysis and graphs is discussed in chapter 2. Ratios are a basic tool for financial analysts and are essential to examine the effectiveness of a bank's risk management process. They are normally the initial points that provide clues for further analysis. Changes in ratios over time offer a dynamic view of bank performance. The outputs of the framework include ratios on balance sheet structure, profitability, capital adequacy, credit and market risk, liquidity, and currency risk. These make up a complete set of a bank's ratios that are normally subject to off-site surveillance. The framework therefore serves as an effective tool to be used in bank supervision.

Graphs. Graphs are powerful tools for analyzing trends and structures. They facilitate comparison of performance and structures over time, showing trend lines and changes in significant aspects of bank operations and performance. In addition, they provide senior management with a high-level overview of risk trends in a bank. Samples of graphs illustrate discussions on risk exposure and risk management in chapters 4 through 13 of this publication. These pertain to asset and liability structures; sources of income; profitability and capital adequacy; composition of loan portfolios; major types of credit risk exposures; and exposure to interest rate, liquidity, market, and currency risk. The graphs produced by the model may also be used during off-site surveillance. In this context, they can serve as a starting point to help with on-site examination and to succinctly present the bank's financial condition and risk management aspects to senior management. They can also help to illustrate points made by external auditors in their presentation to management or by other industry professionals who intend to judge a bank's condition and prospects.

Table 1.3 illustrates the more general use of the analytical tools provided with this publication.

Table 1.3 Possible Uses of Tools Provided

Analytical Phase	Source and Tools Available	Output
Data collection	Questionnaire	Completed input data, questionnaires, and financial data tables
	Financial data tables	
Data processing	Completed input data, questionnaires, and financial data tables	Data processed by the model
Analysis and interpretation of both processed and original input data	Data converted into information	Analytical results (output summary report, tables, and graphs)
Off-site (desk) analysis of a bank's financial condition	Analytical results	Report on a bank's financial condition, risk management, and/or terms of reference for on-site examination
Focused follow-up through an on-site visit, audit, or review engagement	Off-site examination report and/or terms of reference for on-site examination	On-site examination report
Institutional strengthening	On-site examination report	Well-functioning financial intermediary

2

A Framework for Risk Analysis

Key Messages

- The goal of financial management is to maximize the value of a bank.

- The central components of risk management are the identification, quantification, and monitoring of the risk profile.

- The analysis of banks must take place in the context of the current status of a country's financial system.

- Financial sector development encompasses several steps that must be taken to ensure that institutions operate in a stable and viable macropolicy environment with a solid legal, regulatory, and financial infrastructure.

- Risk-based financial analysis requires a framework for transparent disclosure.

- Analytical techniques facilitate an understanding of interrelationships between risk areas within the bank and among different banks.

- Trend analysis provides information regarding the volatility and movement of an individual bank's financial indicators over different time periods.

- The percentage composition of the balance sheet, income statement, and various account groupings enables comparison between time periods, and also between different banking institutions at a given point in time.

- Ratios are often interrelated, and when analyzed in combination, they provide useful risk information. Computation of ratios and trends provides an answer only to what has happened.

2.1 Financial Management

The goal of financial management is to maximize the value of a bank, as defined by its profitability and risk level. Financial management comprises risk management, a treasury function, financial planning and budgeting, accounting and information systems, and internal controls. In practical terms, the key aspect of financial management is risk management, which covers strategic and capital planning, asset-liability management, and the management of a bank's business and financial risks. The central components of risk management are the identification, quantification, and monitoring of the risk profile, including both banking and financial risks.

Risk management normally involves several steps for each type of financial risk and for the risk profile overall. These steps include identifying the risk management objective, risk management targets, and measures of performance. Also important are the identification and measurement of specific risk exposures, including an assessment of the sensitivity of performance to expected and unexpected changes in underlying factors. Decisions must also be made regarding the acceptable degree of risk exposure, the methods and instruments available to hedge excessive exposure, and the choice and execution of hedging transactions. In addition, the responsibility for various aspects of risk management must be assigned, the effectiveness of the risk management process must be assessed, and the competent and diligent execution of responsibilities must be ensured.

Effective risk management, especially for larger banks and for banks operating in deregulated and competitive markets, requires a formal process. In developing economies, especially those in transition, unstable, economically volatile, and shallow market environments significantly expand the range and magnitude of exposure to financial risk. Such conditions render risk management even more complex and make the need for an effective risk management process even more acute. The key components of effective risk management that should be present in a bank and be assessed by the analyst normally include the following:

- An established line function at the highest level of the bank's management hierarchy that is specifically responsible for managing risk and possibly also for coordinating the operational implementation of the policies and decisions of the asset-liability committee. The risk management function should be on par with other major functions and be accorded the necessary visibility and leverage within the bank.

- An established, explicit, and clear risk management strategy and a related set of policies with corresponding operational targets. There are various risk management strategies which have originated from different approaches to interpreting interdependencies between risk factors and differences of opinion concerning the treatment of volatility in risk management.

■ An appropriate degree of formalization and coordination of strategic decision making in relation to the risk management process. Relevant risk management concerns and parameters for decision making on the operational level should be incorporated for all relevant business and functional processes. Parameters for the main financial risk factors (normally established according to the risk management policies of a bank and expressed as ratios or limits) can serve as indicators to business units of what constitutes acceptable risk. For example, a debt-to-equity ratio for a bank's borrowers expresses a level of credit risk. Maximum exposure to a single client is a risk parameter that indicates credit risk in a limited form.

■ Implementation of a process that bases business and portfolio decisions on rigorous quantitative and qualitative analyses within applicable risk parameters. This process, including analysis of a consolidated risk profile, is necessary because of the complex interdependencies of and the need to balance various financial risk factors. Because the risk implications of a bank's financial position and changes to that position are not always obvious, details may be critically important.

■ Systematic gathering of complete, timely, and consistent data relevant for risk management and provision of adequate data storage and manipulation capacity. Data should cover all functional and business processes, as well as other areas such as macroeconomic and market trends that may be relevant to risk management.

■ Development of quantitative modeling tools to enable the simulation and analysis of the effects of changes in economic, business, and market environments on a bank's risk profile and their impact on the bank's liquidity, profitability, and net worth. Computer models used by banks range from simple personal computer–based tools to elaborate mainframe modeling systems. Such models can be built in-house or be acquired from other financial institutions with a similar profile, specialized consulting firms, or software vendors. The degree of sophistication and analytical capacity of such models may indicate early on the seriousness of the bank's efforts to manage risk.

The Basel Capital Accord heightens the importance of quantitative modeling tools and the bank's capacity to use them, as they will provide a basis for implementing the internal ratings-based (IRB) approach to measuring a bank's capital adequacy.

2.2 Why Banks Are Analyzed

The changing environment in which banks find themselves presents major opportunities for banks, but also entails complex, variable risks that challenge traditional approaches to bank management. Consequently, banks must quickly gain financial risk management capabilities to survive in a market-oriented environment, withstand competition by foreign banks, and support private sector–led economic growth.

An external evaluation of the capacity of a bank to operate safely and productively in its business environment is normally performed once each year. All annual assessments are similar in nature, but have slightly different focuses, depending on the purpose of the assessment:

- Public sector supervisory (regulatory) authorities assess if the bank is viable, meets its regulatory requirements, and is sound and capable of fulfilling financial commitments to its depositors and other creditors. Supervisory authorities also verify whether the bank's operations are likely to jeopardize the safety of the banking system as a whole.

- External auditors, who are normally retained by the bank's board of directors, seek to ensure that financial statements fairly present the bank's financial position and the results of its operations. In addition, regulatory authorities in many countries require external auditors to assess whether management meets predetermined risk management standards and to evaluate whether a bank's activities expose the bank's capital to undue risks. Banks are normally required to undergo an external audit that involves at least year-end financial statements and that is considered satisfactory to supervisory authorities.

The financial viability and institutional weaknesses of a bank are also evaluated through financial assessments, extended portfolio reviews, or limited assurance review engagements. Such evaluations often occur when a third party evaluates credit risk that the bank poses, for example, in the context of

- participation in a credit-line operation of an international lending agency or receipt of a credit line or loan from a foreign bank;

- establishment of correspondent banking relationships or access to international markets;

- equity investment by an international lending agency, private investors, or foreign banks; or

■ inclusion in a bank rehabilitation program.

The bank appraisal process normally includes an assessment of the institution's overall risk profile, financial condition, viability, and future prospects. The appraisal comprises off- and on-site examinations to the extent considered necessary. If serious institutional weaknesses are found, supervisory authorities may recommend appropriate corrective actions. If the institution is not considered viable in its current condition, supervisory authorities may suggest actions to restore viability or to lead to the bank's liquidation and closure. The bank review also assesses if the condition of the institution can be remedied with reasonable assistance or if it presents a hazard to the banking sector as a whole.

The conclusions and recommendations of a bank appraisal are typically expressed in a letter to shareholders, a memorandum of understanding, or as an institutional development program. The most common objective of the latter is to describe priorities for improvement, as identified in the analyst's review, that would yield the greatest benefit to the institution's financial performance. To the extent considered necessary, such recommendations are accompanied by supporting documentation, flowcharts, and other relevant information about current practices. The institutional development program often serves as the basis for discussions among the institution's management, government officials, and international lending agencies, which in turn launch implementation of recommended improvements and decide what technical assistance is needed.

The process of bank analysis also occurs within the context of monetary policy making. Central banks have a mission to maintain a stable currency and economy. Three interrelated functions are critical to monetary stability: the implementation of monetary policy, the supervision of banks, and monitoring of the payments system. All three functions must take place to ensure stability. Banking supervision therefore cannot be divorced from the wider mission of monetary authorities. Although the attention of central banking policy focuses on the macroeconomic aspect of general equilibrium and price stability, micro considerations of individual banks' liquidity and solvency are key to attaining stability.

2.3 Understanding the Environment in Which Banks Operate

The compilation and analysis of risk management information from banks is a key task of bank supervisors and financial analysts. For bank management, financial analysts, bank supervisors, and monetary authorities, a risk-based analytical review of individual banks' financial data provides information on the banking sector as a whole, as market trends and relationships are highlighted.

Sectoral analysis is important because it allows norms to be established for the sector as a whole, as well as for a peer group within the sector. The performance of individual banking institutions can then be evaluated on the basis of these norms. Deviations from expected trends and relationships may be analyzed further as they may disclose not only the risk faced by individual banks, but also changes in the financial environment of the banking sector as a whole. By examining sector statistics, an analyst can gain an understanding of changes that are occurring in the industry and of the impact of such changes on economic agents and sectors.

Because banks participate in both the domestic and international financial systems and play a key role in national economies, banking statistics can provide an insight into economic conditions. Financial innovation normally results in changes to measured economic variables, and as a result of this dynamism in the financial system, macroeconomists may find their monetary models no longer reflect reality.

The impact of banking activities on monetary statistics, such as money supply figures and credit extension to the domestic private sector, is also of concern to policy makers. Reviews of banks can serve as a structured mechanism to ensure that monetary authorities recognize and quantify nonintermediated funding and lending, as well as other processes that are important to policy makers in the central bank. The advantage of a structured approach to evaluating banks is that banking sector behavior is considered in a systematic and logical manner, making sector statistics readily available for macroeconomic monetary analysis. Bank supervisors are thereby placed in a position where they are able to meaningfully assist monetary authorities, whose policies are influenced by developments in the banking sector.

Financial System Infrastructure

Bank appraisal in a competitive and volatile market environment is a complex process. The assessment of a bank's financial condition and viability normally centers around the analysis of particular aspects, including ownership structure, risk profile and management, financial statements, portfolio structure and quality, policies and practices, human resources, and information capacity.

To interpret particular findings, estimate future potential, diagnose key issues, and formulate effective and practical courses of action, an analyst must also have thorough knowledge of the particular regulatory, market, and economic environment in which a bank operates. In sum, to do his or her job well, an analyst must have a holistic view of the financial system.

An environment that includes a poor legal framework, difficulties with the enforcement of financial contracts, or unstable macroeconomic conditions presents a higher level of credit risk and makes risk management more difficult. For example, an unstable domestic currency that lacks external convertibility presents a high level of risk. A bank's overall business strategy and its specific policies and practices must both accommodate the economic and regulatory environment within which the bank operates and be attuned to market realities.

Figure 2.1 illustrates the building blocks that are required for sustainable financial sector development and a context for assessing financial risk and risk management.

An unstable **macroeconomic environment**, with uneven economic performance and volatile exchange rates and asset prices, is a principal cause of instability in the financial system. Such an environment makes the realistic valuation of a bank's assets and the accurate evaluation of financial risks very difficult. The political environment is also important because it influences both the principles and the reality under which the financial sector functions. For example, under centrally planned financial systems, markets were greatly limited and banks, as well as their clients, did not have autonomy. **Legal and judicial environments** directly affect many aspects of a bank's operations, such as exercising contractual rights to obtain collateral or to liquidate nonpaying borrowers. A transparent accountability framework establishes the foundation for a well-functioning business environment for banks and other institutions in the financial sector, as well as for their clients.

The **legal and regulatory framework** for **institutions, markets, contracting and conduct**, and **failure resolution** spells out the rules of the game for financial institutions and markets. Before appraising a bank, an analyst should understand the philosophical basis for pertinent laws and regulations and ascertain if the legal and regulatory framework is complete and consistent. The analyst should be thoroughly familiar with the framework not only because bank operations must comply with it, but also because it provides a context for a bank's business, including the objectives and scope of allowed activities. In

Figure 2.1 A Framework for Financial Sector Development

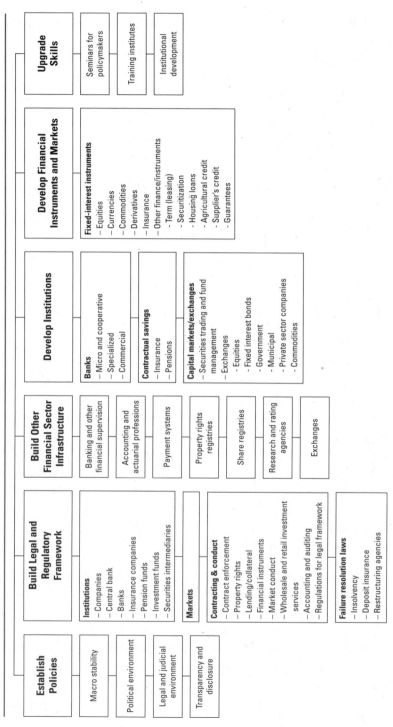

Establish Policies
- Macro stability
- Political environment
- Legal and judicial environment
- Transparency and disclosure

Build Legal and Regulatory Framework

Institutions
- Companies
- Central bank
- Banks
- Insurance companies
- Pension funds
- Investment funds
- Securities intermediaries

Markets

Contracting & conduct
- Contract enforcement
- Property rights
- Lending/collateral
- Financial instruments
- Market conduct
- Wholesale and retail investment services
- Accounting and auditing
- Regulations for legal framework

Failure resolution laws
- Insolvency
- Deposit insurance
- Restructuring agencies

Build Other Financial Sector Infrastructure
- Banking and other financial supervision
- Accounting and actuarial professions
- Payment systems
- Property rights registries
- Share registries
- Research and rating agencies
- Exchanges

Develop Institutions

Banks
- Micro and cooperative
- Specialized
- Commercial

Contractual savings
- Insurance
- Pensions

Capital markets/exchanges
- Securities trading and fund management
- Exchanges
  - Equities
  - Fixed interest bonds
  - Government
  - Municipal
  - Private sector companies
  - Commodities

Develop Financial Instruments and Markets

Fixed-interest instruments
- Equities
- Currencies
- Commodities
- Derivatives
- Insurance
- Other finance/instruments
  - Term (leasing)
  - Securitization
  - Housing loans
  - Agricultural credit
  - Supplier's credit
  - Guarantees

Upgrade Skills
- Seminars for policymakers
- Training institutes
- Institutional development

addition, knowledge of laws and regulations can prompt measures and actions that can be taken in crisis situations.

Key elements of the **institutional legal framework** of the banking system include the central bank law and the banking law. The former defines the central bank's level of autonomy, systemic and functional responsibilities (which often include prudential supervision), regulatory prerogatives, and enforcement powers. The banking law defines the type of financial intermediation to be performed by banks (for example, universal banking), the scope of banking business in the particular country, conditions of entry and exit from the banking system, and capital and other minimum requirements that must be met and maintained by banks. In addition, the banking law specifies the corporate organization and the relationship between banks and the central bank.

Another important element of the legal and regulatory framework involves prudential regulations issued by the regulatory authorities. The objectives underlying such regulations include maintenance of the safety and stability of the banking system, depositor protection, and the minimal engagement of public funds. The most important prudential regulations include bank licensing, corporate governance, closure and exit mechanisms, capital adequacy, and financial risk management. Financial risk management regulations (as elaborated in chapters 4 through 13) aim to limit the degree of a bank's risk exposure, such as through foreign exchange and liquidity. Such measures ensure that a bank has sufficient capital to support its exposure to risk (also known as "capital adequacy requirements") and that it has adequate procedures or systems to assess and hedge and provide against risks, such as asset classification and provisioning procedures and value-at-risk models for market price fluctuations.

A legal framework also encompasses other sections of the financial sector through laws pertaining to insurance companies, pension funds, capital **market authorities**, and the wholesale and retail investment services industry. To protect consumers, a body of laws also exists to regulate contracting and market conduct and behavior.

Other relevant laws relate to **failure resolution**—for example, insolvency, deposit insurance, and restructuring agencies—and to the technical capacity of the judiciary. The mechanisms for failure resolution and the banking sector safety net are intended to enhance the stability of and confidence in the banking system; however, if they are poorly designed, they can undermine market discipline. Elements of the banking safety net include the "lender-of-last-resort" function and deposit-insurance facilities. The specific form of a banking safety net has significant implications for risk management. For example, the existence of lender-of-last-resort facilities—the main purpose of which is to provide temporary liquidity support to illiquid but solvent institutions—may weaken risk management incentives for banks, which tend to maintain less liquidity and lend more when these facilities are in place. Likewise, the existence of deposit insurance, especially where the cost is underwritten by the state, may engender situations of moral hazard, such as the automatic bailout of banks, regardless of the quality of corporate governance or the status of financial risk management.

Financial sector infrastructure strongly influences the quality of bank operations and risk management. Apart from the **supervisory authorities** (discussed in chapter 3), the **payment system**, a key element of financial sector infrastructure, may be organized and managed by the central bank, by members of the banking system, or as an arrangement between individual banks and the central bank. The specific organization of the payment system determines the mechanisms for payment transactions. An inefficient payment system can result in significant cost and settlement risk to the banks.

Infrastructure also encompasses various professions that are central to the financial sector, such as **accounting and auditing**, the actuarial profession, and investment advising. Adherence to international standards of accounting and auditing, coupled with a well-trained cadre of professionals in these fields, can make a significant difference to the fairness and transparency of financial statements. Fair, transparent statements greatly contribute to the facilitation of risk management, bank supervision, and consumer protection.

Property registries are also a part of risk management infrastructure. Such registers define fixed and movable assets and marketable securities and effectively protect property rights. They also facilitate the registration and collection of collateral and subsequent credit risk management. Risk reference registers serve the same purpose through the collection and maintenance of information on the credit history of individuals and firms, which are readily distributed to interested parties.

In addition, **rating agencies** help with risk management by systematically researching banks, companies, and markets and making findings available to both financial professionals and the general public. In many countries, financial infrastructure may also include research institutes, financial advisory services, and similar establishments.

Development of institutions includes forms and rules under which a particular financial institution can be incorporated and, on a broader scale, identifies its potential competitors. Increased competition in banking and finance and the trend toward homogenization of banking business have been major factors that influence changes in national banking systems. The concept of universal banking and the reality of financial markets have, however, increasingly blurred the lines between various institutions. In the context of risk management, the structure and concentration of ownership are key. A banking system dominated by state-owned banks or financial institutions is prone to moral hazard situations, such as implicit guarantees, and tends to have competitive distortions in its markets. A high concentration of ownership or assets also increases risk by subjecting the system to political pressures, because some banks are considered by government entities to be "too big to fail" and may therefore be artificially supported. In exceptional cases where systemic risk is at stake, a supervisory authority may choose to support the too-big-to-fail approach. In addition, the absence of foreign ownership typically indicates closed and inefficient financial markets.

Financial markets and instruments depicts the markets operating in the financial system, their modi operandi, and the terms of their operations. As mentioned previously, modern banks have moved beyond traditional deposit and credit markets to establish a direct presence in practically all aspects of the financial system. Originally established as specialized institutions, banks have sought new customers in wider geographical areas and have come to offer increasingly similar types of accounts, credit, and financial services.

In addition to more intense competition among the different types of banks, the number and diversity of nonbank financial intermediaries have also increased. As a result, effective substitutes for banking products now exist and a broader range of services is available. The threat that nonbanking institutions will expand into banking services has likely been another stimulus for banks to adopt market-oriented behavior. Secondary markets have also grown in importance, which has reduced market segmentation and created more uniform cost structures for different financial institutions.

Each type of market deals with specific financial products. Innovation has brought about a greater variety of financial instruments, the respective markets of which are continuously increasing. In financial risk management terms, the understanding of the risk involved in key products offered by a bank and of the implications of specific markets—for example, in terms of liquidity or price stability—is key to being able to adequately appraise a bank.

The availability and quality of **banking skills** is a central concern in the risk-based appraisal of banks. It is essential that banks have good personnel management and that they are able to systematically develop banking skills within their organization. A good bank should be able to acquire the appropriate skills and to develop a suitable work culture. It should also have a process to optimize the mix of staff skills and experience and to develop staff performance levels in concert with its business and institutional goals.

2.4 The Importance of Quality Data

The objective of financial statements prepared according to International Financial Reporting Standards (IFRS) and Generally Accepted Accounting Principles (GAAP) is to increase transparency and provide information that is useful in making economic decisions. However, even financial statements prepared to exacting international norms do not contain all the information that an individual may need to perform all kinds of risk analysis, because financial statements largely portray the effects of past events and do not necessarily provide nonfinancial information. Nonetheless, IFRS statements do contain data about the *past* performance of an entity (income and cash flows) as well as its current financial condition (assets and liabilities) that are useful in assessing future prospects and risks. The financial analyst must be capable of using the financial statements in conjunction with other information to reach valid investment conclusions.

Financial statement analysis (analytic review) normally consists of a review of financial conditions and specific issues related to risk exposure and risk management. Such reviews can be done off-site, whereas an on-site review would cover a much larger number of topics and be more concerned with qualitative aspects, including quality of corporate governance, physical infrastructure, and management's use of sound management information.

A reliable assessment of the financial condition of banks requires well-trained analysts and supervisors because many bank assets are illiquid and lack an objectively determined market value. New financial instruments make it even more complex to assess the net worth of banks and other financial institutions in a timely manner. The liberalization of banking and capital markets has substantially increased the level of information required to achieve financial stability, while the provision of useful, adequate information on participants and their transactions has become essential for maintaining orderly and efficient markets. For a risk-based approach to bank management and supervision to be effective, useful and timely information must be provided that meets the needs of each key player (see chapter 3). In principle, market participants, depositors, and the general public have no less a need for information than do supervisory authorities.

In theory, the disclosure of information can be gradually improved indirectly through peer pressure from powerful parties in the marketplace. During normal times, such pressure might show banks that disclosure is to their advantage in raising funds, for example, if it prompts potential investors and depositors to provide capital. The desire to hide information—especially that which conveys poor results—unfortunately often translates into a lack of transparency, which is evident even in economies with advanced banking systems. Furthermore, given the sensitivity of bank liquidity to a negative public perception, the information with the strongest potential to trigger sudden and detrimental market reactions is generally disclosed at the last possible moment, usually involuntarily.

Calls for greater transparency often indicate a failure to provide useful and timely information, and this is most acute when the information sought or provided is negative. Regulatory authorities have a responsibility to address the availability of information. While banking legislation has traditionally been used as a way to force disclosure of information, this process has historically involved the compilation of statistics for monetary policy purposes, rather than the provision of information necessary to evaluate financial risks.

A more direct approach, now practiced by most regulatory authorities, involves mandating minimum disclosure, including a requirement that banks publish specified portions of their prudential reports (which do not reveal information that can be used by competitors) and other pertinent information. The value of disclosure depends largely on the quality of the information itself. However, because the provision of information can be costly, information needs have to be examined closely to ensure that the detriments of disclosure are fully justified by its benefits.

Financial disclosure requirements normally focus on the publication of quantitative and qualitative information in a bank's annual financial report, prepared on a consolidated basis and made available to all market participants. The format for disclosure typically mandates a complete, audited set of financial statements, as well as qualitative information such as a discussion of management issues and general strategy. Disclosed information provides the names, interests, and affiliations of the largest shareholders and nonexecutive board members and information on corporate structure; it also clarifies which parts of the financial statements have been audited and, in supplementary disclosures, which have not. Financial statements also contain information on off-balance-sheet items, including quantitative estimates of exposure to shifts in interest or exchange rates.

In addition to minimum disclosure requirements, financial sector disclosure can be improved by the formulation of standards on the quality and quantity of information that must be provided to the public. Given the increasing internationalization of banks and the increasing penetration of national banking systems, there is a strong need for minimum standards to ensure the cross-border comparability of financial statements. This responsibility has been taken by the International Accounting Standards Committee, which has developed a set of international standards to facilitate transparency and the proper interpretation of financial statements. (Full discussion of data quality, transparency, and related accountability issues, including details on international financial reporting standards, is provided in chapter 14.)

Disclosure requirements have to be reviewed periodically to ensure that users' current needs are being met and that the burden on banks is not unnecessarily heavy. Because financial innovations and international influences are likely to expand information requirements, demands made on banks show no sign of diminishing in the future. However, a reliance on full disclosure as a means of monitoring banks requires too much of depositors, who would need an increasing level of analytical sophistication to be able to evaluate the complex business of financial institutions. Furthermore, economies of scale exist in the processing and interpretation of financial information. In the future, professional financial market analysts, rating agencies (which are capable of handling sophisticated financial information), and the highly influential media are expected to play an increasingly important role in applying market discipline to influence or to correct bank behavior.

2.5 Risk-Based Analysis of Banks

The practices of bank supervisors and the appraisal methods of financial analysts continue to evolve. This evolution is necessary in part to meet the challenges of innovation and new developments, and in part to accommodate the broader convergence of international supervisory standards and practices, which are themselves continually discussed by the Basel Committee on Banking Supervision. Traditional banking analysis is based on a range of quantitative supervisory tools for assessing a bank's condition, including ratios. Ratios normally relate to liquidity, the adequacy of capital, quality of the investment portfolio, extent of insider and connected lending, size of exposures, and open foreign exchange positions. While these measurements are extremely useful, they are not in themselves an adequate indication of the risk profile of a bank, the stability of its financial condition, or its prospects.

The central technique for analyzing financial risk is the detailed review of a bank's balance sheet. Risk-based bank analysis includes important qualitative factors and places financial ratios within a broad framework of risk assessment and management and the changes or trends in risks. It also underscores the relevant institutional aspects, such as the quality and style of corporate governance and management; the adequacy, completeness, and consistency of a bank's policies and procedures; the effectiveness and completeness of internal controls; and the timeliness and accuracy of management information systems and information support.

Where appropriate, a bank should be analyzed as both a single entity and on a consolidated basis, taking into account exposures of subsidiaries and other related enterprises at home and abroad. A holistic perspective is necessary when assessing a bank on a consolidated basis, especially if the institution is spread over a number of jurisdictions or foreign markets. A broad view accommodates variations in the features of specific financial risks that are present in different environments.

A risk-based analysis should also indicate whether an individual institution's behavior is in line with peer group trends and industry norms, particularly when it comes to significant issues such as profitability, structure of the balance sheet, and capital adequacy. A thorough analysis can indicate the nature of and reasons for such deviations. A material change in risk profile experienced by an individual institution could be the result of unique circumstances that have no impact on the banking sector as a whole or could be an early indicator of trends.

The picture reflected by financial ratios also depends largely on the timeliness, completeness, and accuracy of data used to compute them. For this reason, the issue of usefulness and transparency is critical, as is accountability, which has become an important topic because of both the growing importance of risk management for modern financial institutions and the emerging philosophy of supervision.

Computation versus Analysis: The Importance of Integrated Financial Analysis

Financial analysis applies analytical tools to financial statements and other financial data to interpret trends and relationships in a consistent and disciplined manner. In essence, the analyst converts data into information and thereby enables the screening and forecasting of information. A primary source of data is the entity's financial statements.

Integrating the various analytical components and techniques discussed in this chapter will distinguish a well-reasoned analysis from a mere compilation of various pieces of information, computations, tables, and graphs. The challenge is for the analyst to develop a storyline, providing context (country, macro-economy, sector, accounting, auditing, and industry regulation, as well as any material limitations on the entity being analyzed), a description of corporate governance, and financial and operational risk and then relating the different areas of analysis by identifying how issues affect one another.

Before starting, the analyst should attempt to answer at least the following questions:

- What is the purpose of the analysis?
- What level of detail will be needed?
- What factors or relationships (context) will influence the analysis?
- What data are available?
- How will data be processed?
- What methodologies will be used to interpret the data?
- How will conclusions and recommendations be communicated?

Too much of what passes for analysis is simply the calculation of a series of ratios and verification of compliance with preset covenants or regulations, without analysis and interpretation of the implications of the calculations, establishing "what happened" without asking the more important questions regarding why and its impact. Once the analyst is sure that the overall approach and reasoning are sound, the analytic review should focus on the following issues:

- What happened, established through computation or questionnaires
- Why it happened, established through analysis
- The impact of the event or trend, established through interpretation of analysis
- The response and strategy of management, established through evaluation of the quality of corporate governance
- The recommendations of the analyst, established through interpretation and forecasting results of the analysis
- The vulnerabilities that should be highlighted, included in the recommendations of the analyst

An effective storyline—supporting final conclusions and recommendations—is normally enhanced through the use of data spanning between 5 and 10 years, as well as graphs, common-size financial statements, and company and cross-sectional industry trends.

The experienced analyst will distinguish between a computation-based approach and an analytic approach. With certain modifications, this process is similar to the approach used by risk-orientated financial supervisors and regulators.

2.6 Analytical Tools

There are many tools to assist with bank analysis, including questionnaires and Excel models that could easily be adapted to any banking environment. These often consist of a series of spreadsheet-based data-input tables that enable an analyst to collect and manipulate data in a systematic manner. This chapter does not discuss detailed steps regarding the use of such tools; rather it provides a conceptual framework to explain their background.

Questionnaires and Data-Input Tables

Bank officials with sufficient authority and experience should complete any questionnaires and data tables used by analysts. Questions should be designed to capture management's perspective on and understanding of the bank's risk management process. The background and financial information requested in the questionnaire will provide an overview of the bank as well as allow for assessment of the quality and comprehensiveness of bank policies, management and control processes, and financial and management information. Questions fall into the following categories:

- Institutional development needs
- Overview of the financial sector and regulation
- Overview of the bank (history and group and organizational structure)
- Accounting systems, management information, and internal controls
- Information technology
- Corporate governance, covering key players and accountabilities
- Financial risk management, including asset-liability management, profitability, credit risk, and the other major types of financial risk

To facilitate the gathering and provisioning of data, an analytical model should contain a series of data-input tables for collecting financial data. The data can then be used to create either ratios or graphs. Data tables are normally related to the major areas of financial risk management. The balance sheet and income statements serve as anchor schedules, with detail provided by all the other schedules. The output of an analytical model (tables and graphs) can assist executives in the high-level interpretation and analysis of a bank's financial risk management process and its financial condition.

Automated Processing of Data

The framework described above envisages the automatic production of tables, ratios, and graphs based on computerized manipulation of input data. This allows the analyst to focus on interpretation and analysis—as opposed to mere processing of data—to measure a bank's performance and to judge the effectiveness of its risk management process. Combined with the qualitative information obtained from the questionnaire, these statistical tables and graphs make up the raw material needed to carry out an informed analysis, as required in off-site (or macro level) reports. The ratios cover the areas of risk management in varying degrees of detail, starting with balance sheet and income statement schedules. The graphs provide a visual representation of some of the analytical results and a quick snapshot of both the current situation in banks (such as financial structure and the composition of investment portfolios) and comparisons over time.

Ratios

A ratio is a mathematical expression of one quantity relative to another. There are many relationships between financial accounts and between expected relationships from one point in time to another. Ratios are a useful way of expressing relationships in the following areas of risk:

- **Activity (operational efficiency):** the extent to which an entity uses its assets efficiently, as measured by turnover of current assets and liabilities and long-term assets

- **Liquidity:** the entity's ability to repay its short-term liabilities, measured by evaluating components of current assets and current liabilities

- **Profitability:** relation between a company's profit margins and sales, average capital, and average common equity

- **Debt and leverage:** the risk and return characteristics of the company, as measured by the volatility of sales and the extent of the use of borrowed money

- **Solvency:** financial risk resulting from the impact of the use of ratios of debt to equity and cash flow to expense coverage

- **Earnings, share price, and growth:** the rate at which an entity can grow as determined by its earnings, share price, and retention of profits

- **Other ratios:** groupings representing the preferences of individual analysts in addition to ratios required by prudential regulators such as banking supervisors, insurance regulators, and securities market bodies

Financial analysis can assist the analyst in making forward-looking projections. Financial ratios aid those projections in the following ways:

- Provide insights into the microeconomic relationships within a firm, which help analysts to project earnings and free cash flow (necessary to determine entity value and creditworthiness)

- Provide insights into a firm's financial flexibility, which is its ability to obtain the cash required to meet financial obligations or to acquire assets, even if unexpected circumstances should develop

- Provide a means of evaluating management's ability

Although they are extremely useful tools, ratios must be used with caution. They do not provide complete answers about the bottom-line performance of a business. In the short run, many tricks can be used to make ratios look good in relation to industry standards. An assessment of the operations and management of an entity should therefore be performed to provide a check on ratios.

Graphs and Charts

Graphs are powerful tools for analyzing trends and structures. They facilitate comparison of performance and structures over time and show trend lines and changes in significant aspects of bank operations and performance. In addition, they provide senior management with a high-level overview of trends in a bank's risk. Graphs can illustrate asset and liability structures; sources of income; profitability; capital adequacy; composition of investment portfolios; major types of credit risk exposures; and exposure to interest rate, liquidity, market, and currency risks. Graphs may be useful during off-site surveillance. In this context, they can serve as a starting point to help with on-site examinations and to present the bank's financial condition and risk management aspects succinctly to senior management. They also help external auditors to illustrate points in their presentation to management and other industry professionals to judge a bank's condition and prospects.

Figure 2.2 shows a bank experiencing significant growth in financial assets held for trading and a worrying decline in cash. Although not illustrated below, the analyst should compare pie charts for several previous years to determine whether the structural change represented in the current chart is representative of a general trend in the business.

In the same manner, a simple line graph can illustrate the growth trends in key financial variables (see figure 2.3). The rapid rise in loans and receivables is clearly illustrated alongside the alarming reduction in cash, creating more concern regarding the entity's liquidity: the increase in trading securities and other investments could have caused the reduction in liquidity (depending on how these increases in working capital were financed).

Figure 2.2 Composition of Assets, by Periods

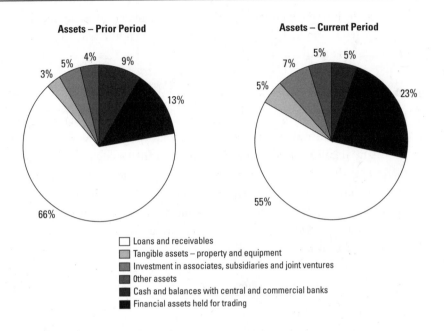

Assets – Prior Period

3%
5%
4%
9%
13%
66%

Assets – Current Period

7%
5%
5%
5%
23%
55%

☐ Loans and receivables
▨ Tangible assets – property and equipment
■ Investment in associates, subsidiaries and joint ventures
▨ Other assets
■ Cash and balances with central and commercial banks
■ Financial assets held for trading

Figure 2.3 Trends in Asset Growth, by Period

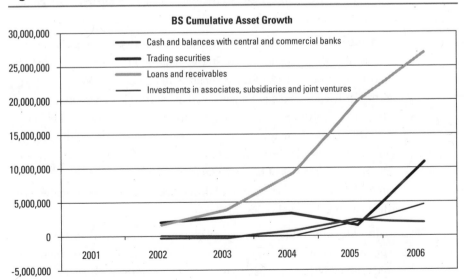

BS Cumulative Asset Growth

— Cash and balances with central and commercial banks
— Trading securities
— Loans and receivables
— Investments in associates, subsidiaries and joint ventures

2.7 Analytical Techniques

Data can be interpreted in many ways. Common analytical techniques include ratio analysis, common-size analysis, cross-sectional analysis, trend analysis, and regression analysis.

Ratio Analysis

Financial ratios mean little when seen in isolation. Their meaning can be interpreted only in the context of other information. It is good practice to compare the financial ratios of a company with those of its major competitors. Typically, the analyst should be wary of companies whose financial ratios are far above or below industry norms. In some cases, evaluating a company's past performance provides a basis for forward-looking analyses. Such an evaluation may suggest that its performance is likely to continue at similar levels or that an upward or downward trend is likely to occur. However, for a company making a major acquisition or divestiture, for a new financial institution, or for a bank operating in a volatile environment, past performance may be less relevant to future performance.

An analyst should evaluate financial information based on the following:

- **Financial institution's goals.** Actual ratios can be compared with company objectives to determine if the objectives are being attained.

- **Banking industry norms (cross-sectional analysis).** A company can be compared with others in the industry by relating its financial ratios to industry norms or a subset of the companies in an industry. When industry norms are used to make judgments, care must be taken, because (a) many ratios are industry specific, but not all ratios are important to all industries; (b) companies may have several lines of business, which distorts aggregate financial ratios and makes it preferable to examine industry-specific ratios by lines of business; (c) differences in accounting methods can distort financial ratios; and (d) differences in corporate strategies can affect certain financial ratios.

- **Economic conditions.** Financial ratios tend to improve when the economy is strong and to weaken during recessions. Therefore, financial ratios should be examined in light of the phase of the business cycle in which the economy is traversing.

- **Experience.** An analyst with experience obtains an intuitive notion of the meaning of transformed data.

Common-Size Analysis

An analytical technique of great value is common-size analysis, which is achieved by converting all financial statement items to a percentage of a given financial statement item, such as total assets or total revenue.

Structure of the Balance Sheet

The structure of the balance sheet may vary significantly depending on the bank's business orientation, market environment, customer mix, or economic environment. The composition of the balance sheet is normally a result of risk management decisions.

The analyst should be able to assess the risk profile of the business simply by analyzing the relative share of various assets and changes in their proportionate share over time (see table 2.1). For example, if any item were to increase rapidly, one would question whether the bank's risk management systems are adequate to handle the increased volume of transactions. In addition, a structural change could disclose a shift to another area of risk. These issues can be raised by an analyst, prior to a detailed review of the management of either credit or market risk. When linked to the amount of net income yielded by each category of assets, this analysis increases in importance, enabling a challenging assessment of risk versus reward.

Table 2.1 Balance Sheet Structure: Common Size Analysis

Balance Sheet Composition	Year 1	Year 2
Cash and balances with central and commercial banks	9.30%	5.50%
Trading securities	13.20%	23.30%
Loans and receivables	65.80%	54.70%
Real estate assets	3.00%	4.80%
Investments in associates, subsidiaries and joint ventures	4.90%	7.10%
Other assets	3.80%	4.70%
Total assets	**100%**	**100%**
Customers' deposits	77.70%	74.10%
Due to banks and other financial institutions	9.50%	7.20%
Other liabilities	3.80%	4.90%
Sundry creditors	0.10%	0.10%
Total equity	8.90%	13.70%
Total liabilities and capital	**100%**	**100%**

Analysis of the Income Statement

Common-size analysis can be used effectively on the income statement as well. The emphasis in the income statement would be on the sources of revenue and their sustainability. A question worth asking pertains to the proportion of income earned in relation to the amount of energy invested through the deployment of assets (see figure 2.4). When analyzing the income structure of a business, analysts should give appropriate consideration to and acquire an understanding of the following aspects:

- Trends in and the composition and accuracy of reported earnings

- The quality, composition, and level of income and expense components

- Dividend payout and earnings retention

- Major sources of income and the most profitable business areas

- Any income or expenditure recognition policies that distort earnings

- The effect of intergroup transactions, especially those related to the transfer of earnings and asset-liability valuations

Figure 2.4 Assets Deployed versus Income Earned

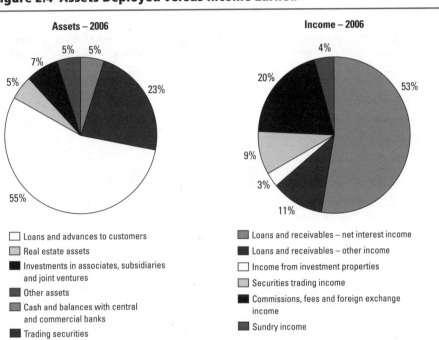

Assets – 2006

5% 5%
7%
5%
23%
55%

Income – 2006

4%
20%
53%
9%
3%
11%

☐ Loans and advances to customers
◻ Real estate assets
■ Investments in associates, subsidiaries and joint ventures
■ Other assets
■ Cash and balances with central and commercial banks
■ Trading securities

▨ Loans and receivables – net interest income
■ Loans and receivables – other income
☐ Income from investment properties
▫ Securities trading income
■ Commissions, fees and foreign exchange income
■ Sundry income

Cross-Sectional Analysis

Ratios are not meaningful when used on their own, which is why financial analysts prefer trend analysis (the monitoring of a ratio or group of ratios over time) and comparative analysis (the comparison of a specific ratio for a group of companies in a sector or for different sectors—see table 2.2). This comparison becomes a useful tool in establishing benchmarks for performance and structure.

Cross-sectional analysis of common-size financial statements makes it easier to compare an entity to other entities in the same sector, even though the entities might be of different sizes and operate in different currencies. If the examples given in figure 2.2 or table 2.1 referred to two different banks, rather than simply the same bank over more than one year, then the conclusions would compare the relative levels of liquidity and structure of assets between the two banks.

Table 2.2 Cross-Sectional Analysis of Two Different Bank Balance Sheet Structures

Balance Sheet Structure	Bank 1	Bank 2
Cash and balances with central and commercial banks	9.30%	5.50%
Trading securities	13.20%	23.30%
Loans and receivables	65.80%	54.70%
Real estate assets	3.00%	4.80%
Investments in associates, subsidiaries and joint ventures	4.90%	7.10%
Other assets	3.80%	4.60%
Total assets	**100%**	**100%**
Customers' deposits	77.70%	74.10%
Due to banks and other financial institutions	9.50%	7.20%
Other liabilities	3.80%	4.90%
Sundry creditors	0.10%	0.10%
Total equity	8.90%	13.70%
Total liabilities and capital	**100%**	**100%**

However, the analyst has to be realistic when comparing entities, because size does influence business results, and entities are seldom exactly the same. Differences in currency are eliminated in the percentage presentation, but the analyst must keep in mind the macroeconomic environment that influences variables such as competition and inflation across currency and national boundaries.

Cross-sectional analysis is not the solution to all problems, as different accounting policies and methods will influence the allocation of transactions to specific line items on the financial statements. For example, some companies could include depreciation in the cost of sales, while others could show it separately. However, if all these aspects are kept in mind, cross-sectional analysis offers the analyst a powerful analytical tool.

Trend Analysis

The trend of an amount or a ratio, which shows whether it is improving or deteriorating, is as important as its current absolute level. Trend analysis provides important information regarding historical performance and growth and, given a sufficiently long history of accurate seasonal information, can be of great assistance as a planning tool for management. The trend analysis could incorporate both currency and percentage changes for the last two years, as a small percentage change could hide a significant currency change and vice versa, prompting the analyst to investigate the reasons despite one of the changes being relatively small. In addition, past trends are not necessarily an accurate predictor of future behavior, especially if the economic environment changes. These caveats should be borne in mind when using past trends in forecasting.

Table 2.3 Balance Sheet Growth, Year-on-Year Fluctuations

Balance Sheet Composition – year-on-year fluctuations	2001	2002	2003	2004	2005	2006
Cash and balances with central and commercial banks	Base year	-16%	7%	66%	74%	-12%
Trading securities	Base year	49%	14%	8%	-25%	165%
Loans and receivables	Base year	21%	21%	43%	62%	25%
Real estate assets	Base year	53%	-10%	8%	-5%	137%
Investments in associates, subsidiaries and joint ventures	Base year					119%
Other assets	Base year	77%	40%	107%	-17%	82%
Total assets	**Base year**	**28%**	**16%**	**34%**	**40%**	**50%**
Customers' deposits	Base year	29%	17%	25%	34%	43%
Due to banks and other financial institutions	Base year	12%	32%	334%	194%	13%
Other liabilities	Base year	14%	11%	49%	27%	94%
Sundry creditors	Base year	22%	26%	11%	166%	82%
Total equity	Base year	28%	8%	75%	29%	130%
Total liabilities and capital	**Base year**	**28%**	**16%**	**34%**	**40%**	**50%**

Variations of Trend Analysis

Changes in currency and percentages focus the analysis on material items. A variation of growth in terms of common-size financial statements is to combine currency and percentage changes. Even when a percentage change might seem insignificant, the magnitude of the amount of currency involved might be significant and vice versa. Such combined analysis is therefore a further refinement of the analysis and interpretation of annual changes.

Annual Growth (Year-to-Year)

Any business that is well positioned and successful in its market is expected to grow. An analysis of balance sheets can be performed to determine growth rates and the type of structural changes that have occurred in a business. Such an analysis indicates the general type of business undertaken by the enterprise and requires an understanding of the structure of its balance sheet and the nature of its assets and liabilities. Even when growth overall is not significant, individual components of the balance sheet normally shift in reaction to changes in the competitive market or economic or regulatory environment (as illustrated in table 2.3). As the balance sheet structure changes, inherent risks also change. The structure of a balance sheet should therefore form part of an assessment of the adequacy and effectiveness of policies and procedures for managing risk exposures. In normal situations, the growth of a business's assets is determined by an increase in the earnings base and access to stable external funding or investment, at a cost that is acceptable to the business.

Businesses that grow too quickly tend to take unjustified risks, and their administrative and management information systems often cannot keep up with the rate of expansion. Businesses that grow too slowly can likewise take risks that are unusual or poorly understood by them. Even well-managed businesses can run into risk management problems arising from excessive growth, especially concerning management of their working capital.

Cumulative Growth from a Base Year

The analysis that can be performed using this technique is not significantly different from looking at year-to-year growth. Reviewing the cumulative effects of change over time, compared to a base year, dramatizes change and the need for remedial action when change outstrips the ability of risk management and administrative systems to keep up with growth or the enterprise's ability to finance its expansion.

Regression Analysis

Regression analysis uses statistical techniques to identify relationships (or correlations) between variables. Examples of such a relationship could be sales and medium-term trade finance over time or hotel occupancies compared to hotel revenues. In addition to analyzing trends over time, regression analysis enables analytic review as well as identification of items or ratios that are not behaving as they should be, given the statistical relationships that exist between ratios and variables.

3

Corporate Governance

Key Messages

- Corporate governance provides a disciplined structure through which a bank sets its objectives and the means of attaining them, as well as monitoring the performance of those objectives.

- Effective corporate governance encourages a bank to operate in a safe and sound manner and to use its resources more efficiently.

- Financial risk management is the responsibility of several key players in the corporate governance structure. Each key player is accountable for a dimension of risk management.

- The key players are regulators/lawmakers, supervisors, shareholders, directors, executive managers, internal auditors, external auditors, and the general public.

- Governance is affected by the relationships among participants in the governance system. To the extent that any key player does not, or is not expected to, fulfill its function in the risk management chain, other key players have to compensate for the gap created by enhancing their own role. More often than not, it is the bank supervisor who has to step into the vacuum created by the failure of certain players.

3.1 Corporate Governance Principles

Corporate governance relates to the manner in which the business of the bank is governed. It is defined by a set of relationships between the bank's management, its board, its shareholders, and other stakeholders. This includes setting corporate objectives and a bank's risk profile, aligning corporate activities and behaviors with the expectation that management will operate the bank in a safe and sound manner, running day-to-day operations within an established risk profile and in compliance with applicable laws and regulations, while protecting the interests of depositors and other stakeholders.

Effective governance practices are one of the key prerequisites to achieve and maintain public trust and, in a broader sense, confidence in the banking system. Poor governance increases the likelihood of bank failures. Bank failures may impose significant public cost, affect deposit insurance schemes, and increase contagion risks.

Banks and banking may affect the welfare of a significant percentage of the world's population. Banks' corporate governance arrangements, therefore, can influence economic development. Sound corporate governance can create an enabling environment that rewards banking efficiency, mitigates financial risks, and increases systemic stability. Lenders and other providers of funds are more likely to extend financing when they feel comfortable with the corporate governance arrangements of the funds' recipient and with the clarity and enforceability of creditor rights. Good corporate governance tends to lower the cost of capital, as it conveys a sense of lower risk that translates into shareholders' readiness to accept lower returns. Good corporate governance has been proven to improve operational performance and reduce the risks of contagion from financial distress. Besides mitigating the internal risk of distress by positively affecting investors' perception of risk and their readiness to extend funding, good governance increases firms' robustness and resilience to external shocks.

The key elements of a sound corporate governance framework in a bank include the following:

- A well articulated corporate strategy against which the overall success and the contribution of individuals can be measured.

- Setting and enforcing clear assignment of responsibilities, decision-making authority, and accountabilities appropriate for the bank's selected risk profile.

- Strong financial risk management function (independent of business lines), adequate internal control systems (including internal and external audit functions), and functional process design with the necessary checks and balances.

- Adequate corporate values, codes of conduct, and other standards of appropriate behavior and effective systems used to ensure compliance. This includes special monitoring of the bank's risk exposures where conflicts of interest are expected to appear (for example, relationships with affiliated parties).

- Financial and managerial incentives to act in an appropriate manner offered to the board, management, and employees, including compensation, promotion, and penalties (compensation should be consistent with the bank's objectives, performance, and ethical values).

- Transparency and appropriate information flows internally and to the public.

Table 3.1 summarizes the responsibilities of the key players involved in bank governance and risk management, including the type of engagement in the governance process.

Table 3.1 Key Players and Their Responsibilities

Key Players	Responsibility	Importance	
		Policy Level	Operational Level
Systemic			
Legal and Regulatory Authorities	Set stage	Critical	n/a
Bank Supervisors	Monitor	Indirect (monitoring)	Indirect
Institutional			
Shareholders	Appoint key players	Indirect	Indirect
Board of Directors	Set policies. Monitor effects. Approve any changes.	Critical	Important
Executive Management	Implement polices and strategies. Manage day-to-day operations	Critical	Critical
Audit Committee/Internal Audit	Test compliance with bank policies regarding corporate governance, risk management processes and control systems	Indirect (compliance)	Critical
External			
External Auditors	Evaluate and express opinion	Indirect (evaluation)	Very important
Outside stakeholders/Public	Act responsibly	n/a	Indirect

The remainder of this chapter discusses latest international and national initiatives in setting the principles for a good governance process. It then discusses the roles and responsibilities of key players in the corporate governance process of a bank. The players directly involved in corporate governance and risk management are considered, as are those parties who determine the regulatory and public policy environment within which a bank operates and who have a major influence on risk management. The activities of third parties, such as bank customers and market participants, are also mentioned.

3.2 Major Developments in Corporate Governance Principles

National authorities are paying more attention to corporate governance, as are institutions engaged in international trade, financial flows, and protecting the stability of international markets (for example, the Organisation for Economic Co-operation and Development [OECD], the Bank for International Settlements, the International Monetary Fund, and the World Bank). This attention can be attributed to several factors: (1) the growth of institutional investors—that is, pension funds, insurance companies, mutual funds, and highly leveraged institutions—and their role in the financial sector, especially in major industrial economies; (2) widely articulated concerns and criticism that the contemporary monitoring and control of publicly held corporations in English-speaking countries, notably the United Kingdom and United States, are seriously defective, leading to suboptimal economic and social development; (3) the shift away from a traditional view of corporate governance as centered on "shareholder value" in favor of a corporate governance structure extended to a wide circle of stakeholders; and (4) the impact of increased globalization of financial markets, a global trend toward deregulation of financial sectors, and liberalization of institutional investors' activities.

Aware of the critical importance of banks' governance, the Basel Committee on Banking Supervision (Basel Committee) published a guidance paper in 1999 to assist banking supervisors in promoting the adoption of sound corporate governance practices. This guidance drew from principles of corporate governance that were published earlier that year by OECD to assist member countries in their efforts to evaluate and improve their corporate governance framework. Further details on OECD Principles of corporate governance are provided in the annex to this chapter.

Since the publication of those documents, issues related to corporate governance have continued to attract considerable national and international attention in light of a number of high-profile breakdowns in corporate governance. Consequently, the improved version of OECD governance principles was published in 2004, and the Basel Committee updated its governance principles for banking organizations in 2006. The governance principles were not intended to be an additional requirement to the revised international framework for capital adequacy (Basel II), in fact, the principles are applicable regardless of whether a country chooses to adopt the Basel II framework.

The philosophy behind the Basel Committee governance principles (see box 3.1) is that sound governance can be achieved regardless of the form used by a banking organization, provided several essential functions are in place. The four important forms of oversight that should be included in the organizational

Box 3.1 Corporate Governance for Banking Organizations

Principle 1 – Board members should be qualified for their positions, have a clear understanding of their role in corporate governance, and be able to exercise sound judgment about the affairs of the bank.

Principle 2 – The board of directors should approve and oversee the bank's strategic objectives and corporate values that are communicated throughout the banking organization.

Principle 3 – The board of directors should set and enforce clear lines of responsibility and accountability throughout the organization.

Principle 4 – The board should ensure that there is appropriate oversight by senior management consistent with board policy.

Principle 5 – The board and senior management should effectively utilize the work conducted by the internal audit function, external auditors, and internal control functions.

Principle 6 – The board should ensure that compensation policies and practices are consistent with the bank's corporate culture, long-term objectives and strategy, and control environment.

Principle 7 – The bank should be governed in a transparent manner.

Principle 8 – The board and senior management should understand the bank's operational structure, including where the bank operates in jurisdictions, or through structures, that impede transparency (that is, "know-your-structure").

Enhancing Corporate Governance for Banking Organizations
Basel Committee on Banking Supervision, February 2006

structure of any bank to ensure appropriate checks and balances include (1) oversight by the board of directors or supervisory board; (2) oversight by individuals not involved in the day-to-day running of the various business areas; (3) direct line supervision of different business areas; and (4) independent risk management, compliance, and audit functions. In addition, it is important that key personnel are fit and proper for their jobs. The implementation of the governance principles set forth by the Basel Committee should be proportionate to the size, complexity, structure, economic significance, and risk profile of the bank and the group (if any) to which it belongs. The application of corporate governance standards in any jurisdiction will depend on relevant laws, regulations, codes, and supervisory expectations.

Parallel to these international efforts, corporate governance has received significant attention in a large number of countries, both in public policy debates and as a reaction to negative developments in the corporate sector and financial markets caused by inadequate governance arrangements. Annex 3A provides a summary of some of the important national initiatives to improve various aspects of corporate governance, such as the work of the Committee of Sponsoring Organizations of the Treadway Commission (commonly referred to as COSO). The most interesting elements of the COSO include an internal control framework and enterprise risk management framework designed to help companies reduce the risk of asset loss, ensure the reliability of financial statements and legal compliance, and promote efficiency.

3.3 Regulatory Authorities: Establishing a Risk-Based Framework

In this publication, regulation of banks refers to the establishment and approval of banking law; supervision of banks refers to the monitoring of bank financial and risk management. Countries use different organizational structures for regulation and supervision—sometimes separating regulation from supervision and housing the regulatory function in a ministry and the supervisory function in the central bank or an independent financial markets authority.

The primary role of bank regulators and supervisors is to facilitate the process of risk management and to enhance and monitor the statutory framework in which it is undertaken. Bank regulators and supervisors cannot prevent bank failures. However, by creating a sound, enabling environment, they have a crucial role to play in influencing the other key players.

A regulatory framework consists of more than just regulations designed to meet specific objectives. The regulatory environment embodies a general philosophy and principles that guide both the content and the implementation of specific regulations. In general, regulators may take either a prescriptive or a market-oriented approach to their task. This choice is determined by the regulator's understanding of the philosophical underpinnings of the economy as a whole.

A **prescriptive approach** usually limits the scope of activities of financial institutions; it often results in regulations for all risks known to the regulators. The danger of such an approach is that regulations quickly become outdated and cannot address the risks stemming from financial innovation.

In contrast, bank regulators that subscribe to a **market-oriented regulatory approach** believe that markets, by definition, function effectively, are capable of managing related financial risks, and should therefore be allowed to operate as freely as possible. With a market-oriented approach, the role of the regulator is focused on facilitating the improvement of risk management. The regulator and the regulated entity should agree on common objectives to ensure an efficient and effective process. In other words, when designing regulations, the regulator should take into account the views of market participants to avoid impractical or ineffective regulations. In practice, regulations in most major countries combine both a prescriptive approach and a market-oriented approach, leaning one way or another depending on individual circumstances.

The new millennium has seen an acceleration of the shift toward a market-oriented approach. Regulations address a broad spectrum of risks and provide principles on how to assess and manage risk without unnecessarily detailed rules and recommendations. In addition, because it is based on principles rather than rules, a market-oriented approach can adapt to changing market conditions. Regulators should therefore concentrate on creating an environment in which the quality and effectiveness of risk management can be optimized and should oversee the risk management process exercised by the boards and management personnel of individual banking institutions.

At the system level, regulators' efforts are typically focused on maintaining public confidence in the banking sector and on creating an equitable market for financial institutions and providers of financial services. Regulators also aim to establish a free-market attitude toward bank supervision and professional supervisory functions, as well as to facilitate public understanding of the bank management's responsibility in the risk management process. In terms of financial risk management, regulators' responsibilities center around improving quality at entry through strict licensing and minimum capital requirements and capital adequacy rules; toughening the fiduciary responsibilities and standards regarding bank owners, directors, and management personnel; providing guidelines on risk management and related policies; setting statutory guidelines with respect to risk positions; and evaluating compliance and overall risk management in a bank or banking system. Most regulators also conduct research on the latest developments in the field of risk management.

As regulators are best positioned to act in the interest of depositors, they should maintain a flexible legal framework and move swiftly and decisively when banking problems are identified. For example, the legal framework in the United States establishes several grounds for intervention by regulatory authorities. These include critical undercapitalization or expected losses great enough to deplete capital, insufficient assets or the inability to meet obligations, substantial dissipation of assets, unsafe and unsound conditions, concealment of books and records, misuse of managerial position, and violation of the law.

Once consensus has been reached that a problem exists that bank management cannot effectively address, the typical recourse has been the removal of responsible managers and directors; fines; and where fraud is involved, criminal prosecution. Unfortunately, situations also arise in which regulators fail to identify problems at an early stage, sometimes as a result of unfavorable laws. Other factors include the highly technical nature of financial machinations, undue political influence, or even corruption because of the large profits or losses at stake. Fraud may also span institutions supervised by multiple regulatory authorities.

3.4 Supervisory Authorities: Monitoring Risk Management

Bank supervision is sometimes applied incorrectly as a legal or administrative function focused largely on regulations related to the business of banking. Such regulations are often prescriptive in nature and impose onerous requirements on banks, which seek to circumvent them by developing innovative products.

Once regulators and supervisors understand that they cannot bear sole responsibility for preventing bank failures, they need to identify clearly what they are capable of achieving and then focus on that specific mission. This process has already taken place in most industrial countries. More and more, the role of a bank's supervisory authority is moving away from monitoring compliance with banking laws and old-style prudential regulations. A more appropriate mission statement today would be "to create a regulatory and legal environment in which the quality and effectiveness of bank risk management can be optimized to contribute to a sound and reliable banking system."

Because transactions of large banks are extremely complex and therefore hard to trace and evaluate, supervisors depend to a substantial degree on internal management control systems. The traditional approach to regulation and supervision has at times caused distortions in financial markets by providing negative incentives for the evasion of regulations, rather than encouraging the adequate management of financial risk. Since the late 1980s, there has been increasing recognition that the old approach to bank supervision does not live up to the challenges of a modern banking environment and turbulent markets. In some jurisdictions, this realization has laid the groundwork for an extensive process of consultation between regulators and banks seeking to establish the legal framework for a shift to a market-oriented, risk-based approach to bank supervision. To establish such a framework, the responsibilities of the different players in the risk management process have to be clearly delineated.

The task of bank supervision becomes monitoring, evaluating, and, when necessary, strengthening the risk management process that is undertaken by banks. However, the supervisory authority is only one of the many contributors to a stable banking system. Other players also are responsible for managing risk, and prudential regulations increasingly stress the accountability of top-level management. Recognizing the high cost of voluminous reporting requirements without corresponding benefits, many countries are moving toward a system of reporting that encourages and enables supervisors to rely more extensively on external auditors in the ordinary course of business, subject to having a clear understanding of their role in the risk management chain. The Basel II capital standard discussed in chapter 6 has introduced three pillars and specifically mentions the role of market discipline evaluated by external parties (for example, rating agencies and external auditors). The move toward shared responsibilities started in the 1990s, with New Zealand being one of the first examples of the new philosophy (see box 3.2).

Box 3.2 A View Opposing On-Site Examination of Banks

The Reserve Bank of New Zealand provides a leading example of a regulatory environment that reflects the new philosophy of banking supervision. In the words of a former governor,
"A further concern we have with on-site examinations or the off-site collection of detailed private information on banks, at least in the New Zealand context, is the risk that these approaches can blur the lines of responsibility for the management of banks. If the banking supervisor has responsibility for regular on-site examinations, it presumably follows that the supervisor also has responsibility for encouraging or requiring a bank to modify its risk positions or make other adjustments to its balance sheet where the supervisor has concerns in relation to the bank's risk profile. This has the potential to erode the incentives for the directors and management of banks to take ultimate responsibility for the management of banking risks, effectively passing some of this responsibility to the banking supervisor. It also has the potential to create public perceptions that the responsibility for the banking risks is effectively shared between a bank's directors and the banking supervisors. In turn, this makes it very difficult indeed for a government to eschew responsibility for rescuing a bank in difficulty . . . I acknowledge that any system of banking supervision creates a risk for the taxpayer in the event that a bank gets into difficulty. However, in order to minimize these risks, the Reserve Bank of New Zealand prefers to keep the spotlight clearly focused on the directors and management of a bank, rather than risk a further blurring of their accountability."

— D. T. Brash, 1997

A related, and important, development has been the toughening of public information disclosure requirements to facilitate the relegation of monitoring responsibilities to the public at large. The new approach to banking regulation and supervision also corresponds, in its essential elements, to the traditional style of regulation and supervision of nonbank financial intermediaries, and thereby contributes to making the regulatory environment for financial institutions more consistent and homogenous. One might easily argue that these changes have occurred in reaction to and as an inevitable consequence of the increasing lack of distinctions between banks and nonbanking financial intermediaries.

3.5   The Shareholders: Appointing the Right Policy Makers

Shareholders play a key role in the promotion of corporate governance. By electing the supervisory board and approving the board of directors, the audit committee, and external auditors, shareholders are in a position to determine the direction of a bank. Banks are different from other companies: the responsibilities of management and the board are not only to shareholders but also to depositors, who provide leverage to owners' capital. Depositors are different from normal trade creditors because the entire intermediation function in the economy, including payments and clearance (and therefore the stability of the financial system), is at stake.

Banking and company laws, as well as regulators, recognize the importance of shareholders and directors. In the modern market-oriented approach to bank regulation, the emphasis on the fiduciary responsibility of shareholders has increased significantly. This is reflected in several ways, including more stringent bank licensing requirements and standards that a bank's founder and larger shareholders must meet to be considered fit and proper. Actions that may be taken against shareholders who fail to properly discharge their responsibilities to ensure the appointment of fit and proper persons for the corporate governance process have also become broader. Bank licensing procedures normally require the identification of major shareholders and mandate a minimum number of shareholders (which varies among jurisdictions).

Explicit approval of the supervisory authority is required for a person to become a bank's founder or "larger" shareholder, which normally implies owning a certain percentage of the bank's shares (typically in the range of 10–15 percent). Such approval is based on the ability of shareholders to meet a certain set of predefined criteria. These criteria are designed to reassure the public that shareholders are able and willing to effectively exercise their fiduciary responsibilities, are able to provide additional capital to the bank in times of need, and do not see the bank as a provider of funds for their favorite projects. The central bank normally approves all changes in the shareholding structure of a bank. The central banks in most jurisdictions also review and approve a bank's charter and the key bylaws that determine the specific relationship of a bank with its shareholders.

Shareholders should play a key role in overseeing a bank's affairs. They are normally expected to select a competent board of directors whose members are experienced and qualified to set sound policies and objectives. The board of directors must also be able to adopt a suitable business strategy for the bank, supervise the bank's affairs and its financial position, maintain reasonable capitalization, and prevent self-serving practices among themselves and throughout the bank as a whole.

In reality, shareholders may not be able to exercise the oversight function in large banks with dispersed ownership structures. Although the founders of a bank must meet certain standards, as a bank becomes larger and shares more widely held, shareholding may become so diffused that individual shareholders have no effective voice in the bank's management and have little recourse but to sell their shares if they don't like the way the bank is being managed. In such cases, effective supervisory oversight becomes critical.

Assessing the Role of Shareholders

Determining a bank's ownership, control structure, and the status of its capital are key elements of bank assessment. This process should include a review of the ownership register, where all shareholders holding more than 2 percent of a bank's capital should be identified by name. The likelihood of a bank engaging in imprudent practices is higher if it is owned by the state than if it is owned by the private sector. An ownership review should therefore also include an assessment of the percentage of direct or indirect shareholding by the state, by the cooperative sector, and by management and employees; it should also state any special rights or exemptions attached to shares. The majority shareholders and therefore the effective owners of the bank can be determined by using a tailored version of table 3.2.

Table 3.2 Shareholder Information

Shareholders	Number of Shareholders	Shares Held		% of Shares
		Number	Unit Size	
Private companies				
Private individuals				
Public sector and government companies (<51% private)				
Names of shareholders who—directly or through intermediaries—control more than 2% of the bank's shares				

Other valuable information concerns the main focus of the larger shareholder businesses and of the people who control them. The bank's corporate charter, any other documents of incorporation, and corporate bylaws should be reviewed to determine the exact nature of the relationship between shareholders and the bank. Special attention should be paid to any situations where more than 75 percent of the votes of shareholders and directors is required to pass a motion as this could create unwarranted special protection (as opposed to legitimate protection of minority interests). A key question to ask is whether resolutions require greater than a simple majority to be accepted, and if so, under what circumstances. In addition, the existence of provisions that either limit voting rights or that allow voting rights to individual shareholders or classes of shareholders that are disproportionate to their shareholding should be considered, as well as whether other options exist to acquire more capital.

Another issue is whether shareholders are carrying out their fiduciary responsibilities effectively and whether they have taken advantage of their ownership position in the bank. In practical terms, this can be ascertained by reviewing select aspects, including the frequency of shareholder meetings, the number of shareholders who are normally present, and the percentage of total shares they represent. The level of direct involvement, if any, that the shareholders have with the bank, the supervisory board (directors), and the management board (executives) should also be taken into account. Such an assessment should include a review of the current composition of the management and supervisory boards; their remaining terms of office; and connections among board members, shareholders, and bank customers. A review should be conducted of the bank's level of exposure to shareholders having more than 1 percent of holdings who are bank customers, including an examination of amounts, terms, conditions, and funding extended to shareholders through instruments such as loans and deposits.

3.6 The Board of Directors: Ultimate Responsibility for a Bank's Affairs

Ultimate responsibility for the way in which a bank's business is conducted lies with the board of directors. The board sets the strategic direction, appoints management, establishes operational policies, and, most important, takes responsibility for ensuring the soundness of a bank. The board is answerable to depositors and shareholders for the lawful, informed, efficient, and able administration of the institution. The members of the board usually delegate the day-to-day management of banking to officers and employees, but board members are responsible for the consequences of unsound or imprudent policies and practices concerning lending, investing, protecting against internal fraud, and any other banking activity.

A board of directors attracts significant interest from regulators because a risk-based approach to bank supervision emphasizes a board's fiduciary responsibilities and seeks to ensure that its directors are qualified and able to effectively carry out such responsibilities. Laws and regulations typically govern the election, required number, qualifications, liability, and removal of board members and officers, as well as disclosure requirements for directors' outside business interests. Other laws and regulations address restrictions, prohibitions, purchases from and sales to board members, commissions and gifts for procuring loans, embezzlement, abstraction, willful misapplication, false entries, penalty for political contributions, and other matters.

The composition of a board of directors is crucial. Studies have found that nearly 60 percent of failed banks had board members who either lacked banking knowledge or were uninformed and passive regarding supervision of the bank's affairs. A strong managing director and a weak board are a recipe for disaster. A board with a strong nonexecutive chairman is more likely to be able to provide objective inputs than a board whose chairman is also the chief executive. A banking institution needs a board that is both strong and knowledgeable. It is essential that the board encourages open discussion and, even more important, that it tolerates conflict well, because conflict indicates that both sides of the coin are being considered. Therefore, shareholders considering the appointment of a board member should review qualifications, career and experience, sector expertise, relations with shareholders, and integrity.

The required number of board members varies among jurisdictions, but in all cases the majority of board members should not be executives of the bank. In banking systems that use the supervisory board model, it is typical that all directors are nonexecutives. Despite the strengths of this approach, the lack of involvement in policy setting by wholly nonexecutive boards is a major disadvantage. Boards with only one executive member typically view the bank in the way that the managing director does. If a board of directors instead includes more than one executive member, board members will have a broader perspective and will be able to look at the company through the eyes of more than one senior executive.

A board must be strong, independent, and actively involved in its bank's affairs. Both the bank directors and the executive management must adhere to high ethical standards and be fit and proper to serve. Although the bank's directors will not necessarily be experts on banking, they should have the skills, knowledge, and experience to enable them to perform their duties effectively (see box 3.3).

Box 3.3 Board of Directors: Effective Exercise of Duties

While not intended to be a "checklist" of requirements, the Committee has observed that boards of directors and their individual members strengthen the corporate governance of a bank when they do the following:

■ Understand and execute their oversight role, including understanding the bank's risk profile;

■ Approve the overall business strategy of the bank, including approval of the overall risk policy and risk management procedures;

■ Exercise their "duty of loyalty" and "duty of care" to the bank under applicable national laws and supervisory standards;

■ Avoid conflicts of interest, or the appearance of conflicts, in their activities with, and commitments to, other organizations;

■ Avoid getting involved in decisions when they have a conflict of interest that makes them incapable of properly fulfilling their duties to the bank;

■ Commit sufficient time and energy to fulfilling their responsibilities;

■ Structure themselves (as a board) in a way, including size, that promotes efficiency and real strategic discussion;

■ Develop and maintain an appropriate level of expertise as the bank grows in size and complexity;

■ Periodically assess the effectiveness of their own governance practices, including nomination and election of board members and management of conflicts of interest, determine where weaknesses exist, and make changes as necessary;

■ Select, monitor and, where necessary, replace key executives, while ensuring that the bank has an appropriate plan for executive succession, and determining that any intended successor(s) are qualified, fit and proper to manage the affairs of the bank;

- Provide oversight of the senior management of the bank by exercising their duty and authority to question and insist upon straightforward explanations from management, and receive on a timely basis sufficient information to judge the performance of management;

- Meet regularly with senior management and internal audit to review policies, establish communication lines and monitor progress toward corporate objectives;

- Promote bank safety and soundness, understand the regulatory environment and ensure the bank maintains an effective relationship with supervisors;

- Provide sound advice and recommend sound practices gleaned from other situations;

- Avoid participation as the board of directors in day-to-day management of the bank; and

- Exercise due diligence in the hiring and oversight of external auditors in jurisdictions where this is the responsibility of the board (in some jurisdictions, external auditors are hired directly by shareholders).

Enhancing Corporate Governance for Banking Organizations
Basel Committee on Banking Supervision, 2004

One of the most important duties of the board is to ensure that the management team has the necessary skills, knowledge, experience, and sense of judgment to manage the bank's affairs in a sound and responsible manner. The management team should be directly accountable to the board, and this relationship should be supported by robust structures. During good times, a board sets tone and direction. It oversees and supports management efforts, testing and probing recommendations before approving them, and makes sure that adequate controls and systems are in place to identify and address concerns before they become major problems. During bad times, an active, involved board can help a bank survive if it is able to evaluate problems, take corrective actions, and when necessary keep the institution on track until effective management can be reestablished and the bank's problems resolved.

An effective board should have a sound understanding of the nature of the bank's business activities and associated risks. It should take reasonable steps to ensure that management has established strong systems to monitor and control those risks. (The board's risk management responsibilities are summarized in box. 3.4.) Even if members of the board are not experts in banking risks and risk management systems, they should ensure that such expertise is available and that the risk management system undergoes appropriate reviews by qualified professionals. The board should in a timely manner take the necessary actions to ensure a capitalization of the bank that reasonably matches its economic and business environment and business and risk profile.

The board should ensure that the bank has adequate audit arrangements and risk management committees in place and that risk management systems are properly applied at all times. Directors need not be experts in these risk management and audit mechanisms, but they should consult experts within and, if necessary, outside the bank to ascertain that such arrangements are robust and are being properly implemented.

The board should also ensure compliance with banking laws and regulations applicable to a bank's business. It should take all reasonable steps to ensure that the information in the bank's disclosure statements is transparent and accurate and that adequate procedures are in place, including external audits or other reviews where appropriate, to ensure that the disclosed information is not false or misleading.

A bank appraisal always includes an assessment of the structure and effectiveness of the board. A major objective of the appraisal is to determine whether the board is staffed with competent and experienced directors who are able and willing to effectively carry out their responsibilities, who fully understand their duties, and who have developed adequate objectives and policies (box 3.4). The appraisal should include review of the minutes of board meetings and, for each functional area, a complete set of reports provided regularly to the relevant director. The follow-up actions undertaken by the directors can be assessed to determine if the board is effectively fulfilling its responsibility to supervise the affairs of the bank and to stay informed of the bank's condition.

A particularly important part of the appraisal is the review of the bank's compliance with laws and regulations and assessment of whether conflicts of interest or self-serving practices exist. A self-serving board is a dangerous board, and when decisions involve a conflict of interest, the director in question should fully disclose the nature of the conflict and abstain from voting on the matter. Such transactions should be scrutinized carefully for the potential of self-serving behavior.

Box 3.4 The Board's Financial Risk Management Responsibilities

Legal principles in banking laws and regulations leave no room for doubt that the board of directors is the primary player in the risk management process. Following are the board's primary responsibilities:

- Formulate a clear policy for each risk management area.

- Design or approve structures that include clear delegation of authority and responsibility at each level.

- Review and approve policies that clearly quantify acceptable risk, specifying the quantity and quality of capital required for the safe operation of the bank.

- Ensure that senior management effectively takes the steps necessary to identify, measure, monitor, and control the bank's financial and operational risks.

- Periodically review controls to ensure that they remain appropriate and make periodic assessment of the long-term capital maintenance program.

- Obtain explanations where positions exceed limits, including reviews of credit granted to directors and other related parties, significant credit exposures, and adequacy of provisions made.

- Ensure that the internal audit function includes a review of adherence to policies and procedures.

- Formally delegate to management the authority to formulate and implement strategies. (The board should, however, critically appraise and ultimately approve the strategic plan.)

- Specify content and frequency of reports.

- Ensure sound staffing and remuneration practices and a positive working environment.

- Perform an annual evaluation of the performance of the chief executive officer.

- Elect a committee, primarily made up of nonexecutive directors, to determine the remuneration of executive directors.

Other self-serving practices of which supervisors and analysts should be aware include the use of a bank's credit potential by directors, officers, or shareholders to obtain loans or to transact other business. The issuance of unwarranted loans to a bank's directors or to their business interests is a serious matter from the standpoints of both credit and management. Losses that develop from such unwarranted loans are bad enough, but the weakening effect on the bank's general credit culture is likely to be even worse. Attention should also be paid to the possibility of gratuities being given to directors for the purpose of obtaining their approval of financing arrangements or of the use of particular services.

3.7 Management: Responsibility for Bank Operations and the Implementation of Risk Management Policies

As highlighted in box 3.5, the financial soundness and performance of a banking system ultimately depend on the boards of directors and on the senior management of member banks. The strategic positioning of a bank; the nature of a bank's risk profile; and the adequacy of the systems for identifying, monitoring, and managing the profile reflect the quality of both the management team and the directors' oversight of the bank. For these reasons, the most effective strategy to promote a sound financial system is to strengthen the accountability of directors and management and to enhance the incentives for them to operate banks prudently. The role of senior management is therefore a fundamental component of a risk-based approach to regulation and supervision. Regulators increasingly aim to strengthen the participation and accountability of senior management to accept key responsibility for the maintenance of a bank's safety and soundness.

Box 3.5 Accountability of Bank Management

The Comptroller of the United States Currency made a study of bank failures between 1979 and 1988 to try to determine the root causes of those failures. The ultimate message of this study was that not all banks in a depressed environment fail: the banks with weak management were the ones that succumbed when times became difficult.

The final words on this trend were offered by a governor of the U.S. Federal Reserve System:
It is important to recognize that bank stockholders suffer losses on their investments, and senior bank management is almost always replaced, regardless of the resolution technique used.

— E. W. Kelley, 1991

The quality and experience of the individuals involved in a senior management team are important. In a financial institution, the process of risk management does not start at the strategy meeting or the planning process or in any other committee; it starts when a prospective employee is screened for appointment to the organization or for promotion to a senior position.

Regulators take several different approaches to ensuring that management is fit and proper. Most regulators have established standards that have to be met by a manager, as listed in box 3.6. Jurisdictions with such standards often require the central bank to confirm the experience, technical capacity, and professional integrity of senior management before its members assume their duties. However, some jurisdictions do not, as a matter of policy, get involved in the appointment of senior management unless a bank is deemed unsafe due to incompetent management.

While the board and management need to support each other, each has its own distinct role and responsibilities to fulfill. The chief executive officer and the management team should run the bank's day-to-day activities in compliance with board policies, laws, and regulations, and they should be supported by a sound system of internal controls. Although the board should leave day-to-day operations to management, the board should retain overall control. The dictation of a board's actions by management indicates that the board is not fulfilling its responsibilities, ultimately to the detriment of the institution.

Management Information Availability to the Board of Directors

Management should provide directors with the information they need to meet their responsibilities and should respond quickly and fully to board requests. In addition, management should use its expertise to generate new and innovative ideas and recommendations for consideration by the board. A bank should have adequate policies in place to increase the accountability of its managers. As the individuals with responsibility for bank stewardship, managers should be given incentives to maintain a well-informed overview of business activities and corresponding risks. The duties and responsibilities of a bank's senior management include appointment to middle-level management positions of people with adequate professional skills, experience, and integrity; the establishment of adequate performance incentives and personnel management systems; and staff training. Management should ensure that the bank has an

Box 3.6 "Fit and Proper" Standards for Bank Management

- No previous convictions for any crime involving fraud, dishonesty, or violence.

- No violation of any law that, in the opinion of the regulator, is designed to protect the public against financial loss from the dishonesty or incompetence of or malpractice by the person concerned. This standard applies when the person is involved in the provision of banking, insurance, investment, and financial services or in the management of juristic persons.

- No indication that a director was the effective cause of a particular company's inability to pay its debts.

- No involvement in any business practice that was deceitful, prejudicial, or that cast doubt on the manager's competence and soundness of judgment.

- Whether any previous application by the person concerned to conduct business has been refused, or whether any license to conduct business has been withdrawn or revoked.

- While filling the role of a director or an executive officer of an institution, no instance of the institution being censured, warned, disciplined, or the subject of a court order by any regulatory authority, locally or overseas.

- No instance of the person concerned being associated with an institution that has been refused a license or has had its license to conduct business revoked.

- No dismissal, debarment, or disciplinary proceedings by any professional or occupational organization, as initiated by an employer or professional body.

- No nonpayment of any debt judged due and payable, locally or elsewhere.

- No declaration of insolvency.

- No convictions of any offenses, excluding traffic violations, political offenses, or offenses committed when the person in question was under the age of 18 years.

- No litigation involving the person in question related to the formation or management of any corporate body.

- No related-party transactions with the institution concerned.

adequate management information system and that the information is transparent, timely, accurate, and complete.

The key managerial responsibility is to ensure that all major bank functions are carried out in accordance with clearly formulated policies and procedures, and that the bank has adequate systems in place to effectively monitor and manage risks. Managerial responsibilities for financial risk management are summarized in box 3.7.

Management's role in identifying, appraising, pricing, and managing financial risk is described well by the Basel Committee on Banking Supervision. The Basel Committee has stated that any corporation that uses new financial instruments has must ensure that all levels of management acquire knowledge and understanding of inherent risks and adapt internal accounting systems to ensure adequate control. Risk management should be an integral part of the day-to-day activities of each and every line manager in a bank so that risk management systems are properly applied and procedures are duly followed.

Box 3.7 Management's Responsibilities with Regard to Financial Risk

- Develop and recommend strategic plans and risk management policies for board approval.
- Implement strategic plans and policies after approval by the board.
- Establish an institutional culture promoting high ethical and integrity standards.
- Ensure development of manuals containing policies, procedures, and standards for the bank's key functions and risks.
- Implement an effective internal control system, including continuous assessment of all material risks that could adversely affect the achievement of the bank's objectives.
- Ensure the implementation of controls that enforce adherence to established risk limits. Ensure immediate reporting of noncompliance to management.
- Ensure that the internal auditors review and assess the adequacy of controls and compliance with limits and procedures.
- Develop and implement management reporting systems that adequately reflect business risks.

Management should also ensure that the bank has adequate internal controls, including appropriate audit arrangements, because risk management failures often result not from unanticipated or extraordinary risks, but from an ineffective decision-making process and weak controls.

Recent changes in international banking have made the management process considerably more demanding. Financial innovation transfers price or market risk from one agent to another, but it does not eliminate the risk itself. The pace of innovation, the growth of off-balance-sheet transactions, and the unbundling of different types of risk have made the analysis of financial statements and the management of a bank's financial position more complex. Management increasingly faces important questions about how best to account for, monitor, and manage risk exposure and how to integrate off-balance-sheet activities into other exposures.

Risk Analysis: Assessment of Management

It is also important that the quality of management be appraised. The assessment of senior management personnel should concentrate on the following:

- Integrity (fit and proper qualities) to manage a bank.

- Adequate technical capacity and experience. These aspects can be evaluated based on the bank's personnel practices in the area of management continuity.

- Systems in place to monitor and control the bank's material risks, including credit, exposure concentration, interest rate, currency, solvency, liquidity, and other risks. Whether these systems are being properly applied and whether management takes appropriate actions, if and when necessary, should also be evaluated.

- Proper managerial guidance and adequate decisions in all key aspects of the bank's business.

- Compliance with all conditions of registration applicable to the bank.

- Regular contact with those persons who are capable of controlling or significantly influencing the bank in a manner that is contrary to the bank's interests. There should be policies that mandate the disclosure of directors' conflicts of interest.

3.8 The Audit Committee and Internal Auditors: An Extension of the Board's Risk Management Function

While the board of directors is the ultimate risk manager, the audit committee can be regarded as an extension of the board's risk management function. An audit committee is a valuable tool to help management with the identification and handling of risk areas in complex organizations. The mission statement of an audit committee that is organized according to modern principles should be "to enhance the management of operational risks on a groupwide basis." Following from this, the goals of an internal audit function are to

- enable management to identify and manage business risks;
- provide an independent appraisal;
- evaluate the effectiveness, efficiency, and economy of operations;
- evaluate compliance with laws, policies, and operating instructions;
- evaluate the reliability of information produced by accounting and computer systems; and
- provide investigative services to line management.

Contrary views exist regarding the value of audit committees. Such committees have been likened to a straw of hope that boards cling to in an attempt to show that they are aware of risk management. It is logical that a board facing risk management problems will rush to the historical source of information about problems in the company, namely the auditors. The proponents of this view often point out that the auditors are simply checklist experts, while risk management has never been such a simple pursuit and should not be delegated to any committee, department, or team.

Audit Committee and Internal Audit Responsibilities

Monitoring and directing the internal audit function is an integral part of the audit committee's overall responsibilities. Both the board and management must have a tool to help ensure that policies are being followed and risks are being managed. Under a market-oriented approach, an audit extends beyond matters directly related to administrative controls and accounting. It comprises all methods and measures adopted within the business to safeguard the business's assets and manage its risks, check accuracy and reliability of accounting and management information, promote operational efficiency, and encourage adherence to management policies. In short, the internal audit can be described as an independent appraisal function and, because it is established within an organization to examine and evaluate its activities, as a valuable service to the organization.

The most important duties of internal auditors are to provide assurance regarding corporate governance, control systems, and risk management processes. Internal auditors should also review annual financial statements prior to their submission to the board of directors, ensuring that appropriate accounting policies and practices are used in the development of financial statements. The review of financial statements must be detailed enough to allow internal auditors to be able to report on a range of aspects, including the fairness of balance sheet and income statement presentation. The internal auditors also consider compliance with regulatory and legislative requirements, identify all significant discrepancies and disclosure problems, highlight differences between the annual report and management accounts, and point to major fluctuations.

Internal auditors and audit committees therefore have a very important contribution to make in the risk management process. In general terms, risk management responsibilities include monitoring the institution's financial risk profile and reviewing management procedures. The responsibilities of audit committees and internal auditors in financial risk management are to

- review management's adherence to board policies and procedures, with periodic reports to the board;
- provide assurance regarding corporate governance, control systems, and risk management processes;
- verify the adequacy and accuracy of the information reported to the board by management;
- improve communication between the board and management;
- evaluate risk management measures for their appropriateness in relation to exposures;
- test all aspects of risk activities and positions;
- ensure effective management controls over positions, limits, and actions taken when limits are exceeded;
- ensure that managers fully understand the established policies and procedures and have the necessary expertise to implement them; and

■ assess operations and suggest improvements.

Internal auditors are also expected to evaluate the external audit function and to ensure follow-up by management of problems identified in auditors' reports. One should, however, appreciate the difficulty of meeting the expectations of the public and regulatory entities. In reality, the ability of internal auditors and committees to satisfy all these requirements is limited. This issue has also received attention, by trying to design an effective framework and better methodologies (e.g., COSO, as discussed in the annex to this chapter) that would make the internal audit process more effective.

3.9 External Auditors: A Reassessment of the Traditional Approach of Auditing Banks

The primary objectives of an audit are to enable the auditor to express an opinion on whether the bank's financial statements fairly reflect its financial condition and the results of its operations for a given period. The external audit report is normally addressed to shareholders, but it is used by many other parties, such as supervisors, financial professionals, depositors, and creditors. The traditional approach to an external audit, according to the requirements of the International Standards of Auditing, typically includes a review of internal control systems. This assessment is undertaken to determine the nature and extent of substantive testing, provide an analytic review or trend analysis, and to undertake a certain amount of detailed testing. Apart from the audit of the income statement, certain line items on the balance sheet are audited through the use of separate programs, for example, fixed assets, cash, investments, or debtors. External auditors have traditionally looked for fraud and mismanagement in the lending function. Audits rarely include a detailed credit analysis of borrowers, as bank supervisors have traditionally performed this function.

A risk-based approach to financial regulation also requires a reassessment of the conventional approach to external audits. External auditors, as an integral part of the risk management partnership, have a specific role to fulfill. If market discipline is to be used to promote banking system stability, markets must first be provided with information and the capacity to hold directors and management accountable for the sound operation of a bank. External auditors play a key role in improving the market's ability to determine which banks to do business with.

External auditors are expected to

- evaluate risks inherent in the banks they are auditing;

- analyze and evaluate information presented to them to ensure that such information makes sense;

- understand the essence of transactions and financial engineering (structures) used by the client bank;

- review management's adherence to board policies and procedures;

- review the information supplied to the board, shareholders, and regulators;

- review adherence to statutory requirements; and

- report to the board, shareholders, and regulators on the fair presentation of information submitted to them.

It is clear that the philosophy of and the approach to external auditing are crucial to the success or failure of a coordinated strategy of risk management. The work of the external auditor is, of course, an added protection for the consumer. It is therefore important that the profession shift from a mere balance sheet audit to an evaluation of the risks inherent in the financial services industry. When such an approach has been fully adopted by all auditors of financial institutions, the risk management process will be significantly enhanced and all users of financial services will benefit.

The role of the accounting and auditing profession has also gained importance as part of the bank supervision process. Management letters and long-form reports submitted by auditors can provide supervisors with valuable insights into various aspects of a bank's operations. This is especially important in situations when auditors become aware of facts that may endanger the stability of a particular bank or of the banking system. In many countries, especially those where supervisory resources are scarce, supervisors may try to avoid repeating the work that external auditors have already performed for client banks. In such situations, auditors have a broader mandate prescribed by law, but at a minimum it is important to establish adequate liaison mechanisms.

3.10 The Role of the General Public

Perhaps the greatest disservice that authorities have done to investors—particularly in jurisdictions where explicit deposit insurance does not exist—is to create the illusion that regulators can guarantee the safety of the public's deposits. When all is said and done, investors must understand that no amount of management or regulatory protection can take away their own responsibility for decisions regarding their investments. Investors and depositors retain responsibility for applying sound principles in the diversification of risk and in the assessment of a financial institution. In those situations where consumers cannot protect themselves, a limited deposit insurance scheme for banks and simplified contractual disclosure for insurance companies and other portfolio managers may be considered.

The only way in which the public can be protected is if it understands who is taking the risk: individuals as investors acting through agents (investment managers and brokers), or the financial intermediaries pooling their funds and acting as principals (banks). When this distinction is clearly established and the public more clearly understands the risks that investment entails, the principal role of financial intermediaries will be to ensure that consumers are protected. This will be particularly true if the "fit and proper" requirement described above is applied to all providers of financial services.

Investors can be assisted in their roles as risk managers if the concept of "public" is broadened to include the financial media and analysts, such as stockbrokers, other advisors, and rating agencies. In addition, the market's ability to provide a basis for informed decisions must be improved through full disclosure of the financial statements of banks, as well as by informed and competent analysis in the media. Investors' interests can be safeguarded in more than one way, but disclosure of what is actually happening is essential.

As a general principle, much of the justification for banking regulation rests on alleged imperfections in information disclosure. A policy of adequate information provision would help to mitigate this underlying problem and possibly allow for the removal of many of the quantitative constraints that are prevalent in banking today. Emphasis on transparency and accountability of management would also reduce the compliance cost and regulatory distortions that are often associated with conventional approaches to banking regulation.

Probably the most promising solution to these problems is legally mandated public disclosure. Louis Brandeis, a U.S. Supreme Court justice, observed in 1913 that sunlight is said to be the best of disinfectants and electric light the most efficient policeman. This quaint-sounding aphorism still holds true. Brandeis made another crucial point: to be effective, disclosure must be made to the public. One of the most important benefits of mandating public disclosure is that the awareness that information has to be publicly disclosed affects the conduct of financial institutions. Boards of directors and management know that, after having been assimilated by the financial press and competitors, even the most highly technical information will filter through to the public. In the United States and other countries with strict information disclosure requirements, the threat of private litigation engendered by public disclosure increases the incentive to management and boards to avoid problems.

Another form of public disclosure occurs when entities such as Standard & Poor's, Moody's Investors Service, and AM Best publish their ratings of companies. Ideally, these private rating agencies balance the needs for public disclosure and confidentiality. (As the agencies receive a great deal of information—which is subsequently made public only in the form of their ratings—from the companies themselves, the agencies must respect the institutions' desire to keep some things confidential.) Through published ratings, the agencies have the ability to act more quickly and have a more subtle effect than regulators commonly do. If rating agencies can build a reputation for reliability among financial analysts, senior management in banking institutions, and the broader public, they can also provide an additional form of risk management for banks.

Market discipline could, therefore, be encouraged as an effective means of reducing the burden on regulators with regard to large, sophisticated investors. The role of financial analysts in assisting the public with risk management should not be underestimated. Financial analysts provide investment advice to clients and are therefore accustomed to presenting financial data from the perspective of investment risk. Investors who buy bank-negotiable certificates of deposit and other wholesale money market instruments should bear risk along with the creditors of bank holding companies. Faced with the possibility of losing their investments, such investors will police banks to protect their interests. Although all regulation can be left to the market, a policy of sharing resources between authorities and the private sector is bound to be more effective than one of the parties acting alone.

Nonetheless, ratings of institutions are sometimes downgraded only when problems have already extensively developed and when substantial, sometimes fatal, damage has been done. The question remains whether the market at large could have recognized deterioration or excessive risk taking at a sufficiently early stage if more information had been available. It will likely take a long time to develop techniques for the evaluation of risk and to standardize them in a way to be adequately captured in published data. Market players are therefore limited in their ability to see credit problems as they develop. The experience of the 1980s, when each major credit problem caused surprise in the market, is likely to remain the general pattern for the foreseeable future.

If market analysts cannot identify and properly evaluate credit and other problems until substantial harm has already been done, market discipline will be insufficient to protect the overall safety of the banking system or of deposit-insurance funds. In fact, the belated imposition of market pressure may complicate the task that supervisors have in dealing with problems. Consequently, the need for mechanisms to protect small and less-sophisticated investors will continue to exist.

Annex 3A: National Initiatives to Improve Corporate Governance

". . . Simply complying with the rules is not enough. They should, as I have said before, make this approach part of their companies' DNA. For companies that take this approach, most of the major concerns about compliance disappear. Moreover, if companies view the new laws as opportunities—opportunities to improve internal controls, improve the performance of the board, and improve their public reporting— they will ultimately be better run, more transparent, and therefore more attractive to investors."

William Donaldson
former U.S. SEC chairman

Given the importance of corporate governance for effective operations and competitiveness, and for the larger economic context in which firms operate, the corporate governance framework has received increased attention, through both international and national initiatives. As mentioned, the most important international initiatives were

- Principles of Corporate Governance of the Organization for Economic Co-operation and Development (OECD), 1999 and 2004, and

- Corporate Governance for Banking Organizations by Basel Committee on Banking Supervision of the Bank for International Settlements, 1999 and 2006.

There were also numerous initiatives in various countries since the early 1990s that have all reinforced the principles by which entities should be governed. Such initiatives were typically triggered by some sort of crisis in the national financial or corporate systems. The most interesting examples that are often referred to include:

- Internal Control – Integrated Framework: issued by the US Committee of Sponsoring Organizations of the Treadway Commission (COSO), 1992 and 2006 (guidance to smaller firms)

- Enterprise Risk Management Framework – issued by COSO, September 2004

- Sarbanes-Oxley (SOX) legislation in the United States, 2002

- Cadbury Code in United Kingdom, 1992 and 2003

- King Reports in South Africa, 1994 and 2002

OECD Principles of Corporate Governance

Aware of the contribution that good corporate governance makes to economic growth, investment and financial market stability, member countries of the

---

Box 3A.1 OECD Principles of Corporate Governance (Revised)

I. *Ensuring the Basis for an Effective Corporate Governance Framework* – The corporate governance framework should promote transparent and efficient markets, be consistent with the rule of law and clearly articulate the division of responsibilities among different supervisory, regulatory and enforcement authorities.

II. *Rights of Shareholders and Key Ownership Functions* – The corporate governance framework should protect and facilitate the exercise of shareholders' rights.

III. *Equitable Treatment of Shareholders* – The corporate governance framework should ensure the equitable treatment of all shareholders, including minority and foreign shareholders. All shareholders should have the opportunity to obtain effective redress for violation of their rights.

IV. *Role of Stakeholders in Corporate Governance* – The corporate governance framework should recognize the rights of stakeholders established by law or through mutual agreements and encourage active co-operation between corporations and stakeholders in creating wealth, jobs, and the sustainability of financially sound enterprises.

V. *Disclosure and Transparency* – The corporate governance framework should ensure that timely and accurate disclosure is made on all material matters regarding the corporation, including the financial situation, performance, ownership, and governance of the company.

VI. *Responsibilities of the Board* – The corporate governance framework should ensure the strategic guidance of the company, the effective monitoring of management by the board, and the board's accountability to the company and the shareholders.

In the original OECD document, each of the main sections is further elaborated in a lot more details.

OECD Secretariat, 2004

Organization for Economic Cooperation and Development (OECD) put governance as one of the priority topic in 1998. The first set of OECD principles was developed in 1999. It has since become an international benchmark for policy makers, investors, corporations and other stakeholders worldwide. The OECD principles define corporate governance as involving "a set of relationships between a company's management, its board, its shareholders, and other stakeholders." Corporate governance also provides the structure through which the objectives of the company are set, and the means of attaining those objectives and monitoring performance are determined. Good corporate governance should provide proper incentives for the board and management to pursue objectives that are in the interests of the company and its shareholders and should facilitate effective monitoring.

In 2002, the initial principles were thoroughly reviewed by the Steering Group on Corporate Governance to take account of new developments and experienced of OECD member and nonmember countries. The new set of principles (box 3A.1) was announced in 2004. In addition to the key topics provided in box 3A.1, further details could be found on OECD site (www.OECD.org). The associated OECD Financial Stability Forum has designated the principles as one of the 12 key standards for sound financial systems.

The OECD principles have also provided a basis for bank governance principles developed by the Basel Committee on Banking Supervision of the Bank for International Settlement. Supervisors have a keen interest in sound corporate governance as it is an essential element in the safe and sound functioning of a bank and may affect the bank's risk profile if not implemented effectively. As the functions of the board of directors and senior management with regard to setting policies, implementing policies and monitoring compliance are key elements in the control functions of a bank, effective oversight of the business and affairs of a bank by its board and senior management contributes to the maintenance of an efficient and cost-effective supervisory system.

Committee of Sponsoring Organizations of the Treadway Commission, United States (COSO)

The Committee of Sponsoring Organizations of the Treadway Commission (commonly referred to as COSO) was convened by the U.S. Congress in response to well-publicized financial irregularities that occurred in the late 1980s. COSO formulated an internal control framework designed to help organizations reduce the risk of asset loss, ensure the reliability of financial statements and compliance with laws and regulations, and promote efficiency. COSO is recognized by many public sector and professional bodies as a standard for the evaluation of internal control and the risk environment.

Integrated Framework for Internal Control of Financial Reporting. Under the COSO framework (see figure 3A.1), the effectiveness of an internal control system is measured by its capacity to provide reasonable assurance to management and to the board of directors of their bank's achievement of its objectives in three categories: (1) effectiveness and efficiency of operations, (2) reliability of financial reporting, and (3) compliance with applicable laws and regulation. The emphasis on behavior in the COSO model is a recognition of reality, namely that policies specify what management wants to happen; what actually happens, and which rules are obeyed, bent, or ignored, is determined by corporate culture.

The COSO internal control model consists of five interrelated components, which are inherent in the way management runs the organization. The components are linked, and serve as criteria for determining whether or not the system is effective. The COSO components include control environment, risk assessment, control activities, monitoring and learning, and information and communication. The COSO enterprise risk management framework and key components of operational risk approaches are summarized in table 3A.1.

Figure 3A.1 COSO – Enterprise Risk Management Framework

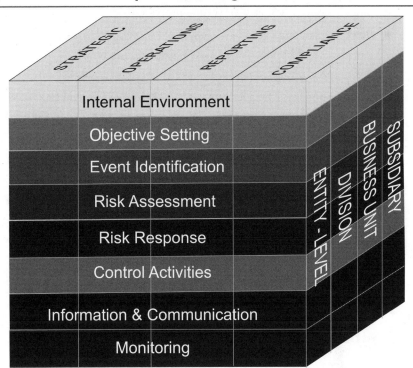

Risk Management Framework. Another important theme addressed by COSO is the enterprise risk management. COSO divides the enterprise risk management (ERM) framework into eight interrelated components (see figure 3A.1), including the following:

- **Internal environment** – Internal environment describes the work environment and risk preferences of an organization and sets the framework for how risk is viewed and addressed by its management and employees. Internal environment includes risk management philosophy, risk appetite, integrity and ethical values, and the environment in which they operate.

- **Objective setting** – Objectives must be set up-front. Risk management function should ensure that there is a process for corporate management to set the objectives, that the chosen objectives support and align with the entity's mission, and that they are consistent with its risk appetite.

- **Event identification** – Internal and external events affecting achievement of an entity's objectives must be identified, distinguishing between risks and opportunities. Opportunities are channeled back to management's strategy or objective-setting processes.

- **Risk assessment** – Risks are analyzed, considering the likelihood of occurrence and impact, as a basis for determining how they should be managed. Risks are assessed on an inherent and a residual basis.

- **Risk response** – Management selects risk responses—avoiding, accepting, reducing, or sharing risk—developing a set of actions to align risks with the entity's risk tolerances and risk appetite.

- **Control activities** – Policies and procedures should be established and implemented to help ensure the risk responses are effectively carried out.

- **Information and communication** – Relevant information is identified, captured, and communicated in a form and timeframe that enable people to carry out their responsibilities. Effective communication also occurs in a broader sense—flowing down, across, and up the entity.

- **Monitoring** – The entirety of enterprise risk management must be monitored and modifications made as necessary.

Other Initiatives

Sarbanes Oxley (SOX) Legislation, United States, was the legislative response to a series of corporate scandals that erupted in the United States in the early 2000s. Section 302 of SOX requires that management certify the following:

- They have viewed their company's financial report.

- To the best of their knowledge, the report contains no untrue statement of a material fact and does not omit any material fact that would cause any statements to be misleading.

- To the best of their knowledge, the financial statements and other financial information in the report fairly present, in all material aspects, the company's financial position, results of operations, and cash flows.

- They accept responsibility for establishing and maintaining disclosure controls and procedures, and the report contains an evaluation of the effectiveness of these measures.

- Any major deficiencies or material weaknesses in controls and any control-related fraud have been disclosed to the audit committee and external auditor.

Table 3A.1 COSO Enterprise Risk Management Framework

COSO Enterprise Risk Management Framework									
Functions	**Activities**	**Internal Environment**	**Management Objectives**	**Risk & Event Identification**	**Risk Assessment**	**Risk Response**	**Control Activities**	**Information Communication**	**Monitoring**
Enterprise:	Activities required to perform each of the 10 separate functions	Tone Integrity Ethics	Strategic	People	Likelihood	Avoid	Policies	Identify relevant information	Monitor entire ERM process
1. Strategic planning									
2. Governance									
3. General management		View of risk	Operational	Processes	Impact	Reduce	Procedures	Capture	Ongoing activities
4. Infrastructure and own capacity development									
5. Business development		Risk management philosophy	Reporting	Systems		Share		Communicate	Separate evaluations
Operational:									
6. New client portfolio set-up									
7. Portfolio management									
8. Settlement & control		Risk appetite	Compliance	External events		Accept		Enable people to carry out responsibilities	Modify processes where needed
9. Valuation & accounting									
10. Risk analytics									

■ The report discloses significant changes affecting internal controls that have occurred since the last report and whether corrective actions have been taken.

The most contentious aspect of SOX is section 404, which is also the most costly to comply with. It requires management and the external auditor to report on the adequacy of the company's internal control over financial reporting (ICFR), as part of each annual reporting cycle. The report must affirm "the responsibility of management for establishing and maintaining an adequate internal control structure and procedures for financial reporting." The report must also "contain an assessment, as of the end of the most recent fiscal year, of the effectiveness of internal control structure and financial reporting procedures." More specifically, the chief executive officer and the chief financial officer must personally report on the adequacy and effectiveness of internal controls over financial reporting, including:

■ the internal control framework used by management,

■ management's assessment of the effectiveness of internal controls,

■ disclosure of any material weaknesses found by the auditor,

■ the result of the external audit required to independently evaluate management's assessment (a requirement of the Securities and Exchange Commission), and

■ a statement of any material weaknesses to be included in the company's annual report.

To do this, managers are generally adopting an internal control framework such as that described in COSO. In late 2006, a new standard was proposed to help alleviate the significant costs of compliance and improve the focus of assessment on the most critical risk areas.

Cadbury Code, United Kingdom, emphasizes the principles of openness, integrity, and accountability. Openness is described as the basis for the confidence necessary between business and all those who have a stake in its success. Open disclosure of information contributes to the efficient working of the market economy, prompts boards to take effective action, and allows shareholders and others to scrutinize companies more thoroughly.

King Report, South Africa, is an example of an initiative to improve governance in a developing country. Unlike its counterparts in other countries at the time, the 1994 King Report in South Africa went beyond the financial and regulatory aspects of corporate governance—it advocated an integrated approach to good governance in the interests of a wide range of stakeholders and the fundamental principles of good financial, social, ethical, and environmental practice. In adopting a participative corporate governance system of enterprise with integrity, the 1994 King Report emphasized the need for companies to recognize that they no longer act independently from the societies in which they operate. King moved away from a single focus on the entity's bottom line by embracing economic, environmental, and social aspects of an entity's activities. The report also distinguished *accountability* from *responsibility*.

4

Balance Sheet Structure

Key Messages

■ The composition of a bank's balance sheet assets and liabilities is one of the key factors that determine the level of risk faced by the institution.

■ Growth in the balance sheet and resulting changes in the relative proportion of assets or liabilities affect the risk management process.

■ Changes in the relative structure of assets and liabilities should be a conscious decision of a bank's policy makers: the board of directors.

■ Monitoring key components of the balance sheet may alert the analyst to negative trends in relationships between asset growth and capital retention capability.

■ It is important to monitor the growth of low, nonearning, and off-balance-sheet items.

■ Balance sheet structure lies at the heart of the asset-liability management process.

4.1 Introduction: Composition of the Balance Sheet

The goal of financial management is to maximize the value of a bank, as determined by its profitability and risk level. Since risk is inherent in banking and unavoidable, the task of financial management is to manage risk in such a way that the different types of risk are kept at acceptable levels and profitability is sustained. Doing so requires the continual identification, quantification, and monitoring of risk exposures, which in turn demands sound policies, adequate organization, efficient processes, skilled analysts, and elaborate computerized information systems. In addition, risk management requires the capacity to anticipate changes and to act so that a bank's business can be structured and restructured to profit from the changes—or at least to minimize losses. Supervisory authorities should not prescribe how business is conducted; they should instead maintain prudent oversight of a bank by evaluating the risk composition of its assets and by insisting that an adequate amount of capital and reserves is available to safeguard solvency.

Until the 1970s, the business of banking primarily consisted of the extension of credit—in other words, a simple intermediation of deposits that had been raised at a relatively low cost—and bank managers faced fairly simple decisions concerning loan volumes, pricing, and investments. The key managerial challenges of the past were controlling asset quality and resulting loan losses, as well as managing overhead expenditures. With the background of recession, volatile interest rates, and inflation during the late 1970s and early 1980s, the management of both assets and liabilities has become necessary to maintain satisfactory margin performance. The complexity of balance sheet management continued to increase as a result of deregulation in the 1980s, with growing competition for funds becoming a primary management concern.

The era of deregulation and increased competition continued in the 1990s, including involvement by financial institutions other than banks. This environment underscored the need for competitive pricing and, in practical terms, for an increase in and engagement of liabilities to maximize spread and control exposure to related risks. Because of the inverse relationship of these two goals, a balancing act between maximizing the spreads versus controlling risk exposures has become a focal point in the financial management, regulation, and supervision of banks.

This chapter highlights the importance of the structure and composition of liabilities and assets, as well as the related income statement items. In addition, it illustrates the ways in which a bank's risk managers and analysts can analyze the structure of balance sheets and income statements, as well as individual balance sheet items with specific risk aspects, for example, liquidity in the case of deposit liabilities or market risk in the case of traded securities. In this process, the interaction between various types of risk must be understood to ensure that they are not evaluated in isolation.

Asset-liability management, which includes raising and utilizing funds, lies at the financial heart of a bank. The asset-liability management process comprises strategic planning and implementation and control processes that affect the volume, mix, maturity, interest rate sensitivity, quality, and liquidity of a bank's assets and liabilities. The primary goal of asset-liability management is to produce a high-quality, stable, large, and growing flow of net interest income. This goal is accomplished by achieving the optimum combination and level of assets, liabilities, and financial risk. Asset-liability management is further discussed in chapter 12.

Figure 4.1 illustrates the composition of a bank's assets and liabilities. An evaluation of the balance sheet structure requires understanding not only the bank, but also its business and competitive environment; the overall regulatory, economic, and policy environment; and the customer mix. The structure of a typical balance sheet, with deposits from customers on the liability side and loans and advances to customers on the asset side, is also reviewed. This pattern reflects the nature of banks as intermediaries, with ratios of capital to liabilities at such a low level that their leverage would be unacceptable to any business outside the financial services industry.

Figure 4.1 Composition of Bank Assets and Liabilities

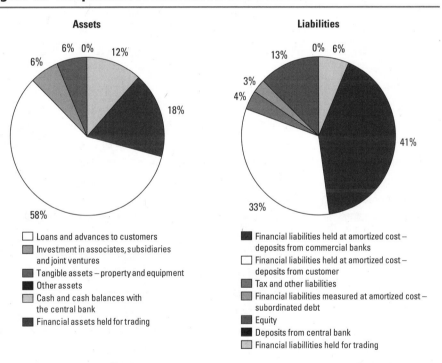

Assets

- Loans and advances to customers
- Investment in associates, subsidiaries and joint ventures
- Tangible assets – property and equipment
- Other assets
- Cash and cash balances with the central bank
- Financial assets held for trading

Liabilities

- Financial liabilities held at amortized cost – deposits from commercial banks
- Financial liabilities held at amortized cost – deposits from customer
- Tax and other liabilities
- Financial liabilities measured at amortized cost – subordinated debt
- Equity
- Deposits from central bank
- Financial liabilities held for trading

4.2 Bank Assets

The analyst should be able to assess the risk profile of the bank simply by analyzing the relative share of various asset items and changes in their proportionate share over time. For example, if the loan portfolio drops significantly, while property lending increases materially, one would question whether the bank's risk management systems are adequate to handle the increased risks. Normally, such a jump would reflect a shift from one to another area of risk. Likewise, an increase or decrease in trading securities would indicate a change in the level of market risk to which the institution is exposed. Such an assessment is possible at a macro level, prior to any detailed review of credit, liquidity, or market risk management. When linked to the amount of net income yielded by each category of assets, this analysis increases in importance, necessitating a challenging assessment of risk versus reward.

A bank's balance sheet (statement of financial position) is normally prepared on a liquidity basis—rather than the noncurrent/current asset basis of nonbank enterprises. An assessment of a bank's liquidity, as evidenced in its balance sheet and statement of cash flows, is of paramount importance to the financial analyst. Banks need assets that are liquid to accommodate expected and unexpected balance sheet fluctuations. In environments where markets are not developed and the liquidity of different claims still depends almost exclusively on their maturity rather than on the ability to sell them, banks tend to keep a relatively high level of liquid assets that bear little or no interest. In such environments, liquid assets typically account for at least 10 percent, or in extreme situations as much as 30 percent, of total assets. Increasing market orientation, the growth of financial markets, and the greater diversity of financial instruments worldwide entail greater short-term flexibility in liquidity management, which in turn reduces the need to hold large amounts of liquid assets. In banking environments with developed financial markets, liquid assets typically account for only about 5 percent of total assets. An appraisal of whether the level of liquid assets is satisfactory must be based on a thorough understanding of money market dynamics in the respective country, as certain assets that appear liquid in good times may not be liquid in more difficult periods. Table 4.1 offers a sample spreadsheet that can be used to assess structural change in the liquidity of a bank's assets.

Table 4.1 Balance Sheet Assets

Assets	Period 01	Period 02
Cash and cash balances with the central bank		
Financial assets held for trading		
Financial assets *designated* at fair value through profit or loss		
Available-for-sale financial assets		
Loans and advances to customers		
Held-to-maturity investments		
Derivatives – Hedge accounting purposes		
Tangible assets		
Intangible assets		
Investments in associates, subsidiaries and joint ventures		
Tax assets		
Other assets		
Noncurrent assets and disposal groups classified as held for sale		
TOTAL ASSETS	**100%**	**100%**

Cash and Balances with the Central Bank

Cash and balances with the central bank represent the holdings of highly liquid assets, such as bank notes, gold coin, and bullion, as well as deposits with the central bank. A percentage of deposits is normally required to be held to meet the central bank's reserve requirements and serve as a monetary policy tool. Flat-rate reserve requirements are used to control the amount of money that a bank is able to extend as credit. However, when banks are required to hold excessive reserve assets, particularly when the assets do not pay interest, the cost to banks increases. This creates incentives for banks to devise instruments that are not subject to reserve requirements, encourages intermediation through new channels, and may give a competitive advantage to institutions that are not subject to reserve requirements. Such practices tend to reduce the effectiveness and the importance of reserve requirements as a monetary policy tool.

Regulators have tried to make reserve requirements more difficult to circumvent and to reduce the incentives for doing so. For example, changes in reserve requirements that have been introduced by regulators include a reduction of the level, type, and volatility of reserve holdings Regulators have also introduced an increase in the various types of compensation made to banks for maintaining reserves.

Financial Assets Held for Trading

These assets represent the bank's investment and proprietary trading books in securities, foreign currencies, equities, and commodities.

Although similar securities are involved, the investment portfolio (chapter 10) must be distinguished from the proprietary trading portfolio (discussed in chapter 11). Proprietary trading is aimed at exploiting market opportunities with leveraged funding (for example, through the use of repurchase agreements), whereas the investment portfolio is held and traded as a buffer/stable liquidity portfolio.

Investment and trading assets are valued in terms of International Accounting Standard (IAS) 39 and can be classified as "trading, available-for-sale, or held-to-maturity." However, these assets would normally be disclosed at fair value (marked-to-market) in the bank's financial statements (see chapter 5, section 5.2 for the treatment of income on such assets and chapter 14 for International Financial Reporting Standards [IFRS] disclosure).

In many developing countries, banks have been or are obligated to purchase government bonds or other designated claims, usually to ensure that a minimum amount of high-quality liquidity is available to meet deposit demands. Frequently, the main purpose of such liquid asset requirements is to ensure a predictable flow of finance to designated recipients. Government is the most frequent beneficiary, often with an implicit subsidy. Such obligatory investments may diminish the availability and increase the cost of credit extended to the economy (and the private sector) and, because of the increased cost of credit, result in a higher level of risk.

In developed countries and financial markets, an increase in bank investment and trading portfolios generally reflects the growing orientation of a bank to nontraditional operations. In such cases, an investment portfolio comprises different types of securities instruments. In risk management terms, such an orientation would mean that a bank has replaced credit risk with market and counterparty risk.

Loans and Advances to Customers

Loans and advances to customers are normally the most significant component of a bank's assets. These include loans for general working capital (overdrafts), investment lending, asset-backed installment and mortgage loans, financing of debtors (accounts receivable and credit card accounts), and tradable debt such as acceptances and commercial paper. Loans and advances are extended in domestic and foreign currency and are provided by banks as financing for public or private sector investments.

In the past decade, innovation has increased the marketability of bank assets through the introduction of sales of assets such as mortgages, automobile loans, and export credits used as backing for marketable securities (a practice known as securitization and prevalent in the United States and the United Kingdom).

An analysis of this trend may highlight investment or spending activity in various sectors of the economy, while an analysis of a foreign currency loan portfolio may indicate expectations regarding exchange rate and interest rate developments. Further, evaluation of trade credits may reveal important trends in competitiveness of the economy and its terms of trade.

Tangible Assets

Tangible assets such as property represent the bank's infrastructure resources and typically include the bank's premises, other fixed property, computer equipment, vehicles, furniture, and fixtures. In certain circumstances, banks may have a relatively high proportion of fixed assets, such as houses, land, or commercial space. These holdings would be the result of collections on collateral, which, under most regulations, banks are required to dispose of within a set period of time. They may also reflect the deliberate decision of a bank to invest in real estate if the market is fairly liquid and prices are increasing. In some developing countries, investments in fixed assets reach such high proportions that central banks may begin to feel obliged to limit or otherwise regulate property-related assets. A bank should not be in the business of investing in real estate assets, and therefore a preponderance of these assets would affect the assessment of the bank. In more developed countries, real estate assets not acquired in the normal course of banking business would be booked in a subsidiary at the holding company level to protect depositors from associated risks.

Investments in Associates, Subsidiaries, and Joint Ventures

Other investments could comprise a bank's longer-term equity-type investments, such as equities and recapitalization/nontrading bonds held in the bank's long-term investment portfolio. This includes equity investments in subsidiaries, associates, and other listed and unlisted entities. The percentage of a portfolio that is devoted to this type of instrument varies among countries, although not necessarily as a result of a bank's own asset-liability management decisions. Such assets are also valued in terms of IAS 39 and will normally be classified as "available-for-sale, or held-to-maturity."

For equity investments, the balance sheet should be reviewed on a consolidated basis to ensure a proper understanding of the effect of such investments on the structure of the bank's own balance sheet, and to properly assess the asset quality of the bank.

Other Assets

Other assets typically include prepaid amounts and other sundry items. These vary with regard to the predictability of income associated with a particular asset, the existence of markets for such assets, the possibility of selling the assets, and the reliability of the assessments of the asset's useful life. The treatment of assets in evaluating capital adequacy can be controversial. For example, such assets may include suspense accounts, which have to be analyzed and verified to ensure that the asset is indeed real and recoverable.

4.3 Bank Liabilities

As explained in section 4.2, the relative share of various balance sheet components—liabilities, in this instance—is already a good indication of the risk levels and types of risk to which a bank is exposed.

An increase in the level of nonretail deposits funding, such as repurchase agreements or certificates of deposit, could expose the bank to greater volatility in satisfying its funding requirements, requiring increasingly sophisticated liquidity risk management. Funding instruments such as repurchase agreements also expose a bank to market risk, in addition to liquidity risk.

The business of banking is traditionally based on the concept of low margins and high leverage. Consequently, a special feature of a bank's balance sheet is its low capital-to-liabilities ratio, which would normally be unacceptable to any other business outside the financial services industry. The acceptable level of risk associated with such a structure is measured and prescribed according to risk-based capital requirements, which are in turn linked to the composition of a bank's assets.

Table 4.2 Balance Sheet Liabilities

Liabilities	Period 01	Period 02
Central bank funding		
Financial liabilities held for trading		
Derivatives held for trading		
Short positions		
Debt certificates (including bonds intended for repurchase in short term)		
Other financial liabilities held for trading – repurchase agreement obligations		
Financial liabilities designated at fair value through profit or loss		
Financial liabilities measured at amortized cost		
Deposits from banks and other credit institutions		
Deposits from customers		
Debt certificates (including bonds) - own securities issued		
Subordinated liabilities		
Financial liabilities associated with transferred financial assets		
Derivatives – Hedge accounting purposes		
Fair value changes of the hedged items in portfolio hedge of interest rate risk		
Provisions		
Tax liabilities		
Other liabilities		
Share capital repayable on demand (e.g. cooperative shares)		
Liabilities included in disposal groups classified as held for sale		
TOTAL LIABILITIES	**100%**	**100%**

While the types of liabilities present in a bank's balance sheet are nearly universal, their exact composition varies greatly, depending on a particular bank's business and market orientation as well as by the prices and supply characteristics of different types of liabilities at any given time. The funding structure of a bank directly affectsits cost of operation and therefore determines a bank's profit potential and risk level. The structure of a bank's liabilities also reflects the specific asset-liability and risk management policies of a bank. Table 4.2 becomes the source used to illustrate a typical liability structure as per figure 4.4.

Central Bank Funding

Borrowings from the central bank may appear among the bank's liabilities. The most frequent reason for borrowing from the central bank is that changes have occurred in the volume of required reserves as a result of fluctuations in deposits. These shifts occur when banks have not correctly forecasted their daily reserve position and have been forced to borrow to make up the difference, or to assist banks to meet temporary requirements for funds. Longer-term credit from the central bank indicates an unusual situation that may be the result of national or regional difficulties or problems related to the particular bank in question. Historically, central bank financing was often directed toward a special purpose determined by government policies—for example, in the areas of agriculture or housing—but this type of activity is increasingly out of date.

Financial Liabilities Held for Trading: Repurchase Agreement Obligations

Instead of resorting to direct borrowing, a bank may sell and simultaneously agree to repurchase securities at a specific time or after certain conditions have been met. Repurchase structures are often used to fund a bank's trading portfolio and to enhance returns on such portfolios.

The proprietary trading portfolio is therefore aimed at exploiting market opportunities with leveraged funding such as repurchase agreements, whereas the investment portfolio is held and traded as a buffer/stable liquidity portfolio—and funded with more stable deposits.

Repurchase agreements may expose banks to interest rate or market risks as they involve underlying securities, and even a credit risk if the buyer is unable to follow through on its commitments. The level of securities sold under repurchase agreements has (in the past) also served as a barometer of the level of disintermediation in the system, as well as the demand for wholesale funds.

Financial Liabilities Measured at Amortized Cost

Deposits from other banks and financial institutions and deposits from customers constitute financial liabilities that are measured at amortized cost.

Deposits from Banks and Other Credit Institutions

Deposits from banks and other credit institutions (interbank funding) includes all deposits, loans, and advances that are extended between banks; they are normally regarded as volatile sources of funding. An analysis of interbank balances may point to structural peculiarities in the banking system, for example, when funding for a group of banks is provided by one of its members.

Given the volatility of such funding sources, however, if a bank is an extensive borrower, its activities should be analyzed in relation to any other aspects of its operations that influence borrowing. The acceptable reasons for reliance on interbank funding include temporary or seasonal loan or cash requirements and the matching of large and unanticipated withdrawals of customer deposits. Money centers or large regional banks engaged in money market transactions tend to borrow on a continuous basis. Otherwise, heavy reliance on interbank funding indicates that a bank carries a high degree of funding risk and is overextended in relation to its normal deposit volume.

Deposits from Customers

Deposits usually constitute the largest proportion of a bank's total liabilities. Deposits from customers—the amount due to other customers and depositors—represent money accepted from the general public, such as demand and savings, fixed and notice, and foreign currency deposits. The structure and stability of the deposit base is critical. Broader trends also come into play. An analysis of private sector deposits (including funding from repurchase agreements and certificates of deposit) highlights economic trends related to the level of spending and its effect on inflation. Furthermore, growth in the money supply is calculated using total deposits in the banking system. A change in the level of deposits in the banking system is therefore one of the variables that influences monetary policy.

Within the deposit structure, some items are inherently more risky than others. For example, large corporate deposits are less stable than household deposits, not only because of their higher degree of concentration but also because they are more actively managed. A large proportion of nonretail or nonstandard deposits can be unstable and tends to indicate that the bank may be paying higher rates of interest than its competitors or that depositors may be attracted by liberal credit accommodations. Cash collateral and various types of loan escrow accounts may also be counted as deposits, although these funds can be used only for their stated purpose.

Competition for funds is a normal part of any banking market, and depositors, both households and corporations, often aim to minimize idle funds. A bank should therefore have a policy on deposit attraction and maintenance and procedures for analyzing, on a regular basis, the volatility and the character of the deposit structure so that funds can be productively utilized even when the probability of withdrawal exists. Analysis of the deposit structure should determine the percentage of hard-core, stable, seasonal, and volatile deposits.

Foreign Borrowings

International borrowing may occur in the same form as domestic funding, except that it normally exposes a bank to additional currency risk. Direct forms of international borrowing include loans from foreign banks, export promotion agencies in various countries, or international lending agencies, as well as vostro accounts. Indirect forms include notes, acceptances, import drafts, and trade bills sold with the bank's endorsement; guarantees; and notes or trade bills rediscounted with central banks in various countries. The existence of foreign funding is generally a good indicator of international confidence in a country and its economy.

4.4 Equity and Other Items

The equity of a bank represents the buffer available to protect creditors against losses that may be incurred by managing risks imprudently. Table 4.3 illustrates the presentation and disclosure of equity in terms of International Financial Reporting Standards (IFRS). According to international norms, banks normally have three tiers of capital components (see chapter 6 for further discussion). The key components of bank capital are common stock, retained earnings, and perpetual preferred stock, all of which are counted as Tier 1 capital. Otherwise, to qualify for Tier 1 or Tier 2 capital, a capital instrument should have long maturity and not contain or be covered by any covenants, terms, or restrictions that are inconsistent with sound banking. For example, instruments that result in higher dividends or interest payments when a bank's financial condition deteriorates cannot be accepted as part of capital. Tier 2 and Tier 3 capital components will often mature at some point, and a bank must be prepared to replace or redeem them without impairing its capital adequacy. When determining capital adequacy, the remaining maturity of Tier 2 and Tier 3 capital components should therefore also be assessed.

Table 4.3 Components of a Bank's Equity

Equity	Period 01	Period 02
Issued capital		
Share premium		
Other Equity		
Revaluation reserves and other valuation differences on:		
Reserves (including retained earnings)		
<Treasury shares>		
Income from current year		
<Interim dividends>		
Minority interest		
Total equity and minority interest		
TOTAL LIABILITIES, MINORITY INTEREST AND EQUITY	100%	100%

Off-Balance-Sheet Items

Financial innovation has also led to a variety of new off-balance-sheet financial instruments. The costs associated with monetary policy regulations, such as minimum reserve requirements, and capital adequacy requirements have frequently been circumvented by the use of off-balance-sheet instruments. Credit substitutes, such as guarantees and letters of credit, and derivative instruments, such as futures and options, do not count as assets or liabilities, even though they expose the bank to certain risks and hence carry a capital requirement. It is a challenge to manage risks in relation to such off-balance-sheet items. Consequently, it is important that management information accurately reflects exposure in relation to these instruments. As part of managing the risk associated with off-balance-sheet items, it is important that the extent of the liability or right is quantified. This can be accomplished by assessing the nature, volume, and anticipated usage of credit commitments, contingent liabilities, guarantees, and other off-balance-sheet items. Sensitivity to market changes that affect such instruments should also be determined in the context of the overall risk to the company.

4.5   Growth and Changes in the Balance Sheet

The banking sector's assets comprise items that are a reflection of individual banks' balance sheets, although the structure of balance sheets may vary significantly depending on business orientation, market environment, customer mix, or economic environment. The composition of a bank's balance sheet is normally a result of asset-liability and risk management decisions. Figures 4.2 and 4.3 illustrate the structure and growth of the asset components of a bank over time. Figure 4.4 shows structural change and growth of capital and liabilities.

The analyst should be able to assess the risk profile of the bank simply by analyzing the relative share of various asset items and the changes in proportionate share over time. For example, if the loan portfolio jumps from 44 percent to 58 percent of on-balance-sheet assets (figure 4.3 – period 4 to current period), one would question if the bank's credit risk management systems are adequate to enable handling of the increased volume of loan transactions and of the loan portfolio. In addition, such a change would disclose a shift from another risk area. Likewise, an increase or decrease in trading securities would indicate a change in the level of market risk to which the institution is exposed. Such observations are possible prior to a detailed review of either the credit or the market risk management areas. When linked to the amount of net income yielded by each category of assets, this analysis increases in importance, necessitating a challenging assessment of risk versus reward.

Figure 4.2 Structural Change and Asset Growth

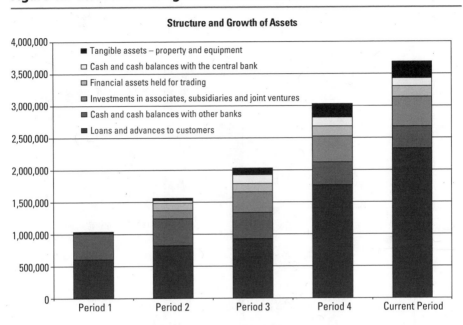

Structure and Growth of Assets

Figure 4.3 Changes in the Structure of a Bank's Assets

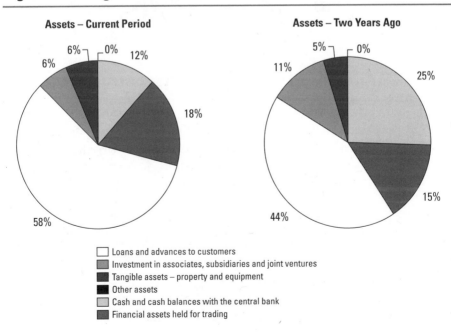

Figure 4.4 Structural Change and Growth of Capital and Liabilities

Structure and Growth of Capital and Liabilities

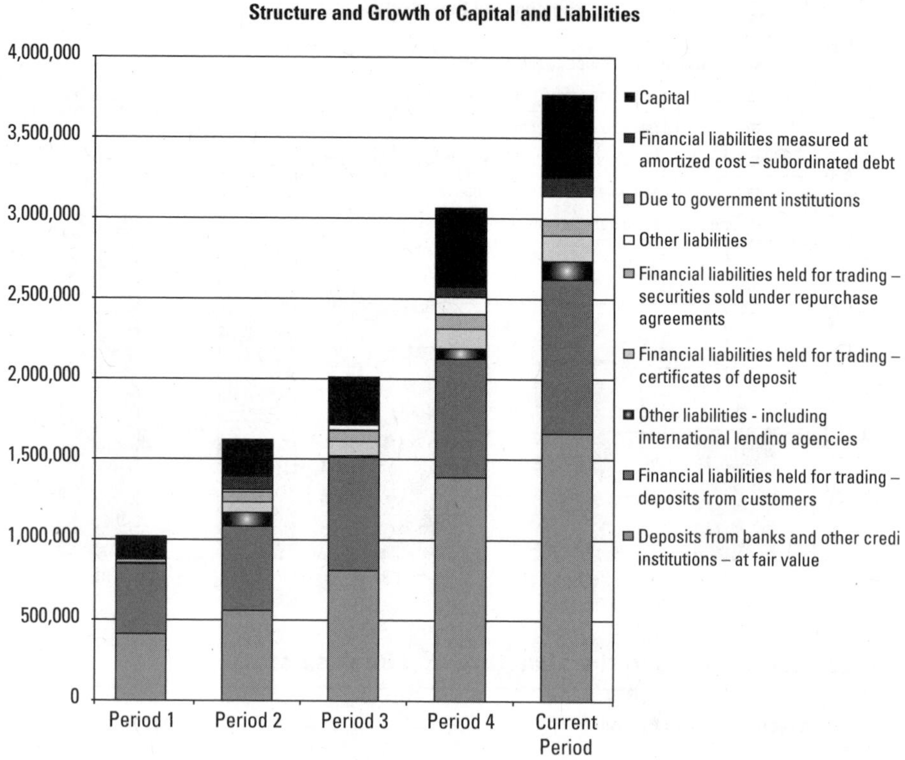

4.6 Risk Analysis of the Balance Sheet Structure and Growth

A bank that is well positioned and successful in its market can be expected to grow. An analysis of balance sheets can be performed to determine growth rates and the type of structural changes that occur in a bank (table 4.4). Such an analysis indicates the general type of business undertaken by a bank and requires an understanding of the structure of its balance sheet and the nature of its assets and liabilities. Even when overall balance sheet growth is not significant, individual components normally shift in reaction to changes in the competitive market or economic or regulatory environments (as illustrated by figures 4.1 to 4.4 above). As balance sheet structure changes, inherent risks also change. The structure of a balance sheet should therefore be a part of an assessment of the adequacy and effectiveness of policies and procedures for managing risk exposures.

Mismatches

Asset-liability mismatches can occur in several areas. A bank could have substantial long-term assets (such as fixed rate mortgages) funded by the short-term liabilities (such as deposits). This creates a maturity mismatch that increases liquidity risk. Alternatively, a bank could have all of its liabilities as floating interest rates bonds, but assets in fixed rate instruments. This creates an interest rate mismatch. Or, a bank that chooses to borrow entirely in one currency and lend in another currency would have a significant currency mismatch.

Mismatches are normally handled by the Asset Liability management functions, which is further discussed in chapter 12.

Growth Trends

Table 4.4 Total Growth of Balance Sheet and Off-Balance-Sheet Items

Total Growth (percent)	Period 2	Period 2	Period 3	Period 4	Current Period
Total assets	100	120	150	190	258
Risk-weighted assets	100	160	205	295	370
Qualifying capital	100	205	254	295	315
Off-balance-sheet items as percentage of total assets	1.09	1.39	15.89	24.62	24.92

Table 4.4 and Figure 4.5 illustrate the overall growth of a bank's assets and capital. In addition, it highlights the extent to which a bank's growth is balanced, or the extent to which the bank has been able to maintain regulatory capital requirements in relation to total assets and risk-weighted asset growth. A graph of this kind could provide an early indicator of capital adequacy problems to come, which in turn could result from rapid expansion.

In normal situations, the growth of a bank's assets is justified by an increase in the stable funding base at a cost that is acceptable to the bank, as well as by profit opportunities. The spread between interest earned and interest paid should normally be stable or increasing. In a stable market environment, increasing margins may indicate the acceptance of higher risk. To avoid increased lending risk, emphasis is often placed on fee-generating income, which does not involve a bank's balance sheet.

Figure 4.5 Total Growth of a Bank's Assets and Capital

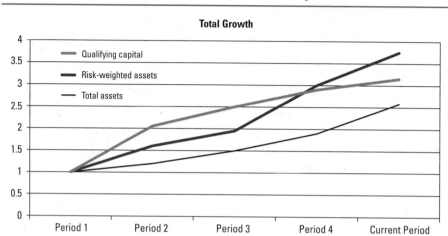

Total Growth

Legend:
- Qualifying capital
- Risk-weighted assets
- Total assets

X-axis: Period 1, Period 2, Period 3, Period 4, Current Period
Y-axis: 0, 0.5, 1, 1.5, 2, 2.5, 3, 3.5, 4

Banks that grow too quickly tend to take unjustified risks and often find that administrative and management information systems cannot keep up with the rate of expansion. Even well-managed banks can run into risk management problems arising out of excessive growth, especially concerning their loan portfolios.

In some countries, monetary policy conduct may limit or significantly affect the rate of growth and the structure of a bank's assets. Despite the shift away from reliance on portfolio regulations and administrative controls, credit ceilings have been and still are a relatively common method of implementing monetary policy in some transitional economies, especially in countries with less-developed financial markets. An alternative method of indirectly manipulating the demand for and level of credit in the economy has traditionally been to influence the cost of credit.

Changes in banking and finance mean that the scope for circumventing credit ceilings and interest rate regulations has increased significantly. A loss of effectiveness, and concerns over the distortions that credit ceiling and interest rate manipulations generate, are the reasons why these instruments are increasingly abandoned in favor of open-market interventions. The use of credit ceilings in countries where such monetary policies have been pursued for long periods of time may have reduced the competitive ability of banks and encouraged innovation and the creation of alternative instruments and channels of financial intermediation. In other words, credit ceilings have inadvertently shaped the evolution of banking systems.

Low-Earning and Nonearning Assets

Banks clearly need to keep a reasonable risk profile on a profitable basis. The cause for declining net interest margins must include the assessment of the level of low-earning or nonearning assets, particularly those with high risk. Figure 4.6 provides a picture of the changing level, over time, of low- and nonearning assets. The proportion of these assets of the total assets of a bank has increased significantly during the periods under observation. This trend should be analyzed not only in relation to industry benchmarks or averages, but also within the context of changes over time. In this particular case, growth may have resulted from changes in the regulatory environment or in the bank's funding structure, whereby the bank may have increased the proportion of funding subject to regulatory requirements. It could also have been due to poor asset management decisions. In many transitional economies, this asset category reflects forced holding of recapitalization bonds issued by governments to save their banking systems.

Figure 4.6 Low-Earning and Nonearning Assets as a Percentage of Total Assets

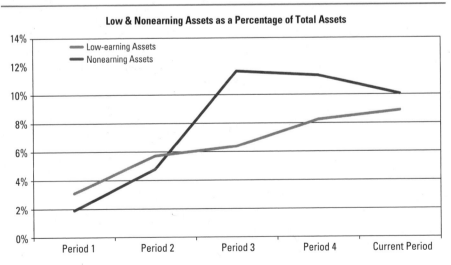

Low & Nonearning Assets as a Percentage of Total Assets

Off-Balance-Sheet Growth

Figure 4.7 similarly illustrates off-balance-sheet growth. This graph can be used to determine the growth of off-balance-sheet items and the proportion that such items constitute in total on- and off-balance-sheet activities. The bank under observation has obviously been increasing its off-balance-sheet activities, although the notional value of many off-balance-sheet instruments may not be directly related to the extent of risk exposure. An analyst should understand why and exactly which instruments have supported this significant trend. Because the off-balance-sheet items do expose a bank to financial risks, a few questions arise, including the risk implications of different instruments not present on the balance sheet. In addition, it is not known whether the return to the bank is equal to the additional risk taken or whether the bank has in place an adequate risk management system for off-balance-sheet exposures.

Figure 4.7 Off-Balance-Sheet Items as a Percentage of Total Assets

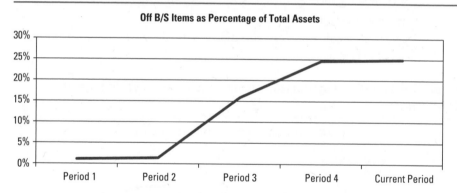

5

Income Statement Structure

Key Messages

- Income and earnings are indicators of a bank's capacity to carry risk or to increase its capital.

- Regulators should welcome profitable banks as contributors to stability of the banking system.

- Profitability ratios should be seen in context, and the potential yield on the "free" equity portion of capital should be deducted prior to drawing conclusions about profitability.

- The components of income could change over time, and core costs should be compared to assumed core income to determine whether such costs are indeed fully covered.

- Management should understand which assets they are spending their energy on and how this relates to the income generated from such assets.

5.1 Profitability

Profitability, in the form of retained earnings, is typically one of the key sources of capital generation. A sound banking system is built on profitable and adequately capitalized banks. Profitability is a revealing indicator of a bank's competitive position in banking markets and of the quality of its management. It allows a bank to maintain a certain risk profile and provides a cushion against short-term problems.

The income statement, a key source of information on a bank's profitability, reveals the sources of a bank's earnings and their quantity and quality, as well as the quality of the bank's loan portfolio and the focus of its expenditures. Income statement structure also indicates a bank's business orientation. Traditionally, the major source of bank income has been interest, but the increasing orientation toward nontraditional business is also reflected in income statements. For example, income from trading operations, investments, and fee-based income accounts for an increasingly high percentage of earnings in modern banks. This trend implies higher volatility of earnings and profitability. It also implies a different risk profile from that of a traditional bank.

Changes in the structure and stability of banks' profits have sometimes been motivated by statutory capital requirements and monetary policy measures such as obligatory reserves. To maintain the public's confidence in the banking system, banks are subject to minimum capital requirements. The restrictive nature of this statutory minimum capital may cause banks to change their business mix in favor of activities and assets that entail a lower capital requirement. However, although such assets carry less risk, they may earn lower returns. Excessive obligatory reserves and statutory liquidity requirements damage profits and may encourage disintermediation. They may also result in undesirable banking practices. For example, the balance sheets of banks in many developing and transitional economies contain large proportions of fixed assets, a trend that adversely affects profitability. Regulatory authorities should recognize the importance of profits and, to the extent possible, avoid regulations that may unduly depress profitability.

Taxation is another major factor that influences a bank's profitability, as well as its business and policy choices, because it affects the competitiveness of various instruments and different segments of the financial markets. For example, taxation of interest income, combined with a tax holiday for capital gains, can make deposits less attractive than equity investments. In general, banks adjust their business and policy decisions to minimize the taxes to be paid and to take advantage of any loopholes in tax laws. Beyond the level and the transparency of profit taxation, key areas to consider when assessing the business environment and profit potential of a bank are if and how fiscal authorities tax unrealized gains and interest income, and whether they allow provisions before taxation. Many fiscal authorities also apply direct taxes to banking transactions.

A thorough understanding of profit sources and changes in the income/profit structure of both an individual bank and the banking system as a whole is important to all key players in the risk management process. Supervisory authorities should, for example, view bank profitability as an indicator of stability and as a factor that contributes to depositor confidence. Maximum sustainable profitability should therefore be encouraged, because healthy competition for profits is an indicator of an efficient and dynamic financial system.

5.2   Income Statement Composition

A bank's Statement of Comprehensive Income (the income statement) is a key source of information regarding the sources and the structure of its income. An example of an analytical income statement is shown in table 5.1.

Table 5.1 Income Statement Composition

Financial & Operating Income and Expenses	Period 01	Period 02
Interest income		
Interest expense		
Interest income – net		
Fee and commission income – net		
Gains (losses) on financial assets and liabilities held for trading		
Exchange differences, net		
Other operating income		
Other operating expenses		
Administration costs		
Impairment losses		
Share of the profit or loss of associates and joint ventures accounted for using the equity method		
Profit or loss from non-current assets and disposal groups classified as held for sale		
TOTAL PROFIT OR LOSS BEFORE TAX FROM CONTINUING OPERATIONS		
Profit or loss after tax from discontinued operations		
Profit or loss attributable to minority interest		
PROFIT OR LOSS ATTRIBUTABLE TO EQUITY HOLDERS OF THE PARENT	100%	100%

Interest Income

Interest income originates from loans and all other advances extended by a bank, such as working capital, investment, and housing, and foreign currency loans, installments, overdrafts, and credit cards. It also includes interest received on the bank's deposits kept with other financial intermediaries. Interest income is normally calculated on an accrual basis, meaning that a bank calculates interest due over the period of time covered by the income statement, regardless of whether or not the interest has been paid. Accounting policies should normally require that a loan be placed in a nonaccrual status if a client is overdue by a specified period of time (say, 60 days) or deemed to be potentially unable to pay (regardless of whether the loan is overdue or not). At that point, all previously accrued but unpaid interest should be reversed out of income. The absence of such a policy normally results in banks with largely overstated interest income and profits.

For management purposes, interest income would normally be further subdivided by sources of income. For example, loan categories can be subdivided into loans to the government, to state enterprises, and to private enterprises (including working capital loans and investment loans categories), and consumer loans to households, mortgage loans, etc. This subdivision is required for supervisory purposes. It may also be the result of a bank's own internal organization, as modern, cost-conscious banks often develop elaborate pricing and costing systems for their various business and product lines to ensure that the contribution of each product to the bottom line is clearly understood.

Interest Expense

Interest expense comprises interest paid on deposits and borrowings related to funding the loan portfolio. A breakdown of interest expenses provides an understanding of a bank's sources of funding and of the corresponding funding cost. The subdivision of interest expense is typically based on both instruments and maturities, such as demand deposits, saving accounts, foreign currency deposits, and certificates of deposit. A bank with low interest expense and thus low funding costs is clearly better positioned than one with high interest expense, as it would be able to lend at market rates with a higher interest margin. The smaller interest expense, however, often involves higher operating expenses. For example, household deposits typically involve lower interest expense but require branch networks to collect them, and the maintenance of deposit accounts is expensive. This is why some banks prefer funding by wholesale deposits, even if this implies higher interest expense.

Net Interest Income

Net interest income is the difference between a bank's interest income and interest expense. The net interest income is the core of a traditional bank's earnings, and the aim of the bank would normally be to keep the net interest income stable and growing. In a floating interest rate environment, this requires active management: banks normally try to adjust lending rates before deposit rates in rising interest-rate markets, and do the opposite in falling markets.

Gains (Losses) on Financial Assets and Liabilities Held for Trading

Gains or losses on financial assets and liabilities held for trading comprises income from the trading and stable liquidity investment books in securities, foreign currencies, equities, and commodities. This income is mostly due to the difference between the purchase and sale price of the underlying instruments, but it also includes interest amounts. The stability or sustainability of trading income affects the viability of a bank and is critically related to the quality of a bank's market risk management function, the effectiveness of the corresponding functional processes, and the proper information technology support. Trading assets would normally be disclosed at fair value (marked-to-market adjustments will flow through the income statement) in the bank's financial statements (see chapters 10 and 14). Available-for-sale assets are also disclosed at fair value, but marked-to-market adjustments are recorded in a reserve account directly in the balance sheet.

Other Operating Income

Other operating income, such as knowledge-based or fee-based income, includes income received from nontraditional banking business such as merchant banking or financial advisory services. This category also includes fee-based income derived from various services to clients, such as accounts or funds management services and payment transaction services. This class of income is generally desirable, as it does not inherently carry any capital charges.

Exchange Differences

Exchange differences often appear in the income statements of banks in developing countries, as such banks are frequently funded by foreign loans. Gains or losses result from exchange rate changes that—depending on whether a bank's net position was long or short and whether the domestic currency has depreciated or appreciated—produce a gain or loss to the bank.

Administrative Costs

Salaries and staff-related expenses, such as social security, pensions, and other benefits, are normally the largest cost item for a bank, because banking is a knowledge- and staff-intensive business. Computers and information technology–related expenses such as software licenses and application system development and maintenance expenses have also become major cost items, especially in modern or internationally active banks that are critically dependent on information support for identifying market opportunities, for transaction processing, and for risk management and management reporting. Administrative expenses also include costs related to rent and utilities, auditing and consulting expenses.

Efficient management of these expenses requires balancing short-term cost-minimization strategies with investments in human and physical resources—especially the banking technology necessary for effective management of banking risks and for the long-term maintenance of the bank's competitive position. Besides loan loss provisions, administrative (operating) expense is the item with the most significant impact on the cost of intermediation, and it is also one of the most controllable items. The level of operating expenses is generally related to a bank's efficiency.

Depreciation

Depreciation results from the reduction in value of a bank's fixed assets. It is conceptually similar to provisions. Banks typically depreciate buildings over 25 to 50 years, movable assets and office equipment over 3 to 5 years, and computers over 2 to 3 years.

Provisions

Loan loss provisions are expenses related to the credit risk inherent in granting loans and advances. Provisions are made to compensate for the impaired value of the related loan principal and interest due. This may include write-offs and recoveries (that is, amounts recovered on loans previously written off), which may be shown as separate line items in the income statement.

Impairment Losses

Impairment expenses relate to loss provisions for all other assets where the value of the asset could be impaired, for example, the assets in a bank's long-term investment portfolio. In many countries, prudential requirements mandate that a bank carries assets at the lower of the nominal value or the market value (in which case loss provisions need to be made), and recognize any appreciation in value only when the investment is liquidated.

Share of the Profit or Loss of Associates Accounted for Using the Equity Method

This category comprises income from a bank's longer-term equity-type investments, such as investments in associated companies and joint ventures held in the bank's long-term investment portfolio. Investment income depends on the respective contractual rates and, for equity investments, on the financial performance of the respective companies. By its nature, the income from equity investments is difficult to accurately predict. Investment assets would be shown on the balance sheet as "investments in associates, subsidiaries, and joint ventures."

5.3 Analyzing the Sources of Banking Income

In today's environment, markets that have traditionally been the sole domain of banks have opened up to competition from other institutions. Banks in turn have diversified into nontraditional markets and therefore no longer perform only a simple intermediation function, that is, deposit taking and lending. In fact, an overview of the industry's profit structure in most developed countries reveals that the traditional banking business is only marginally profitable and that income from other sources has become a significant contributor to the bottom line. Bank profitability appears to be largely attributable to fee income generated from knowledge-based activities, including merchant banking, corporate financing, and advisory services, and from trading-based activities in fixed-income securities, equities, and foreign exchange.

The information contained in a bank's income statement provides an understanding of the institution's business focus and the structure and stability of its profits. To facilitate a comparison between different types of banking institutions, various income statement items—such as interest margins, fee and investment income, and overhead—are usually expressed as a percentage of total assets. By using the asset base as a common denominator, banks are able to compare themselves to the sector average and to other types of banks. When aggregated, such information can also highlight changes that occur within a peer group or the banking sector.

When analyzing a bank's income structure, an analyst should give appropriate consideration to and acquire an understanding of the following aspects:

- Trends in and the composition and accuracy of reported earnings

- The quality, composition, and level of income and expense components

- Dividend payout and earnings retention

- Major sources of income and the most profitable business areas

- The manner and the extent to which accrued but uncollected interest is absorbed into income, in particular when such interest relates to loans that are or should be placed in risk categories of substandard or worse

- The extent to which collateral values (rather than operating cash flows) are the basis for decisions to capitalize interest or roll over extensions of credit

- Any income or expenditure recognition policies that distort earnings

- The effect of intergroup transactions, especially those related to the transfer of earnings and asset-liability valuations

By changing the sequence of income statement items (see table 5.2), the analyst is able to determine the contribution of each of the different sources of banking income—assessing the importance of retail lending versus trading and investment banking activities.

In the current period column of the example in table 5.2, the various components of income and expenses (even gross interest income and gross interest expenses) are disclosed as a percentage of the gross income per line item 5. Net interest income is calculated as the difference between gross interest income and interest expenses related to the loan portfolio and can be seen to make a relatively minor contribution to overall income—especially when the volume of activity to generate the net interest income is taken into account.

Table 5.2 Restructured Income Statement

Restructured Income Statement	Current Period	Prior Period
A. Interest and similar income on loan portfolio and interbank deposits	205	
B. Interest expenses on deposits and loan portfolio funding instruments	170	
1. Net interest income on loan portfolio (A – B)	35	
2. Other banking-related operating income	20	
3. Trading-related income	41	
4. Investment-related income (subsidiaries and associates)	4	
5. Gross Income	100	
6. Specific loan loss provisions and write-offs	6	
7. Operating expenses	55	
8. Expenses related to trading and investment activities	20	
9. Other expenses and interest related to non-deposit borrowings	5	
10. Net income/(loss) before tax	14	
11. Income tax	7	
Effective tax rate	50	
As % of Net income/(loss) after tax		
12. Net income/(loss) after tax	100	
Transfers to general provisions	46	
Dividends declared	14	
Other (+/-)	0	
Retained earnings for the period	40	

5.4 Analyzing Quality of Earnings

The analysis of earnings quality starts by considering the structure of a bank's income and its components—interest income, transactions-based fee income, trading income, and other sources of income—and the trends over the observation period. Figure 5.1 illustrates the composition of a bank's gross income. (Note that the various figures in this chapter are used as an illustration and do not necessarily refer to the same bank.) Such a chart enables an analyst to determine the quality and stability of a bank's profit, including its sources and any changes in its structure. This bar graph shows that the bank's trading and investment income has become an increasing contributor to its gross income, while the contribution of interest income has decreased.

Figure 5.1 Structure of Gross Income

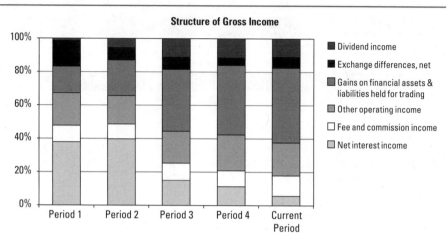

Changes in the income structure of banks has had the effect of improving profitability without increasing the traditional credit risk that results from loan portfolios. For example, many corporate clients are able to attract funding in their own name through the issuance of commercial paper and bonds. Instead of maintaining large corporate loans on their balance sheets, banks increasingly underwrite or service issues of their large corporate clients or perform a market-making function. Doing so generates fee income without increasing credit risk exposure. However, income generated in this manner (for example, through securities trading and merchant banking) is by its nature less stable and predictable because it depends on market conditions and trading performance. The trading portfolio is also subject to market risk (discussed in chapter 10), which can be quite substantial.

Such tendencies normally require scrutiny, as in normal circumstances investment income is less stable than interest income. However, the trend may have been motivated by adverse changes in the bank's macroeconomic or market environment, which would provide good reasons for such an orientation. Another reason would be that the return on investments has been significantly higher than the return on loans. Comparison of the gross income structure and the asset structure normally provides a reasonable basis for an answer to this anomaly; the analysis of income structure may also yield conclusions regarding the quality of asset management.

Figure 5.2 illustrates this process by comparing the composition of various asset categories with the composition of gross income. The purpose of this comparison is to determine exactly how the assets of a bank are engaged and whether the income generated is commensurate with the proportion of assets committed to each specific asset category (in other words, is the income earned where the energy is spent). Assets should normally be engaged in product categories that provide the highest income at an acceptable level of risk. The same analysis can be performed to identify categories of loans and advances that generate proportionately lower yields.

Figure 5.2 Assets Invested Compared with Income Sources

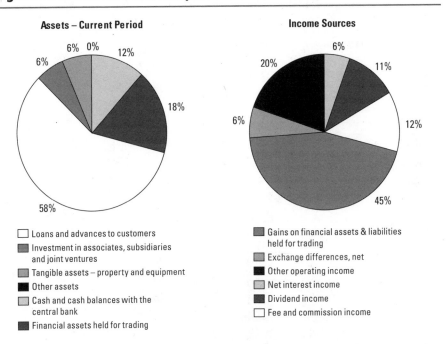

Assets – Current Period

Income Sources

- ☐ Loans and advances to customers
- ◼ Investment in associates, subsidiaries and joint ventures
- ◻ Tangible assets – property and equipment
- ◼ Other assets
- ◻ Cash and cash balances with the central bank
- ◼ Financial assets held for trading
- ◼ Gains on financial assets & liabilities held for trading
- ◻ Exchange differences, net
- ◼ Other operating income
- ☐ Net interest income
- ◼ Dividend income
- ☐ Fee and commission income

An analytical comparison of classes of interest expenses with related liability categories highlights a bank's exposure to specific sources of funding and reveals if structural changes are taking place in its sources of funding. A similar type of graph and analysis can be used to assess whether the components of interest expense in the total expenditures are of the same proportions as the related liabilities. Expensive categories of funding would be clearly highlighted on such a graph, and the reasons for the specific funding decisions would need to be explained. In the long term, this type of analysis would be able to highlight if and what sort of structural changes are taking place in the income and expenditure structure of a bank, and whether they are justified from the profitability perspective.

Figure 5.3 illustrates the next step, the analysis of how a bank's income covers its operating expenses. In the case illustrated, the fee income and trading income significantly contribute to the bank's profitability and to its capacity to carry the operating cost. The stability of the bank's income has likely deteriorated, as fee and trading income are generally considered to be less stable than net interest (that is, intermediation) income. Both the gross income and the operating expenses have shown significant growth in the observation period. In spite of the much higher income level, the bank's bottom line does not appear to have improved. The analysis should determine the reason for the significant increase in operating expenses.

Figure 5.3 Sources of Income versus Costs

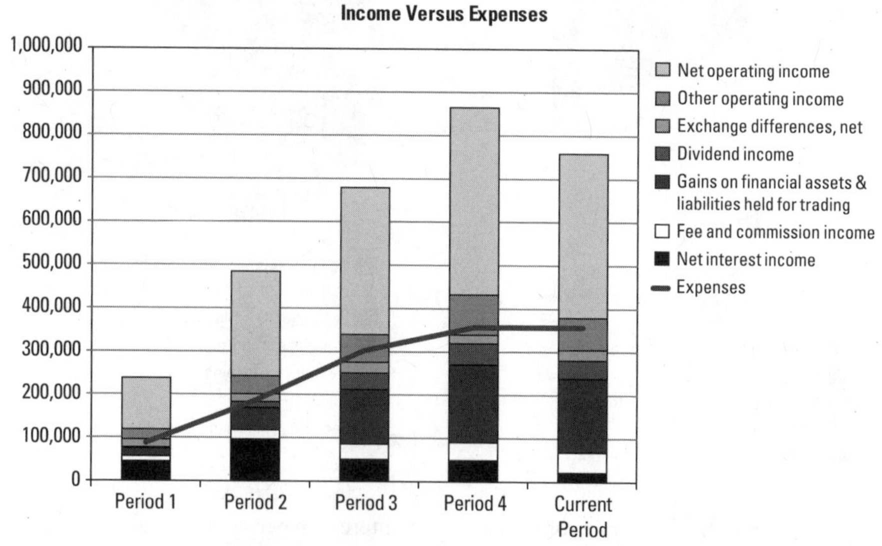

Income Versus Expenses

Operating expenses is one of the items on a bank's income statement that can be controlled. One acceptable reason for the increase in operating expenses would be investments in human resources and banking infrastructure, which could be expected to pay off in the future. If no such reasons can be found, the bank should be asked to rethink its business strategy.

Figure 5.4 illustrates another view of trends in the level of operating expenses in relation to total assets, gross interest income, and gross operating income that could provide the analyst with information on the relationship between a bank's expenses and earning capacity, as well as on whether the bank has optimized its potential. Income and expenses are presented in relation to total assets. When compared with industry norms, such a view can yield important conclusions, for example, that a bank's expenses are high because it is over-staffed. The ratios of operating expenses to interest income and of operating expenses to gross operating income are also very useful, as they clearly indicate the bank's profitability.

Figure 5.4 Operating Income Ratios

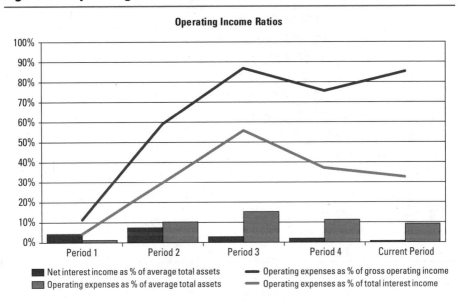

5.5 Analysis of Profitability Indicators and Ratios

Profit is the bottom line or ultimate performance result showing the net effects of bank policies and activities in a financial year. Its stability and growth trends are the best summary indicators of a bank's performance in both the past and the future. Some profitability ratios are shown in table 5.3.

Key indicators include the return on average equity, which measures the rate of return on shareholder investment, and the return on assets, which measures the efficiency of use of the bank's potential. Other ratios measure the profitability of a bank's core business (for example, margin ratios), the contribution to profit of various types of activities, the efficiency with which the bank operates, and the stability of its profits. Ratios are observed over time to detect profitability trends. An analysis of changes of various ratios over time reveals changes in bank policies and strategies and in its business environment.

Table 5.3 Profitability Ratios

Profitability Ratios	Prior Period	Current Period	Benchmark
Net interest income as percentage of average total assets			
Interest income as percentage of average earning assets			
Noninterest income as percentage of average total assets			
Net interest income net of provisions as percentage of total assets			
Interest expense as percentage of average total assets			
Intermediation spread			
Net interest income (net of provisions) as percentage of gross operating income			
Loan loss provisions as percentage of average total assets			
Dividends as percentage of net income after tax			
Return on average equity (pretax)			
Return on average equity (posttax)			
Return on average assets (pretax)			
Return on average assets (posttax)			
Operating expenses/gross operating income			
Staff costs/gross operating income			
Other operating income as percentage of gross operating income			
Other operating expenses as percentage of average total assets			
Total interest expense as percentage of average interest-bearing liabilities			
Interest on subordinated debt as percentage of average subordinated debt			
Noninterest income as percentage of operating income			

Numerous factors may influence a bank's profitability. In some cases, inflation may increase operating costs faster than income. Marking the value of assets to market requires that unrealized gains are recognized as income; because these gains are yet to be realized, this may negatively affect the quality of earnings. Given the traditional narrow margin on which banks operate, a change in the level of interest rates will trigger changes in the gross profit percentage. Banks are influenced by the high level of competition in the banking sector, and many have therefore made significant investments in infrastructure-related assets— especially information technology—as part of their competition strategy. Investments such as these have both increased the overhead cost of banking and negatively affected profitability.

Viewed in the context of the financial items to which they are related, operating ratios enable an analyst to assess the efficiency with which an institution generates income. Industry efficiency norms facilitate a comparison between individual banks and the banking system. A review of interest income in relation to loans and advances allows an analyst to determine the return on the loan assets. Similarly, a comparison of interest expenses and funding indicates the relative cost of funding. This process highlights the impact of monetary policy on the banking system and the effect that changes in official interest rates have on the profitability of a bank.

The ratios can also be used in a broader context. The cost and revenue structure of the banking system can be assessed by calculating and analyzing provisions to loans and advances, interest margin to gross interest income, investment income to investments, and overhead to gross income. The value added by the banking system can be determined by calculating net income after taxes in relation to total average assets (that is, the return on average assets) and net income after taxes in relation to owner equity (that is, the return on equity).

Bankers pay a great deal of attention to the message that is revealed by ratio analysis. Banks usually manage profitability by trying to beat market averages and keep profits steady and predictable as this attracts investors. Ratios are therefore extremely useful tools, but as with other analytical methods, they must be used with judgment and caution because they alone do not provide complete answers about the bottom-line performance of banks. In the short run, many tricks can be used to make bank ratios look good in relation to industry standards. An assessment of the operations and management of a bank should therefore be performed to provide a check on profitability ratios.

The need to generate stable and increasing profits also implies the need to manage risk. Asset-liability management has become an almost universally accepted approach to profitability (risk) management. Because capital and profitability are intimately linked, the key objective of asset-liability management is to ensure sustained profitability so that a bank can maintain and augment its capital resources. Interest margins can be negatively affected by the bank's failure to effectively manage credit risk.

Strong and stable net interest margins have traditionally been the primary objective of bank managers, and they are still the primary determinant of intermediation efficiency and earning performance. An analysis of the interest margin of a bank can highlight the effect of current interest rate patterns, while a trend analysis over a longer period of time can show the effect of monetary policy on the profitability of the banking system. It can also illustrate the extent to which banks are exposed to changes in interest rates, and thus the ability of management to effectively manage interest rate risk.

Figure 5.5 illustrates the intermediation performance of a bank. The net interest margin of the bank has shown a steady increase and then a significant deterioration in the recent period. Such a trend demands further analysis. The analyst should establish if this was due to systemic reasons, for example, if the interest margins were reduced as a result of increased competition. The reduction of interest margins, however, could also be the result of an increase in the cost of funds. Such a trend would negatively affect profitability and ultimately may even affect the solvency of a bank.

Bottom-line profitability ratios—the return on equity and assets—indicate the net results of a bank's operations in a financial year or over time. Figure 5.6 illustrates how to adjust these profitability ratios by deducting an assumed cost of capital to show the real profit of a bank. By comparing the return on equity with the after-tax return on risk-free government securities, one can determine whether equity invested in the bank has earned any additional returns, as compared with risk-free investments. The result, such as the one shown in figure 5.6, may disclose that it could be better for shareholders to simply invest in risk-free government securities or for the bank concerned to cease its intermediation function and close its doors.

Figure 5.5 Average Yield Differential on Intermediation Business

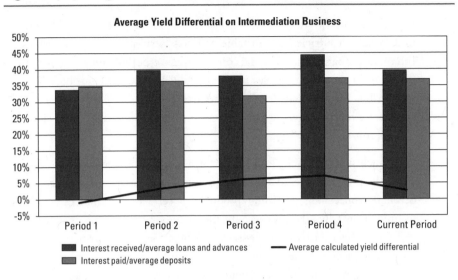

Figure 5.6 Return on Assets (ROA) and Return on Equity (ROE), Adjusted for the Cost of Capital

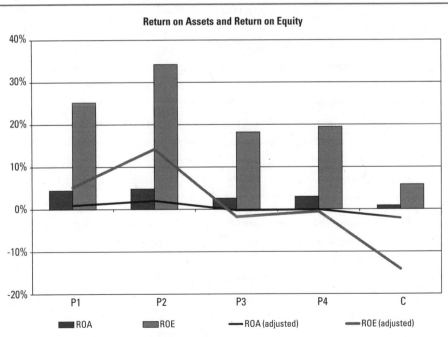

5.6 Assessing Internal Performance

In such an intensively competitive business, modern banks can no longer afford to carry insufficiently profitable products, services, or lines of businesses. International banks and financial conglomerates especially must organize their functions in a way that enables them to establish the exact contribution to the bottom line of their many constituent parts. In the last decade, more refined systems for profitability and performance measurement have been developed to address this need.

The conclusions drawn by internal performance measurement systems directly affect the products offered and their pricing, shaping the bank's entry and exit decisions concerning particular products or services. Internal measurement techniques usually take into account the underlying risk elements (which may negatively affect the bank's expenses), and there-fore also contribute to enhancing risk management techniques. A good measurement system will also enhance the application of a consistent incentive compensation system, based on achievement rather than on hierarchy.

A performance measurement framework comprises a number of elements, including an effective organization that allows a clear allocation of income and expenses to business units related to different lines of a bank's business, products, and market segments; an internal transfer pricing system to measure the contribution of various business units to the bottom line; and an effective and consistent means to incorporate the respective risk elements into the performance measurement framework. Once the net contributions are known, by business lines, products, or markets, it can be clearly established which customer segments are the most promising and which products should be scrutinized concerning their revenue-generating capacity. A good performance measurement framework also allows analysis of the net contribution a relationship with a large customer makes to the bank's bottom line.

Internal transfer pricing systems refers to the cost of funds as they are moved from one business unit to another. A sophisticated internal transfer pricing system will also cover the allocation of overhead costs to business units and will include transfer prices for internal services such as accounting or legal services. Internal transfer prices could, in principle, reflect the respective market prices, including maturities, and the repricing characteristics of the corresponding assets and liabilities. In practice, most banks choose a weighted average based on their specific funding mix.

Branch relationships provide a good example of internal transfer pricing. When making a loan that it cannot fund itself, a business unit will "borrow" funds from the treasury; the same unit will "lend" money to the treasury when it collects excess deposits. Internal transfer prices in both directions should be based on the same principles, but with applicable modifications. For example, the transfer price of deposits may be modified for the cost of obligatory reserves. For consistent application of such a system, a bank must also have a supporting management accounting system.

There are a number of ways to incorporate risk into this framework. For the lending function, as an example, the internal cost of funds could reflect the credit risk of the loan being funded, with a higher transfer price being allocated to lower-quality loans. Loans with higher risk could be expected to generate higher returns. Most banks apply a uniform transfer price for all loans, and the risk element is accommodated by requiring higher returns on lower-quality loans.

Another step is to determine how much capital should be assigned to each of the different business or product lines. The key issue is not how to determine the right amount of capital to be assigned for each business unit, but how to assign capital to all businesses in a consistent manner and based on the same principles. In practice, it is often unnecessary to measure risk using sophisticated modeling techniques for all bank business lines and products in order to determine the appropriate coefficients. And in any case it is nearly impossible to do it in a practical, consistent, and meaningful manner. Instead, banks typically use much simpler "return on risk capital"–type calculations. A practical approach followed by many banks is to use the weights provided under the Basel Accord (discussed in chapter 6) as a basis for calculations.

Transfer pricing should be carefully scrutinized when the analysis concerns a bank that belongs to a banking group or a holding company, especially if the group is domiciled abroad. In some cases, internal transfer prices have been set that allow the parent to take profits from a bank, for example, by charging more than the applicable market price for funds borrowed by the bank from other business units or members of the conglomerate, or by paying less than the market price for funds provided by the same bank. Such cases are especially frequent in countries where there are limits to or complications with dividend repatriation.

6

Capital Adequacy

Key Messages

- Capital is required as a buffer against unexpected losses.

- Capital cannot substitute for bad management or for inadequate risk management policies and practices.

- Capital consists of a strong base of permanent shareholders' equity and disclosed reserves, supplemented by other forms of qualifying capital (for example, undisclosed reserves, revaluation reserves, general provisions for loan losses, hybrid instruments, and subordinated debt).

- International standards for minimum capital and for assessment and measurement of capital adequacy are set by the Basel Accord (Basel II), which defines three tiers of capital. The first two tiers cover credit risk related to on- and off-balance-sheet activities, derivatives, and operational risk; the third tier partially covers market risk.

- Basel II set the total capital adequacy ratio at no lower then 8 percent. The capital ratio is calculated using the definition of regulatory capital and risk-weighted assets.

- The 8-percent ratio must be seen as a minimum. In transitional or volatile environments, a risk-weighted capital adequacy requirement of substantially more than 8 percent would be more appropriate.

- In practice, capital adequacy is calculated according to formulas prescribed by the respective regulatory authorities (Pillar 1). It is monitored by the bank's supervisory authority (Pillar 2). In addition, it is also subject to market discipline (Pillar 3).

6.1 Introduction: The Characteristics and Functions of Capital

Almost every aspect of banking is either directly or indirectly influenced by the availability and cost of capital. Capital is one of the key factors to be considered when the safety and soundness of a particular bank is assessed. An adequate capital base serves as a safety net for a variety of risks to which an institution is exposed in the course of its business. Capital absorbs possible losses and thus provides a basis for maintaining depositor confidence in a bank. Capital also is the ultimate determinant of a bank's lending capacity. A bank's balance sheet cannot be expanded beyond the level determined by its capital adequacy ratio. Consequently, the availability of capital determines the maximum level of assets.

Capital, however, is not a substitute for bad management, poor risk management, poor corporate governance, or weak internal controls.

The cost and amount of capital affect a bank's competitive position. Shareholders expect a return on their equity, and the bank's obligation to earn a reasonable return influences the pricing of bank products. There is also another market perspective: to grant loans and advances, a bank must normally be able to attract deposits from the public. Doing so requires public confidence in the bank, which in turn can best be established and maintained by a capital buffer. If a bank faces a shortage of capital, or if the cost of capital is high, a bank stands to lose business to its competitors.

The key purposes of capital are to provide stability and to absorb losses, thereby providing a measure of protection to depositors and other creditors in the event of liquidation. Consequently, the capital of a bank should have three important characteristics:

- It must be permanent.
- It must not impose mandatory fixed charges against earnings.
- It must allow for legal subordination to the rights of depositors and other creditors.

The total amount of capital is fundamental to the bank's soundness. Also important is the nature of bank ownership, specifically the identity of those owners who can directly influence the bank's strategic direction and risk management policies. A bank's ownership structure must ensure the integrity of the bank's capital and be able to supply more capital, if and when needed. The ownership must not negatively influence the bank's capital position or expose it to additional risk. In addition to owners who are less than "fit and proper" or who do not effectively discharge their fiduciary responsibilities, the structure of financial conglomerates may also negatively affect the capital of banks in such groups.

Banks inherently have a relatively low capital-to-assets ratio. To encourage prudent management of the risks associated with this unique balance sheet structure, regulatory authorities in most countries started to introduce certain capital adequacy requirements. In the late 1980s, the Basel Committee on Banking Supervision took the lead to develop a risk-based capital adequacy standard that would lead to international convergence of supervisory regulations governing the capital adequacy of internationally active banks. The dual objectives for the new framework were to strengthen the soundness and stability of the international banking system and, by ensuring a high degree of consistency in the framework's application, to diminish the sources of competitive inequality among international banks. This initiative resulted in the Basel Capital Accord of 1988 (Basel I Accord). Emergence of new instruments with complex risk profiles—increasing volatility and internationalization—and the trend toward financial conglomerates have prompted ongoing changes to Basel I. Eventually, this led to the introduction of a new and more sophisticated framework, known as the Basel II Accord.

6.2 Capital Adequacy Standards and the Basel Accords

The Basel I Accord offered a definition of regulatory capital, measures of risk exposure, and rules specifying the level of capital to be maintained in relation to these risks. It introduced a de facto capital adequacy standard, based on the risk-weighted composition of a bank's assets and off-balance-sheet exposures, which ensured that an adequate amount of capital and reserves was maintained to safeguard solvency. While the original targets of the Basel I Accord were international banks, many national authorities promptly applied the Basel I Accord and introduced formal regulatory capital requirements. After the introduction of the risk-based capital adequacy standard, risk-based capital ratios have increased significantly in all countries that have adopted the standard.

The Basel I Accord has also played a major role in improving the safety of banking systems in less developed countries and in transitional economies. It has been adopted and implemented in more than 100 countries and now forms an integral part of any risk-based bank supervisory approach. Aware that the banking environment in these countries entails higher economic and market risks, many regulators have introduced even higher standards, with 12 to 15 percent often regarded as the appropriate capital adequacy ratio for transitional and developing environments.

The world financial system has seen considerable changes since the introduction of the Basel I Accord. The volatility of financial markets has increased, and there has been a significant degree of financial innovation. There also have been incidents of economic turbulence leading to widespread financial crisis—for example, in Asia in 1997 and in Eastern Europe in 1998. The risks that internationally active banks must deal with have become more complex. Consequently, there was an increasing concern whether the Basel I Accord provided an effective means to ensure that capital requirements matched a bank's true risk profile; in other words, there was a growing belief that the Basel I Accord was *not* sufficiently risk sensitive. The risk measurement and control aspects of the Basel I Accord needed to be improved.

In 1999, the Basel Committee started consultations that led to a new Capital Accord (Basel II Accord) that is better attuned to the complexities of the modern financial world. While the new framework aims to provide a more comprehensive approach to measuring banking risks, its fundamental objectives remained the same: to promote safety and soundness of the banking system and to enhance the competitive equality of banks.

By 2006, the development of the Basel II Accord had been completed. A significant aspect of the Basel II Accord is the greater use of the banks' internal systems as an input to the capital assessment and adequacy calculations. It provides incentives for banks to improve their risk management practices, with increasingly sensitive risk weights when banks adopt more sophisticated approaches to risk management. It allows greater national discretion on how specific rules may be applied, permitting countries to adapt the standards to different conditions in national financial markets. In addition to the minimum capital requirements, the Basel II Accord includes two additional pillars: an enhanced supervisory review process (Pillar 2) and effective use of market discipline (Pillar 3). All three pillars are mutually reinforcing, and no one pillar should be viewed as more important than another (see figure 6.1).

Figure 6.1 Conceptual Framework for the Basel II Accord

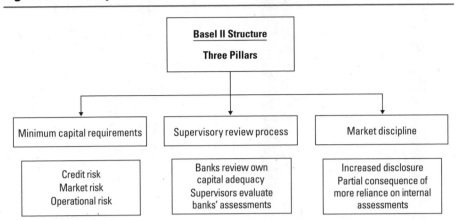

Countries with well-developed financial systems that actively participated in the development of the Basel II Accord promptly started the transition process, although its full implementation may take some time. For example, the European Union issued a new Basel II–based Capital Adequacy Directive in June 2006 obliging member countries to start convergence as of January 1, 2007. The full implementation of all its elements in all member countries is expected by January 1, 2011. Table 6.1 provides a summary of all elements of the Basel II Accord. Further discussion in this chapter is based on and related to the Basel II Accord.

Table 6.1 Summary of the Basel II Accord

	Pillar One — Capital Adequacy Requirement / Basis											Pillar Two — Supervisory Review	Pillar Three — Market Discipline
	Credit Risk			Market Risk		Operational Risk							
	Standardized Approach	Internal Ratings Based Approaches		Standardized Approach	Internal Model	Basic Indicator Approach	Standardized Approach	Alternative Standardized Approach	Advanced Measurement Approaches				
		Foundations Approach	Advanced Approach	Building block Approach	Value-at-Risk (VAR)	One indicator: gross revenue	Same indicator for different business lines	Different indicators for different business lines	Internal Measurement Approach (IMA)	Loss Distribution Approach (LDA)	Scorecard Approach	Regulators must ensure that banks have sound internal processes for capital assessment based on risk commensurate with risk profile.	Enhanced disclosure to facilitate investor decision making. More detail required for banks that use advanced risk management approaches.
Detail	1	2	3	4	5	6	7	8	9	10	11	12	13

Detail	Description
-	Places more emphasis on bank's own internal control and management, the supervisory review process and market discipline
1	Similar to Basel 1, but more reliance on rating agencies.
2	Divide loan portfolio into seven buckets. Probability of default (PD) is provided by bank, with the exposure at default (EAD) and loss given default (LGD) provided by the regulator.
3	Divide loan portfolio into seven buckets. Probability of default (PD), Exposure at default (EAD) and Loss given default (LGD) all provided by the bank, using historical experience
4	Capital requirement calculated separately for market risks. Trading book used for interest, equities, currency and commodities risks, with latter two using the banking book as well
5	Market risk capital is based on higher of average VAR over past 60 days, or previous day's VAR
6	A simplistic approach that uses a single indicator (gross revenue) as a proxy for overall operational risk exposure, to be multiplied by an alpha factor set by the Basel Committee.
7	Bank organizes itself into eight standard business lines—currently all using a common indicator, but flexibility built in for future differentiation of indicators—to be multiplied by a beta factor set by Regulator.
8	Bank organizes itself into eight standard business lines. Retail banking and commercial banking use three-year averages of loans and advances as an indicator, to be multiplied by an m factor set by Regulator. This alternative removes the penalty when banks that engage in high-risk lending also have high profits before provisioning.
9	IMA uses information from standardized approach. Calculates exposure indicator (EI) and loss should an operational risk event occur (LGE). Expected loss (EL) is product of EI*LGE. IMA uses assumptions about relationship between expected and unexpected loss.
10	LDA allows bank to estimate distribution of losses and therefore attempts to assess unexpected losses directly.
11	Bank determines initial level of operational risk capital. Amount is modified over time by capturing underlying risk profile of different business lines. Approach relies on qualitative judgment, less on historical data.
12	Regulator must ensure that banks have sound internal processes for risk-based capital assessment commensurate with risk profile.
13	Enhanced disclosure (quantitative and qualitative): based on materiality, to provide markets with information necessary to make investment decisions.

6.3 Constituents of Capital and Minimum Capital Requirements

Banks' capital consists of three tiers. Tier 1 is the core capital, or regulatory capital. Tier 2 and Tier 3 are classified as supplementary capital, and their recognition is related to the amount of Tier 1 capital. The definition and constituents of capital under the Basel II Accord are practically the same as under the Basel I Accord, but further changes in the definition of eligible capital are likely. Table 6.2 provides an overview of instruments that qualify as equity under Basel Accords.

Table 6.2 Overview of Qualifying Equity Instruments

TIER 1	TIER 2	TIER 3
Equity shares	Asset revaluation reserves	Short-term subordinated debt
Retained earnings	General provisions/loss reserves	
Nonredeemable, noncumulative preference shares	Hybrid (debt/equity) capital instruments	
	Subordinated term debt	

Tier 1 Capital

Tier 1 capital must be permanent, issued, and fully paid; noncumulative; able to absorb losses within the bank on a going-concern basis; junior to depositors, general creditors, and subordinated debt of the bank; and callable only after a minimum of five years with supervisory approval and under the condition that it will be replaced with capital of equal or better quality. The components of a bank's balance sheet that meet the requirements of Tier 1 capital are

- equity shares;
- retained earnings; and
- nonredeemable, noncumulative preference shares.

These Tier 1 components

- are regarded as core capital, or the primary capital of a bank;
- allow a bank to absorb losses on an ongoing basis and are permanently available for this purpose;
- allow a bank to effectively conserve resources when under stress, because common stock provides the bank with full discretion as to the amount

and timing of dividend payments; are the basis on which most market judgments of capital adequacy are made;

- provide an important source of market discipline over a bank's management, through the voting rights attached to the common shares; and

- are expected to be the predominant form of a bank's Tier 1 capital.

Tier 1 capital is common in all banking systems and is always clearly disclosed in published financial statements. It also has a crucial bearing on profit margins and on a bank's ability to bear risk and be competitive. Such capital is regarded as a buffer of the highest quality.

It is important to know whether capital contributions were made in cash or in kind, such as fixed assets. Regulators sometimes limit the amount of contributions in kind and express the limit as a percentage of the total Tier 1 capital. Because contributions in kind may be subject to changes in value, regulators typically require that owners obtain a reliable third-party evaluation before including the corresponding amount in a bank's capital, taking into consideration the fact that revaluation reserves related to fixed assets form part of Tier 2 capital.

The pressure on Tier 1 capital has resulted in the increasing use of innovative capital instruments[1] for capital adequacy purposes. The Basel II Accord limits the amount of innovative capital instruments to a maximum of 15 percent of Tier 1 capital. This limit means that the aggregate of noncommon equity Tier 1 instruments with any explicit feature (other than a pure call option) that might lead to the instrument being redeemed is limited to 15 percent of the bank's consolidated Tier 1 capital.

---

1. The term "innovative capital instruments" refers to special purpose vehicles (SPVs), capital that is cost efficient and can be denominated, if necessary, in nonlocal currency. To be acceptable as Tier 1 capital, an SPV must, at a minimum, meet all the standard requirements for Tier 1 capital. In addition, it must be easily understood and publicly disclosed; proceeds must be immediately available without any limitations; the bank must have discretion over the amount and timing of distributions; distributions can be paid only out of distributable items; and where distributions are preset, they may not be reset based on the credit standing of the issuer. SPV-based step-ups are permitted in conjunction with a call option only if the moderate step-up occurs at least 10 years after the issue date and if it results in an increase over the initial rate that is no greater than either (at national supervisory discretion) (a) 100 basis points, or (b) 50 percent of the initial credit spread, less the swap spread between the initial index basis and the stepped-up index basis. The terms of the instrument should provide for no more than one rate step-up over the life of the instrument. The swap spread should be fixed as of the pricing date.

Tier 2 Capital

Although they do not have the permanence of core capital, other components of a balance sheet may be included in the bank's capital base for the purpose of assessing capital adequacy. These components include capital obligations that would ultimately be redeemed or that contain a mandatory charge against future income, whether or not earnings will be available. Such capital consists of instruments that have the same characteristics as both equity and debt, including asset revaluation reserves, general provisions and general loss reserves, hybrid capital instruments (such as redeemable cumulative preference shares), and subordinated term debt. These types of capital constitute the Tier 2 capital of a bank. The total amount of the Tier 2 capital is limited to 100 percent of Tier 1 capital.

Statutory limitations contained in the Basel Accords define the conditions under which specific instruments may be included in Tier 2 capital:

- *Asset revaluation reserves* may be included, provided that they are prudently valued and fully reflect the possibility of price fluctuations and forced sales. Revaluation reserves arise in two ways. First, in some countries banks are permitted to revalue fixed assets (normally, their own premises) in accordance with changes in market value. Second, revaluation reserves may arise as a result of long-term holdings of equity securities that are valued in the balance sheet at the historic cost of acquisition. For such revaluation reserves, a discount is normally applied to the difference between the historic cost book value and market value to reflect potential volatility, and only 50 percent is included in Tier 2 capital.

- *General provisions/loss reserves,* which are held against future unidentified losses, also qualify. The amount of general provisions/loan loss reserves included in Tier 2 capital may not exceed 1.25 percent of the assets to which they are related.

- *Hybrid (debt/equity) capital instruments* may be included if they are unsecured, subordinated, and fully paid up; are not redeemable without prior consent of the supervisory authority; and are able to support losses on an ongoing basis. In addition, the capital instrument should allow the service obligation to be deferred when the profitability of a bank cannot support payment.

- *Subordinated term debt* includes conventional, unsecured, subordinated debt capital instruments with a minimum original fixed term of maturity of more than five years. During the last five years before maturity is reached, a discount of 20 percent per year should be applied before inclusion as Tier 2 capital. Total subordinated term debt included in Tier 2 capital cannot exceed 50 percent of core capital.

Tier 3 Capital

In 1996, the Basel Committee introduced the concept of Tier 3 capital to allow banks, at the discretion of national regulators, to cover a part of their market risks. Consequently, Tier 3 capital covers only market risks that derive from equities and interest-bearing instruments in the trading book, as well as foreign exchange and commodities in the banking and trading books. The Tier 3 capital instruments consist mostly of short-term subordinated debt. Statutory conditions placed on Tier 3 capital specify that it must have a maturity of at least two years and be subject to a lock-in provision that stipulates that neither interest nor principal may be paid if such payment results in a bank's overall capital dropping below minimum requirements.

Minimum Capital Requirements

The minimum risk-based standard for capital adequacy is set by the Basel Accords at 8 percent of risk-weighted assets, of which Tier 1 should be at least 4 percent. Tier 2 capital amount is limited to 100 percent of Tier 1 capital. The calculation of Tier 2 capital (for example, inclusion of general provisions/loss reserves) depends on methods used to calculate the credit risk.[2] Tier 3 capital is limited to 250 percent of the amount of Tier 1 capital that is allocated for market risks. Tier 2 may be substituted for Tier 3 capital up to a limit of 250 percent, within the overall limits for the applicable limit to the Tier 2 capital.

The capital ratio is calculated using the definition of regulatory capital and risk-weighted assets. The risk-weighted assets are related to credit, market, and operational risk. Total risk-weighted assets are determined by multiplying the capital requirements for market risk and operational risk by 12.5 (that is, the reciprocal of the minimum capital ratio of 8 percent) and adding the resulting figures to the sum of risk-weighted assets for credit risk. Thus, the formula for determining capital adequacy is

---

2   Under the standardized approach to calculating credit risk, general provisions can be included in Tier 2 capital up to the limit of 1.25 percent of risk-weighted assets. Under the internal ratings–based approach to credit risk calculation, general loss reserves must be excluded from Tier 2.

(Tier 1 + Tier 2 + Tier 3) capital divided by (risk-weighted assets + (market risk capital charge × 12.5) + (operational risk capital charge × 1.25)) equals 8 percent

where

- Tier 1 is the entire amount of the bank's Tier 1 capital.

- Tier 2 is limited to 100 percent of Tier 1 capital; subordinated debt included in Tier 2 is limited to 50 percent of total Tier 2 capital.

- Tier 3 is limited to the amount that is eligible to support market risk (that is, subject to the Tier 3 restrictions).

The capital adequacy calculation under the Basel II Accord is subject to certain adjustments, or deductions, related to using the internal ratings–based approach for credit risk and advanced measurement approach for operational risk, including some transitional arrangements. The deductions from Tier 1 also include goodwill and investments in financial institutions. The latter is intended to discourage cross-holding and "double leveraging" of capital in a banking system, which can make the system more vulnerable to the transmission of problems between capital-related institutions.

6.4 Risk-Based Regulatory Capital Allocation: Pillar 1

The capital adequacy standard under the Basel Accords is based on the principle that the level of a bank's capital should be related to the bank's specific risk profile. The capital adequacy requirement was the sole essence of the Basel I Accord and it constitutes Pillar 1 under the Basel II Accord. Measurement of the capital adequacy requirement is determined by three risk components: credit risk, market risk, and (for Basel II) operational risk. For each of these risk components, there are a number of models that can be utilized. In principle, these include some forms of a standardized approach and an approach based on the bank's internal modeling systems.

Credit Risk

Figure 6.2 Basel II: Menu of Credit Risk Assessment Options

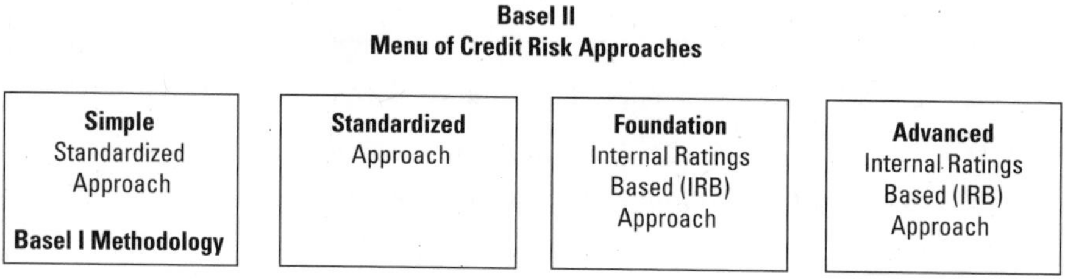

Basel II
Menu of Credit Risk Approaches

Simple Standardized Approach **Basel I Methodology**	**Standardized** Approach	**Foundation** Internal Ratings Based (IRB) Approach	**Advanced** Internal Ratings Based (IRB) Approach

The central focus of the Basel Accords' capital adequacy framework is the assessment of credit risk, including aspects of country risk and counterparty risk. This is because banks are normally exposed to significant credit risk. The credit risk profile of a bank is determined by assigning to its assets and off-balance-sheet commitments various risk weights. The Basel I Accord introduced a fairly **simple standardized methodology** with risk weights based on probability of losses for different classes of assets on a bank's balance sheet. The off-balance-sheet exposures are included using multiplication factors, again related to the expected probability of losses for the respective class of instruments. The risk weighting of assets and off-balance-sheet positions has provided a major step toward improved objectivity in assessing the adequacy of bank capital. The simplicity of this methodology has also enabled it to be introduced in banking systems that are in their early stages of development. A summary of the simple standardized credit risk assessment methodology under Basel I is provided in annex 6A.

However, such simple weighting of assets provided only a crude measure of economic risk, primarily because the methodology is not effectively calibrated to account for different default risks. Consequently, the Basel II Accord provides a broader and better calibrated range of options for credit risk assessment to allow banks and supervisors to select approaches that are most appropriate for their operations and their financial market infrastructure. The new approach also allows a certain degree of national discretion in the way each of the options may be applied in national markets (although this also means continued efforts to ensure the needed consistency in application). The revised framework includes a more complex version of a standardized approach and two versions of an internal ratings–based model.

The Standardized Approach

The standardized approach is based in large part on the *assessments of external rating agencies*. Table 6.3 provides a summary of risk-weight options for different types of banks' clients under the Basel II Accord. For the sovereign rating, the options include direct rating by specialized rating agencies or ratings based on export credit agencies. For the banks, Option 1 implies that the risk weight used for banks will be one rating category below the sovereign risk weight in that country (for AAA to BBB ratings). Option 2 uses a set of risk weights based on the actual rating of the borrowing bank. Lending to foreign banks in countries where there are no ratings agencies will follow the risk weights shown in the "unrated" column. Domestic banks will continue to carry a 20 percent risk weighting. Supervisory authorities could select options, applicable to their jurisdictions, that are best suited for their circumstances.

Eligibility criteria for acceptability of credit assessments made by external credit assessment institutions (or rating agencies) include objectivity, independence, transparency, credibility, international recognition, and access to resources needed to establish and then regularly update the individual ratings. The national supervisors are responsible for determining whether an external credit assessment institution credibly meets the eligibility criteria. Nonetheless, certain reservations about the use of such assessments remain because of the mixed record of agencies when rating less-than-prime borrowers and the use of different credit analysis methodologies by these agencies. In addition, in many developing countries there are no rating agencies or the agencies do not have adequate capacity. (An associated issue is the inadequacy of accounting and financial reporting standards, for both banks and their clients.)

Table 6.3 Standardized Approach: Risk Weights under the Basel II Accord

	Risk Weights under the Standardized Approach of the Basel II Accord						
	AAA to AA-	A+ to A-	BBB+ to BBB-	BB+ to B-	Below B-	Unrated	
Claims on Sovereigns and Central Banks							
Option 1 – Based on Sovereign Credit Risk Assessment (CRA) by Specialized Rating Agencies							Lower weights may be applied to domestic currencies exposures.
Risk Weight	0%	20%	50%	100%	150%	100%	
Option 2 – Based on CRA of Export Credit Agencies (ECAs) risk scores	0–1	2	3	4–6	7		Supervisors may decide to use country risk scores assigned ECAs.
Risk Weight	0%	20%	50%	100%	150%		
Claims on Banks, Public Sector Entities (Noncentral Government), and Securities Firms							
Option 1 – Based on Sovereign CRA	AAA to AA-	A+ to A-	BBB+ to BBB-	BB+ to B-	Below B-	Unrated	Risk weight is one category less favorable than for sovereigns, with 20% floor.
Risk Weight	20%	50%	100%	100%	150%	100%	
Option 2 – Based on CRA of a Bank Itself	AAA to AA-	A+ to A-	BBB+ to BBB-	BB+ to B-	Below B-	Unrated	Claims of three months' or less maturity have more favorable risk weight.
Risk Weight	20%	50%	50%	100%	150%	50%	
Risk Weight, Short-term Claims	20%	20%	20%	50%	150%	20%	
Claims on Private Sector Enterprises and Insurance Companies of Specialized Rating Agencies							
Credit Assessment	AAA to AA-	A+ to A-	BBB+ to BBB-	BB+ to B-	Below B-	Unrated	The risk weights should be increased if warranted by overall default experiences in a country.
Risk Weight	20%	50%	100%	100%	150%	100%	

Off-balance-sheet items under the standardized approach are to be converted into credit exposure equivalents using the conversion factors, which are similar to those established under the Basel I Accord.[3] The treatment of credit risk related to derivative instruments (for example, forward contracts, swaps, options) also remains similar to the version introduced in 1995, with an amendment to the Basel I Accord. With derivative instruments, banks are exposed to credit risk not for the full face value of their contracts, but only to the potential cost of restoring the cash flows if the counterparty defaults. The theoretical basis for assessing the risk on all derivative instruments is the same, with the "credit equivalent" amounts being dependent on the maturity of the respective contract and on the volatility of the rates and prices underlying this type of instrument. For capital adequacy assessment, the derivative instruments are converted according to the same principles as the other types of off-balance-sheet exposures.

In the standardized approach, banks are allowed to use credit risk mitigation techniques (such as collateral, netting, and guarantees) to manage (that is, reduce) their exposures and risk weights. The Basel II Accord provides detailed instructions on the eligibility of credit risk mitigation techniques to reduce credit risk exposures and prescribes the related "haircut" rules.

Internal Ratings–Based (IRB) Approaches

Under the IRB approaches, banks are allowed to use their own internal models and risk estimates in determining the capital requirement for a given exposure. Conceptually, the IRB is *based on asset classes*. Under the IRB approaches, banks must categorize exposures into broad asset classes with different risk characteristics. The asset classes include (a) corporate, (b) sovereign, (c) bank, (d) retail, and (e) equity. There are also subclasses.[4] For each asset class, there are unexpected losses (UL) and expected losses (EL). The Basel II Accord provides specific rules for the capital treatment of expected losses (covered by general loss reserves). The IRB models focus on the risk-weight functions for the unexpected losses.

---

3   One major change is that commitments of less than one year have a credit conversion factor (CCF) of 20 percent, rather then 0 percent established under the Basel I Accord. Only commitments that are unconditionally cancellable are eligible for the 0 percent CCF.

4   For example, the corporate asset class has five subclasses: project finance, object finance, commodities finance, income-producing real estate, and commercial real estate. The retail asset class has three subclasses: exposures to individuals, residential mortgage loans, and loans to small businesses.

The risk measures include probability of default (PD), loss given default (LGD), the exposure at default (EAD), and effective maturity (M). The PD of a borrower or group of borrowers is the central measurable concept on which the IRB approach is founded. Banks' internal measures of credit risk are normally based on assessments of the risk characteristics of both the borrower and the specific type of transaction. In addition, a bank must estimate exactly how much it is likely to lose should a borrower default on an obligation. The magnitude of likely loss is the LGD and is normally expressed as a percentage of a bank's exposure. The actual loss is contingent upon the amount at the time of default, commonly expressed as EAD. The final element normally included in the IRB is the maturity of exposures. These components (PD, LGD, EAD, and M) form the basic inputs to the IRB approach. They combine to provide a measure of the expected intrinsic, or economic, loss; consequently, they form a basis for credit risk–related capital adequacy requirements.

There is a common misconception that using one of the IRB approaches to measure credit risk would result in lower capital charges. This is not true: the measurements under the IRB will normally be more accurate, and the risk-weight curve is far steeper for IRB approaches than for the standardized approach. As a consequence, a poor-quality loan portfolio will produce a higher capital requirement when using an IRB approach. Table 6.4 illustrates the risk weights for unexpected losses prescribed by the Basel II Accord under the IRB approach. It is also worth noting that using an IRB methodology will result in increased volatility in the capital requirement.

Table 6.4 IRB Approach: Risk Weights for Unexpected Losses (UL) for Specialized Lending

IRB Approach: Risk-Weights for Unexpected Losses for Specialized Lending					
Supervisory Category	*Strong*	*Good*	*Satisfactory*	*Weak*	*Default*
External Credit Risk Assessment	BBB- or better	BB- or BB	BB- or B+	B to C-	Not Applicable
Risk weights: unexpected losses for specialized lending	70%	90%	115%	250%	0%
Risk weights: unexpected losses for high-volatility commercial real estate	95%	120%	140%	250%	0%
Specialized Lending: includes project finance, object finance, commodities finance					

For each of the asset classes covered under the IRB framework, there are two options:

Foundation approach, where a bank provides its own estimates for the PD and uses the EAD and LGD provided by the supervisory authority. Once the total probable loss (given the various probabilities of default) is calculated, a capital charge is determined, based on a risk weight for each of the asset (sub)classes.

Advanced approach, where a bank provides its own estimates of PD, EAD, and LGD figures and its own calculation of M, based on historical experience. This alternative opens the door to credit risk modeling and introduces the concept of correlation, which—although not yet accepted by regulatory authorities and not permitted by the capital accord—is common practice among the more sophisticated banks.

In practice, implementation of any of the IRB approaches includes the following elements:

- Classification of exposures by broad asset classes (for example, sovereign, corporate, retail).

- Risk estimates that the bank must assign (using the standardized foundation approach or its own internal estimates) for each asset (sub)class or credit risk exposure.

- Risk-weight function to derive the respective capital requirements for each exposure type.

- A set of minimum requirements established by the supervisory authorities that a bank must meet to be eligible to use an IRB approach. The minimum requirements are related to methods, processes, controls, data collection, and information technology systems that support the assessment of credit risk, the assignment of internal risk ratings, and the quantification of default and loss estimates.

- Supervisory review of a bank's compliance with the minimum requirements, across all asset classes. In principle, the bank may choose one IRB approach for some asset classes and another for other asset classes. Once a bank adopts the IRB approach, it is expected to continue to employ the IRB approach indefinitely.

To be eligible for using the IRB approach, a bank is required to demonstrate to its supervisor that it meets certain minimum requirements, at the outset and on an ongoing basis. The overarching principle for eligibility is that the rating and risk estimation systems and processes to be used by the bank provide for a meaningful assessment of borrower and transaction characteristics, a meaningful differentiation of risk, and reasonably accurate and consistent quantitative estimates of risks that could be easily understood and verified by third parties (for example, supervisors or external auditors). Basel II sets detailed requirements for rating system design and operations, for risk quantification and validation of internal estimates, and for the related corporate governance and oversight.

Market Risk

Market risk is defined as the risk of losses in on- and off-balance-sheet positions that arise from shifts in market prices. More specifically, market risk includes the general and specific interest rate and equity price risks for a bank's trading book of debt and equity instruments and related off-balance-sheet contracts, and general foreign exchange and commodities risks throughout the bank (that is, in the trading and banking books). Trading book valuation methodologies typically include (a) marking-to-market, by daily valuation of positions at readily available, independently sourced, closeout market prices; (b) marking-to-model, which is benchmarked and extrapolated from market inputs; (c) independent price verification, in which market prices are (at least monthly) independently verified for accuracy by outside experts; and (d) valuation adjustments, as needed.

For market risk assessment under the Basel II Accord, banks are allowed to use a *standardized framework or an internal model approach*. Both approaches result in the calculation of an actual capital charge, which is then converted into a notional risk weight, by using the percentage capital requirement set by the respective national regulatory authorities. Market risk could be covered by Tier 1, 2, or 3 capital, subject to the limitations explained in section 6.2. Assets subject to market risk capital requirements are excluded from the credit risk-weighted capital requirements.

Standardized Framework

The standardized framework for market risk assessment is based on a building block approach. It comprises the general market risk that arises from the bank's overall open position in four fundamental markets, and the specific risk associated with the individual securities positions of a bank. The capital requirement is calculated separately for the following risks:

- Interest risk in the bank's trading book

- Equities risk in the bank's trading book

- Currency risk in trading and banking books (see section 13.4 and figure 13.4)

- Commodities risk in trading and banking books

Once quantified, the separate capital charges are added together and multiplied by the reciprocal of the regulatory percentage capital adequacy requirement to create a risk weight for the market risk, from which the allowable portion of the Tier 3 capital adequacy requirement can be calculated. (For example, an 8 percent capital adequacy requirement would result in a 12.5 multiplication factor—see note 1 in section 6.3 and annex 6A for details of the calculation.)

Internal Model Approach: The Use of Value-at-Risk (VAR)

When using an internal model approach, the market risk capital charge is based on whichever is higher: the previous day's value at risk (VAR; see section 11.5) or the average VAR over the last 60 business days. The actual capital requirement is calculated by using a model that falls within the recommended parameters. This figure is then multiplied by the factor k, designated by the national supervisory authorities and related to the quality of a bank's risk management system. (K has a minimum value of 3.0.) Banks are expected by their supervisory authorities to also add to k a "plus" factor—between 0.0 and 1.0—that is determined by the number of times back-testing of the internal model disclosed the predicted VAR to have been exceeded. Because this plus factor is related to the ex post performance of the internal model, its addition is expected to serve as a positive incentive to maintain a good-quality model. The Basel II market risk–related capital standard requires that the VAR must be computed daily and the market risk–related capital requirements met on a daily basis.

The use of internal models for the measurement of market risk is subject to the approval of supervisory authorities, based on a set of detailed requirements related to the following:

- **Market risk management process**. This should be comprehensive, under senior management scrutiny, integrated with but independent from operations, with adequate controls, and with learning capacity.

■ **Coverage**. The risk measurement system should include specific risk factors related to interest rate risk, currency risk, equity price risk, and commodity price risk.

■ **Quantitative parameters of an acceptable internal model**. Included among these are the frequency of VAR computations, an historical observation period, confidence parameters, a holding period, and multiplication factors.

■ **Stress testing and external validation requirements**. These include parameters to ensure that a bank tests against various assumptions and factors that potentially could create extraordinary gains or losses in the trading portfolio or make the control of risk difficult, to ensure that the bank has a system to act on what it learns from the stress test, and to ensure that the system is externally validated in terms of meeting the Basel criteria.

Operational Risk

The Basel II Accord includes capital charges explicitly related to the operational risk. Operational risk is defined as "the risk of loss resulting from inadequate or failed internal processes, people, and systems or from external events." Banking statistics indicate a steady increase in operational risk because of the increasing use of highly automated technology, the increase in retail operations and growth of e-commerce, increased outsourcing, and the greater use of complex instruments and sophisticated techniques to reduce credit and market risk. This recognition has led to an increased emphasis on sound operational risk management by banks, as well as to the inclusion of operational risk in a bank's internal capital assessments and allocation process.

The framework for calculating operational risk related capital charges recognizes three methodologies with increasing sophistication and risk sensitivity: basic indicator approach, standardized approach, and advanced measurement approach. Banks are expected to select the approach that is commensurate to their operational risk profile and risk management capacity. The selection is expected to be endorsed by the supervisory authority based on the quality of operational risk management system, availability of resources in the internal control and audit areas, and the quality of governance.

Basic Indicator Approach

The basic indicator approach uses a single indicator as a proxy for a bank's overall operational risk exposure. Banks using the basic indicator approach must assign capital for operational risk equal to the average of a fixed percentage (denoted as the *alpha* factor) of positive annual gross income over the previous three years. The gross income is defined as net interest income plus net noninterest income (gross of any provisions and operating expenses and excluding profits/losses from sales of securities and any extraordinary or irregular items). The Basel II Accord has established 15 percent as a standard value for *alpha*. This approach will most likely be used by non-G10 banks. The method does not require much work from banks, and it is proposed as the most appropriate method for use until management has in place adequate control processes, board oversight, data reporting, and audit processes related to operational risk.

Standardized Approach

The standardized approach requires a bank to express its business profile through as many as eight standard business lines: corporate finance, trading and sales, retail banking, commercial banking, payment and settlement services, agency and custody services, asset management, and retail brokerage. Within each business line, gross income is again used as an indicator for the scale of business operations and thus the likely scale of operational risk exposures within each of the business lines (see table 6.5). The capital charge for each business line is calculated by multiplying the related gross income by a factor assigned for the respective business line (denoted the *beta* factor). Factor beta is a proxy for the industrywide experience of operational losses for the respective business line. The total capital charge for operational risk is calculated as the three-year average of capital charges on each of the business lines in each year. Banks that use this method do not have to collect operational loss data, but they are required to have effective standards of risk management.

Table 6.5 Operational Risk: Business Lines and Operational Loss Events Types

Operational Risk – Business Lines and Event Types per Basel							
Event types / **Risk Drivers** / **Business lines**	**Internal Fraud** People	**External Fraud** External Events	**Employment Practices and Workplace Safety** People	**Clients, Products and Business Services** People / Processes	**Damage to Physical Assets** External Events	**Business Disruption and System Failures (technology risk)** Systems / External Events	**Execution, Delivery and Process Management** Processes	**Identify Business Line with Highest Incidence of Monetary Losses**
Corporate finance								
Trading and sales								
Retail banking								
Commercial banking								
Payment and settlement								
Agency and custody services								
Asset management								
Retail brokerage								
Identify event types with highest incidence of monetary losses								

* Basel identifies 4 risk drivers – this table allocates the risk drivers to the events where they are most likely to have major impact. It does not preclude all risk drivers from contributing to all event types

Advanced Management Approaches (AMAs)

The most risk-sensitive approaches are the three advanced management approaches (AMAs), which are derived from a bank's internal risk measurement systems and associated operational loss data. Under the AMAs, the capital requirement expected to cover the operational risk is estimated by the bank's internal operational risk measurement system using the quantitative and qualitative criteria determined by the type of AMA used. There are three types of AMAs:

- **Internal measurement approach (IMA).** This approach uses information from the standardized approach, providing for each business line an exposure indicator (EI), the probability of a loss event occurring (PE), and the loss should such an event occur (LGE). The product of these factors and an additional risk factor produces the expected loss (EL).

- **Loss distribution approach (LDA).** This approach allows banks to estimate the likely distribution of operational losses over a given period for each business line or risk type. LDAs attempt to assess unexpected losses directly, whereas IMAs use assumptions about the relationship between expected loss and unexpected loss.

- **Scorecard approach.** Under this approach, banks start with an initial level of capital covering operational risk assigned at the firm or business-line level. This amount of capital is then modified over time by capturing the underlying risk profile of the different business lines. The scorecard approach requires qualitative judgment and relies less on historical data.

In principle, the use of an AMA is subject to supervisory approval, as it provides significant flexibility to banks. The approval is normally conditioned on a bank having a good-quality and independent operational risk management function, operational risk measurement systems integrated into the daily risk management process, and regular reporting of exposures and losses to senior management. The most critical requirement is for the sound operational risk management system, which must be based on a consistent use of internal loss data, relevant external data, scenario analysis, and factors reflecting the business environment and internal control systems.

6.5 Supervisory Review: Pillar 2

Supervisory review is the second pillar of the Basel II Accord and a critical part of the capital adequacy framework. The supervisory review has two objectives:

to assess whether banks maintain adequate capital necessary for the risks inherent in their business profile and business environment, and to encourage banks to have policies and internal processes for assessing and managing capital adequacy that are commensurate with their risk profile, operations, and business strategy. Figure 6.3 illustrates the key Pillar 2 components.

The role of supervisors is to review the bank's internal capital adequacy assessments and management processes, to ensure that the bank's capital targets and capital position are consistent with its overall risk profile and strategy, and to enable supervisory intervention if the bank's capital does not provide a sufficient buffer against risk. In an increasingly risky market environment, this is an increasingly sophisticated process.

Figure 6.3 Supervisory Review: Pillar 2 Components

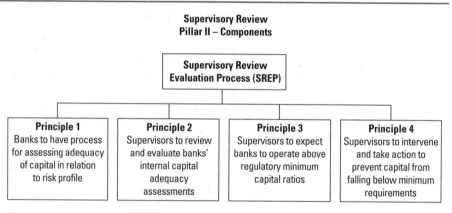

An important aspect of supervisory reviews is the assessment of compliance with the minimum standards and disclosure requirements of a bank using the IRB framework for the credit risk and AMA approaches for the operational risk. Supervisors also are expected to have an approach for identifying and intervening in situations where falling capital levels raise questions about the ability of a bank to withstand business shocks. The Basel II Accord has established certain core principles for supervisory reviews. These principles, as well as the Core Principles for Effective Banking Supervision (Basel, initially issued in September 1997 and updated in October 2006) and other guidance notes related to the supervisory review process published by the Basel Committee on Banking Supervision, are discussed in more details in chapter 15.

Supervisors are expected to take appropriate actions if they are not satisfied with the quality of a bank's internal processes and the results of a bank's own risk assessment and capital allocations. Supervisors are expected to have at their disposal the necessary enforcement powers and tools. For example, they should be able to require banks to hold capital in excess of the minimum, if so mandated by the risk characteristics of a particular bank or its business environment, and to require prompt remedial action if capital is not maintained or restored. The Basel II framework sets special requirements for cooperation between supervisors, especially for the cross-border supervision of complex banking or financial groups. More detailed discussion of the supervisory review process and techniques is provided in chapter 15.

6.6 Market Discipline: Pillar 3

The requirement for market discipline, the third pillar of the Basel II Accord, complements the minimum capital requirements and the supervisory review process. Market discipline is based on disclosure requirements. The banks are asked to disclose reliable and timely information needed by market participants to make well-founded risk assessments, including assessment of the adequacy of capital held as a cushion against losses and of the risk exposures that may give rise to such losses.

The disclosure requirements are based on the materiality concept, that is, banks must include all information where omission or misstatement could change or influence the decisions of the respective information users. The only exception is proprietary or confidential information, the sharing of which could undermine a bank's competitive position. Disclosures are normally made quarterly or semiannually. Banks are expected to have a formal disclosure policy approved by the board of directors, including what will be disclosed, validation reporting frequency, and internal controls over the disclosure process.

The areas that are subject to disclosure are capital structure, capital adequacy, and risk exposure and assessment. The disclosures include qualitative and quantitative aspects. For each risk area (credit, market, operational, equity), qualitative aspects cover strategies, policies, and processes; the structure and organization of the respective risk management function; the scope and nature of the risk measurement and reporting systems; the strategies and policies for hedging and mitigating risks; and processes and systems to monitor their effectiveness. Quantitative aspects involve disclosures of the specific values. Transparency and disclosure are further discussed in chapter 14.

6.7 Management of Capital Adequacy

A bank's management continues to be accountable that its bank has adequate capital. The capital management process should address all material risks faced by the bank. Given its business strategy, a bank must have clearly defined capital adequacy targets; adequate policies and processes to identify, measure, and report all material risks; a capital assessment process that relates its capital to the risk profile; and internal control systems that ensure the integrity of the overall capital assessment and management process.

A bank's board must also devote proper attention to all matters related to the maintenance of capital adequacy. The board has a responsibility to project capital requirements and to determine whether current growth and capital retention are sustainable, to establish sound risk management policies and effective risk management and control systems and procedures, to ensure efficient organization, and to provide adequate resources to attract and retain the necessary professional cadre.

The quality of a bank's assets must also be mentioned in the capital adequacy context. A bank's capital ratios can be rendered meaningless or highly misleading if asset quality is not taken into account. Particularly in developing or transition economies, but also in advanced market economies, many banks report impressive capital ratios when they may in fact be insolvent, because they have overstated asset quality and have provisioned inadequately for losses. An accurate assessment of asset quality and of off-balance-sheet exposures and contingent liabilities is critical for an accurate assessment of capital. Similarly, accurate evaluation of provisions and loan loss reserves is a critical input in the process of capital adequacy assessment.

A bank's capital ratio may be changed by altering either the numerator or the denominator of the ratio. In most cases, to reach or maintain the necessary capital level, banks have done both. They have increased Tier 1 and/or Tier 2 capital by not distributing dividends and by issuing equity or subordinated debt; they have also changed the balance sheet structure by reducing total assets (for example, by cutting back loans) and by shifting into assets that bear a lower risk weight (for example, by moving from corporate loans to government securities or residential mortgages). These decisions have often been motivated by business cycles. In times of high demand, banks are more likely to increase capital; in downturns, they prefer to reduce the size of their balance sheets.

Besides the business cycle aspects, important determinants in selecting the strategy to achieve or maintain capital adequacy include the degree of undercapitalization and the time in which a bank must reach the minimum level of capital. If a bank's condition deteriorates, its options for raising capital become increasingly limited and, at the same time, more expensive. This argues for a bank to maintain capital in excess of regulatory minimums. If its asset quality deteriorates, or if undercapitalization is serious and the time is short, then raising new capital immediately is the only effective solution. Hoping that the problem will solve itself is a fool's game that will cost the bank far more in the long run. Rapid shrinking of the balance sheet often means that a bank is shedding its highest-quality or most liquid assets. This masks the problem in the short run, but creates an even larger problem in the medium term.

The introduction of capital adequacy standards has also motivated regulatory capital arbitrage, reflecting bank efforts to keep their funding cost, including equity, as low as possible. Because the cost of equity is generally perceived as much greater than the cost of debt, banks that would otherwise keep lower capital see the imposition of capital adequacy as a form of regulatory taxation. As with other such forms of taxation, some banks develop methods to minimize the taxes. In practice, capital arbitrage has often exploited the differences between true economic risk and credit risk as measured by the Basel Accords' risk-weighting methodology. Capital arbitrage can be exercised in a number of ways, including shifting the asset composition toward less weighted assets through some form of securitization or by creating credit substitutes (which also carry lower risk weights).

6.8   Analysis of a Bank's Capital Adequacy

Capital adequacy analysis comprises three steps:

(a) analysis of the structure of qualifying capital,

(b) analysis of the bank's risk profile and risk exposures, and

(c) evaluation of the bank's current and future capital needs.

There are no conceptual differences between the Basel I and Basel II approaches to capital adequacy assessments—the approach is essentially the same in both.

However, the analysis of the bank risk profile and risk exposures and the assignment of risk weights are much more complex under the Basel II Accord because of the use of more complex methodologies (which are more sensitive and better attuned to capture the risk profiles of banks' business lines). Therefore, while illustrating the elements of the capital adequacy assessment process, the following discussion will make references to the Basel I Accord to keep the discussion simple and to the point.

Analysis of the Structure of a Bank's Capital

The capital adequacy assessment starts with analysis of the components of a bank's capital, as illustrated in figure 6.4. (The figures presented in this section illustrate the analysis of a bank's capital, but the different figures do not refer to the same bank.) The Tier 1 core capital components, including common stock and retained earnings, should account for more than 50 percent of the total capital. The shareholding structure and the identity of larger shareholders are also important. In extreme circumstances the shareholders may be called upon to increase a bank's capital, either by adding new capital or by forgoing dividend payments. However, no amount of capital would be adequate for a bank with malevolent shareholders, incompetent management, or an incompetent board.

Figure 6.4 Components of a Bank's Capital Structure

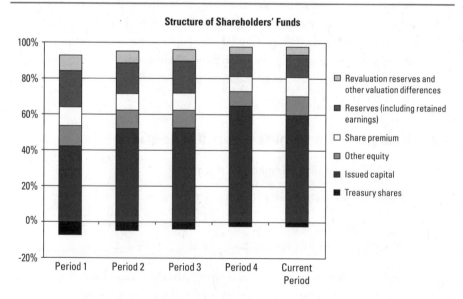

The changes in volume of capital and its structure over time are also significant. For the bank shown in figure 6.4 there were some changes in capital structure. Any changes in capital structure, especially reductions involving core capital, should be credibly explained. A careful analysis is also needed in situations where a reduction of capital is indicated, to explain exactly why and what provoked the loss of capital and to ensure that the bank has learned from the experience and taken adequate measures to prevent a similar situation in the future. The analyst could also compare the changes in capital volume to the bank's risk profile. In general, the changes in capital volume should be in concert with the expected changes in the risk profile to provide an adequate cushion for the bank's risk exposures.

In addition to analyzing the structure of the bank's capital base, one should consider the level and demand for dividends being placed on the bank by shareholders. In periods of economic downturn or situations where the bank's condition is deteriorating, the bank should reduce or eliminate dividend payments to its shareholders.

Analysis of a Bank's Risk Profile

The next step in the capital adequacy assessment is the assessment of the bank's risk exposures. This includes credit risk and market risk under both Basel Accords, plus operational risk under Basel II. Starting with the credit risk, the bank's on- and off-balance sheet assets categories are classified according to the risk categories specified in the Basel I Accord (or subject to the analysis using the approach agreed with the supervisory authority under Basel II) and are assigned the corresponding risk weight.

The analyst should notice the structure of risk-weighted assets and if and how this has changed over time. Whenever there are changes in risk weights, the questions to be addressed are whether this is a result of the bank's business strategy decisions, whether the risk weights reflect actual risk, whether the bank is able to understand and adequately manage the higher level of risk, and what appears to be the trend for the future.

Using the methodology set by Basel I Accord, figure 6.5 illustrates a summary risk profile of a bank, with changes in the risk profile over time in terms of average risk weighting, including on- and off-balance-sheet items. It appears that the weighted average of the bank's total risk profile has been reduced in the observation period. The analyst should understand why and what is the trend. For example, the total average could have been reduced because the bank increased its off-balance-sheet business. The weighted average of on-balance-sheet items could have been reduced because the bank started to engage in regulatory capital arbitrage or because of changes in its demand structure.

Figure 6.5 Risk Profile of On- and Off-Balance-Sheet Items

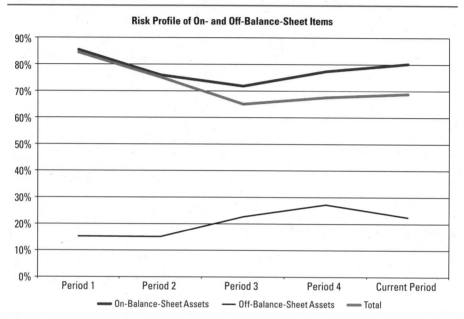

Evaluation of a Bank's Current and Future Capital Needs

Once the denominators corresponding to credit, market, and operational risk of a bank are determined, the capital adequacy ratio calculation is straightforward. Table 6.6 illustrates selected capital adequacy ratios of a bank and their trends over time. A decline in the percentage of core capital in relation to the total qualifying capital would indicate that Tier 2 capital or debt instruments are being used to a greater degree to meet minimum capital requirements. This situation would in turn indicate a relative shift to less permanent forms of capital. The capital adequacy ratio indicates whether or not the bank is meeting the minimum capital requirements.

When a bank's capital adequacy ratio shows deterioration, it is a cause for concern. The reason could be that the bank has increased the size of its balance sheet, while still meeting minimum capital requirements. Should the growth trend continue, it would mean that the bank would have to increase capital to be able to maintain the minimum capital ratio. Another reason for a deteriorating capital ratio could be that the bank has changed its risk profile. In such a case, the analyst should investigate if the bank has adequate policies, procedures, and controls in place to effectively handle the higher risk profile of its operations.

The trend analysis is illustrated in figure 6.6, which traces the capital of a bank over time (in the context of the Basel I Accord). The capital is split into Tier 1, Tier 2, and Tier 3 categories, and these are compared to the capital necessary to meet the 8 percent and 15 percent risk-weighted minimum capital requirement. The bank under review has significantly increased its capital, as well as its risk-weighted capital ratios. This situation likely indicates that this bank is positioning itself for future growth. While capital adequacy is clearly not an issue, this calls for a review of the bank's internal processes and controls to ensure that it is adequately prepared to handle the increasing volume of business and, most likely, the increasing degree of risk.

Figure 6.6 Actual versus Required Capital

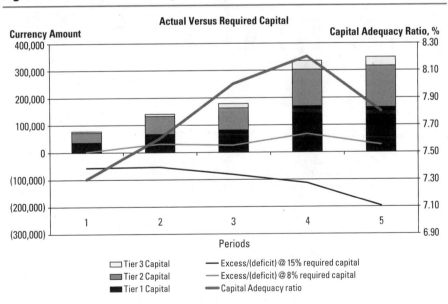

The next question to be addressed is whether a bank can continue to meet its minimum capital requirements in the future. Analysis of this question should include stress tests for situations that might arise in which risk or the bank's capacity to control risk could get out of hand. Figure 6.7 illustrates capital adequacy projections under normal circumstances, made as part of the process of risk management and capital planning. The graph shows the end result of possible situations that a bank may encounter in the future and highlights any projected excess or deficiencies in capital adequacy.

Figure 6.7 Estimating Potential Capital Requirement

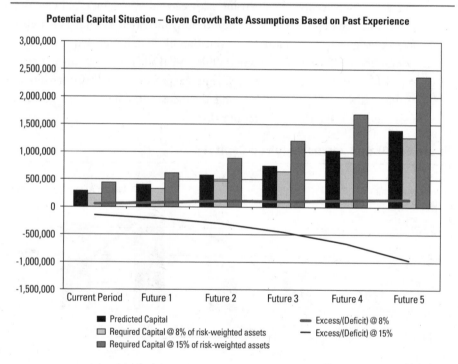

Potential Capital Situation – Given Growth Rate Assumptions Based on Past Experience

The projection in figure 6.7 is based on a simplistic assumption that risk-weighted assets will grow by 10 percent and net qualifying capital by 5 percent, and that the bank's risk profile will remain the same. This expected business growth would clearly result in a capital shortfall. A bank may take a number of actions to address an expected shortfall in capital adequacy, including the following:

- Tier 1 capital increase, by asking shareholders to add capital, by retaining earnings, or by issuing new shares in the market

- Tier 2 capital increase—if there is space for this in the bank's capital structure—by issuing the appropriate instruments

- Change of business policy to focus on business with lower capital requirements

- Reduction in the size of its balance sheet or of its growth

Annex 6A: Credit Risk–Related Weight Assignments Under the Basel I Accord, Covered by Tier 1 and Tier 2 Capital

The Basel I Accord used a fairly simple categorization of credit-related risks, each carrying a weight related to the likelihood of unanticipated losses. Following are the typical risk weights assigned to major categories of loans and advances under Basel I capital adequacy standards.

Credit Risk Related to On-Balance-Sheet Items

- **Cash claims on central governments or on central banks, denominated and funded in the national currency: 0 percent.** This weighting indicates that financial assets related to governments or central banks are internationally regarded as risk free, if denominated in the national currency. This assumption clearly does not hold true when a government's fiscal condition gives reason for concerns or when a government defaults on its debt.

- **Claims on domestic public sector agencies: 0 to 50 percent, at national discretion.** This risk weighting relates to financing, including off-balance-sheet financing and guarantees, made available to the public sector and to quasi-governmental organizations. This relatively low weighting reflects the view that quasi-governmental bodies are also regarded as low risk. Loans guaranteed by or collateralized by securities of such entities are also subject to the same risk weight. National authorities typically assign the weight of 10 or 20 percent, which may not be realistic, especially in developing countries. Although claims on public sector agencies may ultimately be realized, in many situations the point of collection is not within the timeframe of the original financial contract.

- **Claims on banks: 20 percent.** This low weighting is a consequence of the intensive regulation and supervision to which banks are subjected. As a result of formalized risk management procedures and the available central bank accommodation, interbank loans are regarded as less of a credit risk than other loans and advances. For banks outside the Organisation for Economic

Co-operation and Development (OECD), the 20 percent risk weighting applies only to claims with a residual maturity of less than one year.

- **Residential mortgages: 50 percent.** This weighting indicates the traditionally sound nature of such investments. Mortgages, however, are increasingly risky as a result of the high level of consumption expenditures secured by mortgage bonds, which are in turn tied to more flexible mortgage products (for example, home equity loans or advances against capital that has already been paid). Consequently, the relatively low risk weight accorded to residential mortgages could distort the allocation of credit, because loans that finance consumption expenditures can be granted at a price that is not economically justifiable.

- **Other loans: 100 percent.** This weighting generally indicates the higher risk to which a bank is exposed when it extends loans to the private sector or to companies owned by public sector entities. Other claims in this category include claims on governments outside the OECD that are denominated in currencies that are not national currencies; on banks outside the OECD, for claims of residual maturities of more than one year; on real estate and other investments; and on fixed and other assets.

Credit Risk Related to Off-Balance-Sheet Items

The Basel I Accord framework also includes off-balance-sheet items. Off-balance-sheet exposures are treated by converting them into on-balance-sheet credit risk exposures by applying the corresponding credit conversion factors to different types of instruments or transactions. The multiplication factors are derived from the estimated likelihood of default. Credit conversion factors for major off-balance-sheet categories are defined as follows:

- Commitments (such as standby facilities and credit lines) with maturities of up to one year, or those that can be unconditionally cancelled at any time: **0 percent.**

- Short-term, self-liquidating, trade-related contingencies, such as documentary credits subject to collateral by underlying shipments: **20 percent.**

- Certain transaction-related contingent items, such as performance bonds, bid bonds, warranties, and standby letters of credit related to a particular transaction; note issuance facilities and revolving underwriting facilities; and other commitments, such as formal standby facilities and credit lines with maturities of more than one year: **50 percent.**

■ Direct credit substitutes such as general guarantees of indebtedness (for example, standby letters of credit that serve as financial guarantees for loans and securities) and acceptances (for example, endorsements), sale and repurchase agreements, and forward asset purchases: **100 percent**.

The risk weighting of assets and off-balance-sheet positions has provided a major step toward improved objectivity in assessing the adequacy of bank capital. The simplicity of this methodology has also enabled it to be introduced in banking systems that are in their early stages of development. However, this simple weighting of assets provides only a crude measure of economic risk, primarily because the methodology is not effectively calibrated to account for different default risks.

Credit Risk Related to Derivative Instruments

In 1995, the Basel I Accord was amended to include the treatment of forward contracts, swaps, options, and similar derivative contracts. With such derivative instruments, banks are exposed to credit risk not for the full face value of their contracts, but only to the potential cost of restoring the cash flows if the counterparty defaults. The theoretical basis for assessing the risk on all derivative instruments is the same, with the "credit equivalent" amounts being dependent on the maturity of the respective contracts and on the volatility of the rates and prices underlying this type of instrument. For capital adequacy assessment, the derivative instruments are converted according to the same principles as the other types of off-balance-sheet exposures. Table 6A.1 summarizes the weights used for multiplication.

Table 6A.1 Credit Risk Multiplication Factors for Derivative Instruments

Credit Risk Multiplication Factors for Derivative Instruments				
Residual Maturity	Interest Rate	Exchange Rate and Gold	Equity	Commodities
One year or less	0.00%	1.00%	6.00%	10.00%
One to five years	0.50%	8.00%	7.00%	12.00%
More than five years	1.50%	10.00%	8.00%	15.00%

Since the early 1990s, larger banks with more complex business and risk profiles have invested resources in developing models for credit risk arising from their significant business operations. These models are intended to assist banks in better quantifying, aggregating, and managing risks across geographic and product lines. Consequently, such modeling practices prompted development of a new capital accord—Basel II.

Annex 6B: Calculation of the Capital Adequacy Ratio to Include Market Risk (Tier 3 Capital)

Background

1. The Basel I Accord divides capital into two types: core capital (Tier 1) and supplementary capital (Tier 2). These capital elements, taken together, are designed to meet the explicit capital charge for credit risk and allow for a buffer to cover other risks.

2. With the implementation of the 1996 Market Risk Amendment to Basel I, Tier 3 capital, consisting of short-term subordinated debt, was created. Tier 3 capital can be used to partially offset the capital charge for market risks, including foreign exchange risk and commodity risk. However, the amount of Tier 3 capital that can be used for market risks is limited to 250 percent of the amount of Tier 1 capital that is allocated to market risks. Tier 2 capital may be substituted for Tier 3 up to a limit of 250 percent, provided that the overall limits on Tier 2 capital in the 1988 Capital Accord (Basel I) are adhered to.

3. When calculating the market risk capital charge, the result is the actual amount of capital that must be held; when calculating credit risk, the amount of capital needed is determined by multiplying risk-weighted assets by 8 percent. To create a link between credit risk and market risk, the market risk capital charge must be multiplied by 12.5 (the reciprocal of 8 percent) and then added to the risk-weighted assets calculated for credit risk purposes.

4. Thus, the formula for determining capital adequacy can be illustrated as follows:

where

- Tier 1 is the entire amount of the bank's Tier 1 capital.

- Tier 2 is limited to 100 percent of Tier 1 capital; subordinated debt included in Tier 2 is limited to 50 percent of total Tier 2.

- Tier 3 is limited to the amount that is eligible to support market risk, subject to the restrictions in paragraph 2, above.

Example: Calculation of the Capital Adequacy Ratio to Include Market Risk (Tier 3 Capital)

Assumptions:

1. The bank is operating in a regime that requires an 8 percent minimum capital requirement.

2. The bank has calculated its risk-weighted assets as 10,000 and its capital charge for market risk as 500.

3. The bank has 750 of Tier 1 capital, 250 of Tier 2 capital, and 700 of Tier 3 capital.

Solution—see table 6B.1:

1. To calculate the denominator of the equation above, the market risk capital charge must be multiplied by 12.5, the product of which will be added to risk-weighted assets of 10,000. In this example the denominator will be 16,250.

2. One can then determine that in an 8 percent capital environment, the bank will require a minimum of 1,300 in capital (16,250 × 8% = 1,300). Of this amount, 800 is for credit risk (10,000 × 8% = 800), and 500 is for market risk (6,250 × 8% = 500).

3. To determine if the bank has sufficient eligible capital, one must look at the composition of its Tier 1, Tier 2, and Tier 3 capital. Beginning with credit risk, because the minimum capital charge is 800 for credit risk, the bank can use all of its 250 in Tier 2 capital for credit risk. As a consequence, only 550 of Tier 1 capital will be needed for credit risk, leaving an excess of 200 in Tier 1 capital available to meet the market risk capital charge.

4. It is important to note that the amount of Tier 3 capital that may be used to cover market risk is limited to 250 percent of the amount of available Tier 1 capital. In this example, the bank would be limited to 500 of Tier 3 capital for market risk (200 × 250%), despite the fact that it has 700 of Tier 3 capital available. **Wanting to maximize its use of Tier 3 capital, the bank will calculate the amount of Tier 3 capital that is 250 percent of Tier 1 capital and that when summed together with Tier 1 capital will equal 500.** As shown in the table below, the market risk capital charge is 500, and the bank can meet this with 143 of the 200 in Tier 1 capital that remains after the credit risk charge and 357 of Tier 3. The 357 represents 250 percent of the 143, and the two, when added together, equal the 500 market risk capital requirement.

5. Finally, to calculate the bank's capital ratio, all of the Tier 1 capital (750) plus the eligible Tier 2 capital (250) is added to the eligible Tier 3 capital (357). The denominator is 16,250 (as discussed above), resulting in a capital adequacy ratio of 8.35 percent.

Table 6B.1 Calculating the Allowable Portion of Tier 3 Capital

	Available Capital	Risk-Weighted Assets	Minimum Capital Charge @ 8%	Tier 1 and Tier 2 Capital Utilized for Credit Risk	Tier 1 and Tier 3 Capital Required for Market Risk	Minimum Capital Requirement	Eligible Capital (excluding unused Tier 3)	Unused But Eligible Tier 3 – Currently Provided by Tier 1	Unused But Not Eligible Tier 3
	1	2	3	4	5	6	7	8	9
Credit risk	Tier 1: 750 Tier 2: 250	10,000	800	Tier 1: 550 Tier 2: 250		Tier 1: 550 Tier 2: 250	Tier 1: 750 Tier 2: 250		
Market risk	Tier 3: 700	6,250	500		Tier 1: 143 Tier 3: 357	Tier 1: 143 Tier 3: 357	Tier 3: 357	Tier 3: 143	Tier 3: 200
Totals		16,250	1,300	800	500	1,300	1,357		
Capital ratio							8.35%		

1. These amounts are provided in the text.

2. Capital requirement of 500, multiplied by 12.5 (the reciprocal of 8) = 6,250.

3. Risk-weighted assets multiplied by the percentage requirement: 10 000 * 8 % = 800 and 6,250 * 8 % = 500.

4. It would be reasonable for the bank to use all its Tier 2 capital first (up to 100 % of Tier 1 capital).

5. Tier 3 ratio to Tier 1 may not exceed 250:100 (250/350). Tier 3 capital allowed to fulfill requirement = 250/350*500 = 357. The remaining 143 (500 - 357) must come from Tier 1 capital.

6. Consolidation of columns 4 and 5.

7. The required ratio for T3:T1, results in an actual capital adequacy ratio of 8.35% (750 + 250 + 357) /16,250 = 8.35%). This is due to the excess T1 capital in the bank (750 - 550 - 143 = 57)

8. Tier 3 capital can eventually equal the market risk capital requirement of 500. Hence the excess (500-357).

9. The excess Tier 3 capital, above the requirement (700-500), cannot be used unless the current market risk capital requirement of 500 increases.

7

Credit Risk Management

Key Messages

■ Credit risk management lies at the heart of survival for the vast majority of banks.

■ Credit risk can be reduced by implementing policies to limit connected-party lending and large exposures to related parties.

■ Asset classification and subsequent provisioning against possible losses affect not only the value of the loan portfolio, but also the underlying value of a bank's capital.

■ The profile of customers (*who* the bank has lent to) must be transparent.

■ Risks associated with the key banking products (*what* the bank has lent) must be understood and managed.

■ The maturity profile of loan products (*how long* the loans are for) interacts strongly with liquidity risk management.

■ A bank's capacity for credit risk management will contribute significantly to the quality of its risk management practices.

7.1 Establishing Policies for Managing Credit Risk

Credit or counterparty risk is the chance that a debtor or issuer of a financial instrument—whether an individual, a company, or a country—will not repay principal and other investment-related cash flows according to the terms specified in a credit agreement. Inherent to banking, credit risk means that payments may be delayed or not made at all, which can cause cash flow problems and affect a bank's liquidity. Despite innovation in the financial services sector, more than 70 percent a bank's balance sheet generally relates to this aspect of risk management. For this reason, credit risk is the principal cause of bank failures. Although the discussion of the credit risk management function is primarily focused on the loan portfolio, the principles relating to the determination of creditworthiness apply equally to the assessment of counterparties that issue financial instruments.

Financial analysts as well as bank supervisory agencies place considerable importance on formal policies laid down by the board of directors and implemented or administered by management. A lending or financing policy should outline the scope and allocation of a bank's credit facilities and the manner in which a credit portfolio is managed—that is, how investment and financing assets are originated, appraised, supervised, and collected. A good policy is not overly restrictive and allows for the presentation of proposals to the board that officers believe are worthy of consideration, even if they do not fall within the parameters of written guidelines. Flexibility is needed to allow for fast reaction and early adaptation to changing conditions in a bank's mix of assets and the market environment.

Virtually all regulators prescribe minimum standards for managing credit risk. These cover the identification of existing and potential risks, the definition of policies that express the bank's risk management philosophy, and the setting of parameters within which credit risk will be controlled.

There are typically three kinds of policies related to credit risk management. One set aims to *limit or reduce credit risk*. These include policies on concentration and large exposures, diversification, lending to connected parties, and overexposure. The second set aims to *classify assets*. These mandate periodic evaluation of the collectibility of the portfolio of credit instruments. The third set aims to *provision* loss or make allowances at a level adequate to absorb anticipated loss.

7.2 Regulatory Policies to Limit Exposures

To reduce or limit credit risk, regulators pay close attention to three issues: exposure to a single customer, related party financing, and overexposure to a geographic area or economic sector.

Large Exposures to a Single Customer or Connected Parties

Large-exposure and concentration limits usually refer to the maximum permitted exposure to a single client, connected group, or sector of economic activity (for example, agriculture, steel, or textiles). This is especially important for small, regionally oriented or specialized banks. A lending policy should also require that all concentrations be reviewed and reported on a frequent basis.

Modern prudential regulations usually stipulate that a bank refrain from investing in or extending credit to any individual entity or related group of entities in excess of a prescribed percentage of the bank's capital and reserves. Most countries impose a single-customer exposure limit of between 10 and 25 percent of capital. The threshold at which reporting to supervisory authorities becomes necessary should normally be set somewhere below the maximum exposure limit. Supervisors can then devote special attention to exposures above the threshold and require banks to take precautionary measures before concentration becomes excessively risky.

The main difficulty in defining exposure is to quantify the extent to which less-direct forms of credit exposure should be included within the exposure limit. As a matter of principle, contingent liabilities and credit substitutes— such as guarantees, acceptances, letters of credit, and all future commitments— should be included, although the treatment of specific instruments may vary. For example, a financial obligation guarantee may be treated differently than a performance risk guarantee. The treatment of collateral is another contentious issue, as the valuation of collateral can be highly subjective. As a matter of prudence, collateral should not be considered when determining the size of an exposure.

Another conceptual question is the definition of the term "single client." According to international practice, a single client is an individual, legal person, or a connected group to which a bank is exposed. A connected group covers clients that are mutually associated or control other clients, either directly or indirectly, normally through a voting right of at least 15–20 percent, a dominant shareholding, or the capacity to control policy making and management. In addition, the exposure to a number of single clients may represent a cumulative risk if financial interdependence exists and their expected source of repayment is the same. (See figure 7.1 for a hypothetical example.)

In practical terms, a large exposure usually indicates a bank's commitment to support a specific client. Here the risk is that a bank that extends credit to a large corporate client may not be objective in appraising the risks associated with such credit.

Figure 7.1 Exposure to Top 20 Clients

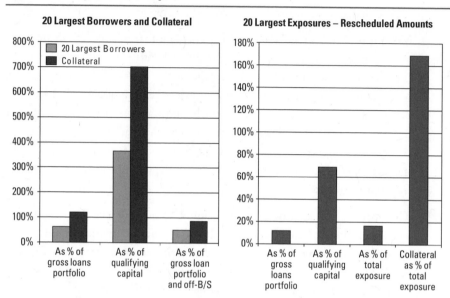

The management of large exposures involves an additional aspect: the bank's ability to identify common or related ownership, to exercise effective control, and to rely on common cash flows to meet its own obligations. Particularly in the case of large clients, banks must pay attention to the completeness and adequacy of information about the debtor. Bank credit officers should monitor events affecting large clients and their performance on an ongoing basis, regardless of whether they are meeting their obligations. When external events present a cause for concern, credit officers should request additional information from the debtor. If there is any doubt that the person or group receiving the investment or financing might have difficulty meeting its obligation to the bank, the concerns should be raised with a higher level of credit risk management, and a contingency plan for addressing the issue should be developed.

Related Party Financing

Dealing with related or connected parties is a particularly dangerous form of credit risk exposure. Related parties typically include a bank's parent, major shareholders, subsidiaries, affiliate companies, directors, and executive officers. Such parties are in a position to exert control over or influence a bank's policies and decision making, especially concerning credit decisions. A bank's ability to identify and track extensions of credit to insiders is crucial (see table 7.1 and figure 7.2).

Table 7.1 Related Party Lending

	Amount of Loans	Amount of Weak Loans	Amount of Loans, as Percentage of Qualifying Capital	Weak Loans as Percentage of Qualifying Capital	Collateral Held
Shareholders holding more than 5 percent of shares					
Shareholders holding less than 5 percent of shares					
Shareholders of any shareholders					
Board of directors					
Executive management					
Entities controlled by the bank					
Entities having control over the bank					
Close relative to any of the above					
Total					

Figure 7.2 Related Party Lending and Affected Loans

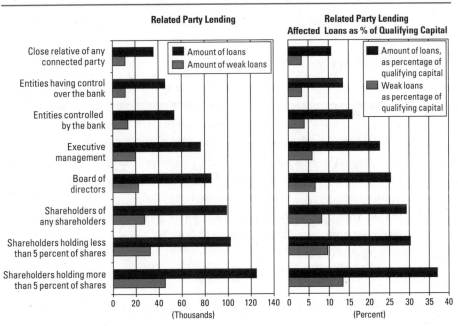

The issue is whether credit decisions are made on a rational basis and according to the bank's policies and procedures. An additional concern is whether credit is based on market terms or on terms that are more favorable with regard to amount, maturity, rate, and collateral than those provided to the general public.

Most regulators establish limits for related parties, typically stipulating that total credit to related parties cannot exceed a certain percentage of Tier 1 or total qualifying capital. If prudential regulations have not established such a limit, the bank should maintain one as a matter of board policy. Prudent banking practice requires board approval of all facilities extended to related parties.

7.3 Management Policies to Reduce Credit Risk

A lending policy should contain an outline of the scope and allocation of a bank's credit facilities and the manner in which a credit portfolio is managed, that is, how loans are originated, appraised, supervised, and collected. As stated earlier, a good lending policy is not overly restrictive, but allows for the presentation of loans to the board that officers believe are worthy of consideration, even if they do not fall within the parameters of written guidelines. Flexibility must exist to allow for fast reaction and early adaptation to changing conditions in a bank's earning assets mix and market environment. A number of elements make up sound lending policies.

Lending Authority

Lending authority is often determined by the size of a bank. In smaller banks, it is typically centralized. To avoid delays in the lending process, larger banks tend to decentralize according to geographical area, lending products, and types of customers. A lending policy should establish limits for all lending officers. If policies are clearly established and enforced, individual limitations may be somewhat higher than would normally be expected, depending on the officer's experience and tenure with the bank. Lending limits could also be based on group authority, which would allow a committee to approve larger loans. Reporting procedures and the frequency of committee meetings should be specified.

Type of Loans and Distribution by Category

A lending policy should specify the types of loans and other credit instruments that the bank intends to offer to clients and should provide guidelines for specific loans. Decisions about types of credit instruments should be based on the expertise of lending officers, the deposit structure of a bank, and anticipated credit demand. Types of credit that have resulted in an abnormal loss should be controlled by senior management or avoided completely. Limitations based on aggregate percentages of total loans in commercial, real estate, consumer, or other credit categories are common. Policies related to such limitations should allow for deviations that are approved by the board.

Appraisal Process

A lending policy should outline where the responsibility for appraisals lies and should define formal, standard appraisal procedures, including reference to re-appraisals of renewals or extensions. Acceptable types and limits on the amount of appraisals should be outlined for each type of credit facility. Circumstances requiring appraisals by qualified independent appraisers should also be described. The ratio of the amount of the loan to the appraised value of both the project and collateral, as well as the method of valuation and differences among various types of lending instruments, should be detailed. A lending policy should also contain a schedule of down payment requirements, where applicable.

Loan Pricing

Rates on various loan types must be sufficient to cover the costs of funds, loan supervision, administration (including general overhead), and probable losses. At the same time, rates should provide a reasonable margin of profit. Rates should be periodically reviewed and adjusted to reflect changes in costs or competitive factors. Rate differentials may be deliberately maintained either to encourage some types of borrowers to seek credit elsewhere or to attract a specific type of borrower. Guidelines for other relevant procedures, such as the determination of fees on commitments or penalty interest rates, are also an element of pricing policy.

Maturities

A lending policy should establish the maximum maturity for each type of credit, and loans should be granted with a realistic repayment schedule. Maturity scheduling should be determined in relation to the anticipated source of repayment, the purpose of the loan, and the useful life of the collateral.

Exposure to Geographic Areas or Economic Sectors

Another dimension of risk concentration is the exposure of a bank to a single sector of the economy or a narrow geographic region (see figure 7.3). This makes a bank vulnerable to weaknesses in a particular industry or region and poses a risk that it will suffer from simultaneous failures among several clients for similar reasons. This concern is particularly relevant for regional and specialized banks or banks in small countries with narrow economic profiles, such as those with predominantly agricultural economies or exporters of a single commodity.

It is often difficult to assess the exposure of a bank to various sectors of the economy, as most bank reporting systems do not produce such information. For example, a holding company of a large diversified group could be used to finance projects in various industries in which the company operates. In any case, banks should have well-developed systems to monitor sector risks, assess the impact of adverse trends on the quality of their portfolios and income statements, and deal with increased risk.

Figure 7.3 Sectoral Analysis of Loans

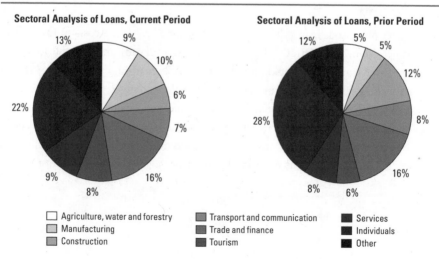

Banks engaged in international lending face additional risks, the most important of which are country (or sovereign) and transfer risks. The country risks encompass the entire spectrum of risks posed by the macroeconomic, political, and social environment of a country that may affect the performance of clients. Transfer risks are the difficulties that a client might have in obtaining the foreign exchange needed to service a bank's obligations. The classification of international loans should normally include both country and transfer risks. A bank may be asked to provision for international loans on a loan-by-loan basis, whereby the level of necessary provisions is raised to accommodate additional risk. Alternatively, a bank may determine aggregate exposures to country and transfer risks on a country-by-country basis and provide special reserves to accommodate risk exposures.

Insistence on Availability of Current Financial Information

The safe extension of credit depends on complete and accurate information regarding every detail of the borrower's credit standing. A possible exception to this rule is the case in which a loan was originally approved with readily marketable collateral to be used as the source of repayment. A lending policy should define the financial statement requirements for businesses and individuals at various borrowing levels and should include appropriate guidelines for audited, unaudited, interim, cash flow, and other statements. It should include external credit checks required at the time of periodic updates. If the loan maturity is longer than one year, the policy should require that the bank's officers prepare financial projections with the horizon equivalent to the loan maturity, to ensure that the loan can be repaid from cash flow. The assumptions for the projections should be clearly outlined. All requirements should be defined so that any negative credit data would clearly indicate a violation of the bank's lending policy.

Collections Monitoring

A lending policy should define delinquent obligations of all types and specify the appropriate reports to be submitted to the board. These reports should include sufficient detail to allow for the determination of the risk factor, loss potential, and alternative courses of action. The policy should require a follow-up collection procedure that is systematic and becomes progressively stronger. Guidelines should be established to ensure that all major problem loans are presented to and reviewed by the board.

Limit on Total Outstanding Loans

A limit on the total loan portfolio is usually expressed relative to deposits, capital, or total assets. In setting such a limit, factors such as credit demand, the volatility of deposits, and credit risks should be considered.

Maximum Ratio of Loan Amount to the Market Value of Pledged Securities

A lending policy should set forth margin requirements for all types of securities that are accepted as collateral. Margin requirements should be related to the marketability of securities. A lending policy should also assign responsibility and establish a timetable for periodic pricing of collateral.

Impairment Recognition

A bank should have policies in place to systematically identify and recognize the impairment of a loan or a collectively assessed group of loans. This should be done whenever a bank will likely be unable to collect the amounts due according to the loan agreement. Impairment can be recognized by reducing the carrying amount of the loan to its estimated realizable value through an existing allowance or by charging the income statement during the period in which the impairment occurs.

Renegotiated Debt Treatment

Renegotiated debt refers to loans that have been restructured to provide a reduction of either interest or principal payments because of the borrower's deteriorated financial position. A loan that is extended or renewed with terms that are equal to those applied to new debt with similar risk should not be considered renegotiated debt. Restructuring may involve a transfer from the borrower to the bank of real estate, receivables or other assets from third parties, a debt-to-equity swap in full or partial satisfaction of the loan, or the addition of a new debtor to the original borrower.

A good practice is to have such transactions approved by the board of directors before concessions are made to a borrower. Bank policies should also ensure that such items are properly handled from an accounting and control standpoint. A bank should measure a restructured loan by reducing its recorded investment to a net realizable value, taking into account the cost of all the concessions at the date of restructuring. The reduction should be recorded as a charge to the income statement for the period in which the loan is restructured. A significant amount of renegotiated debt is normally a sign that a bank is experiencing problems. An exception to this general approach applies in a market environment of falling interest rates, when it may be in the interest of both debtors and creditors to renegotiate the original credit terms.

Written Internal Guidelines

Finally, a lending policy should be supplemented with other written guidelines for specific departments of the bank. Written policies and procedures that are approved and enforced in various departments should be referenced in a bank's general lending policy. The absence of written policies, guidelines, and procedures is a major deficiency and a sign that a board of directors is not properly executing its fiduciary responsibilities.

7.4   Analyzing Credit Risk

Loan Portfolio Structure

The detailed composition of assets usually provides a good picture of a bank's business profile and business priorities as well as the type of intermediation risk that the bank is expected and willing to take. Any analysis should include an overview of *what* products have been lent, to *whom*, and for *how long*.

An aggregate loan portfolio analysis should include the following:

- A summary of the major loan types, including details of the number of customers, average maturity, and the average interest rate earned
- Distribution of the loan portfolio, including various perspectives on the number of loans and total amounts—for example, according to currency, short- (less than one year) and long-term (more than one year) maturities, industrial and other pertinent economic sectors, state-owned and private borrowers, and corporate and retail lending
- Loans with government or other guarantees
- A review of loans by risk classification
- An analysis of nonperforming loans

To illustrate this process, figure 7.4 shows the profile of a bank's borrowers, including individuals and public sector and other enterprises. This profile highlights the target customer segments that pose an acceptable risk to a bank. The figure also traces the shift of target customer profiles from public sector enterprises toward the private sector.

Figure 7.4 Customer Profile: Who We Are Lending To

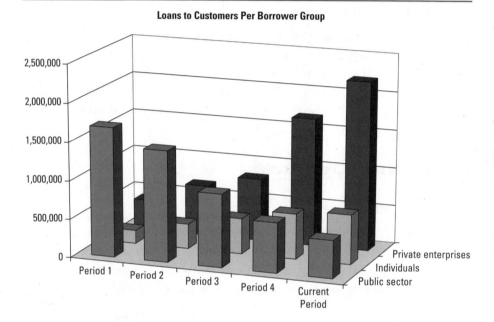

Figure 7.5 illustrates the various products that a bank can lend out in response to market demand. Changes in a bank's target customers clearly affect the distribution of its lending products.

Figure 7.5 Customer Loans by Product

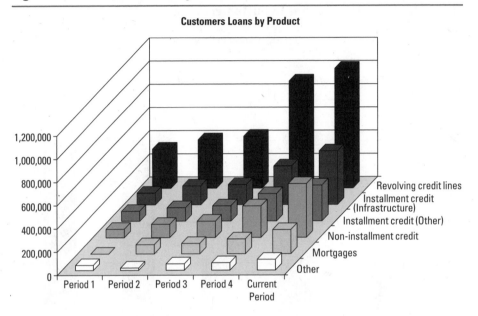

Figure 7.6 traces the evolution of the maturity structure (or length) of a bank's loans to customers. Changes in maturity structure may be influenced by shifts in customers and lending products as well as by a bank's risk factors and macroeconomic trends.

Figure 7.6 Maturity of Loans to Customers

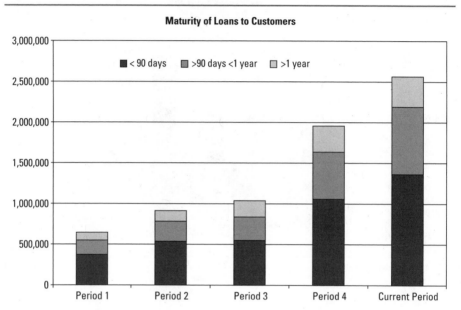

Maturity of Loans to Customers

Loan Portfolio Review

A loan portfolio reflects a bank's market position and demand, its business and risk strategy, and its credit extension capabilities. When feasible, the loan portfolio review (see box 7.1) should normally include a random sampling of loans so that approximately 70 percent of the total loan amount and 30 percent of the number of loans are covered. It should also consider at least 75 percent of the total loan amount and 50 percent of the number of all foreign currency loans and of all loans with maturities greater than one year. In addition, a detailed credit portfolio review should include the following:

■ All loans to borrowers with aggregate exposure larger than 5 percent of the bank's capital

■ All loans to shareholders and connected parties

- All loans for which the interest or repayment terms have been rescheduled or otherwise altered since the granting of the loan

- All loans for which cash payment of interest or principal is more than 30 days past due, including those for which interest has been capitalized or rolled over

- All loans classified as substandard, doubtful, or loss

In each of these cases, a loan review should consider documentation in the borrower's file and involve a discussion with the responsible credit officer of the borrower's business, near-term prospects, and credit history. When the total amount due exceeds 5 percent of a bank's capital, the analysis should also consider the borrower's business plans for the future and the potential consequences for debt service capacity and principal repayment.

Box 7.1 Contents of a Loan Review File

For each of the loans reviewed, a summary file should be made showing the following:

- Borrower's name and line of business

- Use of proceeds

- Date credit was granted

- Loan maturity date, amount, currency, and interest rate

- Principal source of repayment

- Nature and value of collateral/security (or valuation basis, if a fixed asset)

- Total outstanding liabilities, including loan principal and interest due and all other real and contingent liabilities, in cases where the bank is absorbing the credit risk

- Delinquency or nonperformance, if any

- Description of monitoring activities undertaken for the loan

- Financial information, including current financial statements and other pertinent information

- Specific provisions that are required and available

Interbank Deposits

Beyond loans, interbank deposits are the most important category of assets for which a bank carries credit risk. This category may account for a significant percentage of a bank's balance sheet, particularly in countries that lack convertibility but allow their citizens and economic agents to maintain foreign exchange deposits. Other reasons for interbank deposits are the facilitation of fund transfers, the settlement of securities transactions, or because certain services are more economically or efficiently performed by other banks because of their size or geographical location. A review of interbank lending typically focuses on the following aspects:

- The establishment and observation of counterparty credit limits, including a description of existing credit limit policy
- Any interbank credits for which specific provisions should be made
- The method and accuracy of reconciliation of nostro and vostro accounts
- Any interbank credits with terms of pricing that are not the market norm
- The concentration of interbank exposure with a detailed listing of banks and amounts outstanding as well as lending limits

From a credit risk management perspective, interbank deposits should be treated just like any other credit risk exposure. A bank's policy should require that correspondent banks be carefully reviewed for exposure limits, as well as their ability to provide adequate collateral. Banks from regulatory environments that are strict, well supervised, and in tune with international standards are customarily treated as a lesser risk than banks from developing countries.

Off-Balance-Sheet Commitments

All off-balance-sheet commitments that incur credit exposure should also be reviewed. An assessment should be made of the adequacy of credit risk analysis procedures and the supervision and administration of off-balance-sheet credit instruments, such as guarantees. An off-balance-sheet portfolio review should be carried out with the same principles and in a manner similar to a loan portfolio review. The key objective of a review of individual off-balance-sheet items is to assess the ability of the client to meet particular financial commitments in a timely manner.

7.5 Asset Classification and Loan Loss Provisioning

The quality of a bank's loan portfolio is assessed through a classification and loss provisioning process. The specific objective of these reviews is to assess the likelihood that the credit will be repaid, as well as whether the classification of the loan proposed by the bank is adequate. Other considerations include the quality of collateral held and the ability of the borrower's business to generate the necessary cash.

Asset Classification Categories

According to international standards, assets are normally classified in the following categories:

- **Standard, or pass**. When debt service capacity is considered to be beyond any doubt. In general, loans and other assets that are fully secured (including principal and interest) by cash or cash substitutes (for example, bank certificates of deposit and Treasury bills and notes) are usually classified as standard regardless of arrears or other adverse credit factors.

- **Specially mentioned, or watch**. Assets with potential weaknesses that may, if not checked or corrected, weaken the asset as a whole or potentially jeopardize a borrower's repayment capacity in the future. This, for example, includes credit given through an inadequate loan agreement, a lack of control over collateral, or without proper documentation. Loans to borrowers operating under economic or market conditions that may negatively affect the borrower in the future should receive this classification. This also applies to borrowers with an adverse trend in their operations or an unbalanced position in their balance sheet, but which have not reached a point where repayment is jeopardized.

- **Substandard**. This classification indicates credit weaknesses that jeopardize debt service capacity, in particular when the primary sources of repayment are insufficient and the bank must look to secondary sources for repayment, such as collateral, the sale of a fixed asset, refinancing, or fresh capital. Substandard assets typically take the form of term credits to borrowers whose cash flow may not be sufficient to meet currently maturing debts or loans, and advances to borrowers that are significantly undercapitalized. They may also include short-term loans and advances to borrowers for which the inventory-to-cash cycle is insufficient to repay the debt at maturity. Nonperforming assets that are at least 90 days overdue are normally classified as substandard, as are renegotiated loans and advances for which delinquent interest has been paid by the borrower from its own funds prior to renegotiations and until sustained performance under a realistic repayment program has been achieved.

- **Doubtful**. Such assets have the same weaknesses as substandard assets, but their collection in full is questionable on the basis of existing facts. The possibility of loss is present, but certain factors that may strengthen the asset defer its classification as a loss until a more exact status may be determined. Nonperforming assets that are at least 180 days past due are also classified as doubtful, unless they are sufficiently secured.

- **Loss**. Certain assets are considered uncollectible and of such little value that the continued definition as bankable assets is not warranted. This classification does not mean that an asset has absolutely no recovery or salvage value, but rather that it is neither practical nor desirable to defer the process of writing it off, even though partial recovery may be possible in the future. Nonperforming assets that are at least one year past due are also classified as losses, unless such assets are very well secured.

Nonperforming Loans

The concept of nonperforming assets is typically introduced as part of a discussion on asset classification. Nonperforming assets are those not generating income. As a first step, loans are often considered to be nonperforming when principal or interest on them is due and left unpaid for 90 days or more. (This period may vary by jurisdiction.) Loan classification and provisioning entails much more than simply looking at amounts overdue. The borrower's cash flow and overall ability to repay amounts owing are significantly more important than whether the loan is overdue or not.

For financial reporting purposes, the principal balance outstanding, rather than delinquent payments, is used to identify a nonperforming loan portfolio. The nonperforming loan portfolio is an indication of the quality of the total portfolio and ultimately that of a bank's lending decisions. Another such indicator is the bank's collection ratio. Table 7.2 and figure 7.7 illustrate aspects of nonperforming loans over a period of time and the level of provisions put in place to record potential losses.

Table 7.2 Loan Portfolio Statistics

	Period 1	Period 2	Period 3
Gross loans			
Overdue loans			
Overdue loans as percentage of total loans			
Bad debts			
Bad debts as percentage of total loans			
Specific provisions			
Specific provisions as percentage of total loans			
Market value of security held (for assets with specific provisions)			
Coverage ratio (market value of collateral as a percentage of specific provisions)			
Value of loan loss provision as percentage of total loans			
Loans to private sector as percentage of total loans (gross)			
Loans to individuals as percentage of total loans (gross)			
Loans to public sector as percentage of total loans (gross)			
20 largest borrowers as percentage of total gross loans portfolio			
20 largest borrowers as percentage of total off-balance-sheet items			
20 largest borrowers as percentage of net interest income			
20 largest borrowers as percentage of total assets			
20 largest borrowers as percentage of qualifying capital			

Figure 7.7 Loan Portfolio Statistics

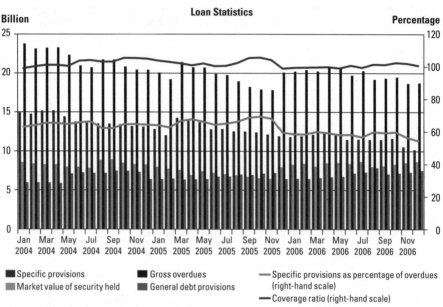

Loan Statistics

Billion / Percentage

- Specific provisions
- Market value of security held
- Gross overdues
- General debt provisions
- Specific provisions as percentage of overdues (right-hand scale)
- Coverage ratio (right-hand scale)

Source: South African Reserve Bank – Supervision Report 2007

When assessed within the context of nonperforming loans, the aggregate level of provisions indicates the capacity of a bank to effectively accommodate credit risk. The analysis of a nonperforming loan portfolio should cover the following aspects:

- Aging of past-due loans, including principal and interest, and classified by more than 30, 90, 180, and 360 days, should be broken down by type of customer and branch of economic activity to determine overall trends and whether all customers are affected equally.

- Reasons for the deterioration of the loan portfolio quality should be determined, which can help identify possible measures the bank can undertake to reverse a given trend.

- A list of nonperforming loans, including all relevant details, should be assessed on a case-by-case basis to determine if the situation is reversible, exactly what can be done to improve repayment capacity, and whether workout or collection plans have been used.

- Provision levels should be considered to determine the bank's capacity to withstand loan defaults. The impact on profit and loss accounts should be considered to determine exactly how the bank will be affected by the deterioration of asset quality.

A number of reasons can explain deteriorating loan portfolio quality. It is unavoidable that banks make mistakes in judgment. However, for most failed banks, the real problems are systemic in nature and rooted in the bank's credit culture. Box 7.2 describes the kinds of problems that indicate distortion in a bank's credit culture.

Box 7.2 Signs of a Distorted Credit Culture

Self-dealing
An overextension of credit to directors and large shareholders, or to their interests, while compromising sound credit principles under pressure from related parties. Self-dealing has been the key issue in a significant number of problem banks.

Compromise of credit principles
Arises when loans that have undue risk or are extended under unsatisfactory terms are granted with full knowledge of the violation of sound credit principles. The reasons for the compromise typically include self-dealing, anxiety over income, competitive pressures in the bank's key markets, or personal conflicts of interest.

Anxiety over income
A situation in which concern over earnings outweighs the soundness of lending decisions, underscored by the hope that risk will not materialize or lead to loans with unsatisfactory repayment terms. This is a relatively frequent problem because a loan portfolio is usually a bank's key revenue-producing asset.

Incomplete credit information
This indicates that loans have been extended without proper appraisal of borrower creditworthiness.

Complacency
This is a frequent cause of bad loan decisions. Complacency is typically manifested in a lack of adequate supervision of old, familiar borrowers, dependence on oral information rather than reliable and complete financial data, and an optimistic interpretation of known credit weaknesses because of survival in distressed situations in the past. In addition, banks may ignore warning signs regarding the borrower, economy, region, industry, or other relevant factors or fail to enforce repayment agreements, including a lack of prompt legal action.

Lack of supervision

Ineffective supervision invariably results in a lack of knowledge about the borrower's affairs over the lifetime of the loan. Consequently, initially sound loans may develop problems and losses because of a lack of effective supervision.

Technical incompetence

This includes a lack of technical ability among credit officers to analyze financial statements and obtain and evaluate pertinent credit information.

Poor selection of risks

This tendency typically involves the following:

- The extension of loans with initially sound financial risk to a level beyond the reasonable payment capacity of the borrower. This is a frequent problem in unstable economies with volatile interest rates.

- Loans where the bank-financed share of the total cost of the project is large relative to the equity investment of the owners. Loans for real estate transactions with narrow equity ownership also fall into this category.

- Loans based on the expectation of successful completion of a business transaction, rather than on the borrower's creditworthiness, and loans made for the speculative purchase of securities or goods.

- Loans to companies operating in economically distressed areas or industries.

- Loans made because of large deposits in a bank, rather than on sound net worth or collateral.

- Loans predicated on collateral of problematic liquidation value or collateral loans that lack adequate security margins.

Commercial Bank Examination Manual
Board of Governors
Federal Reserve System
Division of Banking Supervision and Regulation
December 1985

Overdue Interest

To avoid the overstatement of income and ensure timely recognition of nonperforming assets, bank policies should require appropriate action on uncollected interest. Two basic methods exist for handling both the suspension and nonaccrual of interest. First, in cases where the interest is suspended, it is accrued or capitalized and an offsetting accounting entry is made for a category called "interest in suspense." For reporting purposes the two entries must be netted; otherwise the assets will be inflated.

Second, when a bank places a loan in nonaccrual status, it should reverse uncollected interest against corresponding income and balance sheet accounts. For interest accrued in the current accounting period, the deduction should be made directly from current interest income. For prior accounting periods, a bank should charge the reserve for possible loan losses or, if accrued interest provisions have not been provided, the charge should be expensed against current earnings. A nonaccruing loan is normally restored to accruing status after both principal and interest in arrears have been repaid or when prospects for future contractual payments are no longer in doubt.

In some jurisdictions, a bank may avoid taking action on interest in arrears if the obligation is well secured or the process of collection is underway. A debt is considered to be well secured if it is backed by collateral in the form of liens on or pledges of real or personal property. Such collateral, including securities, must have a realizable value that is sufficient to discharge the debt in full according to contract terms or by a financially responsible party. A debt is "in the process of collection" if collection is proceeding in due course, either through legal action or through collection efforts that are expected to result in repayment of the debt or in its restoration to current status.

Classifying Assets

Asset classification is a key tool of risk management. Assets are classified at the time of origination and then reviewed and reclassified as necessary (according to the degree of credit risk) a few times a year. The review should consider service performance and the client's financial condition. Economic trends and changes in the market for and the price of goods also affect evaluation of loan repayment. Assets classified as "pass" or "watch" are typically reviewed twice a year, and critical assets are reviewed at least quarterly.

Banks determine classifications by themselves but follow standards that are normally set by regulatory authorities.

Primary emphasis is placed on the client's ability and willingness to meet obligations out of prospective operating cash flow. Some jurisdictions require that all credit extended to an individual client should be assigned the same risk classification, while differences in classification should be noted and justified.

Other jurisdictions recommend that each asset be assessed on its own merits. In cases where assets may be classified differently depending on whether subjective or objective criteria are used, the more severe classification should generally apply. If supervisory authorities, and in many cases external auditors, assign more stringent classifications than the bank itself, the bank is expected to adjust the classification.

In some advanced banking systems, banks use more than one rating level for assets in the category of pass or standard. The objective of this practice is to improve the ability to differentiate among different types of credit and to improve the understanding of the relationship between profitability and rating level.

Loan Loss Provisioning

Asset classification provides a basis for determining an adequate level of provisions for possible loan losses. Such provisions, together with general loss reserves that are normally counted as Tier 2 capital and are not assigned to specific assets, form the basis for establishing a bank's capacity to absorb losses. In determining an adequate reserve, all significant factors that affect the collectibility of the loan portfolio should be considered. These factors include the quality of credit policies and procedures, prior loss experiences, loan growth, quality of management in the lending area, loan collection and recovery practices, changes in national and local economic and business conditions, and general economic trends.

Assessments of asset value should be performed systematically, consistently over time, and in conformity with objective criteria. They should also be supported by adequate documentation.

Estimates of the level of necessary loan loss provisions inherently include a degree of subjectivity. However, management discretion should be exercised in accordance with established policies and procedures. An analysis of adequacy of the overall allowance for losses should include the following aspects:

- A survey of the bank's existing provisioning policy and the methodology used to carry it out. In particular, the value attributed to collateral and its legal and operational enforceability should be considered.

- An overview of asset classification procedures and the review process, including the time allotted for review.

- Determination of the current factors that are likely to cause losses associated with a bank's portfolio and that differ from the historical experience of loss. These may include changes in a bank's economic and business conditions or in its clients, external factors, or alterations of bank procedures since the last review.

- A trend analysis over a longer period of time, which serves to highlight any increases in overdue loans and the impact of such increases.

- An opinion of the adequacy of the current policy and, on the basis of the loans reviewed, extrapolation of additional provisions necessary to bring the bank's total loan loss provisions in line with International Financial Reporting Standards.

Policies on loan loss provisioning range from mandated to discretionary, depending on the banking system. The tax treatment of provisions also varies considerably from country to country, although many economists believe that provisions should be treated as business expenses for tax purposes. Tax considerations should not, however, influence prudent risk management policies. In some highly developed countries, it is left to the banks to determine the prudent level of provisions. While some merit exists in estimating loss potential on a case-by-case basis, particularly for large borrowers, it may be more practical to assign a level of required provisions based on each classification category. In many countries, in particular those with fragile economies, regulators have established mandatory levels of provisions that are related to asset classification.

The established level of mandatory provisions is normally determined by certain statistics. In countries where the legal framework for debt recovery is highly developed, such as the United States, studies have demonstrated that approximately 10 percent of substandard assets eventually deteriorate into loss. The percentages for doubtful and loss classifications are approximately 50 percent and 100 percent, respectively. In developing countries where the legal frameworks and traditions for debt collection may be less effective, provisions in the range of 20 to 25 percent of substandard assets may be a more realistic estimate of loss potential. Table 7.3 can be used as a guide to the level of provisions in countries with less-developed legal frameworks.

Table 7.3 Recommended Loan Loss Provisions

Classification	Recommended Provision	Qualification
Pass	1–2 percent	General loss reserve
Watch	5–10 percent	Specific provision
Substandard	10–30 percent	Specific provision
Doubtful	50–75 percent	Specific provision
Loss	100 percent	Specific provision

Loss Assets and Workout Procedures

Two approaches exist for dealing with loss assets. One is to retain loss assets on the books until all remedies for collection have been exhausted. This is typical for banking systems based on the British tradition; in such cases, the level of loss reserve may appear unusually large. The second approach requires that all loss assets be promptly written off against the reserve, that is, removed from the books. This approach is typical of the U.S. tradition and is more conservative— loss assets are considered to be nonbankable but not necessarily nonrecoverable. By immediately writing off loss assets, the level of the reserve will appear smaller in relation to the outstanding loan portfolio. In evaluating the level of provisions established by a bank, an analyst must clearly understand whether the bank is aggressively writing off its losses or is simply providing for them. The approach used in a particular country often depends on the taxation applied to provisions by the fiscal authorities.

Workout procedures are an important aspect of credit risk management. If timely action is not taken to address problem loans, opportunities to strengthen or collect on these poor-quality assets may be missed and losses may accumulate to a point where they threaten a bank's solvency. An assessment of workout procedures should consider the organization of this function, including departments and responsible staff, and assess the performance of the workout units by reviewing attempted and successful recoveries (in terms of both number and volume) and the average time for recovery. The workout methods used and the involvement of senior management should also be evaluated.

During a workout process, each loan and borrower should be considered on their own merits. Typical workout strategies include the following:

- Reducing the credit risk exposure of a bank, for example, by having the borrower provide additional capital, funds, collateral, or guarantees

■ Working with the borrower to assess problems and find solutions to increase loan service and repayment capacity, such as the providing advice, developing a program to reduce operating costs and increase earnings, selling assets, designing a debt restructuring program, or changing loan terms

■ Arranging for a borrower to be bought or taken over by a more creditworthy party, or arranging for some form of joint-venture partnership

■ Liquidating exposure through out-of-court settlement or by taking legal action, calling on guarantees, foreclosing, or liquidating collateral

7.6 Assessing Credit Risk Management Capacity

When carrying out its duties on behalf of both depositors and shareholders, a board of directors must ensure that a bank's lending function fulfills three fundamental objectives:

■ Loans should be granted on a sound and collectible basis.

■ Funds should be invested profitably for the benefit of shareholders and the protection of depositors.

■ The legitimate credit needs of economic agents and households should be satisfied.

The purpose of a review of risk management capacity is to evaluate whether the lending process is well organized; if policies are properly described in internal procedures and manuals; if staffing is adequate and diligent in following established policies and guidelines; and whether the information normally available to participants in the lending process is timely, accurate, and complete.

Lending Processes

The integrity and credibility of the lending process depend on objective credit decisions that ensure an acceptable risk level in relation to the expected return. A review of the lending process should include analysis of credit manuals and other written guidelines applied by various departments of a bank, and of the capacity and actual performance of all departments involved in the credit function. It should also cover the origination, appraisal, approval, disbursement, monitoring, collection, and handling procedures for the various credit functions provided by the bank. Specifically, the review should cover the following:

- A detailed credit analysis and approval process, including samples of loan application forms, internal credit summary forms, internal credit manuals, and loan files

- Criteria for approving loans, determining loan pricing policy and lending limits at various levels of the bank's management, and for making arrangements for lending through the branch network

- Collateral policy for all types of loans, including the actual methods and practices concerning revaluation of collateral and files related to collateral

- Administration and monitoring procedures, including responsibilities, compliance, and controls

- A process for handling exceptions

The review should involve interviews with all middle-level managers of all departments that have a credit function. It should also include reviews of individual credit files. A review of the volume of the credit applications that have been appraised versus those that have been approved in the past 6 or 12 months (in terms of both total numbers and dollar amounts) would be one indication of the quality of credit appraisal.

Human Resources Analysis

This assessment should identify the staff involved in credit origination, appraisal, supervision, and processes to monitor credit risk. Specifically, their number, levels, age, experience, and specific responsibilities should be identified. Staff organization, skills, and qualifications should be analyzed in relation to policies and procedures. All ongoing training programs for a bank's credit staff should be reviewed and their adequacy assessed. The quality and frequency of staff training is usually a good indicator of the level of lending skills.

Information Flows

Because the lending function is usually spread throughout an organization, a bank must have efficient systems for monitoring adherence to established guidelines. This can best be accomplished through an internal review and reporting system that informs the directorate and senior management of how policies are being carried out and that provides them with sufficient information to evaluate the performance of lower-echelon officers and the condition of the loan portfolio. Because information is the basic element of the credit management process, its availability, quality, and cost effectiveness should be analyzed. In addition, because information needed in the credit management process may be dispersed in different parts of the bank, an analysis should pay particular attention to information flows, especially whether the information actually supplied is complete and available in a timely and cost-effective manner. Such an analysis should be closely linked to a review of human resources, organizational and control structures, and information technology.

8

Liquidity Risk Management

Key Messages

■ Liquidity management is a key banking function and an integral part of the asset liability management process.

■ Banks are particularly vulnerable to liquidity problems, on an institution-specific level and from a systemic/market viewpoint.

■ The source of deposits (*who* provides the bank's funding) adds to the volatility of funds, as some creditors are more sensitive to market and credit events than others. Diversification of funding sources and maturities enables a bank to avoid the vulnerability associated with the concentration of funding from a single source.

■ Liquidity management policies should comprise a risk management (decision-making) structure, a liquidity management and funding strategy, a set of limits to liquidity risk exposures, and a set of procedures for liquidity planning under alternative scenarios, including crisis situations.

8.1 The Need for Liquidity

Liquidity is necessary for banks to compensate for expected and unexpected balance sheet fluctuations and to provide funds for growth. It represents a bank's ability to efficiently accommodate the redemption of deposits and other liabilities and to cover funding increases in the loan and investment portfolio. A bank has adequate liquidity potential when it can obtain needed funds (by increasing liabilities, securitizing, or selling assets) promptly and at a reasonable cost. The price of liquidity is a function of market conditions and the market's perception of the inherent riskiness of the borrowing institution.

In the introduction to the June 2008 consultation paper (box 8.1), the Basel Committee on Bank Supervision states the following:

- Liquidity is the ability of a bank to fund increases in assets and meet obligations as they come due, without incurring unacceptable losses.

- The fundamental role of banks in the maturity transformation of short-term deposits into long-term loans makes banks inherently vulnerable to liquidity risk, both of an institution-specific nature and that which affects markets as a whole.

- Virtually every financial transaction or commitment has implications for a bank's liquidity.

- Effective liquidity risk management helps ensure a bank's ability to meet cash flow obligations, which are uncertain as they are affected by external events and other agents' behavior.

- Liquidity risk management is of paramount importance because a liquidity shortfall at a single institution can have systemwide repercussions.

- Financial market developments in the past decade have increased the complexity of liquidity risk and its management.

Box 8.1 Principles For Sound Liquidity Risk Management and Supervision
Draft for Consultation

Principle 1: A bank is responsible for the sound management of liquidity risk. A bank should establish a robust liquidity risk management framework that ensures it maintains sufficient liquidity, including a cushion of unencumbered, high quality liquid assets, to withstand a range of stress events, including those involving the loss or impairment of both unsecured and secured funding sources

Principle 2: A bank should clearly articulate a liquidity risk tolerance that is appropriate for its business strategy and its role in the financial system.

Principle 3: Senior management should develop a strategy, policies and practices to manage liquidity risk in accordance with the risk tolerance and to ensure that the bank maintains sufficient liquidity.

Principle 4: A bank should incorporate liquidity costs, benefits and risks in the product pricing, performance measurement and new product approval process for all significant business activities (both on- and off-balance sheet), thereby aligning the risk-taking incentives of individual business lines with the liquidity risk exposures their activities create for the bank as a whole.

Principle 5: A bank should have a sound process for identifying, measuring, monitoring and controlling liquidity risk. This process should include a robust framework for comprehensively projecting cash flows arising from assets, liabilities and off-balance sheet items over an appropriate set of time horizons.

Principle 6: A bank should actively manage liquidity risk exposures and funding needs within and across legal entities, business lines and currencies, taking into account legal, regulatory and operational limitations to the transferability of liquidity.

Principle 7: A bank should establish a funding strategy that provides effective diversification in the sources and tenor of funding. It should maintain an ongoing presence in its chosen funding markets and strong relationships with funds providers to promote effective diversification of funding sources. A bank should regularly gauge its capacity to raise funds quickly from each source. It should identify the main factors that affect its ability to raise funds and monitor those factors closely to ensure that estimates of fund raising capacity remain valid.

Principle 8: A bank should actively manage its intraday liquidity positions and risks to meet payment and settlement obligations on a timely basis under both normal and stressed conditions and thus contribute to the smooth functioning of payment and settlement systems.

Principle 9: A bank should actively manage its collateral positions, differentiating between encumbered and unencumbered assets. A bank should monitor the legal entity and physical location where collateral is held and how it may be mobilized in a timely manner.

Principle 10: A bank should conduct stress tests on a regular basis for a variety of institution-specific and market-wide stress scenarios (individually and in combination) to identify sources of potential liquidity strain and to ensure that current exposures remain in accordance with a bank's established liquidity risk tolerance. A bank should use stress test outcomes to adjust its liquidity risk management strategies, policies, and positions and to develop effective contingency plans.

Principle 11: A bank should have a formal contingency funding plan (CFP) that clearly sets out the strategies for addressing liquidity shortfalls in emergency situations. A CFP should outline policies to manage a range of stress environments, establish clear lines of responsibility, include clear invocation and escalation procedures and be regularly tested and updated to ensure that it is operationally robust.

Principle 12: A bank should maintain a cushion of unencumbered, high quality liquid assets to be held as insurance against a range of liquidity stress scenarios, including those that involve the loss or impairment of unsecured and typically available secured funding sources. There should be no legal, regulatory or operational impediment to using these assets to obtain funding.

Public disclosure

Principle 13: A bank should publicly disclose information on a regular basis that enables market participants to make an informed judgment about the soundness of its liquidity risk management framework and liquidity position.

Principle 14: Supervisors should regularly perform a comprehensive assessment of a bank's overall liquidity risk management framework and liquidity position to determine whether they deliver an adequate level of resilience to liquidity stress given the bank's role in the financial system.

Principle 15: Supervisors should supplement their regular assessments of a bank's liquidity risk management framework and liquidity position by monitoring a combination of internal reports, prudential reports and market information.

Principle 16: Supervisors should intervene to require effective and timely remedial action by a bank to address deficiencies in its liquidity risk management processes or liquidity position.

Principle 17: Supervisors should communicate with other supervisors and public authorities, such as central banks, both within and across national borders, to facilitate effective cooperation regarding the supervision and oversight of liquidity risk management. Communication should occur regularly during normal times, with the nature and frequency of the information sharing increasing as appropriate during times of stress.

Basel Committee on Bank Supervision
June 2008

Liquidity risk management lies at the heart of confidence in the banking system, as commercial banks are highly leveraged institutions with a ratio of assets to core (Tier 1) capital in the range of 20:1. The importance of liquidity transcends the individual institution, because a liquidity shortfall at a single institution can have systemwide repercussions. It is in the nature of a bank to transform the term of its liabilities to different maturities on the asset side of the balance sheet. Because the yield curve is typically upward sloping, the maturity of assets tends to be longer than that of liabilities. The actual inflow and outflow of funds do not necessarily reflect contractual maturities, and yet banks must be able to meet certain commitments (such as deposits) whenever they come due. A bank may therefore experience liquidity mismatches, making its liquidity policies and liquidity risk management key factors in its business strategy.

Liquidity risk management therefore addresses market liquidity rather than statutory liquidity. The implication of liquidity risk is that a bank may have insufficient funds on hand to meet its obligations. (A bank's net funding includes its maturing assets, existing liabilities, and standby facilities with other institutions. It would sell its marketable assets in the stable liquidity investment portfolio [see chapter 10] to meet liquidity requirements only as a last resort.) Liquidity risks are normally managed by a bank's asset-liability management committee (ALCO), which must therefore have a thorough understanding of the interrelationship between liquidity and other market and credit risk exposures on the balance sheet.

This chapter focuses on the management of expected cash flows. Understanding the context of liquidity risk management involves examining a bank's approach to funding and liquidity planning under alternative scenarios. As a result of the increasing depth of interbank (money) markets, a fundamental shift has taken place in the authorities' attitude toward prudent liquidity management. Supervisory authorities now tend to concentrate on the maturity structure of a bank's assets and liabilities rather than solely on its statutory liquid asset requirements. They do this using maturity ladders for liabilities and assets during specific periods (or time bands), a process that represents a move from the calculation of contractual cash outflows to the calculation of expected liquidity flows.

8.2 Liquidity Management Policies

In day-to-day operations, the management of liquidity is typically achieved through the management of a bank's assets. In the medium term, liquidity is also addressed through management of the structure of a bank's liabilities. The level of liquidity deemed adequate for one bank may be insufficient for another. A particular bank's liquidity position may also vary from adequate to inadequate according to the anticipated need for funds at any given time. Judgment of the adequacy of a liquidity position requires analysis of a bank's historical funding requirements, its current liquidity position and its anticipated future funding needs, the options it has for reducing funding needs or attracting additional funds, and the source of funding.

The amount of liquid or of readily marketable assets that a bank should hold depends on the stability of its deposit structure and the potential for rapid loan portfolio expansion. Generally, if deposits are composed primarily of small, stable accounts, a bank will need relatively low liquidity. A much higher liquidity position normally is required when a substantial portion of the loan portfolio consists of large long-term loans, when a bank has a somewhat high concentration of deposits, or when recent trends show reductions of large corporate or household deposit accounts. Situations also can arise in which a bank should increase its liquidity position—for example, when large commitments have been made on the asset side and the bank expects the client to start utilization.

The liquidity management policies of a bank normally comprise a decision-making structure, an approach to funding and liquidity operations, a set of limits to liquidity risk exposure, and a set of procedures for liquidity planning under alternative scenarios, including crisis situations. The decision-making structure reflects the importance that management places on liquidity: banks that stress the importance of liquidity normally institutionalize the structure for liquidity risk management in the ALCO and assign ultimate responsibility for setting policy and reviewing liquidity decisions to the bank's highest management level. The bank's strategy for funding and liquidity operations, which should be approved by the board, sets specific policies on particular aspects of risk management, such as the target liabilities structure, the use of certain financial instruments, or the pricing of deposits.

Liquidity needs usually are determined by the construction of a maturity ladder (see table 8.1) that comprises expected cash inflows and outflows over a series of specified time bands. The difference between the inflows and outflows in each period (that is, the excess or deficit of funds) provides a starting point from which to measure a bank's future liquidity excess or shortfall at any given time.

Table 8.1 Maturity Profile of Assets and Liabilities (Liquidity Mismatches)

	2001	2002	2003	2004	2005	2006
Assets						
Less than 3 months	8,440,268	9,306,606	10,272,647	11,497,545	15,203,780	31,725,644
3 months to 1 year	1,748,961	1,779,905	2,946,684	6,068,174	5,896,048	10,908,547
Over 1 year	5,144,749	8,511,279	9,558,988	13,047,642	21,898,451	21,799,745
Total assets	**15,333,978**	**19,597,790**	**22,778,319**	**30,613,361**	**42,998,279**	**64,433,936**
Liabilities						
Less than 3 months	7,861,928	9,924,646	12,533,008	18,103,033	21,738,876	38,536,352
3 months to 1 year	6,308,929	8,059,233	8,520,962	9,498,927	17,543,080	17,638,551
Over 1 year	1,163,121	1,613,911	1,724,349	3,011,401	3,716,323	8,259,033
Total liabilities	**15,333,978**	**19,597,790**	**22,778,319**	**30,613,361**	**42,998,279**	**64,433,936**
Liquidity Mismatches						
Less than 3 months	578,340	-618,040	-2,260,361	-6,605,488	-6,535,096	-6,810,708
3 months to 1 year	-4,559,968	-6,279,328	-5,574,278	-3,430,753	-11,647,032	-6,730,004
Over 1 year	3,981,628	6,897,368	7,834,639	10,036,241	18,182,128	13,540,712

Once its liquidity needs have been determined, a bank must decide how to fulfill them. Liquidity management is related to a net funding requirement; in principle, a bank may increase its liquidity through asset management, liability management, or (and most frequently) a combination of both. In practice, a bank may meet its liquidity needs by disposing of highly liquid trading portfolio assets or assets that are nearly liquid, or by selling less-liquid assets such as excess property or other investments. On the liabilities side, this can be achieved by increasing short-term borrowings and short-term deposit liabilities, by increasing the maturity of liabilities, and ultimately by increasing capital.

Many banks, particularly smaller ones, tend to have little influence over the total size of their liabilities. Their liquid assets enable such banks to provide funds to accommodate fluctuations in deposit levels and to satisfy increases in loan demand. Banks that rely solely on asset management to maintain liquidity in the face of shifts in customer asset and liability preferences concentrate on adjusting the price and availability of credit and the level of liquid assets that they hold.

Asset liquidity, or how "salable" the bank's assets are in terms of both time and cost, is central to asset-liability management. To maximize profitability, bank management must weigh the full return on liquid assets (yield plus insurance value) against the higher return associated with less-liquid assets. In most cases, liquid assets normally are maintained only as a liquidity buffer that banks can use should they encounter funding problems and depositors have to be refunded. Banks otherwise prefer to invest in assets with higher yields. Income derived from higher-yield assets nonetheless may be offset by a forced sale, which may in turn become necessary as a result of adverse balance sheet fluctuations.

The number of banks that rely solely on manipulation of the asset structure to meet liquidity needs is declining rapidly, as the interbank (money) markets develop. Seasonal, cyclical, or other factors often can cause aggregate outstanding loans and deposits to move in opposite directions, resulting in a loan demand that exceeds available deposit funds. A bank that relies on asset management should restrict loan growth to a level that can be supported by available deposit funds. As an alternative, liquidity needs may be met through liability sources such as money markets.

Another challenge for liquidity management is contingent liabilities, such as letters of credit or financial guarantees. These represent potentially significant cash outflows that are not dependent on a bank's financial condition.

Although outflows in normal circumstances typically may be low, a general macroeconomic or market crisis can trigger a substantial increase in cash outflows because of the increase in defaults and bankruptcies in the enterprise sector that normally accompanies such events. Low levels of market liquidity, further exacerbating funding shortfalls, often accompany banking crises.

Foreign Currency Aspects

The existence of multiple currencies also increases the complexity of liquidity management, particularly when the domestic currency is not freely convertible. A bank may have difficulty raising funds or selling assets in foreign currencies in the event of market disturbances or changes in domestic monetary or foreign exchange policies. In principle, a bank should have a management system (that is, measuring, monitoring, and control) for its liquidity positions in all major currencies in which it is active. In addition to assessing its aggregate liquidity needs, a bank should also perform a separate analysis of its liquidity strategy for each currency. Key decisions in managing liquidity in individual foreign currencies center on the structure of such management: who is responsible for liquidity and liquidity risk in each currency, and within what parameters.

A bank that operates in foreign currencies but does not maintain branch offices abroad usually manages liquidity of foreign currencies at its headquarters. A typical scheme for a bank with offices abroad is that policy setting and overall coordination and supervision are kept at headquarters, but the responsibility for the bank's liquidity in a major foreign currency is delegated to the branch office in the country issuing that currency. The liquidity strategy for each currency, or exactly how its foreign currency funding needs will be met, should be a central concern of the bank. The bank must also develop a back-up liquidity strategy for circumstances in which its usual approach to liquidity funding is disrupted. Depending on the size of its foreign exchange operations and its portfolio in each currency, the bank may define a back-up liquidity strategy for all currencies or may draw up a separate contingency plan for each.

8.3 The Regulatory Environment

The most significant development in prudential liquidity regulation in the past two decades has been the assessment of liquidity needs by calculating expected cash flows based on the maturity structure of a bank's assets and liabilities. However, even regulators that have adopted the cash-flow methodology believe that the stock (of liquid assets) approach has an important, if supplementary, role to play and should not be neglected (see box 8.1 and figure 8.1). This stance is based on the perception that the increasingly important role of liquidity management, in addition to being an asset-liability management tool, has significant implications for the stability of the banking system as a whole. Certain crucial premises influence this stability, including the confidence of banks in each other, the confidence of major suppliers of funds in banks, and the existence of normal market conditions.

Figure 8.1 Statutory Liquidity Required versus Actual Liquid Assets Held

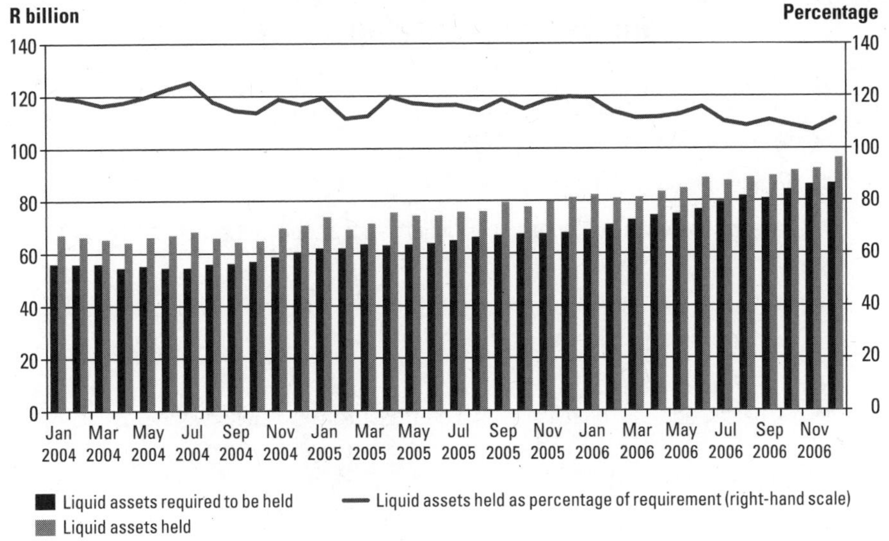

Source: South African Reserve Bank – Supervision Report 2007

Banking legislation normally contains specific liquidity requirements that banks must meet. These prudential requirements should not be viewed as the primary method for managing liquidity risk; the opposite in fact is true. Given the importance of liquidity, a bank with prudent management should establish certain policy guidelines for risk management in addition to determining responsibility for planning and day-to-day fund management. Typical liquidity regulations (or a bank's own liquidity guidelines) are summarized in box 8.2.

Box 8.2 Typical Liquidity Regulations or Internal Liquidity Guidelines

- A limit on the loan-to-deposit ratio
- A limit on the loan-to-capital ratio
- Guidelines on sources and uses of funds
- Liquidity parameters: for example, liquid assets should not fall below "X" percent or rise above "Y" percent of total assets
- A percentage limit on the relationship between anticipated funding needs and available resources to meet these needs: for example, the ratio of primary sources over anticipated needs should not fall below "X" percent
- A percentage limit on reliance on a particular liability category: for example, negotiable certificates of deposit should not account for more than "X" percent of total liabilities
- Limits on the minimum/maximum average maturity of different categories of liabilities: for example, the average maturity of negotiable certificates of deposit should not be less than "X" months

Trends in the prudential supervision of liquidity, as in other areas of regulation, have tended to lag behind market trends. In addition, less progress has been made in the international coordination and convergence of liquidity regulation than, for example, in the field of capital adequacy. Nevertheless, some important changes have taken place, including the following:

- A relative decline in the importance of liquid asset requirements as a supervisory tool, in favor of the cash-flow or maturity-profile approach
- Emphasis on the continual need for a stock of stable liquid assets as a supplementary method of controlling risk
- A shift away from statutory requirements toward a more flexible approach to setting guidelines and monitoring liquidity
- Greater emphasis on evaluating the liquidity of individual banks, rather than an across-the-board approach
- Greater efforts by supervisors to improve bank standards for the information and control systems that are used to manage liquidity

■ Incorporation into the regulatory framework of off-balance-sheet products and new methods of asset-liability management

The approach to supervision is therefore increasingly focused on the independent evaluation of a bank's strategies, policies, and procedures and its practices related to the measurement, monitoring, and control of liquidity risk. The emphasis increasingly is on the management structures necessary to effectively execute a bank's liquidity strategy and on the involvement of senior management in the liquidity risk management process.

Most countries now make a clear distinction between instruments of prudential supervision and monetary control. This applies particularly to the holding of specific liquid assets. In recent years, a greater reliance on control of the money supply as a major policy instrument—together with structural changes in the banking environment—has highlighted the incompatibility of and inconsistency between prudential supervision and monetary control. When banks attempt to circumvent the impact of monetary policy instruments such as the cash-reserve requirement, which forms part of the prudential liquid asset requirements (for example, by moving liabilities related to repurchase agreements off the balance sheet), liquidity risk management may be negatively affected.

8.4 The Structure of Funding

Funding structure is a key aspect of liquidity management. A bank with a stable, large, and diverse deposit base is likely to have fewer liquidity problems than a bank lacking such a deposit base. The assessment of the structure and type of deposit base and evaluation of the condition (that is, the stability and quality) of the deposits thus is the starting point for liquidity risk assessment. The type of information that is necessary to conduct this assessment includes the following:

■ **Product range.** The different types of deposit products available should be noted, along with the number of accounts and the balance raised for each. This information is best presented in a schedule that shows the product type, such as savings or checking account, six-month deposit, or deposit with maturity greater than six months. (Product types are defined according to a bank's own product offerings.) The nature of the depositor (for example, corporate or retail) should also be shown, because each type of depositor has a certain behavioral pattern. Breakdowns by the terms of deposit, including currency, maturity, and interest rates, should also be included.

■ **Deposit concentration.** The assessment should look at an itemization for all customers with deposits that aggregate to more than a certain percentage of total assets, with terms and pricing shown for each.

■ **Deposit administration.** Information should be gathered on the adequacy of the systems that record and control depositor transactions and internal access to customer accounts, as well as on the calculation and form of payment of interest (for example, average daily or period-end balance).

Because of the competition for funds, most corporations and individuals seek to minimize their idle funds and the effect of disintermediation on a bank's deposit base. A bank's management therefore typically will adopt a development and retention program for all types of deposits. In addition to deposit growth, management also must look at the quality of the deposit structure to determine what percentage of the overall deposit structure is based on stable or hard-core deposits, fluctuating or seasonal deposits, and volatile deposits. This step is necessary if funds are to be invested with a proper understanding of anticipated and potential withdrawals. Figure 8.2 illustrates the source of deposits (that is, from whom they have been received, including households and public and private sector enterprises) for the particular bank under observation. Deposit management is a function of a number of variables, some of which are not under the direct control of bank management.

Figure 8.2 Deposit Sources

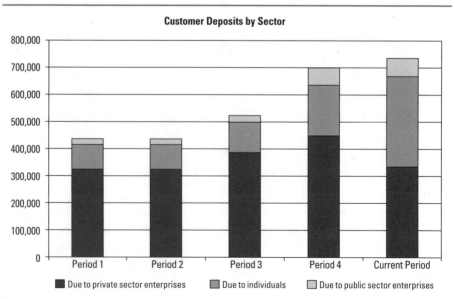

Interbank Funding

Another key ingredient of a liquidity profile is a bank's ability to obtain additional liabilities (also known as its liquidity potential). The marginal cost of liquidity (that is, the cost of incremental funds acquired) is of paramount importance in evaluating the sources of liquidity. Consideration must be given to such factors as the frequency with which a bank needs to refinance maturing purchased liabilities and its ability to obtain funds through the money market. For a bank that operates frequently in short-term money markets, the crucial determinant of the ability to borrow new funds is its standing in the market.

The obvious difficulty of estimating the ability to borrow is that until a bank enters a market, the availability of funds at a price that will give a positive yield spread cannot be determined with certainty. Changes in money market conditions may cause a bank's capacity to borrow at a profitable rate to decline rapidly. In times of uncertainty, large investors and depositors tend to be reluctant to trade with small banks because they are regarded as risky. The same pattern may also apply to larger banks if their solvency comes into question.

8.5 Cash Flow Analysis

Maturity mismatches are an intrinsic feature of banking, including the short-term liability financing of medium-term and long-term lending. The crucial question is not whether mismatching occurs—because it always does—but to what extent, and whether this situation is reasonable or potentially unsound. Put another way, one can ask how long, given its current maturity structure, a bank could survive if it met with a funding crisis, and what amount of time would be available to take action before the bank became unable to meet its commitments. These questions should be asked by banks, regulators, and, ultimately, policy makers. This aspect of liquidity risk management also implies that access to the central bank, as the lender of last resort, should be available only to solvent banks that have temporary liquidity problems.

Figure 8.3 provides a view of a bank's maturity ladder. The trends are reviewed over time to determine whether the mismatches are increasing. An increased mismatch could be the result of problems in obtaining long-term funding for the bank or could reflect a deliberate decision based on the bank's view of future interest rate movements. For example, banks tend to increase their short-term mismatches if they expect interest rates to fall.

Figure 8.3 Liquidity Mismatches

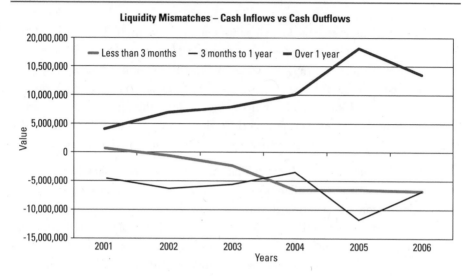

The focus of such an analysis is not only the size of the mismatch but also its trends over time, as these could indicate if the bank has a potential funding problem. When reviewing the short-term mismatch as a percentage of total liabilities, an analyst will need to determine the proportion of the total funding that has to be renewed on a short-term basis. Liquid assets actually held can then be compared with the value of the short-term mismatch to assess how much of the latter is in fact covered by a buffer stock of high-quality liquid assets. In addition, other readily marketable securities should be considered.

The contractual maturity-term structure of deposits over time can also be used to ascertain if the funding structure is changing. If it is, the analyst should determine whether the bank is experiencing funding shortages or is deliberately changing its funding structure. Figure 8.4 provides a trend analysis of the maturity profile of the deposit base. This analysis can be used to evaluate whether a bank's policy change is of a permanent or erratic nature, as well as to assess the regularity of funding problems (that is, the amount of funding that has to be renegotiated contractually on a short-term basis).

Figure 8.4 Maturity Profile of Deposit Base

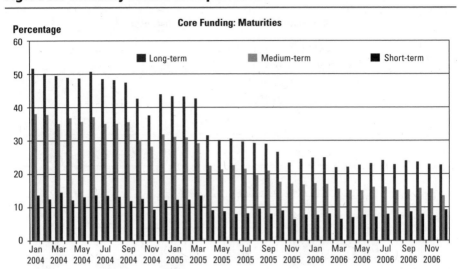

While it is apparent that the maturity structure of deposits for the observed bank has changed, the reasons are not straightforward or easy to determine. For example, in volatile economies characterized by high inflation and in countries where the public lacks confidence in the banking system, the maturity of deposits tends to be much shorter than in stable economies. The worsening of the observed bank's economic environment could have triggered the shortening of maturities. At the same time, it is apparent that the bank's source of deposits changed during the period, with individual household deposits as a percentage of total deposits increasing and private enterprise deposits decreasing (see figure 8.2). The change in average maturity could therefore be at least partly attributed to changes in funding sources.

Once the contractual mismatch has been calculated, it is important to determine the expected cash flow that can be produced by the bank's asset-liability management model. The cash flow statement in a bank's annual report can be useful in this regard (see figure 8.5).

Figure 8.5 Cash Flows (Derived from Cash Flow Statement)

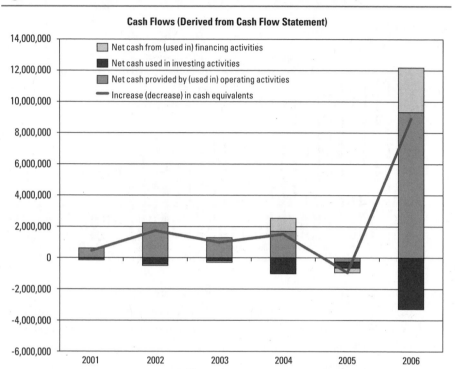

Neither the contractual nor the expected mismatch will be accurate, but both will indicate the amount of funding that a bank might be required to obtain from nonclient sources. The sources available to banks could include the central bank's liquidity support facilities (geared toward liquid assets held by the individual banks) and money market funding. The amount remaining for use of central bank facilities indicates the size of the expected money market shortage. Money market committees of central banks use this critical variable to determine the monetary policy options that are available to them for market interventions.

An additional aspect that should also be assessed is the potential impact of credit risk on liquidity. If large exposures or excessive sector risk were to materialize, there could be significant consequences for liquidity. The type of credit risk exposure, especially sector concentration, should be considered and specifically evaluated. For example, in the early 1980s and again in 2008, many banks in the United States suffered huge losses as a result of poor real estate lending practices.

8.6 Volatility of Funding and Concentration of Deposits

Another critical aspect of liquidity risk management is dependence on a single source of funding (also known as concentration risk). If a bank has a few large depositors and one or more withdraw their funds, enormous problems will occur if alternative sources of funding cannot quickly be found. Most banks therefore monitor their funding mix and the concentration of depositors very closely, to prevent excessive dependence on any particular source. The sensitivity of banks to large withdrawals in an uncertain environment cannot be overemphasized.

Regulators increasingly are focusing on mismatches in liquidity flows and on the ability of banks to fund such mismatches on an ongoing basis, rather than on statutory liquid assets and traditional access to the central bank.

An appraisal of a bank therefore must give adequate attention to the mix between wholesale and retail funding and, in connection to this, to the exposure to large depositors and whether or not an undue reliance on individual sources of funds exists. Figures 8.6 and 8.7 illustrate an assessment of concentration in the bank under observation. The aim of such an assessment is to establish if the bank is exposed to a creditor large enough to cause a liquidity crisis if it were to withdraw its funding.

By calculating the percentage of the short-term mismatch that large deposits represent, an analyst can obtain a picture of the sensitivity of the bank or of the banking sector as a whole to withdrawals by large suppliers of funds. The proportion of wholesale funding to retail funding is another means of measuring sensitivity to large depositors. Overall, the increasing volatility of funding is indicative of the changes in the structure and sources of funding that the banking sector is undergoing.

To assess the general volatility of funding, a bank usually classifies its liabilities as those that are likely to stay with the bank under any circumstances—for example, enterprise transaction accounts—and those that can be expected to pull out if problems arise. The key issues to be determined for the latter are their price sensitivity, the rate at which they would pull out, and which liabilities could be expected to pull out at the first sign of trouble.

Figure 8.6 Ten Largest Sources of Deposits as a Percentage of the Total Deposits

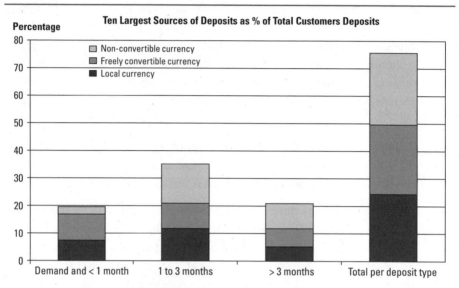

Figure 8.7 Funding Concentration

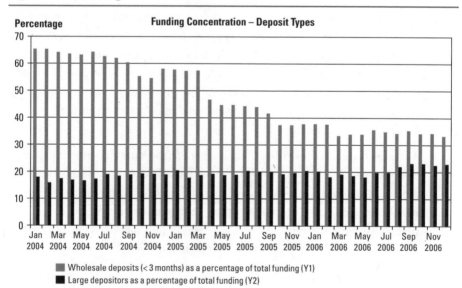

Source: South African Reserve Bank – Supervision Report 2007

8.7 Liquidity Risk Management Techniques

The framework for liquidity risk management has three aspects: measuring and managing net funding requirements, market access, and contingency planning. Forecasting possible future events is an essential part of liquidity planning and risk management. The analysis of net funding requirements involves the construction of a maturity ladder and the calculation of the cumulative net excess or deficit of funds on selected dates. Banks should regularly estimate their expected cash flows instead of focusing only on the contractual periods during which cash may flow in or out. For example, cash outflows can be ranked by the date on which liabilities fall due, by the earliest date a liability holder can exercise an early repayment option, or by the earliest date that contingencies can be called.

An evaluation of whether or not a bank is sufficiently liquid depends on the behavior of cash flows under different conditions. Liquidity risk management must therefore involve various scenarios. The "going-concern" scenario has established a benchmark for balance sheet–related cash flows during the normal course of business. This scenario is ordinarily applied to the management of a bank's use of deposits. A second scenario relates to a bank's liquidity in a crisis situation when a significant part of its liabilities cannot be rolled over or replaced—implying contraction of the bank's balance sheet. This scenario relates to many existing liquidity regulations or supervisory liquidity measures.

A third scenario refers to general market crises, wherein liquidity is affected in the entire banking system, or at least in a significant part of it. Liquidity management under this scenario is predicated on credit quality, with significant differences in funding access among banks. From the perspective of liquidity management, an implicit assumption can be made that the central bank will ensure access to funding in some form. The central bank in fact has a vested interest in studying this scenario because of the need it would create for a total liquidity buffer for the banking sector—and for a workable means of spreading the burden of liquidity problems among the major banks.

Table 8.2 provides a simple forecasting tool for liquidity needs under normal business conditions, under conditions of liquidity crisis, and under conditions of general market crisis. Projections for a bank's liquidity in a crisis situation should start to be derived systematically and rigorously as soon as the bank foresees persistent liquidity shortfalls or experiences difficulties rolling over or replacing its liabilities. Projections of liquidity during a market crisis should start to be derived at the first indication that the macroeconomic situation is changing, or that assumptions regarding the behavior of the bank's assets or liabilities under normal business conditions are not holding. A bank may preempt a potential crisis by deliberately changing the behavior of its assets or liabilities—for example, by becoming more aggressive in the market, by forgoing expected profits, or by severing its relationships with certain types of borrowers.

Table 8.2 Maturity Ladder under Alternative Scenarios

Cash Inflows	Normal Business Conditions	Bank-Specific Crisis	General Market Crisis
Maturing assets (contractual)			
Interest receivable			
Asset sales			
Drawdowns			
Others (specify)			
Total inflows			
Cash inflows			
Maturing liabilities (contractual)			
Interest payable			
Disbursements on lending commitments			
Early deposit withdrawals			
Operating expenses			
Others (specify)			
Total outflows			
Liquidity excess (shortfall)			

Diversified liabilities and funding sources usually indicate that a bank has well-developed liquidity management. The ability to readily convert assets into cash and access to other sources of funding in the event of a liquidity shortage also are very important. For example, to bridge short-term fluctuations and to prevent problems from occurring, banks may ensure that lines of credit or funding are available through other financial institutions. The level of diversification can be judged according to instrument types, the type of fund provider, and geographical markets.

In practice, however, it may be difficult to obtain funding when a dire need for it exists. Certain unusual situations also may have an impact on liquidity risk, including internal or external political upheavals (which can cause large withdrawals), seasonal effects, increased market activity, sector problems, and economic cycles.

Management must evaluate the likely effect of these trends and events on funding requirements. All banks are influenced by economic changes, but sound financial management can buffer the negative changes and accentuate the positive ones. Management must also have contingency plans in case its projections prove to be wrong. Effective planning involves the identification of minimum and maximum liquidity needs and the weighing of alternative courses of action to meet those needs.

Large banks normally expect to derive liquidity from both sides of the balance sheet and maintain an active presence in interbank and other wholesale markets. They look to these markets as a source for the discretionary acquisition of short-term funds on the basis of interest rate competition, a process that can help them meet their liquidity needs. Conceptually, the availability of asset and liability options should result in a lower cost for liquidity maintenance. The costs of available discretionary liabilities can be compared with the opportunity cost of selling various assets, because banks also hold a range of short-term assets that can be sold if necessary. These assets also serve as reassurance to the potential suppliers of funds, thus enhancing a bank's ability to borrow.

The major difference between liquidity in larger and smaller banks is that, in addition to deliberately determining the asset side of the balance sheet, larger banks are better able to control the level and composition of their liabilities. They therefore have a wider variety of options from which to select the least costly method of generating required funds. Discretionary access to the money market also reduces the size of the liquid asset buffer that would be needed if banks were solely dependent upon asset management to obtain funds.

When large volumes of retail deposits and lending are at stake, outflows of funds should be assessed on the basis of probability, with past experience serving as a guide. Banks with large volumes of wholesale funds can also manage liquidity through maturity matching. This means that an appropriate degree of correspondence between asset and liability maturities must be sought, but not that an exact matching of all assets and liabilities is necessary.

Table 8.3 and figure 8.8 illustrate the liquidity management of a bank and how the bank's liquidity position has deteriorated over time. The percentage of loans funded from the bank's internally generated sources has steadily decreased. In contrast, the percentage of volatile liabilities has increased, and volatility coverage has become significantly worse. Unfortunately, simple graphs such as that in figure 8.8 cannot tell the whole story. The assessment of bank liquidity, whether by banks themselves, by their supervisors, or by outside analysts, is a complex process that cannot be reduced to any single technique or set of formulas.

Table 8.3 Liquidity Ratios

Liquidity Ratios	Period 1	Period 2	Period 3
Readily marketable assets as percentage of total assets			
Volatile liabilities as percentage of total liabilities			
Volatility coverage (readily marketable assets as percentage of volatile liabilities)			
Bank run (readily marketable assets as percentage of all deposit-type liabilities)			
Customer loans to customer deposits			
Interbank loans as percentage of interbank deposits			
Net loans and investments as percentage of total deposits			
Demand deposits as percentage of customers deposits			
Deposits with maturities longer than three months as percentage of customer deposits			
Less-than-90-days deposits as percentage of customer deposits			
Certificates of deposit as percentage of customer deposits			
Ten largest deposits as percentage of customer deposits			

Figure 8.8 Liquidity Ratios: Trend Analysis

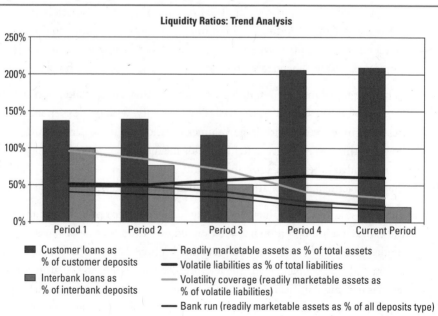

Liquidity Ratios: Trend Analysis

Legend:
- Customer loans as % of customer deposits
- Interbank loans as % of interbank deposits
- Readily marketable assets as % of total assets
- Volatile liabilities as % of total liabilities
- Volatility coverage (readily marketable assets as % of volatile liabilities)
- Bank run (readily marketable assets as % of all deposits type)

In reality, a bank's position and reputation within the financial community influence its liquidity management options. This connection is based on many factors, the most crucial of which is the bank's past and prospective profitability. Properly understood, a maturity profile can be a useful indicator of a bank's position and may yield important information, for example, when a sudden increase in maturity mismatches occurs. However, maturity profiles should be analyzed in conjunction with information about the bank's off-balance-sheet business, management objectives, and systems of control. Some banks are better positioned than others to quickly alter the maturity pattern of their balance sheet.

Although the acquisition of funds in a market at a competitive cost enables profitable banks to meet the expanding customer demand for loans, the misuse or improper implementation of liability management can have severe consequences. The following risks are associated with the practice of market funding–based liquidity management:

- Purchased funds may not always be available when needed. If the market loses confidence in a bank, the bank's liquidity may be threatened.

- Overreliance on liability management may cause a tendency to minimize the holding of short-term securities and to relax asset liquidity standards, which may result in a large concentration of short-term liabilities that support assets with longer maturities. During times of tight money, this tendency could squeeze earnings and give rise to illiquid conditions.

- As a result of rate competition in the money market, a bank may incur relatively high costs when obtaining funds and may be tempted to lower its credit standards to invest in high-yield loans and securities.

- If a bank purchases liabilities to support assets that are already on its books, the high cost of purchased funds may result in a negative yield spread.

- When national monetary tightness occurs, interest rate discrimination may develop, making the cost of purchased funds prohibitive to all but a limited number of large banks. Small banks with restricted funding should therefore avoid taking excessive loans from money market sources.

- Preoccupation with obtaining funds at the lowest possible cost and with insufficient regard to maturity distribution can greatly intensify a bank's exposure to the risk of interest rate fluctuations.

9

Managing Liquidity and Other Investment Portfolios

Key Messages

- The objective of investment management is to maximize the return on a portfolio within policy constraints that address liquidity and market value volatility.

- A bank's liquidity portfolio serves as a source of prudential liquidity to cover short-term liabilities when the bank may not have access to normal sources of funding.

- The liquidity portfolio is also a source of return and is usually actively managed against a benchmark to generate a positive spread over the cost of funds.

- A liquidity policy typically sets the minimum size of the liquidity portfolio, usually in terms of coverage of short-term liabilities.

- The liquidity policy also sets risk limits to control credit risk, interest rate risk, and foreign currency risk to ensure the necessary level of liquidity and to protect earnings and capital. The liquidity portfolio typically is managed against a benchmark portfolio based on the underlying funding or on the holder's liabilities.

9.1 Nature of the Liquidity Portfolio

For commercial banks, the liquidity portfolio traditionally was one of the key tools for liquidity management, providing a back-up source of funds to meet unexpected levels of withdrawals or net redemptions.[1] The development of deep and liquid interbank markets, however, means that banks

---

1   The term "liquidity portfolio" is used firstly to distinguish it from the proprietary trading portfolio, and secondly to accentuate the prudential nature and minimum level of liquidity that it signifies.

borrow to meet any funding shortfalls, with the result that day-to-day liquidity operations have become a liability management issue.

The liquidity portfolio nonetheless has remained as a fallback source of funds to meet liabilities coming due if a bank won't or can't access alternative sources of funding. The tightening or closing of interbank markets can occur during periods of systemic risk, when lenders will not provide funds because of broad risk aversion, or because of a negative event specific to the institution.

The objective of investment management is to maximize the return on a portfolio within policy constraints that address liquidity and market value volatility. In most cases, the liquidity portfolio is structured to generate positive carry (that is, the return is higher than the cost of funds and contributes positively to the net income of the bank). This is typically achieved by the assumption of credit risk and interest rate risk. In the case of credit risk, the bank invests in securities that have a lower credit standing and thus a higher yield than the bank's funding instruments. This is called credit transformation. In the case of interest rate risk, management will take advantage of the upward slope of the yield curve and invest in assets that have a slightly longer duration than its funding instruments. This is called maturity transformation. Both of these positions normally result in a profit for the bank, but income and capital can be at risk in the case of credit deterioration, yield curve inversion, or upward shifts in yields. These risks need to be tightly controlled to protect bank income and capital from unacceptable levels of loss.

For commercial banks, the size of the liquidity portfolio relative to total assets will tend to increase during periods of slow economic growth, when the demand for commercial and industrial loans is low and credit worthiness of clients deteriorate. Conversely, an increase in economic growth typically leads to a decline in the liquidity portfolio as funds are redeployed toward loans with higher expected returns. For prudential liquidity portfolios, the investment policy should specify a minimum size relative to short-term liabilities to ensure that the portfolio can fulfill its role as a provider of liquidity in times of stress.

9.2 Investment Policy

The investment policy sets out the rationale for holding a liquidity portfolio and defines any target levels, usually in terms of short-term liability coverage. From a regulatory perspective, the target level normally would be described as a liquid asset ratio. The investment policy also sets out broad credit and market risk parameters.

Benchmark Position

The most neutral market risk position, from the perspective of the balance sheet, matches the risk profile of the liquidity portfolio with the risk profile of the liabilities with respect to currency, duration, and credit. This neutral position is generally referred to as the benchmark position. Any deviation from this position would expose a bank's income and capital to risk. At the policy level, it is important to specify the baseline position for the liquidity portfolio (the benchmark) and the tolerance for risk resulting from active management. One efficient way to express this tolerance is in terms of a "risk budget," whereby the board (or its delegates) approves an acceptable level of income or capital loss. This risk budget can then be implemented into a risk management structure, wherein risks are independently measured and limited to ensure that the board's risk tolerance is not exceeded.

9.3 Strategic Asset Allocation

The objective of the strategic asset allocation (SAA) process is to maximize the expected return within the asset-liability management (ALM) constraints relating to liquidity, income, and capital volatility. This process is critical in central banks and banks with large asset management portfolios, but may be less important in a commercial banking environment.

The goal of SAA is therefore to determine the policy mix of asset classes that becomes the benchmark portfolio—which, subject to the constraints mentioned above, maximizes the value of that portfolio (or minimizes its cost). SAA uses a quantitative framework to optimize the risk and return characteristics of assets through projections of contingencies that may affect the future liability structure.

SAA should specify the neutral currency composition, portfolio duration, and eligible instruments. Reserves adequacy and any minimum return requirements should be the main determinants of the desirable risk-return profile for the reserves; this profile should then be embodied in a benchmark portfolio.

The SAA framework is used by asset managers to make a periodic determination of the optimal policy mix of asset classes. The process is a two-step exercise: the first step is to propose duration, liquidity, and asset class constraints that are acceptable and that would enable net worth and liquidity goals to be met; the second step is to select a benchmark that is replicable and that would maximize expected return within these constraints. Critical senior management inputs to the SAA exercise are normally expressed by the board of directors through an investment policy statement, the elements of which are as follows:

Investment policy objectives (earnings and risk tolerance):

- Minimum income requirement

- Credit risk (the tolerance of outright default)

- Market risk (the tolerance of volatility of returns over the investment horizon)

- Business risks (consideration of any correlation between asset classes and the core business of the bank)

Investment policy constraints:

- Liquidity requirements

- Investment time horizon under normal and adverse circumstances

- Legal, regulatory, and tax considerations

- Unique needs, such as foreign currency composition, based on currency composition of actual or contingent liabilities

The importance of the SAA process in terms of the returns generated by each dimension of the portfolio management function is underscored by the finding that SAA typically accounts for more than 90 percent of long-term performance. Tactical trading is therefore a much less significant driver of portfolio risk and return.

Central Bank Aspects

In the case of central banks, foreign currency reserves portfolios are held to meet a country's need for foreign currency when it is unable to borrow from other sources. In broad terms, the optimal long-term risk profile for these reserves is set with respect to the rationale for holding such reserves, rather than the composition of the central bank's balance sheet. This is particularly true for emerging markets and other countries that do not enjoy deep and certain access to the capital market borrowings that otherwise could serve to finance any external imbalances. The investment policy for a central bank therefore should set out an SAA based jointly on the rationale for holding reserves and on the amount of reserves that could be considered adequate relative to any actual and contingent claims.

9.4 Benchmark Portfolio

A benchmark portfolio represents the optimal risk profile for the liquidity (investment) portfolio with respect to the rationale for holding funds and the characteristics of the underlying liabilities. A good benchmark is a replicable, transparent portfolio strategy that complies with risk constraints. The benchmark provides the baseline for measuring both risk and performance.

From an investment perspective, a benchmark portfolio can be defined as a replicable notional portfolio, approved by senior management, that embodies the investment objectives of the financial institution. A benchmark portfolio represents the best feasible passive strategy, given the objective of holding liquidity, the risk tolerance of the institution, and other constraints (such as capital preservation). The setting of an investment benchmark can also be described as the "operationalization" of the SAA process.

Benchmarks are critical for evaluating performance versus long-term strategy; they also are used as fallback positions when the portfolio manager has a neutral market view or a stop-loss is triggered. In essence, the long-term objective of the benchmark function—a neutral strategy—is to provide a replicable portfolio with a constant risk profile versus the market. It is used to evaluate both the value added in returns and the risk exposure resulting from active management.

Benchmarks can be set for liabilities as well as assets. A liability benchmark could compare the cost of funding of the institution to that of comparable bond issues of similar institutions with the same credit rating and market standing. However, establishment of a funding benchmark is complicated, as there are no standard funding transactions in the market. The credit rating of the issuer is only one factor that influences price; maturity of the issue and specific call or other features also have a major effect on the cost of funding. Only the market environment is really common to all issuers.

The construction of a benchmark focuses on areas that are less emphasized during the SAA process. Benchmarks typically specify a target currency composition, allocation to specific assets or indexes, and a duration target. Figure 9.1 illustrates the bridging aspects of the benchmarking process—providing a context for the evaluation of managers' portfolio performance, in line with the policies decided on during the SAA phase.

Figure 9.1 Benchmarking: Link between Strategic Asset Allocation and Portfolio Management

Benchmarking: Link Between Strategic Asset Allocation and Portfolio Management		
Strategic Asset Allocation (SAA)		**Portfolio Management**
Responsibilities		**Responsibilities**
Management or Board of Directors		Portfolio managers
Investment Horizon		**Investment Horizon**
Medium to long-term (> 1 year)		Daily trading to three-month horizons
Decision-Making Parameters	**Investment Benchmark**	**Decision-Making Parameters**
Risk-return tradeoff for various asset classes and sectors		Performance – expected excess return versus the benchmark
Stress testing for worst-case scenarios		Risk or possible deviation of returns versus the benchmark
Positions / Holdings		**Positions / Holdings**
Long – actual SAA view		Deviation from the benchmark (security / sector / duration / currency selection)
Value-Added		**Value-Added**
Policy framework		Active management – excess return

Benchmarking is a critical risk management tool, providing a yardstick for the measurement of performance and actual risk from active management. For a benchmark to be realistic, it must represent a simple and unambiguous, flexible, investable, and replicable portfolio, easily implemented with no influence on market prices. Rules pertaining to the benchmark must be transparent. Its characteristics, constituents, and rebalancing rules have to be agreed upon in advance and be available or easily accessible for portfolio risk management purposes.

A benchmark is typically constructed using externally available market indexes. These indexes may be made up of a set of specific securities that meet defined characteristics, or the indexes may be based on a synthetic market indicator such as LIBOR (London Interbank Offered Rate) or a swap rate. These indexes should be combined in such a way as to create a benchmark portfolio that meets the currency, duration, liquidity, and credit constraints set out in the investment policy. A few examples of the market indexes generated and made available by index providers are shown in table 9.1.

Table 9.1 Examples of U.S. Dollar Market Indices

Market Sector	Indices
U.S. government securities	1–12-month Treasury bills, 1–10-year Treasury bonds
Banks	Overnight federal funds 3-month LIBID
Mortgage-backed securities	Master Mortgage Index
AAA Asset-backed securities	Floating rate: ROF1; Fixed rate: ROA1
Large capitalization equities	Standard & Poor's 500

A good benchmark should be comprehensive and should include all opportunities under normal market conditions. It should provide a fair, realistic baseline strategy. Changes must be few and understandable, and the benchmark should not preclude participants that may not invest in the specific segments or countries addressed by the benchmark. Transaction and tax costs ought to be predictable and transparent. If the above criteria are met, performance can be measured against objective indexes.

9.5 Eligible Instruments

Financial instruments are approved for the investment policy when they meet certain criteria based on the rationale for holding these funds. For liquidity portfolios, the main criterion should be the instrument's liquidity—that is, the ability to realize funds in a timely fashion, without negatively affecting the price of the instrument. The precondition for liquidity is the existence of deep and broad markets with multiple market makers that stand ready to buy (bid for) the assets. Liquidity is provided through both cash and futures markets because dealers generally are more willing to make continuous markets in instruments in which they can, in turn, offset their risk by using futures.

In assessing the required level of liquidity, policy makers need to consider the investment horizon over which the funds would need to be drawn down. Instruments suitable for working capital or daily liquidity needs are quite different from those that would be liquidated over several months or more. For prudential liquidity portfolios, it is also important to consider the liquidity of the instruments during times of systemic crisis. As noted, systemic crises may exogenously affect a bank's ability to access funds. During such a crisis, the bank may be selling assets in stressed markets, characterized by much lower levels of liquidity.

9.6 Credit Risk

In the context of the liquidity portfolio, credit risk refers to the risk of default. But it is also related to liquidity, as markets for low-rated credits generally are thinner than those for higher-rated credits, and the liquidity of assets with low credit ratings will significantly worsen during systemic crises. For both of these reasons, the investment policy should constrain the credit risk of the investment instrument both at the specific-issuer level and at the portfolio level.

With respect to specific-issuer credit risk, most banks rely on multiple independent credit rating agencies when establishing minimum ratings for eligible assets. When different agencies have split ratings, the policy should specify which rating prevails. The allowable level of exposure to any one institution typically also is constrained, with the exposure level set usually as a percentage of the creditor institution's own funds.

At the portfolio level, credit risk is controlled through global limits, expressed as a percentage of the total portfolio. A fundamental risk management tool is diversification; typically the liquidity portfolio will constrain the exposure to any one institution as a maximum percentage of the total portfolio. In addition, the investment policy may seek to minimize the vulnerability of the portfolio to systemic risks. Systemic risk is defined as a risk that affects a class of institutions that share a common business, country of origin, or type of asset. The investment policy may thus also set a percentage limit to the share of the portfolio that may be exposed to any single country, industry, or sector.

Table 9.2 gives a breakdown of types of credit risk and risk management tools.

Table 9.2 Credit Risk in Liquidity Portfolios

Credit Risk	Risk Tool	Benchmark Limits
Specific- creditor risk	Credit rating	Minimum rating requirements
	Size of exposure	Maximum exposure as a percentage of the institution's capital base
	Diversification	Maximum exposure to any one institution as a percentage of total assets
Systemic risk	Not applicable	Maximum exposure to any industry or sector in a single country as a percentage of total assets
Country risk	Credit rating	Maximum exposure per country as a percentage of total assets
		Minimum credit ratings
Sector risk	Sector groupings	Maximum exposure per sector as a percentage of total assets

9.7 Market Risk

Market risk is defined as the volatility of income or market value resulting from fluctuations in underlying market factors such as currency, interest rates, or credit spreads. For commercial banks, the market risk of the liquidity portfolio arises from mismatches between the risk profile of the assets and their funding. The benchmark portfolio, which should be based on the currency, duration, and credit characteristics of the underlying liabilities, stands as a proxy for the liabilities. Any deviation from the benchmark portfolio would thus give rise to risk and should be constrained.[2]

9.8 Active Management

Active management is the investment process by which an institution's portfolio is repositioned versus the benchmark portfolio, within the risk level authorized by the board, to seek excess returns (performance against the benchmark portfolio). The investment process of the institution ought to be well defined and repeatable, with clear objectives, processes, and accountabilities.

There is no standard investment process. Individual institutions may emphasize different styles of risk taking according to their investment policy, business philosophy, and strengths relative to the market. Some investment processes are fairly centralized, using team-based decisions; others are completely decentralized, allocating to individual risk takers a part of the risk budget within which they manage quite independently. Other investment processes are hybrids, with teams making the fundamental decisions relating to sector exposures, and individual managers implementing these decisions through security selection and tactical trading decisions.

Portfolio management decisions may be based on fundamental analysis of the macro- and microeconomic drivers of value, on technical analysis (charting) of the market, or on exploitation of arbitrage possibilities between different markets using quantitative pricing models. A few institutions, particularly hedge funds, may focus on only one of these techniques, but most banks will use a

---

2   For central banks in developing countries, the rationale for holding foreign currency reserves is typically that these reserves provide backing for some portion of the country's foreign currency liabilities and assist its management of the exchange rate. The strategic asset allocation and ensuing benchmark portfolio in such cases thus reflect these underlying contingent liabilities, rather than balance sheet values.

combination of fundamentals, technical analysis, and modeling to develop their investment strategies.

In assessing the adequacy of risk management systems, it is important to understand the process and style with which investments are made, because the approach of an institution to risk taking dictates the level of sophistication that is required of the risk management system. For example, a highly leveraged portfolio management style would require sophisticated risk measurement and monitoring systems, because any losses would be multiplied by the leverage factor. Even low-risk, so-called arbitrage trades can result in devastating losses when highly leveraged, as was seen in the Long-Term Capital Management (LTCM) failure of 1999.

At the other extreme, some banks or institutions take much more conservative positions with regard to the benchmark, opting for minimal outright market exposure. This management style obviously requires a less-sophisticated risk management support system. Figure 9.2 illustrates the relationship between passive management (managing the portfolio to the benchmark), active trading and directional trading.

Figure 9.2 Portfolio Management Styles

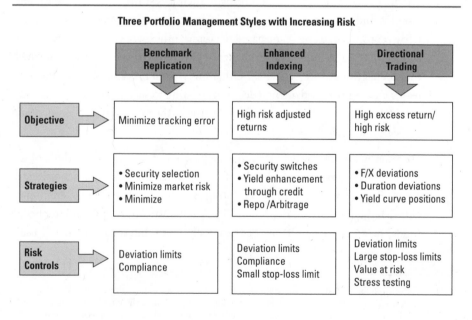

Three Portfolio Management Styles with Increasing Risk

	Benchmark Replication	**Enhanced Indexing**	**Directional Trading**
Objective	Minimize tracking error	High risk adjusted returns	High excess return/ high risk
Strategies	• Security selection • Minimize market risk • Minimize	• Security switches • Yield enhancement through credit • Repo /Arbitrage	• F/X deviations • Duration deviations • Yield curve positions
Risk Controls	Deviation limits Compliance	Deviation limits Compliance Small stop-loss limit	Deviation limits Large stop-loss limits Value at risk Stress testing

9.9   Risk Budgets

A risk budget establishes the tolerance of the board to income or capital loss from market risk over a given horizon, typically one year due to the accounting cycle. Institutions that are not sensitive to annual income requirements may have a longer horizon, which would also allow for a greater degree of freedom in portfolio management.

Once an annual risk budget has been established, a system of risk limits must be put in place to guard against actual or potential losses exceeding the risk budget. There are two types of risk limits, and both are necessary to constrain losses to within the prescribed level (the risk budget). The first type is **stop-loss limits**, which control cumulative losses from the mark-to-market of existing positions relative to the benchmark. The second is **position limits**, which control potential losses that could arise from future adverse changes in market prices.

Stop-Loss Limits

Stop-loss limits are set relative to the overall risk budget. The allocation of the risk budget to different types of risk is as much an art as it is a science, and the methodology used will depend on the set-up of the individual investment process. Some of the questions that affect the risk allocation include the following:

- What are the significant market risks of the portfolio?
- What is the correlation among these risks?
- How many risk takers are there?
- How is the risk expected to be used over the course of a year?

The risk positions arising from different markets and risk takers generally are not perfectly correlated, and the aggregate of individual stop-loss limits may exceed the risk budget. Compliance with stop-loss limits requires frequent, if not daily, performance measurement. Performance is the total return of the portfolio less the total return of the benchmark. The measurement of performance is a critical statistic for monitoring the use of the risk budget and compliance with stop-loss limits.

Position Limits

Position limits also are set relative to the overall risk budget and are subject to the same considerations discussed above. The function of position limits, however, is to constrain potential losses from future adverse changes in prices or yields (see also chapter 11). Table 9.3 lists the main market risks or market factor sensitivities and the types of position limits that are commonly used to constrain these risks to acceptable levels.

Table 9.3 Market-Risk Management Tools

Market Risk	Factor Sensitivity	Risk Management Tool (Benchmark Limits)
Foreign currency	Open position	Percent deviation
Interest rate risk	Modified duration DV01 DV01	Duration deviation limits Net DV01 limits
Yield curve exposure	Key rate duration	***
Credit spread risk	DV01 of credit positions	Net DV01 limits
Options: Directional risk Convexity Volatility	 Delta position Gamma Vega	
Portfolio risk	Value at risk (VAR)	*** (percent of capital)

Note: *** Important risk statistics, but not conducive to implementation as hard limits.

The DV01 is the dollar value of a basis point and gives the change in the market value in absolute terms for a basis-point change in yields. The modified duration gives the percentage change in the market value for a basis-point change in yields.

9.10 Management Reporting

A key element in the delegation of risk-taking authority is accountability for the risks taken. This usually is effected through management reports. These reports should focus on key statistics relating to

- the composition of the portfolio versus the benchmark,
- the performance to date of the portfolio and the benchmark, and
- the existing portfolio risk as measured by the tracking error or value at risk.

Management reports should also include descriptive analysis of market strategies, market movements, and results. Performance attribution is also extremely useful, as it allows for an ex post critique of the results from specific risk-taking activities. This can help an institution refine its investment process to focus on those activities in which it has a proven track record and to eschew those activities in which it has been unable to generate excess returns.

10

Market Risk Management

Key Messages

- Banks use leveraged funds with shorter-term maturity—often repurchase agreements—for their own trading activities.

- All securities classified as available for sale or fair value through the profit and loss, are subject to market risk measurement, whereas portfolios held to maturity eliminate the necessity to recognize fluctuations in market valuations.

- Market risk results from the volatility of positions taken in the four fundamental economic markets: interest-sensitive debt securities, equities, currencies, and commodities.

- The volatility of each of these markets exposes banks to fluctuations in the price or value of marketable financial instruments.

- In sophisticated market environments, with sufficient depth, banks can normally hedge against market volatility. The resulting net effective open position determines the amount of the portfolio that remains exposed to market risk.

- Capital has to be retained as a buffer against potential losses from market risk; such capital is referred to as Tier 3 capital.

10.1 Sources of Market Risk: Selected Concepts

Market risk is the risk that an entity may experience loss from unfavorable movements in market prices resulting from changes in the prices (volatility) of fixed-income instruments, equity instruments, commodities, currencies, and related off-balance-sheet contracts. In addition, market risk comes from the general foreign exchange and commodities risks throughout the bank (that is, in the trading and banking books).

The major components of market risk are therefore interest rate risk, equity risk, commodities risk, and currency risk. Each component of risk includes a general market risk aspect as well as a specific risk aspect that originates in the specific portfolio structure of a bank.

Exposure to market risk may arise as a result of the bank taking deliberate speculative positions or may come from the bank's market-making (dealer) activities.

The increasing exposure of banks to market risk is due to the trend of business diversification away from the traditional intermediation function toward market-making and trading activities, whereby banks set aside "risk capital" for deliberate risk-taking activities. The trading portfolio must be distinguished from the liquidity portfolio (see chapter 9). Trading is aimed at exploiting market opportunities with leveraged funding (for example, through the use of repurchase agreements), whereas the liquidity portfolio is held and traded to provide a buffer against risk. Both proprietary trading and liquidity portfolios are subject to market risk.

Volatility

The price volatility of most assets held in securities portfolios is often significant. Volatility occurs even in mature markets, although it is much higher in new or illiquid markets. The presence of large institutional investors—such as pension funds, insurance companies, or investment funds—has also had an impact on the structure of markets and on market risk. Institutional investors adjust their large-scale, stable liquidity investment and trading portfolios through large-scale trades, and in markets with rising prices, large-scale purchases tend to push prices up. Conversely, markets with downward trends become more nervous when large, institutional-size blocks are sold. Ultimately, this leads to a widening of the amplitude of price variances and therefore to increased market risk. The advent of electronic trading has widened this phenomenon.

Recognizing Price Changes and Marking to Market

Marking to market refers to the repricing of a bank's portfolios to reflect changes in asset prices from market price movements. This policy requires that the asset be repriced at the market value of the asset in compliance with IAS 39. Because assets in a trading portfolio are constantly sold and bought, price positions related to a bank's trading portfolio should be evaluated and marked to market at least once per day. The reports prepared in this process should be submitted to and reviewed by the senior bank managers responsible for the bank's investment, asset-liability, and risk management.

IAS 39 requires that trading (and available-for-sale) positions be marked to market in the balance sheet, with the fluctuations in market value for the trading portfolio then to flow through the income statement. The fluctuations in available-for-sale portfolios are taken to equity. Although the process is conceptually simple, marking to market can be difficult in markets that are shallow or lack liquidity. Most banks quantify market risks by tracing the historical loss experienced by various instruments and markets, but banks in volatile or illiquid market environments, often without the benefit of sophisticated technology, face the problem of how to transform this complex analysis into a workable solution that can be effectively applied to their everyday business.

Interest Rate Risk

Positions in fixed-income securities and their derivatives (for example, exchange-traded futures, forward rate agreements, swaps, and options) present interest rate risk. The risk factors refer to the aggregate market sensitivity of the bank's portfolio, where the short and long positions in different instruments may be offset. Risk factors related to interest rate risk are estimated in each currency in which a bank has interest-rate-sensitive on- and off-balance-sheet positions.

Equity Risk

Equity risk relates to taking or holding trading-book positions in equities or instruments that display equity-like behavior (for example, convertible securities) and their derivatives (for example, futures and swaps on individual equities or on stock indexes). Equity-related risk is calculated for the specific risk of holding a security (*beta*) and for the position in a market as a whole. For derivatives, the risk is measured by converting the derivative into a notional equity position in the relevant underlying instrument.

Commodity Risk

Holding or taking positions in exchange-traded commodities, futures, and other derivatives presents commodity risk. Commodity prices may be volatile as commodity markets are often less liquid than financial markets, and changes in supply and demand can have dramatic effects on prices. Managing a commodity book can be a complex task, as it entails directional risk from changes in spot prices; basis risk from changes in the price relationship between two similar, but not identical, commodities; and gap risk, which captures the changes in forward prices arising from maturity mismatches. Another operational aspect of commodities risk relates to delivery risk and the necessity to close out positions before delivery.

Currency Risk

Currency risk refers to trading positions in currencies and gold. Excluded from this treatment are the so-called "structural positions"—that is, positions of a nondealing or nontrading nature such as investments in foreign branches (see chapter 11). The net open position in a currency normally includes the spot position, the forward position, the *delta*-based equivalent of the total book of foreign currency options, and any other items in the trading books that represent profit or loss in foreign currencies.

Other Risks

Underdeveloped infrastructure in a secondary market could increase risk and complicate risk measurement. For example, in some markets settlement takes place several days after transactions are concluded. This lengthy settlement period necessitates an accurate assessment of counterparty risk—that is, the risk that the position will move into the money during the settlement period but the counterparty fails to deliver. Certain volatility specific to individual securities cannot be explained by other factors and should be factored into overall risk assessment and management. In some countries, markets in financial instruments are not liquid, resulting in potentially much higher market price volatility and therefore greater exposure to risk. The widespread development of derivative instruments has allowed banks to hedge their open positions in ever-more-sophisticated ways; however, because market liquidity is a crucial precondition for the use of such instruments, concern has grown regarding the valuation and effectiveness of hedges made in less-developed markets.

10.2 Measuring Interest Rate Sensitivity

The combination of a volatile interest rate environment, deregulation, and a growing array of on- and off-balance-sheet products have made the management of interest rate risk a growing challenge. At the same time, informed use of interest rate derivatives—such as financial futures and interest rate swaps—can help banks manage and reduce the interest rate exposure that is inherent in their business. Bank regulators and supervisors therefore place great emphasis on the evaluation of bank interest rate risk management, particularly since the implementation of market risk–based capital charges, as recommended by the Basel Committee.

Interest-Rate Risk Sources

The sensitivity of interest income when interest rates change, originates from four types of interest rate risk, namely, repricing risk, yield curve risk, basis risk, and optionality.

Repricing risk. Variations in interest rates expose a bank's income and the underlying value of its instruments to fluctuations. The most common type of interest rate risk arises from timing differences in the maturity of fixed rates and the repricing of the floating rates of bank assets, liabilities, and off-balance-sheet positions. The basic tool used for measuring repricing risk is duration, which assumes a parallel shift in the yield curve.

Yield curve risk. Repricing mismatches also expose a bank to risk deriving from changes in the slope and shape of the yield curve (nonparallel shifts). Yield curve risk materializes when yield curve shifts adversely affect a bank's income or underlying economic value. For example, a bank's position may be hedged against parallel movements in the yield curve; for instance, a long position in bonds with 10-year maturities may be hedged by a short position in 5-year notes from the same issuer. The value of the longer-maturity instrument can still decline sharply if the yield curve increases, resulting in a loss for the bank. As figure 10.1 illustrates, yield curves do not necessarily shift in a parallel fashion. In such cases key rate duration is employed to measure the price impact of the shift.

Figure 10.1 Illustration of Nonparallel Shifts in the Yield Curve

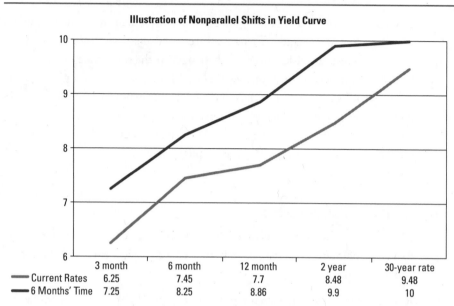

Illustration of Nonparallel Shifts in Yield Curve

	3 month	6 month	12 month	2 year	30-year rate
Current Rates	6.25	7.45	7.7	8.48	9.48
6 Months' Time	7.25	8.25	8.86	9.9	10

Basis risk, also described as spread risk, arises when assets and liabilities are priced off different yield curves and the spread between these curves shifts. When these yield curve spreads change, income and market values may be negatively affected. Such situations can occur when assets that are repriced monthly—based on an index rate (such as U.S. Treasury bills) or at the prime rate offered on loans to customers—are funded by a liabilities that may also reprice monthly, but possibly based on a different index rate (such as LIBOR or swaps). Basis risk thus derives from an unexpected change in the spread between the two index rates.

Optionality. An increasingly important source of interest rate risk stems from the options embedded in many bank assets and liabilities (for example in mortgage-backed securities). Options may be stand-alone derivative instruments, such as exchange-traded options, or they may be embedded within otherwise standard instruments. The latter may include various types of bonds or notes with call or put provisions, nonmaturity deposit instruments that give depositors the right to withdraw their money, or loans that borrowers may prepay without penalty. Such options lead to increased volatility risk as well as prepayment risk.

Duration

Duration is a measure of price sensitivity to changes in interest rates. Specifically, duration which is expressed as a numbers of years, gives the percentage change in the price of a fixed-income security for a specified change in interest rates. There are three measures of duration: *Macauley, modified, and effective duration.* Duration has become the single most common measure of interest rate risk for fixed-income investment portfolios and trading positions. Originally duration was used exclusively to measure interest rate risk for these portfolios because they were marked to market and the change in the market value would flow through income. Corporate finance specialists, however, have increasingly focused attention on the economic value of the firm in addition to its current earnings. Given this change in focus, modified duration was introduced to measure the sensitivity of the economic value of capital to a change in interest rates.

Duration is based on the time to receipt of future cash flows. When interest rates rise, the net present value of a fixed set of future cash flows will decline. For marketable securities, this will translate into a commensurate decline in price. Conversely, when interest rates decline, the net present value or price of a series of future cash flows will increase (see figure 10.2).

Figure 10.2 Duration as an Indicator of Interest Rate Risk in a Portfolio

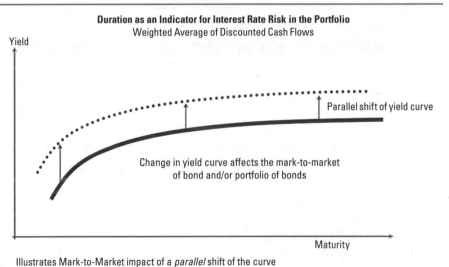

Duration as an Indicator for Interest Rate Risk in the Portfolio
Weighted Average of Discounted Cash Flows

Yield

Parallel shift of yield curve

Change in yield curve affects the mark-to-market
of bond and/or portfolio of bonds

Maturity

Illustrates Mark-to-Market impact of a *parallel* shift of the curve

The impact of duration can be illustrated in a very simple example using the effective duration of a 10-year bond with a nominal value of $1 million, which pays a coupon of 5 percent. If market rates are also 5 percent at the issue date, the coupon is paying the required market yield, and the value of the bond must be 100 percent of $1 million—or simply referred to as 100.

Assume that the market rates decline to 4 percent. The value of the bond will then increase as the bond pays a higher coupon than the market requires. The new market value will be 108.18. Similarly, if the market rates move to 6 percent, the value of the bond will decrease as the bond pays a lower coupon than the market requires. The new market value will be 92.56.

The effective duration formula now uses these observed values to calculate interest rate sensitivity, expressed in years, as follows:

108.18 – 92.56 / 2 * 100 * 1% = 15.62 / 200 * .01 = 7.8

The new price of the bond when market rates fall <u>less</u> the price of the bond if interest rates were to rise

<u>divided by</u>

two times the market value of the bond before the rate movements <u>multiplied by</u> the size of the movement

Given that the effective duration of the bond above is 7.8 years, one can conclude the following:

- For each 1 percent (or 100 basis point [bp]) move in interest rates, the percentage value of the bond will change by 7.8 percent, calculated as follows:

$$.01 * 7.8 = .078 = 7.8\%$$

- For each 100 bp change in interest rates, the value of a bond with a market value of $ 1 million will change by $78,000, calculated as follows:

$$.01 * 7.8 * \$1,000,000 = \$78,000$$

- For each 1 bp change in interest rates, the value of a bond with a market value of $1 million will change by $780 (normally referred to as DV01 or PV01), calculated as follows:

  .0001 * 7.8 * $1,000,000 = $780

Knowing the change in value caused by a one basis point move is useful for the calculation of **value at risk** (section 10.4).

Duration is additive. The duration for each bond in a bond portfolio can be calculated separately (known as key rate duration) and then added together to determine the duration of the portfolio. **Key rate duration** is a refinement of duration. It incorporates the fact that the pricing of individual bonds can be determined by different parts of the yield curve and that each part of the yield curve reacts differently to an exogeneous price shock (in a nonparallel manner as illustrated in figure 10.1 above).

10.3 Portfolio Risk Management

By its very nature, market risk requires constant management attention and adequate analysis. Prudent managers should be aware of exactly how a bank's market risk exposure relates to its capital. Market risk management policies should specifically state a bank's objectives and the related policy guidelines that have been established to protect capital from the negative impact of unfavorable market price movements. Policy guidelines should normally be formulated within restrictions provided by the applicable legal and prudential framework. While policies related to market risk management may vary among banks, certain types of policies are typically present in all banks.

Other matters that should be addressed by the marking-to-market policy are pricing responsibility and the method used by a bank to determine the new (market) price of an asset. Risk management policy should stipulate that prices be determined and the marking to market be executed by officers who are independent of the respective dealer or trader and his or her managers. Some jurisdictions have enacted prudential regulations that specifically cover the process of marking to market the value of a bank's assets, sometimes with a high level of detail. In practice, the pricing of positions would be less than effective if independent, third-party price quotes were not taken into consideration. A bank should routinely acquire the latest price and performance information available from external sources on assets held in its portfolios.

Position Limits

A market risk management policy should provide for limits on and monitoring of positions (long, short, or net positions in markets and products), bearing in mind the liquidity risk that could arise on execution of unrealized transactions such as open contracts or commitments to purchase and sell securities (for example, option contracts or repurchase agreements). Such position limits should be related to the capital available to cover market risk. Banks, especially those with large, stable liquidity investment and trading portfolios, would also be expected to set limits on the level of risk taken by individual traders and dealers. These limits are related to several factors, including the specific organization of investment and trading functions and the technical skill level of individual dealers and traders. The sophistication and quality of analytical support that is provided to the dealers and traders may also play a role, as do the specific characteristics of a bank's stable liquidity investment or trading portfolios and the level and quality of its capital. This type of policy should specify the manner and frequency of position valuations and position limit controls.

Stop-Loss Provisions

Market risk management policy should also include stop-loss sale or consultation requirements that relate to a predetermined loss exposure limit (risk budget). The stop-loss exposure limit should be determined with regard to a bank's capital structure and earning trends, as well as to its overall risk profile. When losses on a bank's positions reach unacceptable levels, the positions should automatically be closed or consultations initiated with risk management officers or the asset and liability committee to establish or reconfirm the stop-loss strategy.

Limits to New Market Presence

Financial innovations involve profits that are much higher than those of standard instruments, because profit is a key motivating factor to innovate. In a highly competitive market environment, innovation also places pressure on competitors to engage in new business to make profits or to not lose a market presence. However, innovation involves a special kind of risk taking, requiring that a bank be willing to invest in or trade a new instrument even though its return and variance may not have been tested in a market setting—or even though the appropriate market for the instrument may not yet exist.

A prudent bank should have risk management policies that proscribe its presence in new markets and its trading in new financial instruments. Limits related to a new market presence should be frequently reviewed, monitored and adjusted. Because the high spreads initially available in new market segments attract competitors, markets may pick up at a fast pace. Increasing use of a new instrument also helps to increase the breadth and depth of related secondary markets and to increase their liquidity. Once a market becomes established and sufficiently liquid, a bank should readjust the limits to levels applicable to mature markets.

Figure 10.3 Monitoring Market Presence

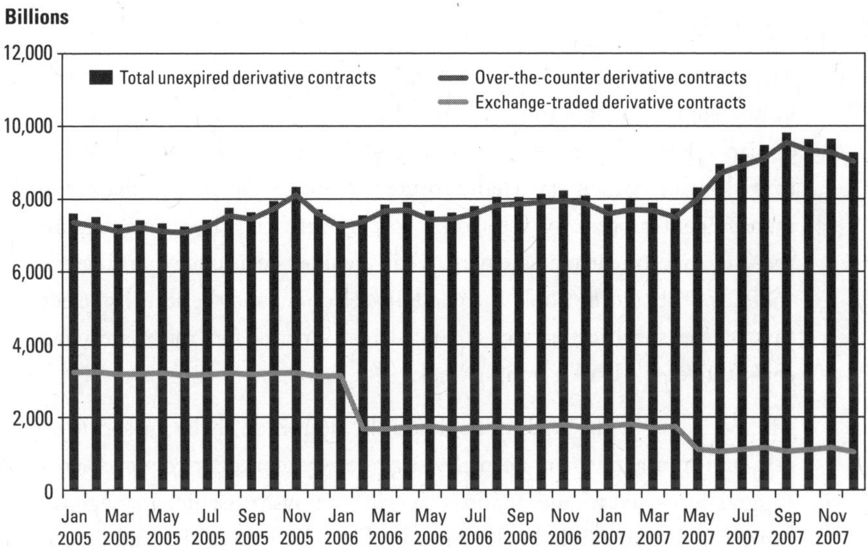

Billions

Legend:
- Total unexpired derivative contracts
- Over-the-counter derivative contracts
- Exchange-traded derivative contracts

Information Technology

The availability of sophisticated computer technology in recent years has been instrumental in developing many new financial instruments. Technology has improved the quality of and access to information, and this in turn has increased the efficiency and liquidity of related secondary markets. Modeling and analytical tools that are supported with timely and accurate information and that are internally consistent provide the technical support necessary to conduct transactions and make decisions. In addition, sophisticated computer programs have enabled the simultaneous processing and risk evaluation of transactions, providing bank management and staff with the information needed to understand in real time the exact nature of risk and the value of open positions.

It is this technological capacity that has enabled banks to engage in trading—that is, to take positions in financial instruments, including positions in derivative products and off-balance-sheet instruments. The bank takes these positions with the intention of benefiting in the short term from actual or expected differences between buying and selling prices, or from other price or interest rate variations. A bank's trading book may also include positions arising from brokering or market making, as well as certain instruments taken to hedge the risk exposures inherent in some trading activities.

Organization

Trading activities in most banks are carried out in organizational (treasury) units that are separate from standard banking activities. Most banks also recognize a portion of capital that is specifically allocated to cover the risk related to trading and which is partially covered by Tier 3 capital (see chapter 6). The management process for the bank's trading activities has elements similar to those of investment management. This includes decisions regarding the total volume of the trading book, the portfolio selection, and the security selection—that is, the specific types of financial instruments and the shares that they constitute of the bank's trading book.

The positions in the trading book are, by definition, held for short-term resale, and transactions are normally triggered by market price movements. The triggers proposed to and endorsed by the responsible senior management are expressed in terms of bid-offer spreads. The structure of the trading portfolio therefore is in constant flux throughout the trading day.

10.4 Market Risk Measurement: Value at Risk (VAR) as a Possible Tool

Given the increasing involvement of banks in investment and trading activities and the high volatility of the market environment, the timely and accurate measurement of market risk is a necessity, including measurement of the exposures on a bank's liquidity and trading portfolios and on- and off-balance-sheet positions.

Trading activities require highly skilled analytical support. Traders must use some form of technical analysis to gauge market movements and market opportunities. A fundamental analysis of classes of securities and of market behavior is also needed for the trader to be able to anticipate price movements and position the portfolio accordingly. Ex post analysis is also important to understand how market movements have affected profit and loss.

Because of the fast-changing nature of a bank's trading book and the complexity of risk management, banks engaged in trading must have market risk measurement and management systems that are conceptually sound and that are implemented with high integrity. This reinforces the fact that risk management structures and related strategies should be embedded in a bank's culture and not be dependent on just one or two people. The Basel Committee on Banking Supervision's capital adequacy standard for market risk specifies a set of qualitative criteria that must be met for a bank to be eligible for application of the minimum multiplication factor for market risk capital charges. These criteria include the following:

■ An independent risk control unit responsible for the design and implementation of the bank's market risk management system. The unit should be independent from business trading units and should report directly to senior management of the bank. It should produce daily reports on and analysis of the output of the bank's risk measurement model, as well as analysis of the relationship between the measures of risk exposure and trading limits.

■ Board and senior management who are actively involved in the risk control process and who regard risk control as an essential aspect of business. The daily reports prepared by the independent risk control unit should be reviewed by management that has sufficient seniority and authority to enforce reductions in the positions taken by individual traders and reductions in the bank's overall risk exposure.

■ A market risk measurement system that is closely integrated into the daily risk management process of a bank and that is actively used in conjunction with trading and exposure limits. The risk measurement system should be subject to regular back-testing—that is, to ex post comparison of the risk measure generated by the bank's internal model against daily changes in portfolio value and against hypothetical changes based on static positions. The ultimate test remains actual profits or losses compared to the budgeted profits.

■ A routine and rigorous program of stress testing to supplement the risk analysis provided by the risk measurement model. The results of stress testing should be subject to review by senior management and should be reflected in the policies and limits to market risk exposure, especially when stress tests reveal particular vulnerability to a given set of circumstances.

■ A process to ensure compliance with a documented set of bank policies, controls, and procedures concerning the trading activities and the operation of the risk measurement system.

The capacity to systematically assess and measure risk and to effectively manage the net open position is crucial. Methods range from calculation of the net open position (or market factor sensitivity) to value at risk and other more sophisticated estimates of risk. Table 10.1 provides an example of a simplistic but practical method to aggregate assets, as reflected on the balance sheet, to arrive at a net open position. Once forward and unsettled transactions are taken into account, a projected position is determined at book value, translated into market value, and then disclosed in terms of a common denominator representing the equivalent position in the cash markets. This methodology belongs to the static type of market risk measurement tools known as standard or table-based tools. Based on the net open position one can estimate the potential earnings or capital at risk by multiplying the net open position (market risk factor sensitivity) by the price volatility. This estimate provides a simple, one-factor value at risk; it does not, however, take into consideration the correlation between positions. Figure 10.4 illustrates the concept.

Table 10.1 Simplistic Calculation of Net Open Positions

Position	Commodities	Fixed-income	Equities	Currencies
Net book value of assets per balance sheet				
Forward and unsettled transactions				
Position at book value				
Position at market value before transactions in derivatives				
Position in derivatives (delta-equivalent position in options)				
Net effective open position after transactions in derivatives				
Possible movements in market prices (price volatility)				
Impact on earnings and capital				

Figure 10.4 Potential Amount of Qualifying Capital Exposed

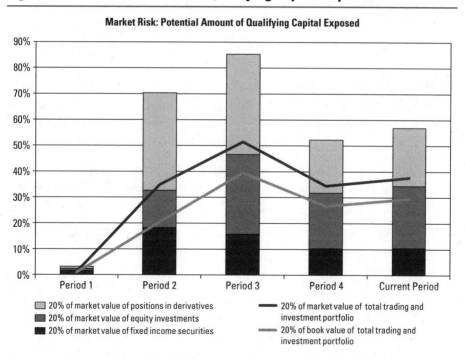

Market Risk: Potential Amount of Qualifying Capital Exposed

Legend:
- 20% of market value of positions in derivatives
- 20% of market value of equity investments
- 20% of market value of fixed income securities
- 20% of market value of total trading and investment portfolio
- 20% of book value of total trading and investment portfolio

Such a simplistic approach to market risk assessment treats every market to which the bank is exposed as a separate entity and does not take into account the relationships that may exist among various markets. Each risk is therefore measured on an individual basis. A more comprehensive approach assumes risk assessment from a consolidated perspective, which takes into consideration the relationships among markets and the fact that a movement in one market may affect several others. For example, a fluctuation in the exchange rate may also affect the price of bonds issued in a particular currency. The potential solution to this conceptual problem lies in the use of statistical techniques such as value at risk.

Risk is based on probabilistic events, and it is apparent that no single measurement tool can capture the multifaceted nature of market risk. Even the simplest aspects of market risk management can present a problem in real-life situations—particularly so when a bank does not have adequate systems. At an absolute minimum, marking to market is a fundamental measure that should be taken to protect a bank's capital. Both the stable liquidity investment portfolio and the trading book should be marked to market on a daily basis to ensure that the real value of positions is maintained. For a bank's managers, analysts, and supervisors such a figure indicates the actual value of the stable liquidity investment and trading portfolios and indicates the steps that should be taken to protect capital.

Value at Risk

VAR is a modeling technique that typically measures a bank's aggregate market risk exposure and, given a probability level, estimates the amount a bank would lose if it were to hold specific assets for a certain period of time.

It is a forward-looking method that expresses financial market risk in a form that anybody can understand, namely currency. It measures the predicted

- ■ worst loss (maximum movement of the yield cure),
- ■ over a target horizon (for example, 10 days, which provides the benefit of early detection),
- ■ within a given confidence level (99 percent is the level chosen by the Basel Committee).

The effect of a yield curve movement of one bp on the market value of a bond has already been explained in section 10.2. What remains in terms of the above definition of VAR is to determine the maximum movement that can take place over a given time horizon at a specified confidence level. The Basel Committee specifies a confidence level of 99 percent over 10 days.

Box 10.1 VAR Calculation

If the value of a one bp move is $780, a specific bond's VAR would be determined by the potential overall basis point move, multiplied by the dollar value of $780.

For example, if the potential movement could be 30 bp over a 10-day period, the VAR of the bond will be 30 times $780, or $23,400.

Inputs to a VAR-based model include data on the bank's positions and on prices, volatility, and risk factors. The data should be sufficiently comprehensive to capture all risks inherent in a bank's on- and off-balance-sheet positions. The risks covered by the model should include all interest, currency, equity, and commodity and option positions inherent in the bank's portfolio.

VAR-based models combine the potential change in the value of each position that would result from specific movements in underlying risk factors with the probability of such movements occurring. The changes in value are aggregated at the level of trading book segments and across all trading activities and markets. The VAR amount may be calculated using one of a number of methodologies:

- The **historical simulation approach** calculates the hypothetical change in value of the current portfolio, based on the historical past movements of risk factors. (At a 99 percent confidence level, one could take the lowest of 100 daily observations and apply that return to the current portfolio to determine the maximum loss over the following day.)

- The **delta-normal or variance/covariance** methodology is the methodology most widely used by portfolio managers. This approach assumes that the distribution of asset returns is normal and that returns are serially independent (that is, are not influenced by the previous day's return). To calculate the potential change in value of the current portfolio, one computes the mean and standard deviation of asset returns to achieve a combination of risk factor sensitivities of individual positions in a covariance matrix, representing risk factor volatilities and correlations between each asset.

- The **Monte Carlo simulation** method constructs the distribution of the current portfolio using a large sample of random combinations of price scenarios, the probabilities of which are typically based on historical experience. This approach is more flexible than the other two methodologies and does not rely on assumptions regarding the normality of returns, but the number of scenarios grows rapidly with the complexity of a portfolio and its risk factors.

The measurement parameters include a holding period, a historical time horizon at which risk factor prices are observed, and a confidence interval that allows for the prudent judgment of the level of protection (that is, that identifies the maximum acceptable losses). The observation period is chosen by the bank to capture market conditions that are relevant to its risk management strategy.

An appraisal of capital charges or mark-to-market exposures depends on availability of information that meaningfully expresses a bank's exposure to market risk. The information provided (to senior management, the board, and third parties such as bank supervisors) should include both aggregated and disaggregated exposures at certain control points (in time) and performance information about risk and return, including a comparison of risk and performance estimates with actual outcomes. The disaggregation could be either by standard risk categories or asset classes (for example, equity, fixed-income, currency, commodity) or by some other criterion that more correctly characterizes a bank's risk profile (for example, by business units or risk types). According to the Basel Committee on Banking Supervision, the disclosure requirements for each portfolio should include

- VAR calculations, broken down by type of risk or asset class and in the aggregate, estimated for one-day and two-week holding periods, and reported in terms of high, medium, and low values over the reporting interval and at period end;

- information about risk and return in the aggregate, including a comparison of risk estimates with actual outcomes, such as a histogram of daily profit/loss (P/L) divided by daily VAR, or some other representation of the relationship between daily P/L and daily VAR;

- qualitative discussions to assist with a comparison of the P/L to VAR, including a description of differences between the basis of the P/L and the basis of the VAR estimates; and

- quantitative measure of firmwide exposure to market risk, broken down by type of risk, that in the bank's judgment best expresses exposure to risk, reported in terms of high, medium, and low values over the reporting period and at period end.

Most of the large banks that are major players with high market risk exposures have developed sophisticated risk indexes and tools for risk assessment and measurement that can be applied across different markets. Although specific arrangements may differ, these internal risk measurement models usually fit a common conceptual framework. The models typically measure a bank's aggregate market risk exposure and, given a probability level, estimate the amount the bank would lose if it were to hold specific assets for a certain period of time. Because such VAR-based models cover a number of market risks, the bank is able to fine-tune its portfolio structure, drawing on a range of options for portfolio diversification to reduce the risk to which it is exposed and the associated capital requirements.

As stated above, the Basel Committee has established certain quantitative standards for internal models when they are used in the capital adequacy context. The quantitative standards include a 99th percentile, one-tailed confidence interval; a holding period of 10 trading days; and a historical observation period of at least one year. (If recent price volatility has been high, however, a shorter observation period would yield a higher value than the horizon, covering a longer but overall less volatile period.) VAR numbers should be aggregated on a simple-sum basis across risk factor categories, taking into consideration cross-correlations within each category.

The Basel Committee market risk capital standard (see also chapter 6) requires that the VAR be computed daily and the market risk–related capital requirements met on a daily basis. The capital requirement is expressed as the higher of the previous day's VAR and the average of the daily VAR measures for each of the last 60 business days. This is then multiplied by an additional factor k (which has a minimum value of 3.0), designated by national supervisory authorities and related to the quality of a bank's risk management system.

Supervisors will increase k by a factor of between 0.0 and 1.0 according to the number of times that back-testing of the internal model has shown the projected VAR to have been exceeded. Because this "plus" factor is related to the ex post performance of the internal model, this measure is expected to introduce a positive incentive to maintain a good-quality model.

VAR, however, is based on assumptions that historical experiences may be repeated in future. As such it has limitations—an issue which is further discussed in section 10.6 (stress testing and scenario analysis). It should therefore be used as one tool in an integrated set of tools—and not as the only measure of a portfolio's exposure.

10.5 Risk and Performance Measurement

Management reports (for examples, see tables 10.2 to 10.5) should include descriptive analyses of market strategies, market movements, and performance results. Risk reporting should include an analysis of the portfolio's risk characteristics, such as

- modified duration,
- price (currency) value of a one bp change—PV01, and
- key rate duration.

Risk reports should also cover return characteristics, which emphasize the total return of the portfolio, not only realized profits and coupon receipts, but also unrealized marked-to-market gains and losses.

Performance Reporting

Accountability for risks taken is normally demonstrated through an effective management reporting system, which allows an assessment of a portfolio's performance and enables management to determine the value added of investment decisions relative to a benchmark. A performance report should cover

- overall value added of active versus passive management,
- value-added of each strategy and manager, and
- tracking of progress toward investment objectives.

In addition to the value-added objectives discussed above, performance measurement provides a very effective risk control tool for portfolio management, as discussions between the performance measurement staff and the trading staff inevitably lead to the detection of errors and instilling of discipline in the organization.

Performance reports should focus on the following key statistics (see table 10.2):

- The composition of the portfolio compared with the benchmark
- The performance to date of the portfolio and the benchmark
- The existing portfolio risk as measured by the tracking error or VAR

Table 10.2 Reporting Performance and Market Risk: Portfolio versus the Benchmark

Performance or Risk Measure	Portfolio	Benchmark	Excess / Deviation
Ex ante: risk reporting			Basis Points (bp or $)
Portfolio duration (months) – interest rate			
Portfolio duration (months) – credit spread			
Tracking error (bp) – credit spread			
Value-at-Risk (at 90, 95 and 99% confidence level) – time horizon is 1 day, 1 Week, 1 month, 6 months)			
Ex post: performance reporting			
Return – current month in %			
Return – current year-to-date in %			
Return – inception to date in %			
Holding period in years			
Tracking error (bp) – interest rate (tracking error equals standard deviation of excess returns)			
Information ratio (excess return divided by the tracking error)			

When measuring (calculating) performance, risk analytics staff must keep in mind the following issues:

- The same market prices must be used for securities that are held in both the portfolio and the benchmark.

- Performance income must be reconciled with accounting.

- The concept of total return means that unrealized price gains and losses as well as realized coupon and other income are considered in the income (profit and loss) statement.

Risk analytics staff must also take into consideration the following:

- Cash flows to and from the portfolio, over which the portfolio manager has no control

- Various rate-of-return formulas

- Time-weighted methods

- Internal rates of return

- Linking returns of multiple periods

- Annualizing returns

Performance attribution—analyzing the components of performance—is also extremely useful, as it allows for an ex post critique of the results from specific risk-taking activities. This can help an institution refine its investment process to focus on those activities in which it has a proven track record and to eschew those activities in which it has been unable to generate excess returns.

Interest Rate Risk Measurement Using Key Rate Duration

For a fixed-income (bond) portfolio, measuring the sensitivity to interest rates is a crucial activity. In table 10.3, a one bp parallel move to the yield curve (PV01 or DV01—see 10.2 discussion of duration) is used to determine the following:

■ The portfolio duration (interest rate sensitivity) is 1.73 years, whereas the benchmark portfolio is marginally less sensitive to interest rate movements at a duration of 1.64 years.

■ The benchmark portfolio is exposed to interest rates up to three years.

■ The portfolio manager has engaged in active management and not simply followed the benchmark, as there are exposures to the four -and five-year key rates and portions of the yield curve.

■ The portfolio's greatest absolute sensitivity to interest rates is at the two-year key rate, where it would gain $36,979 if interest rates moved downward by one bp.

■ The greatest relative exposure of the portfolio against the benchmark exists in the 2.5-year part of the yield curve, where it would lose $8,062 more than the benchmark portfolio, were interest rates to move downward by one bp.

■ The bank's portfolio is more exposed to an across-the-board, one bp interest rate movement, and would stand to gain $5,641 in such an unlikely case.

Table 10.3 Interest Rate Sensitivity of a Portfolio versus the Benchmark

Key Rates	Portfolio	Benchmark	PV01
O/N	-29	0	-30
1 WEEK	-29	2	-31
1 MONTH	-753	41	-795
3 MONTH	-4,322	158	-4,479
6 MONTH	5,190	329	4,861
9 MONTH	-2,535	669	-3,204
1 YEAR	21,587	16,524	5,063
1.5 YEAR	31,990	35,565	-3,574
2 YEAR	36,979	29,148	7,831
2.5 YEAR	12,367	20,430	-8,062
3 YEAR	13,618	10,942	2,676
4 YEAR	3,822	0	3,822
5 YEAR	1,567	0	1,567
6 YEAR	0	0	0
7 YEAR	0	0	0
8 YEAR	0	0	0
9 YEAR	0	0	0
10 YEAR	0	0	0
15 YEAR	0	0	0
20 YEAR	0	0	0
30 YEAR	0	0	0
TOTAL	119,443	113,803	5,641
Duration (years)	1.73	1.64	0.08
Duration (months)	20.70	19.72	0.98

Credit Spread Risk Measurement Using Key Rates

We can learn more about the two portfolios (bank and benchmark) by analyzing the sensitivity of the key rates to a widening of the credit spreads. In table 10.4, a one bp widening of credit spreads (swap rate against the treasury rates, CR01) is used to determine the following:

Table 10.4 Sensitivity of a Portfolio to Widening of Credit Spreads versus the Benchmark

DV01	Portfolio	Benchmark	CR01
O/N	-29	0	-29
1 WEEK	-29	0	-29
1 MONTH	-774	0	-774
3 MONTH	-4,395	0	-4,395
6 MONTH	5,051	0	5,051
9 MONTH	-3,785	0	-3,785
1 YEAR	15,012	0	15,012
1.5 YEAR	13,134	0	13,134
2 YEAR	26,641	0	26,641
2.5 YEAR	11,787	0	11,787
3 YEAR	2,274	0	2,274
4 YEAR	458	0	458
5 YEAR	0	0	0
6 YEAR	0	0	0
7 YEAR	0	0	0
8 YEAR	0	0	0
9 YEAR	0	0	0
10 YEAR	0	0	0
15 YEAR	0	0	0
20 YEAR	0	0	0
30 YEAR	0	0	0
TOTAL	65,336	0	65,336
Duration (years)	1	0	1
Duration (months)	11	0	11

- The benchmark portfolio has to be a government securities portfolio as it is clearly free of any credit risk, that is, a risk-free portfolio. The portfolio credit spread sensitivity is 1 year (11 months), whereas the benchmark portfolio must have a zero credit spread duration.

- The portfolio's greatest absolute sensitivity to credit spreads is at the two-year key rate, where it would gain $26,641 if credit spreads narrowed (downward) by one bp.

- The greatest relative exposure of the portfolio against the benchmark must also exist in the two-year part of the yield curve, where it would gain the same amount as the absolute amount of $26,641 more than the benchmark portfolio, were credit spreads to narrow by one bp.

- The bank's portfolio exposure to credit spread narrowing could gain it $65,336.

In the unlikely situation where both interest rates and credit spreads moved downward by exactly one bp—across all parts of the yield curve—the bank's portfolio would gain $70,977 ($5,641 + $65,336) more than the benchmark portfolio.

10.6 Stress Testing and Scenario Analysis

The Basel Committee recommendation also includes a requirement that banks establish and regularly use a "routine and rigorous program" of stress tests to identify events or influences that can negatively affect a bank's capital position.

Stress testing is fast becoming the norm for risk measurement and analysis. As part of the fallout from the 2007 – 2008 financial sector crisis, some critics are questioning the value of tools such as VAR. The problem is not VAR itself. It is still a useful indicator, but remains a statistical tool, using historical information and with at most a 99 percent confidence level; always leaving some potential exposure.

The solution lies in applying common sense when using tools. Risk managers should know the characteristics of their portfolios and apply scenario analyses to ask the "what if" questions that appear to have been sorely lacking in many instances.

The purpose of stress testing is to identify events or influences that may result in a loss—that is, have a negative impact on a bank's capital position. Stress tests should be both qualitative and quantitative in nature. Quantitative criteria should identify plausible stress scenarios that could occur in a bank's specific market environment. Qualitative criteria should focus on two key aspects of stress testing: evaluation of the bank's capacity to absorb potentially large losses, and identification of measures that the bank can take to reduce risk and conserve capital.

It is virtually impossible to develop a standard stress test scenario that has a consistent impact on all banks. Stress-testing methodology therefore usually entails a number of steps, including the following (see table 10.5):

Table 10.5 Current Portfolio Price Movements during Major Historic Market Crises

Market Crisis	Portfolio Losses After: 1 Day	1 Week	1 Month	3 Months	6 Months
1. BAHT devalues	-33,792	-130,300	-133,572	-816,255	-1,280,952
	-0.49	-1.88	-1.93	-11.79	-18.50
2. Ruble devalues	-28,829	-184,603	-9,795	-661,150	-1,365,128
	-0.42	-2.67	-0.14	-9.55	-19.72
3. Euro weakens	10,161	-198,632	-468,165	-1,190,649	-1,844,777
4. Dotcom falls	-23,802	-102,202	-329,826	-1,309,357	-1,300,675
	-0.34	-1.48	-4.76	-18.91	-18.79
5. US in recession	-84,290	-112,331	-272,146	-559,127	-59,209
	-1.22	-1.62	-3.93	-8.08	-0.86
6. September 11 terror attacks	15,112	286,579	477,924	135,269	193,305x
	0.22	4.14	6.90	1.95	2.79
7. Major corporate bankruptcy	33,687	-31,941	15,066	-734,156	-466,133
	0.49	-0.46	0.22	-10.60	-6.73

■ Review of information on the largest actual losses experienced during a specific period, compared to the level of losses estimated by a bank's internal risk measurement system. Such a review provides information on the degree of peak losses covered by a given VAR estimate.

■ Simulation of extreme stress scenarios, including testing of a current portfolio against past periods of significant disturbance. Such testing should incorporate both the large price movements and the sharp reductions in liquidity that are normally associated with these events.

■ Evaluation of the degree of sensitivity of a bank's market risk exposure to changes in assumptions about volatilities and correlations. In other words, the bank's current position should be compared to extreme values within the historical range of variations for volatilities and correlations.

■ Execution of bank-specific test scenarios that capture specific characteristics of a bank's trading portfolio under the most adverse conditions.

The complexity of stress tests normally reflects the complexities of a bank's market risk exposures and respective market environments. The results of stress tests should be reviewed periodically by senior management and the board and should prompt, as necessary, changes in specific risk management policies and exposure limits. If the stress tests reveal a particular vulnerability, the bank should promptly address the situations and risks that give rise to that vulnerability. The stress-test scenarios and the testing results normally are subject to supervisory attention.

Estimates derived from stress tests can also be used for portfolio evaluation and as a management tool. For example, the estimates can be compared to actual profit earned or loss incurred during the period under review. Comparison of the potential impact on profits with reported profits and losses is an added tool for evaluating a bank's market risk management.

11

Currency Risk Management

Key Messages

- Currency risk results from changes in exchange rates and originates in mismatches between the values of assets and liabilities denominated in different currencies.

- Other types of risk that often accompany currency risk are counterparty risk, settlement risk, liquidity risk, and currency-related interest rate risk.

- When assessing currency risk, one must distinguish between the risk originating in political decisions, risk resulting from traditional banking operations, and the risk from trading operations.

- Currency risk is managed by establishing position limits.

- The key currency risk management limit is the net effective open position. The net effective open position of all currencies, added together as absolute values and expressed as a percentage of qualifying capital, should not exceed a predetermined value.

- Currency risk management forms part of the asset-liability management process.

11.1 Introduction: Origin and Components of Currency Risk

Currency risk results from changes in exchange rates between a bank's domestic currency and other currencies. It originates from a mismatch when assets and liabilities are valued in different currencies. That mismatch may cause a bank to experience losses as a result of adverse exchange rate movements when the bank has an open on- or off-balance-sheet position, either spot or forward, in an individual foreign currency. In recent years, a market environment with freely floating exchange rates has practically become the global norm. This has opened the doors for speculative trading opportunities and increased currency risk. The relaxation of exchange controls and the liberalization of cross-border capital movements have fueled a tremendous growth in international financial markets. The volume and growth of global foreign exchange trading has far exceeded the growth of international and capital flows and has contributed to greater exchange rate volatility and therefore currency risk.

Currency risk arises from a mismatch between the value of assets and that of capital and liabilities denominated in foreign currency (or vice versa), or because of a mismatch between foreign receivables and foreign payables that are expressed in domestic currency. Such mismatches may exist between both principal and interest due. Currency risk is speculative and can therefore result in a gain or a loss, depending on the direction of exchange rate shifts and whether a bank is net long or net short in the foreign currency. For example, in the case of a net long position in foreign currency, domestic currency depreciation will result in a net gain for a bank and appreciation will produce a loss. Under a net short position, exchange rate movements will have the opposite effect.

In principle, the fluctuations in the value of domestic currency that create currency risk result from changes in foreign and domestic interest rates that are, in turn, brought about by differences in inflation. Fluctuations such as these are normally motivated by macroeconomic factors and are manifested over relatively long periods of time, although currency market sentiment can often accelerate recognition of the trend. Other macroeconomic aspects that affect the domestic currency value are the volume and direction of a country's trade and capital flows. Short-term factors, such as expected or unexpected political events, changed expectations on the part of market participants, or speculation-based currency trading may also give rise to currency changes. All these factors can affect the supply and demand for a currency and therefore the day-to-day movements of the exchange rate in currency markets. In practical terms, currency risk comprises the following:

- **Transaction risk,** or the price-based impact of exchange rate changes on foreign receivables and foreign payables—that is, the difference in price at which they are collected or paid and the price at which they are recognized in local currency in the financial statements of a bank or corporate entity.

- **Economic or business risk** related to the impact of exchange rate changes on a country's long-term or a company's competitive position.

For example, a depreciation of the local currency may cause a decline in imports and greater exports.

- **Revaluation risk or translation risk,** which arises when a bank's foreign currency positions are revalued in domestic currency or when a parent institution conducts financial reporting or periodic consolidation of financial statements.

Other risks related to international aspects of foreign currency business are incurred by banks conducting foreign exchange operations. One such risk is a form of credit risk that relates to the default of the counterparty to a foreign exchange contract. In such instances, even a bank with balanced books may find itself inadvertently left with an uncovered exchange position. Another form of credit risk peculiar to exchange operations is the time-zone-related settlement risk. This arises when an exchange contract involves two settlements that take place at different times due to a time-zone difference, and the counterparty or the payment agent defaults in the interim. The maturity mismatching of foreign currency positions can also result in interest rate risk between the currencies concerned: a bank can suffer losses as a result of changes in interest rate differentials and of concomitant changes in the forward exchange premiums, or discounts, if it has any mismatches with forward contracts or derivatives of a similar nature.

11.2 Policies for Currency Risk Management

Policy-setting responsibilities. There are many activities of banks that involve risk taking, but there are few in which a bank may so quickly incur large losses as in uncovered foreign exchange transactions. This is why currency risk management deserves the close attention of the bank's board and senior management. The board of directors should establish the objectives and principles of currency risk management. These should specifically include setting appropriate limits to the risks taken by the bank in its foreign exchange business and establishing measures to ensure that there are proper internal control procedures covering this area of the bank's business. Within this framework, specific policies and limits should be determined by a risk management committee such as the asset-liability management committee (ALCO) The policy guidelines should be periodically reviewed and updated to properly match the bank's risk profile with the quality of its risk management systems and staff skills.

The policy guidelines should also reflect changing circumstances in domestic and international currency markets, accommodating possible changes in the currency system—for example, in the form of capital controls introduced as the result of political decisions or underlying macroeconomic conditions of particular countries that would affect the currency exchange rate. In addition, the policies should specify the frequency of revaluation of foreign currency positions for accounting and risk management purposes. In principle, the frequency of revaluation and reporting should be commensurate with the size and specific nature of the bank's currency risk exposures.

For management and control purposes, most banks make a clear distinction between foreign currency exposure resulting from dealing and trading operations, and exposures resulting from a more traditional banking business involving assets, liabilities, and off-balance-sheet exposures denominated in a foreign currency. These may include loans, investments, deposits, borrowings, or capital, as well as guarantees or letters of credit. Because of the different nature of operations and the concomitant risk exposures, banks also typically maintain two types of currency risk management processes. Currency risk management involving dealing/trading operations must be an information-intensive, day-in/day-out process under close scrutiny by senior management and the risk management committee. Management of traditional banking operations, on the other hand, is in most cases carried out on a monthly basis.

Risk Exposure Limits

A bank has a net position in foreign currency and is exposed to currency risk when its assets (including spot and future contracts to purchase) and its liabilities (including spot and future contracts to sell) are not equal in a given currency. Banks should have written policies to govern their activities in foreign currencies and to limit their exposure to currency risk and therefore to potential incurred losses. In principle, limits are established based on the nature of currency risk and the type of business by which that risk is incurred. These limits, whether they are expressed in absolute or relative terms, should be related to a bank's risk profile and capital structure and to the actual history of a currency's market behavior.

Limits may be applicable in various timeframes depending on the dynamics of the particular activity. Limits on dealing/trading are typically established for overnight positions, but for some extremely dynamic activities, such as spot trading, intraday limits may be necessary. The less liquid a currency market is and/or the more volatile the currency is, the lower the currency risk exposure limit should be set.

Net Open Position Limits

The net open position limit is an aggregate limit of a bank's currency risk exposure. Normally expressed as a percentage of the bank's capital, it may also be shown in relation to total assets or to some other benchmark. Logically, the net open position limit represents a proxy for the maximum loss that a bank might incur from currency risk. If the exchange rates of currencies in which a bank holds open positions are perfectly correlated, the limit on a net open position would be sufficient for currency risk management purposes. In terms of aggregation of a bank's exposure to various currencies, the perfect correlation would imply that long and short positions in various currencies could simply be netted.

Because currencies are not perfectly correlated, a bank's choice on how to aggregate net open positions in various currencies to arrive at a total net open position (also known as the gross aggregate position) for currency risk management purposes is an indication of the bank's risk management stance. A conservative bank aggregates by adding together the absolute values of all open positions in specific currencies, implying that the exchange rates of all currencies are expected to move in such a way that all positions would result in simultaneous losses. A less conservative bank often chooses a middle route, such as aggregating all short positions and all long positions in various currencies and taking the larger of the two as an indicator of the aggregate (total) net open position. This latter method, known as the "shorthand method," has been accepted by both the Basel Committee and the European Union.

In many countries, prudential regulations specifically limit the net open position, that is, a bank's total exposure to currency risk. In some countries limits are common for all banks holding a foreign exchange license, while in others the limits are established on a bank-by-bank basis according to the supervisors' assessments of the quality of risk management and the technical capacity of staff. International efforts also have been made to reach agreement on capital requirements related to currency risk, with a view to promoting these capital requirements as an international standard.

In principle, the prudential limit established in a particular country should be related to exchange rate volatility. In practice, the prudential limit to the net open position is frequently set at 10–15 percent of a bank's qualifying capital. In periods when significant domestic currency devaluation is expected, the central bank may further restrict short positions in foreign currencies. In countries with relatively stable exchange rates and external convertibility, net open position limits tend to be higher or nonexistent.

Currency Position Limits

A well-managed bank should also maintain a set of specific limits on its risk exposure to specific currencies—in other words, it should establish limits on net open positions in each currency. Currency position limits can apply to balance sheet revaluation points, overnight positions, or intraday positions. These limits can be adjusted on a case-by-case basis, depending on the bank's expectations of shifts in the exchange rate between the domestic currency and the foreign currency.

Other Position Limits

If engaged in currency dealing/trading, a bank should normally maintain limits on spot positions in each currency. Within these limits it also should establish limits for its individual currency dealers/traders. If a bank is engaged in business with derivatives, it should establish limits on the size of mismatches in the foreign exchange book. These limits are typically expressed as the maximum aggregate value of all contracts that may be outstanding for a particular maturity. Procedures may vary among banks, but specific limits are generally set on a daily basis for contracts maturing in the following week or two, on a biweekly basis for contracts maturing in the next six months, and on a monthly basis for all other contracts.

Stop-Loss Provision

Most banks that actively participate in currency markets also maintain "stop-loss" provisions, or predetermined loss exposure limits on various positions and currencies. Stop-loss exposure limits should be determined based on a bank's overall risk profile, capital structure, and earning trends. When losses reach their respective stop-loss limits, open positions should automatically be covered. In volatile or illiquid markets, however, the stop-loss limit may not be fully effective, and the market may move past a stop-loss trigger before an open position can be closed.

Concentration Limit

The market value of a foreign currency–denominated contract is normally sensitive to both the contract's maturity and the exchange rates between the relevant currencies. High concentration always increases risk. A bank should therefore establish limits on the maximum face value of a contract in specific currencies or on aggregate face values of all contracts combined.

Settlement Risk

Settlement can become complex in the context of foreign currency operations, as it may involve parties in different time zones and hours of operation. An open position may last for several hours. And while actual losses rarely materialize, the size of a potential loss can be large. Settlement risk can be mitigated by a request for collateral, but a bank should also establish specific limits on exposure to settlement risk. These limits should be related to the total amount that is outstanding and subject to settlement risk on any given day. A bank may also establish limits on settlement risk within the total exposure limit placed on a counterparty. In such cases, a limit could be viewed as a component of credit risk.

Counterparty Risk

All transactions involving foreign contracts or foreign currency receivables also involve counterparty risk—the exposure to loss because of the failure of a counterparty to a contract to make the expected payments. Such risk may in turn be a result of circumstances in the country in which the counterparty conducts business. This risk is particularly pronounced in countries that lack external convertibility and where the government imposes restrictions on access to the foreign exchange market and on cross-border foreign exchange transactions. To minimize the risk, a bank should establish counterparty risk limits, especially for counterparties in countries that lack convertibility or where potential exists for the development of a shortage of foreign exchange. Overnight and forward positions to individual counterparties are typical. Conservative banks may also establish country limits related to the total exposure to all counterparties based in a specific country.

Revaluation

Revaluation or translation refers to the points in time when a bank revalues its on- and off-balance-sheet positions to estimate the potential losses that existing positions might produce. Revaluation is essentially the same as "marking to market," except that it pertains to changes (as a result of exchange rate fluctuations) in the domestic currency value of assets, liabilities, and off-balance-sheet instruments that are denominated in foreign currencies. Revaluation is an important risk management tool, regardless of whether gains and losses have to be recognized for tax or supervisory purposes under applicable accounting regimes.

The frequency of revaluation for internal risk management purposes must be attuned to specific market conditions and to the degree of currency risk that is implicit in a bank's operations. When estimating potential gains and losses, a bank should use conservative estimates of potential future exchange rate movements. The determination of realistic exchange rates for revaluation purposes can be complex. Estimates are easiest to make for countries with freely convertible domestic currency and are typically derived from historical exchange rate movements. For countries lacking convertibility or where rates are subject to manipulation or government intervention, estimates are difficult to make because rates can change significantly and unexpectedly. Conservative banks also conduct revaluations under worst-case scenarios. Clearly, not all positions can always be closed out, particularly in countries where there is restricted convertibility or market access. The objective is to determine early enough what measures may need to be taken to protect the bank.

Liquidity Risk Concerns

Currency risk management should incorporate an additional liquidity risk-related aspect. Foreign currency transactions, whether originating on the balance sheet or off the balance sheet, may introduce cash flow imbalances and may require the management of foreign currency liquidity. This process can be carried out using a liquidity or maturity ladder that indicates mismatches and commitments over time in each currency. A bank may also establish limits on mismatches in specific currencies for different time intervals.

In countries where the national currency does not have external convertibility, maturity mismatches result in higher liquidity risk, because a bank may have difficulty acquiring the necessary amount of foreign currency in a timely manner. In such countries, the central bank is often an active participant in foreign exchange markets and may provide the liquidity in foreign exchange that is needed for current account transactions. When assessing the adequacy of a bank's foreign exchange liquidity management in a country that lacks external convertibility, an analyst should, for liquidity support purposes, be thoroughly familiar with the applicable foreign exchange market arrangements.

Accounting Treatment

The accounting treatment of currency risk–related losses is of key importance for a bank's management, as well as for analysts and supervisors. Accounting treatments may vary among countries, depending on the purpose of revaluation. An analyst should be thoroughly familiar with the rules that are locally applicable on the accounting treatment of gains or losses arising from currency risk. The analyst should also be familiar with the process of revaluation and with the accounting rules used by a bank under review for risk and internal management reporting purposes.

Making rules for the recognition of gains or losses that have immediate tax and other implications requires careful consideration by authorities and bank regulators. This is particularly important in unstable and volatile economies that lack external convertibility and that are characterized by frequent and drastic domestic exchange rate adjustments. In many transition economies, a depreciation of the national currency against the currencies of major trading partners by 200 percent per annum is not uncommon, and depreciation by 30–50 percent is frequent. Analysts and supervisors must be extremely careful when interpreting the financial statements of banks in such environments.

For tax and supervisory purposes, revaluations of balance sheet positions are usually considered to be realized gains or losses, and revaluations of off-balance-sheet positions are considered unrealized. The most conservative approach requires that all gains and losses be promptly reflected in earnings. Some regulators require that only realized gains or losses and unrealized losses be reflected in earnings. Some countries also permit the deferment of recognition of both unrealized gains and unrealized losses, resulting in misstated capital and earnings.

In developing countries, the apparent application of a standard accounting treatment of gains and losses may be counterproductive if the taxation system requires tax payment on all gains, even if the assets are subject to sale restrictions. In a country with a currency that is depreciating rapidly, even a small open position may create accounting adjustments in amounts that are comparable to or even greater than a bank's business in the domestic currency. An example that illustrates this point is a situation that occurred in a transition economy where accounting adjustments of bank balance sheets resulting from exchange rate movements were considered realized gains or losses. In the process of banking system rehabilitation, assets of impaired value were replaced by government securities denominated in freely convertible currencies, such as U.S. dollars. This created large net long positions in the banking sector. In the case in question, banks were not allowed to sell or trade bonds if the discount factor was greater than 10 percent, making it impossible for them to close or reduce long positions. Subsequent significant devaluation of the national currency created large "realized" foreign exchange gains that were duly taxed. This in turn resulted in the drain of liquidity from the banking sector and significant damage to the banking sector and the entire economy.

11.3 Currency Risk Exposure and Business Strategy

Most banks, especially those operating in countries with unstable currencies, are keenly aware of the risks associated with foreign currency business. The degree of currency risk exposure is therefore a matter of business orientation and is often related to a bank's size. Smaller and new banks often limit their business to servicing the foreign currency needs of their customers. This involves selling or buying foreign currency on the customer's behalf, a process whereby the open currency positions that such transactions create normally are closed within minutes. Such banks, exposed to currency risk for very short periods of time and to a limited extent, therefore do not need elaborate currency risk management.

Banks that maintain correspondent banking relationships with foreign banks or that support customer transactions denominated in foreign currencies are exposed to much higher levels of currency risk. The risk is higher still for banks that lend and borrow in foreign currency, as this may result in open currency positions or maturity mismatches. This business profile is typical of medium-size banks or larger banks in developing countries. Figure 11.1 illustrates the potential volume of foreign currency business as part of a bank's balance sheet structure in a developing country.

Figure 11.1 Currency Structure of Assets and Liabilities

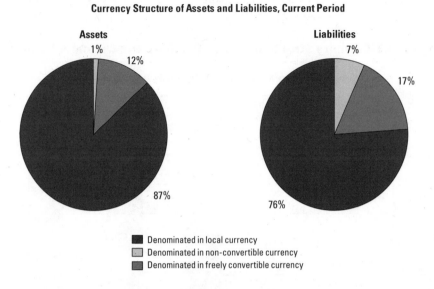

Currency Structure of Assets and Liabilities, Current Period

■ Denominated in local currency
☐ Denominated in non-convertible currency
■ Denominated in freely convertible currency

Banks that are engaged in such activities should operate the appropriate currency risk management policies. The extent of operations and risk taking should correspond to the quality of the bank's risk management process and its capital position—and should be in line with the regulatory, macroeconomic, and financial market environment of each respective country. In practical terms, currency risk management can be an especially challenging task in countries that lack external convertibility. Exchange rate stability can be contrived because conditions in the currency markets of such countries—such as the right of access and the type of transactions that are allowed in the market—are often subject to manipulation by the authorities. Markets that are shallow can be greatly influenced by expectations, and exchange rate adjustments, when they occur, tend to be drastic and are often introduced at unexpected times. Banks operating in such environments are exposed to a much higher degree of currency risk, and it is much more difficult to determine sound limits to such exposure.

Figure 11.2 illustrates a bank's currency structure of loans and deposits. The bank is clearly on a fast growth path. Its loan portfolio significantly exceeds the funding capacity provided by its deposit base and indicates that the growth has been fueled by nondeposit borrowings, which probably includes foreign borrowings. The bank is therefore exposed to funding and currency risk. For a bank in a developing country, where access to international markets may be limited, subject to restrictions, or even closed by circumstances over which the bank has no control, a foreign exchange position such as this entails a high-risk exposure.

Figure 11.2 Currency Structure of Loan Portfolio and Customer Deposits

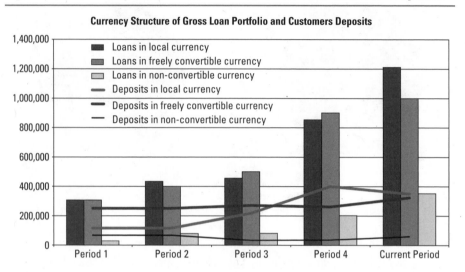

Currency Structure of Gross Loan Portfolio and Customers Deposits

Recognition of the increased risk and of the needed technical skills associated with the foreign exchange business has prompted regulators in almost all countries that do not maintain external convertibility to introduce two types of bank licenses. For a license to operate only in its domestic currency, a bank has to satisfy only minimum capital and technical requirements. A bank wishing to also operate in foreign currencies must meet much higher minimum capital and other requirements to obtain a license. The minimum capital needed for a foreign exchange license is typically two to three times more than is required for a domestic currency license.

Spot Trading

Large and well-capitalized banks, including so-called internationally active banks, look to foreign exchange operations as a source of profits. Such banks actively engage in currency trading and may play the role *of market makers*; in other words, they may become dealers in foreign currencies. Banks engaged in currency markets and spot trading may carry sizeable net open positions, although for relatively brief periods of time. In certain circumstances, however, spot rate movements may become so rapid that an open position results in losses in hours or even minutes. In addition to adequate foreign exchange risk management policies, spot trading requires effective organization and technically competent staff, sophisticated technology and effective information systems, and access to up-to-the-minute information. Banks that lack adequate information resources are much more vulnerable to sudden spot rate movements prompted by temporarily unbalanced supply-and-demand conditions, inside information, or rumors.

A bank may deliberately maintain open positions to take advantage of expected exchange rate movements. This usually takes a form of currency market arbitrage, or sometimes speculation, and involves the buying and selling of foreign currencies, securities, or derivatives. This arbitrage is motivated by discrepancies between spot exchange rates prevailing at the same time in different markets, or differences between forward margins for various maturities or interest rates that exist concurrently in different markets or currencies. Buying a currency in one market for simultaneous sale in another market is termed arbitrage in space; the creation of an open position in a currency in anticipation of a favorable future exchange rate movement is arbitrage in time. Switching from one currency to another to invest funds at a higher yield is currency-related interest arbitrage. From the point of view of the supervisory authorities, however, any deliberate assumption of risk on an open position is usually characterized as speculation, rather than arbitrage.

Forward Transactions

Banks may also be engaged in forward foreign exchange transactions, which are settled on the agreed date and at agreed exchange rates. the maturity of the forward contract can be a few days, months, or years. Forward rates are affected not only by spot rates, which are normally influenced by market conditions, but also by interest rate differentials. A change in differentials may therefore result in a profit or a loss on a forward position, requiring that these be actively managed. This in turn requires a significant capacity for information processing. In this case, a bank should maintain a forward book, which is usually managed on a gap (mismatch) basis. A forward book typically necessitates a close look, on a weekly or a biweekly basis, at forward positions for contracts nearing maturity, and a look on a monthly basis for other contracts. A bank may take a view regarding expected movements in interest rate differentials and then manage its forward positions in a way that is compatible with expected movements.

Currency Swaps

Banks averse to risk may avoid dealing in forward contracts altogether and instead engage in currency swaps. Two parties to a currency swap agreement exchange a series of payments in different currencies at agreed dates and a preagreed exchange rate. A single period swap is referred to as a forward rate agreement. A currency swap avoids a net open currency position but still has to be marked to market. In any case, in a normally dynamic trading environment, it is virtually impossible for a bank active in currency markets to maintain covered positions in all currencies at all times. Short or long positions in various currencies alternate any number of times during the course of a day. At certain times, established by its currency risk management procedures, a bank therefore typically determines its open positions and takes the necessary actions to cover excessive risk exposures, usually by arranging for swaps.

Prudent risk management for a bank normally engaged in a large number of spot and forward transactions each day requires the establishment of a formal procedure for computing unrealized profits and losses at least on a daily basis—and calculations more frequent than this are desirable. Such calculations should normally include the entire foreign exchange book. This is a precondition for effective portfolio management and provides a bank's management with a meaningful insight into the performance of its foreign exchange operations and the associated risk.

11.4 Review of Currency Risk Management Procedures

The volume of a bank's foreign currency operations, including its standard on- and off-balance-sheet operations in foreign exchange and trading operations, should normally be determined by the access conditions of and liquidity in respective markets. When assessing a bank's exposure to currency risk and the adequacy of its risk management techniques, an analyst must be aware of the regulatory environment and market conditions in the relevant countries and of the bank's access to those markets. Currency markets in developing countries often have restricted access and may lack liquidity, and the availability of adequate hedging instruments may be limited. These factors should be reflected in the bank's policies and operations.

A key aspect of currency risk management review is the assessment of whether or not a bank has the capacity to adequately handle its level of operations in foreign exchange. The bank's currency risk exposure policies, the extent to which risks are taken, risk management procedures, and exactly how exposures are managed all must be taken into consideration. A review should also take into consideration the bank's regulatory and market environment, its asset size, capital base, customer volume in foreign exchange, the experience of its staff, and other relevant factors. The nature and availability of instruments that can be used to hedge or offset currency risk are also critical.

The key determinant of currency risk management is the policies that place limits on currency risk exposure. Policies should be reassessed on a regular basis to reflect potential changes in exchange rate volatility and an institution's over-all risk philosophy and profile. The limits should be established in the context of an institution's overall risk profile to reflect aspects such as capital adequacy, liquidity, credit quality, market risk, and interest rate risk. The relative impor-tance of each policy depends on a particular bank's circumstances and opera-tions. All applicable policies and procedures, including operational guidelines, should be clearly defined and adjusted whenever necessary. Senior management responsible for policy making must fully understand the risks involved in for-eign exchange operations. The basis upon which specific policies and exposure limits are formed must be clearly explained in a consistent and logical manner.

The Basel recommendation for supervisors and management is to ensure that a bank has in place appropriate limits and that it implements adequate internal controls for its foreign exchange business. Risk procedures should cover the level of foreign currency exposure that an institution is prepared to assume and, at a minimum, should include intraday, overnight, and forward limits for cur-rencies in which an institution is authorized to have an exposure—individually and for all currencies combined. Stop-loss limits and settlement limits should also be determined.

Currency risk management can be based on gap or mismatch analysis using the same principles as liquidity risk and interest rate risk management. The pro-cess should aim to determine the appropriate mismatch or imbalance between maturing foreign assets and liabilities. This mismatch can be evaluated in light of basic information such as current and expected exchange rates, interest rates (both locally and abroad), and the risk-return profile that is acceptable to bank management. (The market risk related to currency trading is discussed in detail in chapter 10.)

Table 11.1 illustrates a simplistic method to calculate the net effective open position. The calculation of a net effective open position in a currency should consider the exposures reflected both on and off the balance sheet and should include the net spot position (that is, all asset items minus all liability items, including accrued interest denominated in the currency in question); net forward position (that is, amounts to be received minus amounts to be paid under forward foreign exchange transactions, plus the principal on currency swaps not included in the spot position); mismatched forward commitments; net positions in derivatives; and positions resulting from operations in foreign branches.

Table 11.1 Currency: Reporting Net Effective Open Position

Net Effective Open Position in Foreign Currencies (FX)	US Dollars	UK Sterling	Euro	Swiss Francs	Japanese Yen	Total
Total foreign currency assets						
Total foreign currency liabilities						
Net spot position						
Mismatched forward commitment						
Foreign branches/ operations						
Net position in derivatives						
Net effective open position after hedging						
Maximum net open position during the month						

The net position in all currencies should be aggregated and attention paid to the exact method of aggregation of the open positions that is used by the bank. A conservative bank should aggregate by adding the absolute value of open positions, thereby projecting the worst possible scenario for exchange rate movements.

Banks in many developing countries often handle freely convertible currencies as a single currency for risk management purposes. The rationale for this approach is that risk exposure arising from movements in the exchange rates of hard currencies is much less than that arising from fluctuations in domestic currency. In addition, the grouping of freely convertible currencies simplifies currency risk management. While this system is usually adequate in countries where banks are not engaged in forward contracts or derivatives, situations exist in which this system may backfire. For example, environmental disasters, political events, and announcements of unexpectedly bad macroeconomic indicators may promptly and significantly increase cross-currency risk.

When mismatches in the maturity structure occur, interest rate and liquidity risk develops. A bank should have well-defined procedures for the management of such mismatches to maximize income and limit potential loss. Figure 11.3 illustrates the analysis of a foreign currency deposits maturity structure. The maturity structure of loans funded by these deposits should fully correspond to the deposit maturity structure. If a bank's risk management policies permit the running of mismatches, the analyst should look for evidence that the bank is performing effective "what if" studies. Doing so will help the bank attain an effective limit structure.

Managing maturity mismatches is a challenging task. With regard to maturity gaps in the forward book, the key issue is not the expected behavior of interest rates in relation to the various maturities of a single currency, but the expected differential between the interest rates of two currencies for various maturities and the respective risk implications. This is obviously a more complex situation than the management of interest rate risk for a single currency. Furthermore, the elimination of maturity gaps on a contract-by-contract basis is practically impossible for a bank that is actively involved in currency markets and that has a foreign exchange book made up of hundreds of outstanding contracts.

Maturity gaps are typically handled by the use of swaps. This is a relatively sound risk management practice as long as any changes in exchange rates are gradual and the size and the length of maturity gaps managed systematically and reasonably well. This procedure, however, can result in high costs for bridging maturity gaps in situations where sudden and unexpected changes in interest rates occur that can momentarily influence the market quotations for swap transactions.

Figure 11.3 Freely Convertible Currency Deposit Maturities as a Percentage of Total Customer Deposits

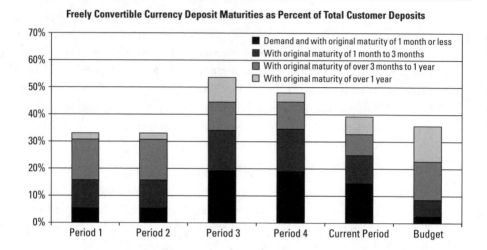

Freely Convertible Currency Deposit Maturities as Percent of Total Customer Deposits

Legend:
- Demand and with original maturity of 1 month or less
- With original maturity of 1 month to 3 months
- With original maturity of over 3 months to 1 year
- With original maturity of over 1 year

X-axis: Period 1, Period 2, Period 3, Period 4, Current Period, Budget

Capital Charges

Currency risk exposure implies certain capital charges that are added to the charge calculated for market risk (see chapter 6). A bank clearly should be able to prudently carry currency risk. According to various country guidelines, the net open foreign currency position established by a bank should not exceed 10–15 percent of qualifying capital and reserves. Using the shorthand method, capital adequacy is calculated as 8 percent (or the regulatory percentage for the country, if different from 8 percent) of the overall net open position. The overall net open position is measured as the greater of the sum of the net short positions and the sum of the net long positions, plus the net position (short or long) in gold, regardless of the sign. Figures 11.4 and 11.5 illustrate the open positions of a bank in the various currencies in which it operates, expressed as a percentage of its capital and including aggregate exposure—that is, the net (absolute) open foreign currency position.

Figure 11.4 Currency Risk Exposure as a Percentage of Qualifying Capital

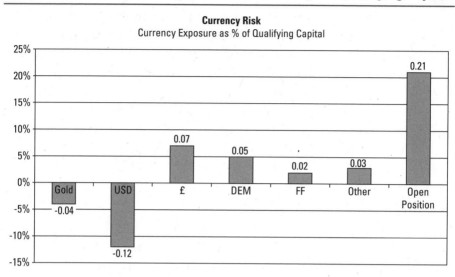

Currency Risk
Currency Exposure as % of Qualifying Capital

Figure 11.5 Maximum Effective Net Open Foreign Currency Position as a Percentage of Net Qualifying Capital and Reserves

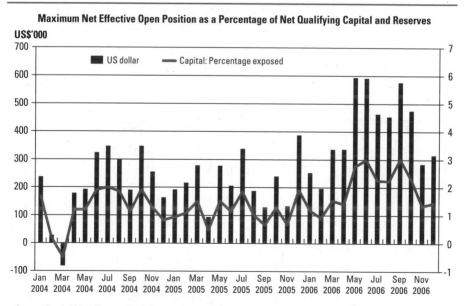

Maximum Net Effective Open Position as a Percentage of Net Qualifying Capital and Reserves

Source: South African Reserve Bank, Banking Supervision Department Annual Report 2006

273

Alert Systems

A bank also should maintain a system of alerts for situations in which limits are exceeded. An analyst should expect the bank to have well-defined procedures, including clear assignments of responsibilities, to handle alerts. Adequate procedures and internal controls should be in place for all other key functions related to foreign exchange operations. The analyst also should assess the procedures and practices for revaluation and for measuring foreign exchange trading gains and losses. A prudent bank should carefully review the names of institutions and individuals with which it does forward exchange business and should request margin cover wherever it is deemed appropriate.

Staffing

The efficient organization and quality of staff are a crucial part of currency risk management. In sum, the skills and experience of staff should be commensurate with the scope of a bank's operations. Responsibility for trading, standard foreign exchange operations, processing of transactions and payments, front- and back-office (operations) support and account reconciliation, risk management, and revaluation functions should all be clearly separated. Especially critical is the separation of foreign exchange dealing, accounting, and internal control functions. Policies should be formulated by the board and determined by ALCO. Line management should be responsible for overseeing foreign currency transactions and ensuring compliance with risk limits.

Information Systems

The analyst should assess information systems; reporting requirements; and the accounting, auditing, and internal control systems that support foreign exchange operations and the currency risk management function and that allow for proper surveillance. Accurate and timely information support is especially critical: a bank with a high volume of foreign exchange operations must have proper information support if it is to develop strategies for trading operations and executing specific transactions. Information support also is needed to manage open currency positions, account for transactions and keep the foreign exchange book, revalue the financial position, estimate potential gains and losses, and ensure compliance with risk management policies. An analyst should be able to identify the subsystems or modules that support these functions.

In addition, information systems should be capable of generating timely and complete management reports on spot and forward positions, mismatches and liquidity positions, foreign currency–related interest rate risk positions, and counterpart and country exposure positions. Information systems should have the capacity to highlight any exceptions to policy or exposure limits and to bring such exceptions to the attention of management. Information support should include regular reporting to senior management.

12

Asset-Liability Management

Key Messages

■ Interest rate risk management is one of the key aspects of asset-liability management.

■ The asset-liability management committee addresses the protection of both income and capital from interest rate risk. The goal of interest rate risk management is to maintain interest rate risk exposures within authorized levels.

■ Nontrading interest rate risk is the sensitivity of capital and income to changes in interest rates.

■ Nontrading interest rate risk originates in mismatches in the repricing of assets and liabilities, growth rates of interest-bearing assets and liabilities, changes in relationships between rate indexes (basis risk), changes in the shape of the yield curve, and the potential exercise of explicit or embedded options.

■ Banks generally attempt to ensure that the repricing structure of their balance sheet generates maximum benefits from expected interest rate movements. This repricing structure may also be influenced by liquidity issues, particularly if the bank does not have access to interest rate derivatives to separate its liquidity and interest rate views.

■ Banks measure these risks and their impact by identifying and quantifying exposures through use of sophisticated simulation and valuation models, as well as a repricing gap analysis.

12.1 Objective of Asset-Liability Management

Asset-liability management (ALM)—the management of the overall balance sheet—comprises the strategic planning and implementation and the control processes that affect the volume, mix, maturity, interest rate sensitivity, quality, and liquidity of a bank's assets and liabilities. These key elements are highly interdependent.

The central objective of this process—to stabilize and maximize the spread between interest paid to raise funds and interest earned on the bank's assets, and at the same time to ensure adequate liquidity and to constrain risk to acceptable levels—is as old as banking business itself. The practices, norms, and techniques of asset-liability management have, however, changed substantially in recent years, with many commercial banks using the ALM process to take more risk to enhance income. Moreover, given the complexity and volatility of modern financial markets, the need for good asset-liability management has significantly increased. Adoption of a formal approach to asset-liability management is therefore a prerequisite for an integrated approach to managing the risks associated with balance sheet and off-balance-sheet items.

The operational aspects of asset-liability management center around the structuring of a bank's balance sheet so the bank can maintain an adequate liquidity and risk profile throughout an interest rate cycle. Bank balance sheets are not totally flexible, in part because assets with long maturities are difficult to securitize or sell. Because it can take some time to change the asset portfolio structure, raise alternative sources of funding, and execute the necessary transactions, the repositioning process normally starts even before the next interest rate cycle begins.

All financial institutions face interest rate risk. When interest rates fluctuate, a bank's earnings and expenses change, as do the economic value of its assets, liabilities, and off-balance-sheet positions. The net effect of these changes is reflected in the bank's overall income and capital.

Broadly speaking, interest rate risk management comprises the various policies, actions, and techniques that a bank can use to reduce the risk of diminution of its net equity as a result of adverse changes in interest rates. This chapter discusses various aspects of interest rate risk and reviews the techniques available to analyze and manage it. These include, in particular, repricing and sensitivity analyses.

Asset-Liability Management Committee

The ALM strategy and related decisions should take into account and be able to accommodate all relevant limitations and potential distractions. The actions of both bank and nonbank competitors can affect (re)pricing potential. Unforeseen developments on the domestic or international front, such as the financial crisis in East Asia, or changes in expectations can influence customer or market behavior and require complex adjustments.

ALM decisions should be coordinated across the relevant operational divisions and must be effectively executed (see box 12.1). This necessitates the establishment of a formal institutional structure responsible for ALM. In most banks, this structure typically is an asset-liability management committee (ALCO), the membership of which should include senior line managers of all relevant functional and business processes.

For ALCO decisions to be meaningful, the committee should have at its disposal a broad range of essential information related to investment and trading portfolios; the historical, current, and projected structure of the bank's assets and liabilities; and relevant information on maturities, yields, interest rates and spreads, and repricing capacity and structure. The ALCO should also be informed about the competitive position of the bank's assets, liability rates, and yields in relation to both the market and the bank's major competitors. The projected balance sheet structure and the repositioning strategy should normally be based on a quantitative model of the balance sheet, following a simulation of various interest rates and (re)pricing scenarios and their effects on the bank's earnings, liquidity, and capital.

Box 12.1 ALM Objective

In managing the Bank's balance sheet, our objective is to ensure that the currency, interest rate, and maturity characteristics of the Bank's liabilities and assets are well-aligned, so that the Bank is not exposed to material currency, interest rate, or maturity mismatch risks.

We aim to ensure adequate funding for each product at the most attractive cost, and to manage the currency composition, maturity profile, and interest rate sensitivity characteristics of the portfolio of liabilities supporting each lending product in accordance with the particular requirements for that product and within prescribed risk parameters.

We shall achieve our objectives through implementation of an asset and liability management (ALM) framework leading to a portfolio-wide assessment and monitoring of balance sheet risks. This framework will enable us to advance broader balance sheet risk management issues such as

- upgrading the Bank's approach to management of its equity, income immunization techniques, and loan portfolio credit risk management;

- consolidating the portfolio-wide approach to hedging and managing the balance sheet risks so as to exploit transaction netting opportunities and reduce transaction costs;

- executing and implementing currency and interest rate swap transactions as needed to manage all aspects of the Bank's balance sheet risks.

—Example from a Treasury ALM Group

12.2 Interest Rate Risk Management Responsibilities

In principle, the sound management of interest rate risk requires systematic and adequate oversight by senior management. Also needed are risk management policies and procedures that are clearly spelled out and that are commensurate to the complexity and nature of a bank's activities and the level of its exposure to interest rate risk; appropriate risk measurement, monitoring, and control functions; and adequate internal controls. Interest rate risk should be monitored on a consolidated basis, including the exposure of subsidiaries. This does not imply the use of conventional accounting consolidation—which may allow offsets between positions from which a bank may not in practice be able to benefit, because of legal or operational constraints—but rather the use of proper mechanisms to ensure the completeness and integrity of the information on which the risk management decisions are made.

The bank's board of directors has ultimate responsibility for the management of interest rate risk. The board approves the business strategies that determine the degree of exposure to risk and provides guidance on the level of interest rate risk that is acceptable to the bank; on the policies that limit risk exposure; and on the procedures, lines of authority, and accountability related to risk management. The board also should systematically review risk to fully understand the level of risk exposure and to assess the performance of management in monitoring and controlling risks in compliance with board policies.

Senior management must ensure that the structure of a bank's business and the level of interest rate risk it assumes are effectively dealt with, that appropriate polices and procedures are established to control and limit risk, and that resources are available to assess and control it. Reports to senior management should provide aggregate information and a sufficient level of supporting detail to facilitate a meaningful evaluation of the level of risk, the sensitivity of the bank to changing market conditions, and other relevant factors.

In most cases, day-to-day risk assessment and management is assigned to a specialized committee, such as ALCO. Duties pertaining to key elements of the risk management process should be adequately separated to avoid potential conflicts of interest—in other words, a bank's risk monitoring and control functions should be sufficiently independent from its risk-taking functions. Larger or more complex banks often have a designated, independent unit responsible for the design and administration of balance sheet management, including interest rate risk. Given today's widespread innovation in banking and the dynamics of markets, banks should identify any risks inherent in a new product or service before it is introduced and ensure that these risks are promptly considered in the assessment and management process.

Banks should also have an adequate system of internal controls to oversee the interest rate risk management process. A fundamental component of such a system is a regular, independent review and evaluation to ensure the system's effectiveness and, when appropriate, to recommend revisions or enhancements. Supervisory authorities often require the results of such reviews.

The defined limits of risk should be enforced and banks should introduce adequate procedures to keep risk exposures within those limits and to change the limits when they prove inadequate. At a senior level, limits are normally established relative to a bank's total income or capital and then are broken down by portfolios, activities, or business units. The design of the system of limits should ensure that positions that exceed assigned limits are promptly addressed by management.

The goal of interest rate risk management in the balance sheet is, therefore, to maintain risk exposure within authorized levels, which may be expressed in terms of risk to income, the market value of equity, or both.

12.3 Models for the Management of Interest Rate Risk in the Balance Sheet

Banks should have clearly defined policies and procedures for limiting and controlling interest rate risk. The interest rate risk measurement system employed by a bank should comprise all material sources of interest rate risk and should be sufficient to assess the effect of interest rate changes on both earnings and economic value. The system should also provide a meaningful measure of the bank's interest rate exposure and should be capable of identifying any excessive exposures that may arise. It is important that it be based on well-documented and realistic assumptions and parameters. The system should cover all assets, liabilities, and off-balance-sheet positions, should use generally accepted financial concepts and risk measurement techniques, and should provide bank management with an integrated and consistent view of risk in relation to all products and business lines.

"Gap" Model

It was common practice in the 1980s and early 1990s for financial institutions to analyze their exposure to interest rate risk using the "gap" approach. This approach is so named because it aims to allocate assets and liabilities to maturity "buckets," defined according to their repricing characteristics, and to measure the "gap" at each maturity point.

In a gap model, the components of the balance sheet are separated into items that are sensitive to interest rates and those that are not. These are in turn sorted by repricing period (or modified duration) and allocated to time periods known as time or maturity buckets. Maturity buckets should be set up based on key rates (described as specific maturity points on the spot rate curve) and should take into consideration the correlation of yields.

It is important to note that the focus of this analysis is on repricing (that is, the point at which interest rates may be changed) and not on the concept of liquidity and cash flow. In terms of this approach to risk management, the gap is closed when the repricing of rate-sensitive assets and liabilities is adequately matched. Table 12.1 illustrates a simplified framework for conducting a repricing gap analysis.

A positive gap indicates that a higher level of assets than liabilities reprice in the time frame of the maturity bucket—a balance sheet position that is also referred to as asset sensitive. This would give rise to higher income should the specific yield increase. The opposite balance sheet position is referred to as liability sensitive or as negative gap, and describes a situation in which a similar increase in the yields associated with a specific time interval would produce a decrease in net interest income.

Theoretically, once a balance sheet repricing position is known, a framework is put into place to judge the overall exposure of a bank to interest rate fluctuations. Management then has the option of structuring a balance sheet to produce a zero gap, which would presumably immunize a bank from interest rate fluctuations. Such protection may, however, also result in a lower level of net interest margins. Banks generally attempt to ensure that the repricing structure of their balance sheet generates maximum benefits from expected interest rate movements. For example, if a bank expects short-term yields to increase, it would want more assets than liabilities to be repriced in the short term. This is not always possible in practice because of the structural difficulties in illiquid markets, or because exchange controls limit access to offshore markets and to instruments that are designed to help manage risk exposure.

Table 12.1 A Repricing Gap Model for Interest Rate Risk Management

Balance Sheet Items – Duration / Economic Value of Equity							
1	2	3	4	5	6	7	8
Assets / Repricing – Key Rates	Balance Sheet $ million	6 months	12 months	2 years	30	Zero	Key Rate Duration
Assets and Approximate Duration (years)	Amount	0.25	0.5	1	15	0	Calculated
Cash and balances with the Central Bank	4.000	4						0.25
Securities portfolio (includes stand-alone and hedging derivatives)	34.000	1	3	22	8		4.23
Fair value of positions in derivatives	4.000	4					0.25
Inter-bank placements	14.000	10		4			0.46
Loans and advances to other customers	76.000		15	46	15		3.66
Fixed assets net of depreciation	2.000					2	0.00
Other assets (net of provisions)	6.000					6	0.00
Total Assets	**140.000**	**19**	**18**	**72**	**23**	**8**	**3.08**
Weighted Duration of Assets	**3.08**	**0.03**	**0.06**	**0.51**	**2.46**	**0.00**	**3.08**
ALM Derivatives							
Weighted duration of assets – after ALM derivatives							
Liabilities and Owners Capital							
Due to other banks and credit institutions	14.000	14					0.25
Core funding – retail and corporate core deposits	45.000	14	11	5	15		5.31
Non-core funding	8.000	8					0.25
Foreign funding	24.000	12	12				0.38
Fair value of liabilities in respect of derivatives	0.000						
Other borrowings	23.000	8	9		6		4.20
Other liabilities	4.000					4	0.00
Subordinated Debt	2.000				2		15.00
Total Liabilities	**120.000**	**56**	**32**	**5**	**23**	**4**	**3.17**
Weighted Duration of Liabilities	**3.17**	**0.12**	**0.13**	**0.04**	**2.88**	**0.00**	**3.17**

Table 12.1 continued

Balance Sheet Items – Duration / Economic Value of Equity							
1	2	3	4	5	6	7	8
Assets / Repricing – Key Rates	Balance Sheet $ million	6 months	12 months	2 years	30	ZERO	Key Rate Duration
Shareholder's Equity	20.000						
Total Liabilities & Capital	140.000						0.00
GAP	-0.09	-0.08	-0.07	0.47	-0.41	0.00	-0.09
Duration of Equity – prior to hedging	2.54						
ALM Derivatives							
Weighted duration of liabilities – after ALM derivatives							
Duration of Equity – after using ALM derivatives							
Calculation of EVE: 2.54 = [3.08*140 - 3.17*120]/20							

One of the benefits of a repricing gap model is the single numeric result, which provides a straightforward target for hedging purposes. Unfortunately, a repricing gap is a static measure and does not give the complete picture. Where management uses only current-year income to judge rate sensitivity, the repricing approach tends to overlook or downplay the effects of mismatches on medium- or long-term positions. Gap analysis also does not take into account variations in the characteristics of different positions within a time band; in other words, all positions within a time band are assumed to mature or reprice simultaneously. In reality, this will happen only to the extent the yields within the maturity bucket are highly or perfectly correlated and reprice off the same yield curve. A cumulative gap can arise from a number of different incremental gap patterns and may obscure yield curve exposures, that is, sensitivity to the changes in the shape of the yield curve. In addition, gap analysis does not consider expected changes in balance sheet structure and ignores both basis risk and the sensitivity of income to option-related positions.

There are other limitations also to the efficacy of gap analysis. The level of net interest margin (the ultimate target of interest rate risk management) is normally determined by the relative yields and volumes of balance sheet items, the ongoing dynamics of which cannot be fully addressed by a static model. Moreover, a static gap model assumes linear reinvestment—a constant reinvestment pattern for forecast net interest income—and that funding decisions in the future will be similar to the decisions that resulted in the bank's original repricing schedule. A static gap model thus usually fails to predict the impact of a change in funding strategy on net interest margins.

Repricing gap models nonetheless are a useful starting point for the assessment of interest rate exposure. Banks also have over time progressed from simple gap analysis to more sophisticated techniques. Ideally, a bank's interest rate measurement system will take into account the specific characteristics of each interest-sensitive position and will capture in detail the full range of potential movements. As this is in practice extremely difficult to accomplish, in most instances an ALCO will employ a variety of methodologies for interest rate risk analysis.

Sensitivity Analysis

This process applies different interest rate scenarios to a static gap model of a bank's balance sheet. (See also table 10.3.)

Simulation

This process involves constructing a large and often complex model of a bank's balance sheet. Such a model will be dynamic over time and will integrate numerous variables. The objective of a simulation exercise is to measure the sensitivity of net interest income, earnings, and capital to changes in key variables. The risk variables used include varying interest rate paths and balance sheet volumes. Simulation is highly dependent on assumptions, and it requires significant time before the inputs made yield meaningful results; it may therefore be more useful as a business planning tool than for interest rate risk measurement. If it is used as a risk measurement tool, the parameters should be highly controlled to generate as objective a measure of risk as possible.

Duration Analysis

Table 12.1 illustrates the importance of bank management focusing on the duration of the balance sheet as a whole, including the duration contribution of any derivatives position.

Interest rate risk is measured by calculating the weighted average duration of *all* assets, liabilities, and off-balance-sheet positions and then measuring the sensitivity of the equity to a change in interest rates.

The duration analysis model is then used to determine the effective duration of equity (or the economic value of equity, EVE, the exposure of the bank's equity to interest rate risk). It has the advantage of providing a longer-term perspective than other models, such as simulation and interest rate gap models, which focus on current earnings, and is thus typically used as a complementary measure to set acceptable bands within which the duration exposure of capital may vary.

Current Market Practice

The more sophisticated banking institutions use a mixture of risk management strategies. Banks increasingly use derivative instruments such as swaps, options, and forward-rate agreements to hedge interest rate exposure, and techniques such as simulation and duration analysis, still provide useful information regarding the impact of these instruments on a bank's interest rate position.

Banks should measure their vulnerability to loss under stressful market conditions, including the breakdown of the key assumptions on which their interest rate models are built, and should consider the results of any such assessment when establishing and reviewing their policies and limits on interest rate risk. The stress test should be tailored to the risk characteristics of a bank; it should also be designed to provide information on the circumstances in which the bank would be most vulnerable—when the assumptions and parameters on which the interest rate risk measurement or simulation models are based would experience sudden or abrupt changes. Test scenarios should consider such abrupt changes in the general level of interest rates and in the relationships among key market rates (especially those commonly used as index rates), and also should address potential changes in the volatility and liquidity conditions in all markets where the bank maintains a presence.

Because interest rate risk can have adverse effects on both a bank's earnings and its economic value, two separate but complementary approaches exist for assessing risk exposure: net interest income (NII) simulation and economic value of equity (EVE) analysis. The following information comes from a very informative discussion of NII and EVE contained in several annual reports of Sun Trust Bank.

Net Interest Income

From the perspective of earnings, which is the traditional approach to interest rate risk assessment, this analysis focuses on the impact of interest rate changes on a bank's net interest income.

Future interest rates cannot be predicted, but management can simulate the impact on net interest income under a variety of scenarios, including gradual changes in rates, rapid changes, economic shocks, and growing and shrinking yield curves. The simulation may incorporate likely customer behavior under a given set of facts, or it may test possible outcomes assuming unlikely behaviors or an extreme event. The simulation can be used to analyze the effect of alternative strategies on NII levels.

Figure 12.1 depicts the estimated sensitivity of NII to gradual changes in interest rates. The sensitivity is measured as a percentage change from the forecasted NII assuming stable interest rates for the next 12 months.

As shown in figure 12.1, a gradual decrease in interest rates (during period 3) would increase NII, and a gradual increase in interest rates would reduce NII.

Figure 12.1 Net Interest Income Sensitivity

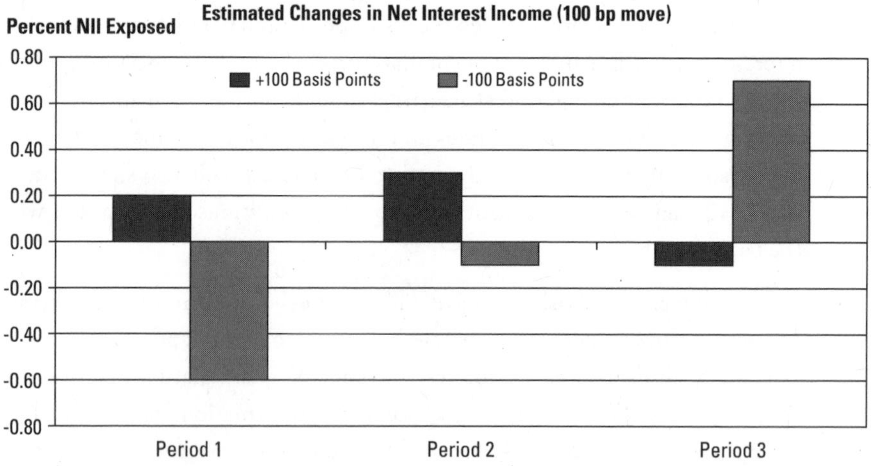

Economic Value of Equity

The impact of interest rate changes on the economic value of equity (EVE) reflects the sensitivity of the bank's net worth to fluctuations in interest rates.

EVE provides a more comprehensive measure of the potential long-term effects of interest rate changes than models that focus on earnings.

While NII simulation highlights interest rate risk over a relatively short time, EVE analysis incorporates all cash flows over the estimated remaining life of all balance sheet and derivative positions. The sensitivity of EVE to changes in the level of interest rates is a measure of the longer-term repricing risk and options risk embedded in the balance sheet. In contrast to the NII simulation, which assumes interest rates will change *gradually* over a period of time, EVE uses *instantaneous* changes in rates.

Because EVE measures the discounted present value of cash flows over the estimated lives of instruments, the change in EVE does not directly correlate to the degree that earnings would be affected over a shorter period, such as the current fiscal year. Further, EVE does not take into account factors such as future balance sheet growth, changes in product mix, changes in yield curve relationships, and changing product spreads that could mitigate the adverse impact of changes in interest rates.

Figure 12.2 reflects the estimated sensitivity of equity to changes in interest rates. The sensitivity is measured as the percentage change in equity.

Figure 12.2 Equity Sensitivity to Interest Rates (EVE)

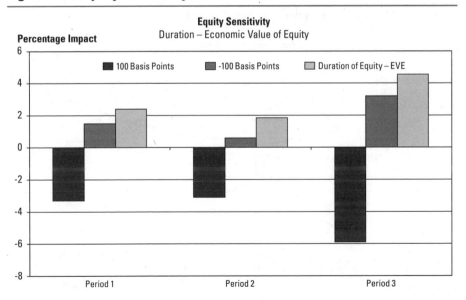

12.4 The Impact of Changes in Forecast Yield Curves

In addition to the traditional repricing gap method having the limitations of any static model in a dynamic environment, the interpretation of a repricing schedule can also be rather complex and requires in-depth knowledge of a bank's operating characteristics. One can obtain yield curve forecasts from a bank and develop an understanding of the institution's interest rate view. This is a crude but, for the purposes of a bank assessment, effective way to understand the potential impact of a given change in interest rates on an income statement and capital and reserves.

The market's forward yield curves offer a more objective view on the paths interest rates may follow, indicating the market's expectations and providing a "best guess" estimate. The market additionally can provide objective measures of the expected volatility of yields that can be used, within a given confidence level, to measure risk.

It must be accepted that, in certain markets, a balance sheet repricing structure cannot easily be changed. Figure 12.3 illustrates forecast yield curves for a range of instruments and a range of points in time, starting from the current period (displaying the actual yield curve) to a period one year into the future (displaying a forecast yield curve in the future).

Figure 12.3 Current and Forecast Yield Curves

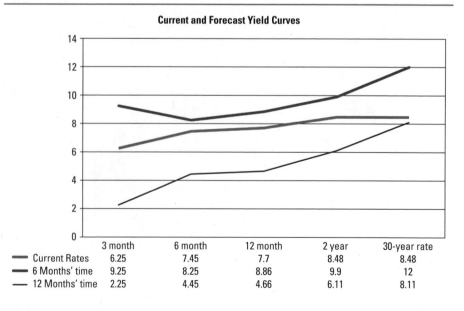

Current and Forecast Yield Curves

	3 month	6 month	12 month	2 year	30-year rate
Current Rates	6.25	7.45	7.7	8.48	8.48
6 Months' time	9.25	8.25	8.86	9.9	12
12 Months' time	2.25	4.45	4.66	6.11	8.11

Repricing Gaps and Sensitivity Analysis

Figure 12.4 illustrates the effect on income and capital that is caused by a change in a key market rate (such as the central bank discount rate). The objective of such a sensitivity analysis is to highlight the effect of a specific key rate on the income statement and on capital and reserves. Interest rate risk may not necessarily result in a loss, but it should be monitored to identify those banks that assume particularly significant levels of risk.

A bank normally should set limits to the impact it is prepared to absorb to its earnings and to the economic value of its equity in the event of changes in market interest rates. The form of limits should be related to the size and complexity of the bank's positions. For banks engaged in traditional banking activities and that do not hold derivatives or instruments with embedded options, simple limits are enough. For banks with complex and diversified business, a detailed limits system may be needed to take into account all possible sources of interest rate risk. Such a system should also consider specific scenarios of movements in market interest rates and historic rate volatilities.

Figure 12.4 Potential Effect on Capital as a Result of a Movement in Interest Rates

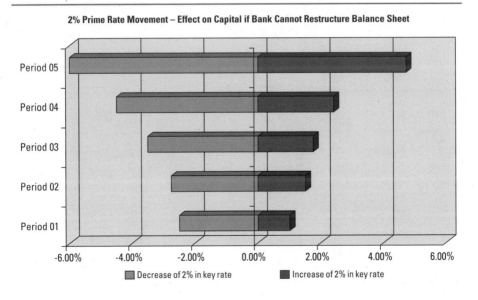

2% Prime Rate Movement – Effect on Capital if Bank Cannot Restructure Balance Sheet

13

Operational Risk Management in a Treasury Environment

"Operational risk is the risk of loss resulting from inadequate or failed internal processes, people, and systems or from external events."
—Basel Committee on Banking Supervision, October 2006

Key Messages

- Operational risk has to be *minimized* whereas credit and market risk is normally *optimized.*

- Operational risk management has become increasingly important as the Basel Committee has finalized its capital and reporting requirements.

- Operational risks assessments must identify business functions and activities in the same manner as line managers manage the life cycle of those functions for each business line. Such functional activities must be clearly aligned to management's strategic, operational, reporting, and compliance objectives.

- Risk assessments should include more than traditional internal controls to ensure a holistic approach that integrates all aspects of risk, especially technology, information security, new product and project risk, as well as externalities such as business disruptions.

- Control objectives should be established by considering an entity's business objectives (strategic, operational, financial, and compliance) and then modifying those objectives after due consideration of the risk environment in which they have to be achieved.

- Key controls should be streamlined and reviewed regularly to assess the efficiency of business processes.

- Compliance with laws, regulations, policies, and guidelines is paramount; it is the culture of compliance that determines the environment within which trading decisions are made.

- Operational risk management requires clear reporting, with performance and risk indicators linked to the control of risks arising from business activities.

- Operational risk reports should be designed to ensure that questions related to trends in indicators address *what* happened, *why* it happened, the *impact* of events, as well as subsequent management *action* and *accountability,* and are integrated into the reporting mechanism.

13.1 Operational Risk Management and the Basel Committee Initiatives

Managing operational risk presents some unique challenges to banks. As operational risk events are largely internal to institutions, the causes or risk factors may not be universally applicable. Moreover, the magnitude of potential losses from specific risk factors is often not easy to project. Very large operational losses have been considered to be rare or isolated occurrences, which causes the perception that it is difficult to get management to focus on the often mundane work required to design an effective mechanism for systematic reporting of trends in a bank's operational risks.

Risk managers attempt to optimize credit and market risk, whereas management strives to minimize operational risk.

Despite these challenges, senior management and the board must be actively involved in the monitoring and reporting of operational risk management by line managers.

The objectives of an operational risk management framework and supporting systems are therefore to:

- Define and explain exposures and incidents that result from people, processes, systems, and external events; and generate enterprise-wide understanding of the drivers of operational risk incidents.

- Provide early warning of incidents and escalation of potential risk by anticipating risks and identify problem areas through ongoing monitoring of key risk indicators.

- Reduce vulnerability to external and systemic effects.

- Clearly define the roles and responsibilities of line personnel in managing operational risk and empower business units to take necessary actions.

- Strengthen management oversight.

- Provide objective measurement tools.

- Integrate qualitative and quantitative data and other information.

- Influence business decisions.

Accomplishing these objectives may require a change in the behavior and culture of the firm. Management must not only ensure compliance with the operational risk policies established by the board, but also report regularly to senior executives. Several tools that can assist them in this task will be discussed in this chapter:

- Identification of key performance and risk indicators

- Loss-incident databases

- Risk mapping: graphical representation of the probability and severity of risks

- Self-assessment of the controls in place to manage and mitigate operational risk

The Basel Committee initiative has increased the attention on operational risk because in the modern environment, the level of risk for banks has increased. Increased reliance on sophisticated technology, expanding retail operations, growing e-commerce, outsourcing of functions and activities, and greater use of structured finance (derivative) techniques that claim to reduce credit and market risk have all contributed to the higher level of operational risk.

The traditional definition of operational risk relies on the sources of risk or events that subject a bank to losses from its methods of operations. The traditional sources of risk are

- people,

- processes,

- systems, and

- external events.

These very sources of risk are also the resources available to a bank when performing its business line functions and risk management activities.

The Basel Committee's Core Principles on Banking Supervision address operational risk in Principle 15, which requires supervisors to ensure that banks have risk management policies and processes to identify, assess, monitor, and control or mitigate operational risk. These policies and processes should be commensurate with the size and complexity of the bank (see box 13.1).

Box 13.1 Basel Committee on Banking Supervision – Core Principle 15 – Operational Risk

Supervisors must be satisfied that banks have in place risk management policies and processes to identify, assess, monitor, and control/mitigate operational risk. These policies and processes should be commensurate with the size and complexity of the bank.

Essential criteria

1. The supervisor requires individual banks to have in place risk management policies and processes to identify, assess, monitor and mitigate operational risk. These policies and processes are adequate for the size and complexity of the bank's operations, and the supervisor confirms that they are periodically adjusted in the light of the bank's changing risk profile and external market developments.

2. The supervisor requires that banks' strategies, policies and processes for the management of operational risk have been approved and are periodically reviewed by the board. The supervisor also requires that the board oversees management in ensuring that these policies and processes are implemented effectively.

3. The supervisor is satisfied that the approved strategy and significant policies and processes for operational risk are implemented effectively by management.

4. The supervisor reviews the quality and comprehensiveness of the bank's business resumption and contingency plans to satisfy itself that the bank is able to operate as a going concern and minimize losses, including those that may arise from disturbances to payment and settlement systems, in the event of severe business disruption.

5. The supervisor determines that banks have established appropriate information technology policies and processes that address areas such as information security and system development, and have made investments in information technology commensurate with the size and complexity of operations.

6. The supervisor requires that appropriate reporting mechanisms be in place to keep the supervisor apprised of developments affecting operational risk at banks in their jurisdictions.

7. The supervisor confirms that legal risk is incorporated into the operational risk management processes of the bank.

8. The supervisor determines that banks have established appropriate policies and processes to assess, manage, and monitor outsourced activities. The outsourcing risk management program should cover

- conducting appropriate due diligence for selecting potential service providers;
- structuring the outsourcing arrangement;
- managing and monitoring the risks associated with the outsourcing arrangement;
- ensuring an effective control environment; and
- establishing viable contingency planning.

Outsourcing policies and processes should require the institution to have comprehensive contracts and/or service level agreements with a clear allocation of responsibilities between the outsourcing provider and the bank.

Additional criterion

The supervisor determines that the risk management policies and processes address the major aspects of operational risk, including an appropriate operational risk framework that is applied on a groupwide basis. The policies and processes should include additional risks prevalent in certain operationally intensive businesses, such as custody and correspondent banking, and should cover periods when operational risk could increase.

In its 2003 document, *Sound Practices for the Management and Supervision of Operational Risk*, the Basel Committee provided guidance to banks for managing operational risk, in anticipation of the implementation of the Basel II Accord, which requires a capital allocation for operational risks. These guidelines contained 10 operational risk principles under the following headings:

Developing an appropriate risk management environment. The first three principles outline the obligations of the board of directors (or the level of executives with the ultimate executive decision-making function) and senior management in managing operational risk. Principle 1 states that the board must recognize operational risk as a distinct risk category; provide a definition of operational risk that applies to all units within the firm; and establish the policies for identifying, assessing, monitoring, and controlling it. Principle 2 states that the board should ensure that there are comprehensive internal audits of adherence to the operational risk policies, and that audits are conducted by competent staff who are not directly responsible for managing operational risk. Principle 3 gives senior management the responsibility for implementing firmwide operational risk policies and for developing specific policies to manage operational risk for all of the bank's material products, activities, processes, and systems.

Risk management: identification, assessment, monitoring, and mitigation or control. The next four principles address operational risk management in the day-to-day activities of the banking organization. Under Principle 4, banks should assess the operational risk inherent in all of their existing material products, activities, processes, and systems. Before new products, activities, processes, and systems are introduced, an assessment of the operational risk should be implemented. Principle 5 requires that there be an established process to monitor operational risk profiles and potential exposures to losses on an ongoing basis. Regular reports on risk management should be submitted to the board of directors and senior management. Under Principle 6, banks should periodically review their operational risk control procedures and strategies and make adjustments as necessary. Principle 7 advises banks to adopt contingency and business continuity plans to ensure their ability to maintain operations and limit losses in the event of severe business disruption.

Role of supervisors. Principle 8 states that banking supervisors should require all banks, regardless of size, to have an effective framework in place to identify, assess, monitor, and control/mitigate material operational risks as part of an overall approach to risk management. Under Principle 9, supervisors should conduct, directly or indirectly, regular independent evaluations of a bank's policies, procedures, and practices related to operational risks. Supervisors should ensure that there are appropriate mechanisms in place to apprise them of developments at banks under their jurisdiction.

Role of disclosure. Principle 10 states that banks should make sufficient public disclosure to allow market participants to assess their approach to operational risk management.

Table 13.1 provides a graphic image of the Basel model. It also provides a possible match of the Basel risk sources (events) to the traditional risk drivers, namely people, processes, systems, and external events. The model identifies eight potential business lines and seven event types for which operational risk should be assessed, which is a departure from the textbook description of event types or the sources of risks mentioned previously.

Table 13.1 Basel II Operational Risk Business Lines and Risk Event Types

Operational Risk – Business Lines and Event Types per Basel

Event types / Business lines / Risk Drivers	Internal Fraud — People	External Fraud — External Events	Employment Practices and Workplace Safety — People	Clients, Products and Business Services — People / Processes	Damage to Physical Assets — External Events	Business Disruption and System Failures (technology risk) — Systems / External Events	Execution, Delivery and Process Management — Processes	Identify Business Line with Highest Incidence of Monetary Losses
Corporate finance								
Trading and sales								
Retail banking								
Commercial banking								
Payment and settlement								
Agency and custody services								
Asset management								
Retail brokerage								
Identify risk source with highest incidence of monetary losses								

13.2 A Framework for Managing and Reporting Operational Risk

The problem with the presentation of the Basel model in table 13.1 is that it does not provide information regarding the functions and activities required to complete the life cycle of a transaction for a given business line. In addition, many entities view some of the Basel-identified "business lines" (for example, payment and settlement) as functions serving more than one business line— rather than as business lines in their own right.

Business Life Cycle-Based Framework

Using the proprietary securities trading business line within a bank's treasury as an example, the functions required can be divided into enterprise-wide functions and operational-level functions. The enterprise-wide functions are

- strategic planning,
- governance,
- general management,
- capacity development (own infrastructure), and
- business development.

On an operational level, the functions of securities trading include

- new client portfolio set-up,
- portfolio management,
- settlement and control,
- valuation and accounting, and
- risk analytics.

Reflecting back on figure A3.1 (annex to Chapter 3), which summarized the COSO (Committee of Sponsoring Organizations of the Treadway Commission) approach to enterprise risk management (ERM), the implementation of an operational risk methodology that incorporates both the COSO ERM and Basel requirements is illustrated as shown in table 13.2.

Table 13.2 ERM Model Expanded to Include Enterprise Functions Required to Complete the Life Cycle of a Transaction for a Business Line

Functions	Activities	ERM Model – Linked to Business Functions and Activities							
		Internal Environment	Objectives	Risk & Event Identification	Risk Assessment	Risk Response	Control Activities	Information Communication	Monitoring
Enterprise: 1. Strategic planning 2. Governance 3. General management 4. Infrastructure and own capacity development 5. Business development **Operational:** 6. New client portfolio set-up 7. Portfolio Management 8. Settlement & control 9. Valuation & accounting 10. Risk analytics	Activities required to perform each of the 10 separate functions	Tone Integrity Ethics	Strategic	People	Likelihood	Avoid	Policies	Identify relevant information	Monitor entire ERM process
		View of risk	Operational	Processes	Impact	Reduce	Procedures	Capture	Ongoing activities
		Risk management philosophy	Reporting	Systems		Share		Communicate	Separate evaluations
		Risk appetite	Compliance	External events		Accept		Enable people to carry out responsibilities	Modify processes where needed

Benefits of a Structured Approach to Operational Risk Management

Most organizations appear to adopt risk and control assessments to satisfy their financial controllers and internal auditors—and seldom to leverage the principles of COSO that can be adapted easily to facilitate the implementation of an operational risk management approach, that mimic transaction flows, and that provide line management with an intuitive tool for managing operational risk.

In many organizations, the basic COSO requirement to communicate, inform, and monitor is almost ignored by controllers and auditors—who appear quite satisfied to attest that controls were *designed efficiently and operating effectively*. This situation leads to endless waste of resources and encourages line management to avoid the burdensome control activities.

Managers themselves often disagree about definitions and approaches. Entities that have had some success in implementing a coherent approach to operational risk management agree that a willingness to experiment is important; too much analysis can lead to a lack of decision making, proving the old adage that "you don't plow a field by turning it over in your mind."

Adopting a consistent framework to operational risk management throughout an entire organization allows an organization to achieve the following:

- Specific improvements in controls or documentation processes
- Improvements in the control environment of the organization
- Automation of activities and control processes
- Better analysis of risk drivers and more efficient linkage of controls to sources of risk
- Increased risk management awareness by process owners (line managers and staff)
- Management understanding of its responsibility to manage and monitor risk and controls effectively
- Senior management reporting that is clear, comprehensive, integrated, and actionable
- Leveraging activities rather than duplication
- Consistent standards

- Strategic questions asked, and shifting corporate mindset and culture

- Single repository of risk and control data—as well as action items

- Enhanced learning and end-user support

Adopting a structured approach will result in greater efficiency. The regulatory burden will be converted into a sound business requirement. By avoiding duplication, audit fatigue can be reduced as multiple redundant audit and control questionnaires are virtually eliminated. Such questionnaires often satisfy only a single unit's objectives and seldom benefit line management.

Business process reengineering. Management buy-in can be obtained by ensuring that the risk assessment and control phase is used to streamline cumbersome manual processes or detective controls, which may require time-consuming reconciliations after the event, when certain controls may easily be automated. For example, performing risk analysis before the introduction of new projects and products could promote a successful launch by alerting management to potential problems in advance. Moreover, it would be more cost effective than having to alter processes after the fact, if a postevent analysis identifies unacceptable risk.

Table 13.3 builds on table 13.2 to illustrate how all the COSO objectives (as well as Sarbanes-Oxley requirements) can be achieved while remaining relevant to the business objectives of line managers.

It provides an overview of the steps required to implement a structured approach to operational risk assessment and management, while including reporting and monitoring functions as well. Implementation of a structured approach to operational risk management should eliminate the need for additional questionnaires to satisfy internal or external auditors—or any other risk, control, or compliance function in the organization.

Table 13.3 Operational Risk Management

Functions	Activities	Business Objectives	Process Flows	Risk Assessment and Response	Key Controls	Reporting & Monitoring	Information & Communication	Data / Metrics
		Provide business rationale for performing tasks	Prepare flowchart of activities – by function	Identify **drivers** of risk: People Processes Systems External events	Define control objectives and ensure that they are aligned with business objective as modified by risk assessment Decide on policies and procedures	How can one know that entity is meeting its business objectives	How can one know that entity is meeting its control objectives – risk environment deteriorating	Metrics required Frequency
Enterprise: 1. Strategic planning 2. Governance 3. General management 4. Infrastructure and own capacity development 5. Business development	**Activities required to perform each of the 10 separate functions**	Classify objectives into 4 categories Strategic Operational Reporting Compliance	Describe manner in which functions / activities performed	Consider all **sources** of risk: Activity process flows IT Information security Business continuity Adequacy of facilities Regulatory compliance New project implementation Management concerns	What measures (key controls) are in place to achieve risk management objectives regular monitoring (by whom) ensuring accuracy completeness validity correct period appropriateness classification?	Key Performance Indicators: Link to drivers of performance Determine why is indicator a KPI What business question answered What is benchmark / standard Decisions influenced Actions taken Backward looking	Key Risk Indicators: Link to drivers of risk Determine why is indicator a KRI What control objective reflected What is benchmark / standard Decisions influenced Actions taken Early warning of developing risks Forward looking	Determine sources of data
Operational: 6. New client portfolio set-up 7. Portfolio Management 8. Settlement & control 9. Valuation & accounting 10. Risk analytics		Align objectives with appropriate functions		Formulate risk response How likely is it that a risk will materialize? How badly will it affect my business if risks do materialize (impact) Where will the impact be felt: Monetary (M) Reputational (R) Compliance (C)	Determine whether controls are: manual (M) or automated (A) preventive (P) or detective (D)?	Report and ensure action and monitoring by senior management	Report and ensure action and monitoring by senior management	Ensure efficiency of data collection Responsibility
		Ensure that business objectives are reviewed regularly		Decide on a risk response: Avoid Accept Reduce Share	Evaluate design & operating effectiveness	Modify processes where needed use framework for business process re-engineering		Investigate automated data mining possibilities

The framework answers the following questions from a line manager's perspective:

- What businesses/business lines am I in?
- What generic functions are required for the completion of the (transaction) life cycle of the business line?
- What activities are necessary to perform each function?
- What are my business objectives (why am I doing this)? Are my functions and activities aligned with these objectives?
- How am I currently achieving my business objectives (understanding process flows)?
- What will prevent me from achieving my business objectives (risk areas, risk drivers, and my response to the risks identified—can I live with the risk)?
- How can I manage the obstacles that could prevent me from achieving my objectives (controls)?
- Which indicators will tell senior management that the obstacles that could prevent achievement of objectives are well managed, escalating, or have outdated management processes (KPI/KRI)? In order to communicate results effectively, analysts should analyze trends and determine reasons for trends and events; thereby convincing management to:
  - ❏ evaluate performance effectiveness
  - ❏ take action when risk indicators demand attention
  - ❏ re-engineer cumbersome manual processes
  - ❏ re-engineer inefficient manual and detective (after-the-fact) controls
- How can we improve information management—database construction and data mining?

When implementing any framework, risk managers should avoid falling into the trap of allowing a software model to dictate the operational risk management methodology. Software should be acquired that allows managers to collect data that support the firm's objectives. Tools should not manage operational risk.

13.3 Identification of Business Line Functions and Activities

Key questions in determining which functions are required and useful for the transaction cycle are why a particular function is necessary and how it contributes to achieving the business line's business objectives. Once the key functions are determined, management must decide on actionable activities that will achieve functional objectives in the most efficient manner.

Table 13.4 identifies the functions and activities of the securities trading business line and indicates how the activities align with business objectives. The process requires answering two questions:

- What are the major functions performed during the life cycle of a transaction or a given business line?

- What activities are required to achieve each functional objective?

Some risk specialists disagree with the notion of mixing enterprise functions such as strategy, governance, and general management with line management operational functions. However, when one reviews each function's activities, it becomes clear that lack of a well-communicated strategy will quickly lead to an organization that is not structured correctly for achieving its stated business objectives. That, in turn, will almost inevitably place staff career planning in jeopardy: resource allocation could be haphazard as any new idea that is proposed could take priority, to the detriment of achieving longer-term goals.

When human and systems capacity is not developed prior to marketing new business opportunities—prior to training staff and installing automated systems infrastructure (where practical)—the result will be unnecessary manual and other workaround processes, controls after the event (detective rather than preventive controls), losing operational efficiencies, and exposing the enterprise to needless human and systemic stress. In the long run, a situation like this will play out in the way, for example, client portfolios are set up, adversely affecting settlement, accounting, and risk analytics functions—all directly related to operational risk management.

Table 13.4 Securities Trading (Business Line) Functions and Activities

Functions	Activities
Strategic planning	Formulate and accept a mission that supports the overall IBRD mission (values & core beliefs)
	Formulate a three- to five-year vision
	Articulate and communicate strategic objectives
	Select appropriate achievement measurement criteria
Governance	Structure business lines and units to facilitate achievement of the mission and strategic objectives
	Recommend appropriate Strategic asset allocation model and external performance benchmarks to relevant policymakers
	Implement policies and guidelines in accordance with board decisions
	Implement an effective risk management process
	Reengineer inappropriate or outdated business processes
	Determine appropriate risk reporting and managerial criteria to internal and external clients
General management	Manage people
	Manage staff careers in alignment with strategic plan
	Plan and manage facilities
	Plan and manage budget resources
	Report on managerial activities
Capacity development (own infrastructure)	Develop products, publications, and projects aligned to mission
	Develop human resource skills (staff training)
Business development	Agree on a business development and target market strategy
	Adopt a marketing and communications strategy
	Adopt a standard approach to assessing new client needs
	Assess risk and reward for potential new clients
New client portfolio set-up	Conclude legal and investment management agreements (IMA) with clients
	Set up new client portfolio
	Set up agreed-on counterparty arrangements
Portfolio management	Construct and/or rebalance portfolio according to client directives
	Perform pretrade compliance
	Execute trades (choose trading platform)
	Determine and agree on overall liquidity needs
Settlement and control	Confirm and settle transactions
	Make and receive payments (e.g., SWIFT)
	Investigate transactions when necessary
	Manage cash transaction flows and reconciliations
	Maintain static data
	Manage bank and custodian relations
Valuation and accounting	Value portfolios
	Accounting for portfolios
	Manage external (CTR) and other reporting requirements
	Agree on level of service to internal and external clients
Risk analytics	Design, test, and implement risk models
	Measure risk and communicate to BLs and TREVP
	Measure portfolio performance and compare with agreed-on benchmarks
	Monitor compliance activities

13.4 Process Flows: Documenting the Manner in Which Functions Are Performed

The manner in which activities are performed exposes an entity to operational risk and inefficiencies. Management must select the technologies most likely to ensure optimal cost effectiveness at the lowest possible risk exposure. To select the proper technologies, management must first determine the business rationale for performing functional activities:

■ What business objectives are satisfied by performing the activities?

■ How does the business perform the activities, that is, what is the process flow?

Figure 13.1 provides an example of the activities involved in processing a fixed income investment, using flowcharts.

Figure 13.1 Trade Process Flow—From Risk-Analytics Perspective

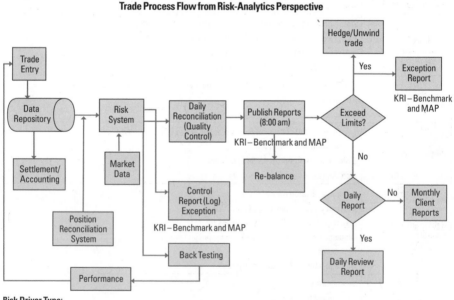

Trade Process Flow from Risk-Analytics Perspective

Risk Driver Type:

People – Key person risk, staffing

Process – Transaction (execution error), Control Operations (limit exceedance, volume, complexity), Model (mark to market, methodology)

System – System failure (downtime, inadequacy)

External Event – Business continuity, natural disaster

Indicator Measurement:

Benchmark

Minimum Acceptable Performance (MAP)

Source: Cheryl Troy – World Bank Treasury

13.5 Risk Assessment: Contribution of People, Processes, Systems, and External Events

There is sometimes a temptation in treasury environments to think of risk as being exclusively quantitative. Therefore, the challenge is to find a framework for the measurement of operational risk and governance that appeals to quantitatively oriented people and into which nonquantitative risk can be seamlessly integrated.

Risk is defined as anything that hinders the ethical achievement of sustainable business objectives and results. This includes the failure to exploit opportunities and to maintain organizational relevance. Every organization faces a variety of risks from external and internal sources that must be assessed. Risk assessment is the identification and analysis of those risks that potentially jeopardize the achievement of business objectives. Risk assessment forms a basis for determining how risks should be managed. A precondition to risk assessment is establishment of business objectives that are internally consistent and aligned with an organization's strategy and mission.

When undertaking a risk assessment, a bank must ask the following key questions regarding each function and its related activities (see table 13.5):

- What are the sources of risk (people, processes, systems, external events)?
- What risks are covered by the internal control framework?
- What are the information technology (IT) and systems risks?
- What are the information security risks?
- What are the risks related to business continuity?
- What are the risks related to facilities and location?
- What special risks may result from servicing external clients and complying with regulatory requirements?
- What are the additional risks from planning and implementing new products or projects?
- What else is bothering management?
- How likely is it that a risk will materialize?
- How badly will business be affected if risks do materialize, and will the impact be monetary, reputational, or related to compliance?

Once the risks have been identified, management must determine whether to accept the risks (because the low impact or likelihood of occurrence does not justify the expense of controlling them) or to mitigate the risks by avoiding, reducing, or sharing them.

Risk (and control) assessments normally work best when the questioning process is guided by an experienced neutral observer.

Table 13.5 Risk Assessment: Questions for Each Functional Activity—Linked to Basel and ERM Models

Risk Questions and Response	Risk Assessment Questions for Each Functional Activity - Linked to Basel and ERM Models											
	What risks are covered by internal control framework	What IT (Info Technology) risks have to be considered	What Information Security risks have to be considered	What risks related to Business Continuity have to be considered	What risks related to Facilities & Location have to be considered	What special risks result from servicing External Clients / Clients as well as complying with Regulatory Requirements	New Products? What additional downstream risks result from planning and implementing new products or projects	What else is bothering management	How likely is it that a risk will materialize	How badly will it affect the business if risks do materialize	Where will the impact be felt:	What is the response to the risks identified
Basel Event Types	Internal fraud External fraud	Business disruption and system failures	Business disruption and system failures Internal fraud External fraud	Business disruption and system failures Damage to physical assets	Damage to physical assets Employment practices and workplace safety	Clients products and business services	Clients products and business services Execution delivery and process management	Execution delivery and process management				
Operational Risk Definition Drivers of Risk	People External events	Systems External events	People External events Systems External events	External events	External events	People Processes Systems External events	People Processes Systems External events	People Processes Systems External events				
ERM: Enterprise Risk Management COSO Model									Likelihood	Impact	Monetary (M) Reputational (R) Compliance (C)	Avoid risk Reduce risk Accept risk Share risk
Function	**Activities**											

13.6 **Control Assessment**

Internal control is a process intended to provide reasonable assurance of achieving effectiveness and efficiency of operations, reliability of financial reporting, and compliance with applicable laws and regulations. This includes safeguarding assets.

The control environment sets the tone of an organization, providing discipline and structure. It includes integrity and ethical values, the competence of the staff, management's philosophy and operating style, the way management assigns authority and responsibility, the way management trains and develops staff, and the attention and direction provided by the board of directors. Policies and procedures are the control activities that help ensure that management directives are carried out and the organization achieves its objectives. Control activities—such as approvals, authorizations, verifications, reconciliations, reviews of operating performance, security of assets, and segregation of duties—occur throughout the organization, at all levels, and in all functions.

Controls can be either formal or informal. Formal controls include policy manuals, procedures, hierarchy, and regulations. Informal controls include ethics, competence, morale, trust, skills, leadership, processes, culture, information, resources, measurements, policies, communication, teamwork, and procedures.

When assessing a control process, management should address the following issues (see table 13.6):

- Considering the business rationale and related risks, what is the risk management (control) objective?
- Who is responsible for monitoring this risk?
- What measures (key controls) are in place to achieve the risk management objective (for example, regular monitoring, accuracy, completeness, validity and correct period, appropriateness, classification)?
  - ❑ Is this control manual or automated?
  - ❑ Is this control preventive or detective?
- Who performs the risk management activity?
- Is there evidence (including from external parties or other divisions) that the control activity is routinely carried out?

- Is the effectiveness of any key control dependent on more than one individual or business unit?

- How does this risk management activity differ from current best market practice?

Usually management must satisfy its auditors that it has complied with its own stated risk management processes. One way of integrating compliance testing into routine management activities would be to require that any analysis or discussion of significant financial and risk trends and fluctuations, and any performance or reporting problems highlighted in quarterly financial reports, be linked to management's own description of its risk management procedures. Including the risk matrix as an agenda item in quarterly reporting would ensure that any changes to processes or risk management controls made during the financial reporting cycle are documented in a timely manner. Such reviews should also identify new risks and necessary changes to existing processes and internal controls.

Table 13.6 Control Assessment Questions

Functions	Activities	Considering the business rationale and related risks, what is the risk management (control) objective?	Who is responsible for monitoring this risk?	What measures (key controls) are in place to achieve the risk management objective (for example, regular monitoring, accuracy, completeness, validity and correct period, appropriateness, classification)?	Is the control manual (M) or automated (A)?	Is the control preventive (P) or detective (D)?	Who performs the risk management activity and what evidence exists that it is done (include explicit references to reliance on external parties and other divisions)?	Design: How do these risk management activities differ from current best market practice?	Operating: Are people actually doing what they should be doing in terms of control procedures?	How would management know that they are meeting their business objectives? Key performance Indicators	How would management know when risk management controls are not working as planned or the risk environment is deteriorating? Key Risk Indicators

Control Design & Operating Effectiveness (spanning the columns beginning with "Is the control manual (M) or automated (A)?" onward)

13.7 Key Indicators of Performance and Risk

Managing operational risk requires identifying appropriate indicators of performance and risk. This requires collecting data (metrics)—internally and externally—which are representative of business processes. Such data is normally presented in relationship with a given frequency, for example, wages per hour. When compared to an independent or previously agreed benchmark, a metric becomes a risk or performance indicator.

Many operational risk managers choose not to define key performance indicators and key risk indicators separately. If one has to differentiate, one could begin by defining a key performance indicator (KPI) as a metric expressed in terms of a target. KPIs are seen as backward-looking and describing past performance (see table 13.7).

Table 13.7 Difference between Metrics and Indicators

Activity: Confirm and Settle Transactions	Month 1	Month 2	Month 3
Trade volumes – use data mining	1000	1100	900
Metric: Number of errors – use data mining	14	21	19
Benchmark / Threshold	1.5%	1.5%	1.5%
Upper limit – immediate action required	2.0%	2.0%	2.0%
Trades with errors	1.4%	1.9%	2.1%
KPI: error rate as % of benchmark	93%	127%	141%
KRI: excess errors above benchmark	-6.7%	27.3%	40.7%
Risk factor compared to: Benchmark and upper limit of acceptability	1	2	3

A key risk indicator (KRI) is defined as an operational or financial variable that provides a reliable basis for estimating the likelihood and the severity of one or more operational risk events. It can be a specific causal variable as well as a proxy for the drivers of the events and losses related to an operational risk. A KRI can be strictly quantitative, like the turnover rate in a business unit or the number of settlement errors, or more qualitative, like the adequacy of a system or the competence of personnel. It can be perfectly objective, like the number of hours of system downtime, or more subjective, like the overall complexity of a portfolio of derivatives. But to be useful, a KRI will always have to be somehow linked to one of the risk drivers—or even better, to one of the mechanisms generating an operational failure. It follows that indicators have to be regularly reviewed and updated by discarding those that have become irrelevant or redundant, changing the way key data are collected and processed, and developing new indicators according to the evolution of the risk and the control environment.

KRIs are measurable indicators that track exposure or loss and show a status at a given point in time or, as one person put it, "trouble." Anything that can perform this function may be considered a risk indicator. Although credible key risk indicators are of utmost importance, managers should not spend endless hours trying to define such indicators. Advice from experienced risk managers is that a risk indicator should be defined and then used; if it is not appropriate, it will sort itself out over time and modifications can then be made.

KRIs may be financial indicators, but more often they are operational statistics that are combined and manipulated into KRIs and then included in an operational risk management report. The report informs the board of directors if controls are operating effectively and if trends in risk management remain within acceptable limits. Examples might include statistics on trading volumes, settlement errors, trade fails, and so forth.

Unlike KPIs (which look backward at past performance), KRIs look forward at potential risks. KRIs should be validated for different types (for example, exposure and control), different risk classes (people, technology, and processes), and for different units as well as treasury-wide. KRIs should quantify all tangible and intangible aspects needed for risk-based decision making, that is, system failures, compliance, internal audits, turnover, and so forth.

A good KRI should have at least the following characteristics and abilities:

- Based on objective standards that are accepted by line managers and preferably having external benchmarks available
- Useful
- Easy to apply and be understood by the end users
- Developed using an objective and consistent methodology
- Providing a clear understanding of the risk variables underlying the indicator, such as the likelihood and impact of occurrence
- Containing advance warning features
- Quantifiable (numbers, dollars, or percentages)
- Tied to management objectives, risk owners, and risk categories

- Demonstrating clearly where problems might arise

- Timely and cost effective to produce, utilizing automated data mining techniques where possible

KRIs are particularly useful in providing senior management with assurance that the control framework is functioning as intended (and as documented). Business managers should identify KRIs for each control in their jurisdiction.

For example, as a metric such as the number of trade entry errors increases, the probability of some underlying and potentially systemic mistakes and errors of judgment is likely to rise. In other words, changes in the value of this metric above a predetermined threshold are likely to be associated with changes in operational risk exposure or operational loss experience. One can establish this point by determining who needs the information, what business or control objective–related question is being answered, why that specific metric is unique in answering the question, and which decisions are influenced or actions taken based on the KPI or KRI requiring this metric as input (see table 13.8).

Management should determine what data are needed for developing indicators and how that data can be collected. The data collected should disclose a clear understanding of which risks management should be and are monitoring. The following questions should help management prepare operational risk reports in a cost-effective manner:

- How does management know that it is meeting its business objectives (KPIs), and what is the target success rate (benchmark) aimed for by management?

- How does management know when risk management controls are not working as planned or the risk environment is deteriorating (KRIs)?

- Why are these aspects reflective of success or escalating risks?
  - ❏ Who needs this information?
  - ❏ What business or control objective question is answered by this metric?
  - ❏ How is this metric unique in answering business question?
  - ❏ What decisions are influenced by these data?
  - ❏ What actions should be taken based on the KPIs and KRIs?

- How will data collection take place?
  - ❏ What data should be collected?
  - ❏ How often should data be collected?
  - ❏ Where can the data be found?
  - ❏ How should the data be collected?
  - ❏ Who will be responsible for collecting the data?

When designed properly and reported in a timely manner, risk and performance indicators provide a predictive warning of potential issues that may adversely affect the business. However, credible risk and performance indicators emerge only when risk managers fully understand the end-to-end operational flow of the business.

With a detailed mapping of the business process, a risk manager can design indicators that will yield the best information, based on high-quality metrics.

A practical way to map the business process is described by Sergio Scandizzo.[1]

---

1   Sergio Scandizzo, *The Operational Risk Manager's Guide—Tools and Techniques of the Trade*, London: Riskbooks, 2007.

Key Risk Indicators

Table 13.8 Determination of Metrics for Inclusion as KPIs and KRIs

Function	Activity	Metric/ Statistic — unit / time scale of measurement	KPI — metric as % of target	KRI — metric as indicator of future risks	Who Needs this Information	What Business or Control Objective Question is Answered by this metric — How is this Metric linked to Risk Drivers	Why is metric unique in answering business question	Decisions Influenced	Actions Taken based on KPI/ KRI	Data Source	Frequency of collection
	Confirm (validate) transaction, automatically update positions and enter into settlement system										
	Make and receive payments (e.g. Swift)										
Settlement & Control	Investigate transactions when necessary										
	Manage cash transaction flows and reconciliations										
	Maintain static data										
	Manage bank & custodian relations										

13.8 Operational Risk Reporting: Analysis, Actions, and Accountability

Reporting and Monitoring Operational Risk

Principle 5. Banks should implement a process to regularly monitor operational risk profiles and material exposures to losses. There should be regular reporting of pertinent information to senior management and the board of directors that supports the proactive management of operational risk.

Principle 6. Banks should have policies, processes and procedures to control and/or mitigate material operational risks. Banks should periodically review their risk limitation and control strategies and should adjust their operational risk profile accordingly using appropriate strategies, in light of their overall risk appetite and profile.

Sound Practices for the Management and Supervision of Operational Risk
Basel Committee on Banking Supervision
December 2003

Well-structured management information, reviewed regularly as part of the governance process, will contribute significantly to the identification and management of operational risk. By linking operational risk management functions to key performance and key risk indicators, management is provided with risk-based management information that focuses on risk management processes that pertain to each business line function and its related activities. The risk metrics include operational issues related to the trading activity, such as the monitoring of rate resets and other triggers on structured trades, settlement issues, and legal confirmations with respect to derivatives and debt service.

Internal control systems need to be monitored, a process that assesses the quality of the system's performance over time. This is accomplished through ongoing monitoring activities and separate evaluations. Ongoing monitoring occurs in the course of business and includes regular management and supervisory activities and other actions staff may take in the performance of their duties. The scope and frequency of separate evaluations will depend primarily on an assessment of risks and on the effectiveness of ongoing monitoring procedures. Internal control deficiencies should be reported upstream as part of regular reporting to senior management. Identified deficiencies should, in turn, initiate analytical investigation of the reasons for fluctuations and errors, to determine if such occurrences are the result of the development of new risks or the failure of existing risk management processes. This approach operationalizes the risk management process as a normal part of the management process, ensuring that risk assessment is not merely something that is performed once a year to satisfy some external reporting requirement.

Pertinent information must be identified, captured, and communicated in a form and within a time frame that enables people to carry out their responsibilities. Information systems produce reports containing the operational, financial, and compliance-related information that make it possible to run and control a business. They deal not only with internally generated data, but also with the information about external events, activities, and conditions that is necessary for informed decision making and external reporting. Effective communication must also occur in a broader sense, flowing down, across, and from the bottom. In a healthy control environment, communications are open. When a business objective is in jeopardy, bad news flows rapidly, enabling timely corrective action to be taken. All personnel must receive a clear message from top management that their control responsibilities must be taken seriously. They must understand their own role in the internal control system and understand how their individual activities relate to the work of others. They must have a means of communicating significant information upstream. There also needs to be effective communication with external parties, such as customers, suppliers, regulators, and shareholders.

An operational and enterprise risk dashboard should address key questions for management:

- Are any strategic, operational, reporting, or compliance objectives at risk?
- Which key risk and performance indicators require immediate action?
- Are all policies, limits, and laws complied with?
- Who should be accountable for actions required as a result of issues highlighted?
- Are key messages highlighted in the most efficient manner to convey critical information?
- Are required actions and accountabilities clearly conveyed?

A prototype operational risk report is shown in figure 13.2. The report is EXCEL based and can be used together with inexpensive software such as XCELSIUS.

Figure 13.2 Sample Operational Risk Management Report

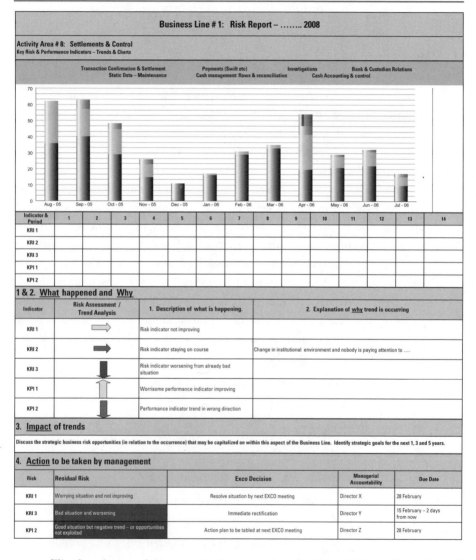

The foundation of the report is that a trend analysis should be performed on all key risk indicators, identifying significant fluctuations and asking the following four important questions:

- What has happened that draws attention?

- Why has it happened?

- What is the impact of the trend or situation?

- What actions need to be taken to reverse an unacceptable trend? Who is responsible for taking the action, and when should it be done?

It is a pity that internal auditors are not more involved with operational risk issues—so much of what is implicit in modern internal auditing can be used almost "as is," to enhance operational risk management.

Internal auditors leave out the most powerful tool in the arsenal provided by their auditing standards—namely the power and impact of "analytic review" or "financial analysis."

This leads to undue emphasis on control design and detailed testing, rather than an evaluation of whether the impact of risks and controls are actually being monitored by management. And how will management know that the controls are functioning? Not through theoretical work but by analyzing trends in key performance and key risk indicators and determining whether managers pay heed and take action when unsatisfactory trends emerge.

It is not enough to analyze operational risk on a business line basis—one has to understand the life cycle of transactions within a business line, because the life cycle clarifies the various functions and activities required to manage a business line. Although this may seem natural because of the need to allocate responsibility and reward performance and good behavior, it will give a biased view of operational risk exposures and may even miss some of them altogether. In fact, failures in one part of the process can generate failures in others as well as materialize into losses within units that are organizationally separate, while being part of the same business line process.

Some people distinguish between "scorecards" and "dashboards." A scorecard presents risk or performance indicators focused on the *strategic* level, providing management with information regarding execution of strategic objectives. A dashboard (see figure 13.2) contains performance indicators, risk indicators, and metrics—all focused on the *functional* level, for example, settlements and control, or accounting/valuation. In order to design a dashboard, background information must be easy to complete and assist with the analytical standards required of a good dashboard. Table 13.9 provides guidance in this regard.

Table 13.9 Design of Dashboard—Input Table to Facilitate Analysis

Operational Report Design						
If Metric Is not Automated – Be Critical						
Input Information	**Time Series**	**Chart types required**	**Analysis**	**Issues**	**Projects**	**Items to Escalate to Dashboard**
		trend line bar chart and trend line pie charts	what happened / why did it happen / what is the impact of the trends or events / what action should management take / date (original and revised) / accountable senior manager	Bullet / Description / Action required	Bullet / Description / Action required	
KRI – by function						
KRI 1						
KRI 2 etc						
KPI – by function						
KPI 1						
KPI 2						
Benchmark – by indicator						
Target rate for each KPI						
Excess risk rate for selected KRIs						
Operational Metrics – by activity						
Operational metric 1						
Operational metric 1						
Financial Metrics – by activity						
Financial metric 1						
Financial metric 2						

Annex 13A. Overview of Functions and Activities in a Treasury Environment

Establishing the Overall Policy Framework

Prior to the commencement of any funding, market operations, or risk management activities, senior management decides on policies governing the various treasury functions. Typically the board of directors or a delegated senior committee specifies the types of funding and investments in which a bank might engage. The authorization thus issued normally would include a list of eligible instruments and their derivatives and would specify rules pertaining to allowable counterparties, currencies, and maturity structures. These general policy directives may also specify the principles underlying the asset-liability management of the balance sheet and may authorize the use of an external asset management firm for managing the bank's investments.

Responsibility for the establishment and maintenance of a control framework (risk management framework) and the list of officers authorized to transact on behalf of the bank normally is specified in internal guidelines. Unlike corporate policy, which should be approved by the board of directors, these operational guidelines may be approved at a treasury or investment policy committee level.

As financial markets are constantly changing, it is imperative that policy guidelines be reviewed on a regular basis.

Portfolio Management (Market Operations)

Financial intermediaries must necessarily transform the duration (interest rate exposure) of their liabilities to different interest exposures on the asset side of the balance sheet. At the same time, intermediaries must be able to meet their commitments (such as deposits or bond repayments) when they come due or are called. The actual inflow and outflow of funds will not necessarily be reflected in contractual terms and may vary according to market conditions. A financial intermediary therefore is inherently exposed to liquidity mismatches. Consequently, liquidity policies and liquidity risk management are key elements of its business strategy. (The importance of managing liquidity risk is more fully discussed in chapter 8.)

Access to cost-effective funding for the bank's treasury can be influenced by interest rates and the spread environment, by the activities of competitors in the market, by demand for credit, by a bank's credit rating, and by the local environment (for example, the availability of arbitrage markets). The structure of a bank's funding is a key aspect of liquidity management.

A bank with a stable, large, and diverse deposit base is likely to have fewer liquidity problems than one lacking such a deposit base. Assessment of the structure and type of deposit base and the evaluation of the condition (stability and quality) of the deposits, therefore, is the starting point for liquidity risk assessment. The following information is necessary to conduct an assessment of the funding environment:

■ Product range

■ Deposit concentration

■ Deposit administration

■ Funding structure

■ Approach to potential sources of funding

With respect to borrowings, management should ensure that the funding risks are properly managed. Unauthorized transactions or changes (that is, those without proper approval or those made by unauthorized staff) could cause potential financial and reputation risks for the bank. Transaction information that is not captured correctly or promptly—especially when complex funding structures such as index-linked bonds and swaps are utilized—could result in settlement delays or failures, and the poor timing of transaction execution may cause opportunity costs. Inappropriate behavior on the part of employees (for example, favoring certain counterparties) or imperfect execution could also cause potential monetary losses and harm to the bank's reputation.

From an operational risk perspective, some funding structures require manual intervention during the life of the instrument, because treasury computer software may be unable to capture the required rates or intervention triggers. Where derivatives are used as a part of the funding structure, transactions executed in excess of a counterparty's credit line limit would increase exposure. Incorrect determination of derivative parameters, such as notional amounts, periodic coupon cash flows, dates, and day count conventions, also can cause potential financial losses.

Investment and Cash Flow Management

In a commercial banking environment, the investment and trading process assists in smoothing short-term liquidity shortfalls and surpluses, to maximize returns with minimum cash balances and to provide cash flows to all internal and external clients. The investment function also manages longer-term assets as a contingent source of liquidity, while earning a reasonable return on the investment portfolio. (Management of liquidity and other investment portfolios is discussed in chapter 9, and market risk management is discussed in chapter 10.)

As the risk profiles of different classes of instruments can differ markedly, individual portfolio managers normally take responsibility for subportfolios in different asset classes and of differing maturity profiles. A complicating factor in the investment management process arises when a bank requires collateral from counterparties (for example, for swaps). The calculation and secure management of such collateral usually involves a custodian, which requires a mechanism to ensure accurate computation and recordkeeping capacity.

Use of External Asset Managers

Bank boards of directors may sometimes authorize outsourcing the management of a specific percentage of liquid assets or investments to try to obtain a higher portfolio return or to secure a transfer of technology. The use of external managers is an effective way to obtain professional management of a bond portfolio while a bank is building internal capacity. It is important to recall, however, that at least 90 percent of the risk and return of the portfolio will come from the selection of the benchmark (through the strategic asset allocation process); no more than 10 percent is likely to come from active management by external managers.

To avoid any negative surprises, it is therefore critical that management understands the differences in expected risk and return from different benchmarks, and that the benchmarks selected for external managers have acceptable risk/return attributes. In addition, it is essential to determine how much risk external managers will be permitted, compared with the benchmark. This can be expressed in terms of an acceptable level of underperformance as measured in basis points of return.

Before embarking on an external manager program, there are important steps to take:

- Determine the selection criteria and the selection process.

- Determine the benchmarks and risk limits to be incorporated into the investment management agreements.

- Determine the fee basis (that is, flat versus performance fees).

- Establish performance review and criteria (for example, tracking error, Sharpe ratios) for firing managers.

- Monitor the manager's compliance with risk limits.

- Arrange payment of management fees.

- Establish service requirements for training.

Bank management may choose to outsource targeted amounts in stages to enable evaluation of how well the external managers are fulfilling their mandate. Knowing that the size of their mandate could be increased could also be an important incentive for the external managers to do well.

Treasury Operations

Management of the treasury operations function has become increasingly complex with changes in the financial markets, regulatory requirement changes, and technological advances.

Risk in this area is considered to be the highest when manual interventions take place. The management response has been a focus on automation of the activities of recording and settling trades—"straight-through" processing. Automation of the treasury operations function focuses a significant portion of the risk on the market operations activity where electronic inputs are made, necessitating greater control over the payment approval and release function, including enhanced control over the confirmation of transactions and the reconciliation of bank accounts at other institutions (nostro accounts).

In recent years many traditional treasury operations functions have been outsourced, but those that often remain in the treasury are

- cash management,

- banking relations,

- settlement of trades, and

- accounting, valuation, and reporting for treasury activities (asset-liability management, funding, and investing).

Settlement of Trades

Settlement risk is the risk that settlement in a transfer system will not take place as expected because one party defaults on its clearing obligations. A default on settlement leads to both credit (counterparty) and liquidity risk. The best manner in which to mitigate settlement risk is clearly to have a safe and efficient payment system.

The settlement function must ensure the proper settlement of transactions executed by the portfolio management and funding sides of the treasury. The role of settlement staff is to minimize the operational risk associated with the settlement process by strictly adhering to stated controls. To summarize, the settlement function must

- ensure that all transactions are confirmed (verbally or through SWIFT, Society for Worldwide Interbank Financial Telecommunication) on a timely basis;

- ensure that all payments are made accurately and in a timely manner;

- ensure that all receipts are recorded accurately and in a timely manner;

- ensure that all securities are delivered and received accurately and in a timely manner; and

- maintain all standard reference and static data, such as standard settlement instructions, authentication and test keys between banks, and customer information files (including phone and telex/fax numbers, bank contacts, and addresses).

All failed transactions must be monitored and followed up until resolved. Lack of notification regarding failed transactions can lead to prolonged exposure to financial and reputational risk. All failed transactions should be communicated to the trading floor, as a lack of communication between settlement staff and traders regarding fails will prevent the teams from exploring ways to eliminate avoidable failed transactions in the future.

Risks associated with the settlement function include the following:

- Transactions may be improperly entered in the trading system software. Inaccurate or incomplete trade entry could result in settlement, accounting, financial reporting, and valuation errors.

- Actionable events (reset triggers, reset rates, or other "ticklers") may be missed, resulting in errors in interest accruals, cash flows, settlement, accounting, financial reporting, and valuation.

- Derivative (legal) documentation between the bank and its counterparties may not be executed and finalized, creating possible differences in the understanding of trade details.

Cash Management and Banking Relations[2]

The major objectives of the cash management and banking relationship functions are to optimize cash planning and to facilitate the straight-through processing of funds. To achieve these objectives, staff in these areas must ensure the timely processing of payments and receipts, provide an efficient correspondent banking infrastructure, foster a high customer service level for client investigations, and minimize the operational risk associated with cash processing by following through on outstanding and suspense items.

Following are some of the risks associated with this dual function:

- Unauthorized instructions for transfers may occur if access to terminals is not strictly enforced.

- Transactions can be delayed or rejected if data are not entered in the system correctly.

- Loss and misappropriation of funds or fraud may occur as a result of improper unauthorized changes to SWIFT messages.

- Checks may be misplaced, deposited to a wrong account, or not deposited at all.

- Delivery of funds to the wrong account can delay receipt of funds by the rightful beneficiary. This creates a reputational risk and may result in monetary claims for late delivery.

---

2   Although the banking relations function could justifiably be considered to belong outside of the treasury operations area, for the sake of simplicity it is discussed here.

- Delivery of payment to the incorrect beneficiary will result in loss of funds should those payments prove unrecoverable.

- Discrepancies in value date, mismatching, and human error may result in inaccurate data and therefore incorrect cash reconciliations.

- Incorrect cash positions may be reported to trading floor cash managers, resulting in potential financial losses to the bank.

Accounting and Reporting of Treasury Activities

Accurate recordkeeping is crucial in risk management. A sound recordkeeping system should keep track of transactions on a trade-date basis and should maintain all supporting information. Postings to the general ledger and memorandum accounts should originate with and be reviewed by persons who do not have the authority to execute transactions. Ledgers should be reconciled frequently with the respective account statements and confirmations held by the staff executing the transactions. Recordkeeping should be subject to internal audit on a regular basis.

The role of the accounting function in treasury operations is to measure treasury results and reflect them in the financial statements and supporting reports. Accountants have to ensure the accuracy of any market data used in valuations and generate any accounting entries required by generally accepted accounting practice, such as the adjustment of financial assets and liabilities to fair values.

These are challenging requirements, as they require the treasury accounting function to field a full complement of personnel who are trained not only in the accounting function, but also in the substance of the various trading and derivative products. The challenge is compounded by the fact that the essential investment data typically must be sourced from many different systems, and few of these systems provide reports that could be described as user-friendly. Consequently, some management information reports must be prepared manually, with the attendant risk of data integrity errors. One way in which treasury operations managers attempt to address multiple data sources is by relying on integrated operational databases, or "data warehouses," from which management reports can be customized.

To ensure the consistency of data and reporting sources, the accounting function also may be split into two areas: one for pure reporting, and the other for reconciling key data and reports produced by different systems. The two areas involve different activities.

Accounting-related activities include

- ensuring that accounting is set up to accommodate new business requirements and products in a timely manner,
- performing daily accounting data review and control for all portfolios,
- reviewing performance reports for all portfolios as an additional validation and control of accounting information,
- reviewing new and changed trades,
- reviewing profit and loss accounts,
- preparing regulatory reports, and
- reviewing accounting entries, especially manual ones.

Reconciliation activities include

- reconciling data from different systems for accuracy, completeness, and agreement;
- reconciling the accounting system with the custodian system to ensure that all securities are accounted for (a custodian is a financial institution that keeps custody and records of a bank's or other institution's securities); and
- ensuring that all manual entries are appropriate.

Quantitative Strategies

The primary objective of a quantitative strategies function is to help strengthen the investment processes by increasing the use of analytical tools and techniques and by conducting quantitative modeling and research. Quantitative strategies apply to the disciplines of strategic asset allocation and market analysis; the quantitative strategies function also conducts financial modeling for the benefit of the investment, liquidity, funding, and asset-liability management businesses of a bank. In major banks, this function supports external clients or even other asset managers.

Models and analytical tools are used to support risk management decision making at the day-to-day business level as well as strategic risk/reward decision making at the portfolio level. As it is essential that the data used for modeling are consistent and reliable, the modeling function should be responsible for ensuring that the infrastructure by which data are centralized is adequate.

The responsibilities of the quantitative strategies function include the development and production of monthly market analysis charts, the tracking and dissemination of the market views and sentiment indicators of market strategists and participants, and the systematic synthesis and dissemination of investment research and views. These analyses should be performed internally by economists and financial analysts and externally by market and industry experts. For this function to be credible, it must develop and maintain extensive relationships with external quantitative market strategists working at broker dealers, as well as with pension fund managers and asset managers.

Model Validation

Implementation of models and handling of any system changes are operational risk issues; improper use of a model or using incorrect data with a model exposes an entity to significant operational risk.

Validation of the models used in the treasury environment is raised as a policy issue to ensure that the analyst is aware of the importance of segregating the responsibility for model development and usage from the checking and validation of such models. Table 13.5 places model development in the risk analytics function and identifies model validation as a policy issue to highlight the importance of independent checks and balances.

A Sobering Thought on Risk Models

The LTCM (Long-Term Capital Management) risk model told them that the loss they incurred on one day in August 1998 should have occurred once every 80 trillion years. It happened again the following week.

Howard Davies
Former Chairman
UK Financial Services Authority

Risk Measurement

Risk measurement and risk management focus on providing a disciplined approach to risk control in portfolio management. The objective of the function is to provide an independent assessment of the market risks being taken across the various treasury businesses. This assessment is for the benefit of risk budget decision makers (traders) as well as management. The risk factors normally covered by market risk measurement include interest rates, exchange rates, equity prices, and commodity prices.

Risk measurement requires the periodic computation of risk positions (daily, monthly, quarterly). It normally provides daily risk reporting to the portfolio managers to assist in their investment decisions and to support periodic benchmark rebalancing. It therefore benefits the risk decision makers by providing them with feedback on their positions and by facilitating the determination of future positions. Management in turn uses the outputs of the risk analytics and compliance function to monitor the risks being taken across the various business lines and to ensure compliance with established guidelines.

A prerequisite of the risk measurement function is to ensure that all securities are properly valued (that is, are marked to market). This is achieved by mapping investments to an appropriate pricing source. Proper pricing will lead to accurate measurement of total returns and performance.

Because the models used to assess the risks on treasury businesses are often run on a variety of systems and, in some cases, by third-party vendors, the risk measurement function should take responsibility for managing the complex array of risk systems and vendors. To maintain their knowledge of best practice and leading-edge technologies and techniques, staff working in this area should maintain extensive relationships with the vendors of risk management and measurement systems as well as with their market counterparts, such as pension fund and asset managers, and with broker dealers and other industry experts.

Performance Measurement and Analysis

The objective of performance measurement is to determine the total return of the benchmark and the total return of the portfolio, and to report the results to management.

Performance analysis (and attribution) is the process of decomposing the total return or cost of a portfolio into a series of primary risk factors, quantifying the extent to which key risk decisions (such as sector allocations, security selection, and benchmark or manager risk) have contributed to portfolio performance. This can be done on either an absolute or a relative basis (that is, versus an index). The objective of the performance analysis function is to develop tools and methodologies capable of measuring the contributions to performance of different levels of decision making. The goal is to have models that assess and attribute performance on an absolute basis and also relative to benchmarks, thus providing a basis for refining and improving the decision-making process. Performance attribution both contributes to and facilitates the development of the risk budgeting and risk management frameworks.

Performance and Risk Reporting

Accurate and timely reporting is essential to support decision-making processes and to support the monitoring of a treasury's performance in pursuit of its objectives. Risk-based reporting thus is a critical part of investment management and of the risk management of portfolios.

A risk reporting team should have a library of standard reports to evaluate the key performance and risk statistics needed for the assessment of investment and funding decisions; it should also have the necessary tools for ad hoc, in-depth analysis.

Portfolio reports must deliver information that is both adequate and timely enough to enable portfolio managers to evaluate their portfolio risk and size their positions such that they remain within a tolerable risk level. This information should include performance and risk measures such as duration, sensitivity, value at risk, and yield curve risk.

Each functional area should be responsible for its own reports. For example, daily compliance and risk reports should be produced respectively by the compliance and risk management teams; daily performance reports for a fixed-income portfolio (and monthly performance and attribution reports) may be generated by the treasury operational unit in collaboration with the performance attribution function. Responsibility for regular and ad hoc market-related reports may be assigned to a quantitative strategies function. Where information from multiple functional areas in a treasury is presented in a joint report, the risk analytics and compliance unit's role should be to coordinate the preparation and ensure the consistency and timely production of the report.

Compliance

The purpose of the compliance function is to ensure that all treasury transactions and business activities comply with appropriate laws, regulations, policies, guidelines, and ethical standards. A strong compliance function is an important cornerstone to counterparty and client confidence that the treasury function will act appropriately and in their best interests. It is important that the monitoring of compliance with investment, borrowing, swap authorities, and other guidelines be centralized for an entire banking group and its asset management clients.

Additional areas of responsibility of the compliance function include

- participating in due diligence meetings with external service providers and asset managers to ensure they have the capacity to assess compliance with given guidelines;

- assisting in drafting guidelines that are measurable and consistent;

- designing portfolio management policies for treasury portfolios, for example, trading limits, selection of vendors, procedures, reporting requirements, and introduction of new financial instruments;

- liaising with both the internal and external auditors; and

- assisting in the development of a treasury code of ethics.

The compliance staff must monitor compliance with guidelines and report exceptions; they must also work internally with colleagues and externally with counterparties to remedy infractions and prevent their recurrence. A mature compliance function will be able to assist with the development of treasury systems infrastructure and to participate in data quality meetings with colleagues from treasury operations and other areas.

Technology Support, Security, and Business Continuity (IT)

Although the IT function may be housed outside of the treasury, systems security requirements would necessitate that the treasury IT function be closely aligned with treasury operations. In whatever unit IT is located, it should provide the systems mechanism and infrastructure to support treasury activities. The primary success indicator of the IT function is the ability of the treasury to participate competitively in financial markets without suffering financial losses due to systems-related problems.

The IT specialist in a treasury has to provide trading floor and accounting systems capable of capturing in real time all market data, from all providers, that are needed to value any type of financial instrument. Market data should be retrievable for repricing, reporting, historical analysis, and other purposes, and the treasury systems should support trade maintenance applications, including automated rate resetting, money market rollovers, and other repetitive tasks.

The main risks and difficulties facing the treasury IT specialist include the following:

- High dependence on outside vendors. The lack of the necessary IT skills within the organization usually results in outsourcing of the activity.

- "Scope creep." Documentation of user requirements for system development projects may be threatened by the tendency of users to make changes well into the implementation phase.

- Consistent reporting from a centralized database. The production of official reports can involve numerous workflow procedures, raising the risk that data—translated into different spreadsheets using different calculation routines—will be altered.

- Information security of data, workstations, and application systems. The IT industry is advancing too quickly for most treasury security teams to keep pace, and the risks of virus attacks and break-ins are increasing.

- An adequate disaster recovery facility. Particularly in remote locations, there is a risk that business continuity could not be sustained in a major systems failure.

- Outsourcing of hardware and systems management. External standards of support may not be as stringent as those maintained internally.

- Maintaining support of application systems that utilize diverse development software. The rapid advance of IT exposes legacy systems to the inevitable danger of market expertise becoming increasingly hard to find.

14

Transparency and Data Quality

Key Messages

- Accounting information has to be useful.

- Relevance, reliability, comparability, and understandability are attributes of useful information.

- Financial statements should strive to achieve transparency through the fair presentation of useful information.

- International Financial Reporting Standards (IFRS) contain sufficient disclosure requirements to ensure fair presentation.

- Perceived deficiencies in financial reporting standards often relate to inadequate enforcement of and nonadherence to existing standards.

14.1 Introduction: The Importance of Useful Information

The provision of transparent and useful information on market participants and their transactions is an essential part of an orderly and efficient market, as well as a key prerequisite for imposing market discipline. For a risk-based approach to bank management and supervision to be effective, useful information must be provided to each key player. These players (as discussed in chapter 3) include supervisors, current and prospective shareholders and bondholders, depositors and other creditors, correspondent and other banks, counterparties, and the general public. Left alone, markets may not generate sufficient disclosure. Although market forces normally balance the marginal benefits and costs of disclosing additional information, the end result may not be what players really need.

Banking legislation traditionally has been used to force disclosure of information. However, legally mandated disclosure has involved the provision of prudential information required by bank supervisors and the compilation of statistics for monetary policy purposes, rather than the provision of information that enables a comprehensive evaluation of financial risks. Nevertheless, even such imperfect information has improved the functioning of markets.

The financial and capital market liberalization trends of the 1980s have brought increasing volatility to financial markets and consequently have increased the information needed to ensure financial stability. With the advance of financial and capital market liberalization, pressure has increased to improve the usefulness of available financial sector information through the establishment of International Financial Reporting Standards and minimum disclosure requirements. These requirements address the quality and quantity of information that must be provided to market participants and the general public. The provision of information is essential to promote the stability of the banking system, and regulatory authorities have made the improvement of information quality a high priority. Banks are also encouraged to improve their internal information systems and develop a reputation for providing quality information.

In the 1990s, the changing structure of financial intermediation further strengthened the case for enhanced disclosure. The substitution of tradable debt securities for bank lending and the increased use of financial instruments to transfer risk have reduced the importance of banker-client relationships while expanding the role of markets and market prices in the allocation of capital and risks in the financial system. This shift has also affected disclosure requirements: to make informed choices, investors need sound information about the profile and nature of risks involved.

The public disclosure of information is predicated on the existence of quality accounting standards and adequate disclosure methodology. The process normally involves publication of relevant qualitative and quantitative information in annual financial reports, which are often supplemented by biannual or quarterly financial statements and other important information. Because the provision of information can be expensive, its usefulness for the public should be weighed against cost when disclosure requirements are determined.

It is also important to time the introduction of information well. Disclosure of negative information to a public that is not sufficiently sophisticated to interpret it could damage a bank—and possibly the entire banking system. In situations where low-quality information is put forth or users are not deemed capable of properly interpreting what is disclosed, public requirements should be carefully phased in and progressively tightened. In the long run, a full-disclosure regime is beneficial, even if some immediate problems are experienced, because the cost to the financial system of not being transparent is ultimately higher than that of revealing information.

14.2 Transparency and Accountability

Transparency refers to creating an environment where information on existing conditions, decisions, and actions is made accessible, visible, and understandable to all market participants. Disclosure refers more specifically to the process and methodology of providing the information and of making policy decisions known through timely dissemination and openness. Accountability refers to the need for market participants, including the relevant authorities, to justify their actions and policies and accept responsibility for both decisions and results.

Transparency is a prerequisite for accountability, especially to borrowers and lenders, issuers and investors, and national authorities and international financial institutions. The following section discusses the benefits of transparency, emphasizes what transparency is not, and elucidates the constraints on transparent behavior.

Over the past decade, the issues of transparency and accountability have been increasingly and strongly debated as part of economic policy discussions. Policy makers in some countries have long been accustomed to secrecy, which has been viewed as a necessary ingredient for the exercise of power in sensitive situations; it also has the added benefit of hiding incompetence! However, secrecy also hinders the emergence of the desired effects of policies. The changed world economy and financial flows, which have entailed increasing internationalization and interdependence, have placed the issue of openness at the forefront of economic policy making. There is growing recognition on the part of national governments, including central banks, that transparency improves the predictability and therefore the efficiency of policy decisions. Transparency forces institutions to face up to the reality of a situation and makes officials more responsible, especially if they know they will be called upon to justify their views, decisions, and actions. For these reasons, timely policy adjustment is encouraged.

In part, the case for greater transparency and accountability rests on the need for private sector agents to understand and accept policy decisions that affect their behavior. Greater transparency improves economic decisions taken by other agents in the economy. Transparency is also a way to foster accountability, internal discipline, and better governance, while both transparency and accountability improve the quality of decision making in policy-oriented institutions. Such institutions—as well as other institutions that rely on them to make decisions—should be required to maintain transparency. If actions and decisions are visible and understandable, monitoring costs can be lowered. In addition, the general public is more able to monitor public sector institutions, shareholders and employees have a better view of corporate management, creditors monitor borrowers more adequately, and depositors are able to keep an eye on banks. Poor decisions therefore do not go unnoticed or unquestioned.

Transparency and accountability are mutually reinforcing. Transparency enhances accountability by facilitating monitoring, while accountability enhances transparency by providing an incentive to agents to ensure that their actions are properly disseminated and understood. Greater transparency reduces the tendency of markets to place undue emphasis on positive or negative news and thus reduces volatility in financial markets. Taken together, transparency and accountability can also impose discipline that improves the quality of decision making in the public sector. This can result in more efficient policies by improving the private sector's understanding of how policy makers may react to events in the future.

What transparency cannot ensure. Transparency and accountability are not, however, ends in and of themselves, nor are they panaceas to solve all problems. They are instead designed to assist in increasing economic performance and may improve the working of international financial markets by enhancing the quality of decision making and risk management among market participants. In particular, transparency does not change the nature of banking or the risks inherent in financial systems. Transparency cannot prevent financial crises, but it may moderate the responses of market participants to bad news. Transparency also helps market participants anticipate and assess negative information, and thereby mitigates panic and contagion.

Constraints on transparency. The dichotomy that exists between transparency and confidentiality should also be noted. The release of proprietary information may enable competitors to take advantage of particular situations, a fact that often deters market participants from full disclosure. Similarly, monitoring bodies frequently obtain confidential information from financial institutions, an event that can have significant market implications. Under such circumstances, financial institutions may be reluctant to provide sensitive information without the guarantee of client confidentiality. However, both unilateral transparency and full disclosure contribute to a regime of transparency. If such a regime were to become the norm, it would ultimately benefit all market participants, even if in the short term it might create discomfort for individual entities.

14.3 Transparency in Financial Statements

The objective of financial statements is to provide information about an entity's financial position (balance sheet), performance (income statement), and changes in financial position (cash flow statement). The transparency of financial statements is secured through full disclosure and by providing fair presentation of the information necessary for making economic decisions to a wide range of users. In the context of public disclosure, financial statements should be easy to interpret.

As can be expected, specific disclosure requirements vary among regulators. Nonetheless, there are certain key principles whereby standards should be evaluated, according to a report submitted to the G7 finance ministers and central bank governors in 2000. These key principles are summarized in box 14.1.

Box 14.1 Criteria for Evaluating International Financial Reporting Standards

Financial reporting (accounting) standards should **contribute** to—or at least be consistent with (and not hamper)—sound risk management and control practices in banks. They should also provide a prudent and reliable framework for generating high-quality accounting information in banks.

Accounting standards should **facilitate** market discipline by promoting transparent reporting of banks' financial position and performance, risk exposures, and risk management activities. Accounting standards should facilitate and **not constrain the effective** supervision of banks.

Disclosure should be sufficiently comprehensive to allow assessment of a bank's financial position and performance, risk exposures, and risk management activities. International financial reporting standards should be suitable for implementation not only in the most advanced financial markets but also in emerging markets.

Certain specific criteria underpin high-quality accounting. Accounting principles should generate relevant and meaningful accounting information. They should generate prudent, realistic, and reliable measurements of financial position and performance and consistent measurements of similar or related items.

There are also certain internationally accepted criteria for financial reporting standards. Accounting standards should not only have a sound theoretical foundation, but also be workable in practice. Accounting standards should not be overly complex in relation to the issue addressed. They should be sufficiently precise to ensure consistent application, and they should not allow alternative treatments. When alternative treatments are permitted, or judgments are necessary in applying accounting principles, balanced disclosures should be required.

Source: Basel Committee on Banking Supervision,
Report to G7 Finance Ministers and Central Bank Governors, April 2000

The adoption of International Financial Reporting Standards (IFRS) has been a necessary measure to facilitate transparency and proper interpretation of financial statements. In 1989, the Framework for the Preparation and

Presentation of Financial Statements was included in the IFRS to accomplish the following:

- Explain concepts underlying the preparation and presentation of financial statements to external users
- Guide those responsible for developing accounting standards
- Assist preparers, auditors, and users in interpreting the IFRS and in dealing with issues not yet covered by the standards

Financial statements are normally prepared under the assumption that an entity will continue to operate as a going concern and that events will be recorded on an accrual basis. In other words, the effects of transactions and other events should be recognized when they occur and be reported in the financial statements for the periods to which they relate.

Qualitative characteristics are those attributes that make the information provided in financial statements useful. If comprehensive, useful information does not exist, managers may not be aware of the true financial condition of their bank and key governance players may be misled. This would in turn prevent the proper operation of market discipline. In contrast, the application of key qualitative characteristics and appropriate accounting standards normally results in financial statements that present a true and fair picture. Following are the requisite qualitative characteristics of financial information:

- **Relevance.** Information must be relevant because it influences the economic decisions of users by helping them to evaluate past, present, and future events or to confirm or correct past assessments. The relevance of information is determined by its nature and material quality. Information overload, on the other hand, can force players to sift through a plethora of information for relevant details, making interpretation difficult.

- **Reliability.** Information should be free from material errors and bias. The key aspects of reliability are faithful representation, priority of substance over form, neutrality, prudence, and completeness.

- **Comparability.** Information should be presented consistently over time and be congruous with related information and with other entities to enable users to make comparisons.

- **Understandability.** Information should be easily comprehended by users with reasonable knowledge of business, economics, and accounting, as well as the willingness to diligently study the information.

The process of producing useful information comprises the following critical points to ensure the comprehensiveness of the information provided:

- **Timeliness.** A delay in reporting may improve reliability, but could simultaneously result in decreased relevance.

- **Benefit vs. cost.** Benefits derived from information should normally exceed the cost of providing it. Banks in developing countries often lack adequate accounting systems and therefore have a lower capacity for providing relevant information. The level of sophistication of the target audience is also important. Both of these aspects affect the costs and benefits of improved disclosure. However, the mere fact that that a bank might not have accounting systems capable of producing useful information should not be accepted as an excuse for not obtaining and providing it for the markets.

- **Balancing qualitative characteristics.** Providers of information must achieve an appropriate balance of qualitative characteristics to ensure financial statements are adequate for their particular environment.

In the context of fair presentation, it is better to not disclose information than to disclose information that is misleading. It is therefore not surprising that when an entity does not comply with specific disclosure requirements, the IFRS require full disclosure of the fact and the reasons for noncompliance. Figure 14.1 summarizes how transparency is secured through the proper application of the concepts making up the IFRS framework.

Figure 14.1 Transparency in Financial Statements

Transparency in Financial Statements

OBJECTIVE OF FINANCIAL STATEMENTS
To provide a fair presentation of
• Financial position
• Financial performance
• Cash flows

TRANSPARENCY AND FAIR PRESENTATION
• Fair presentation achieved through providing useful information (full disclosure), which secures transparency
• Fair presentation equals transparency

SECONDARY OBJECTIVE OF FINANCIAL STATEMENTS
To secure transparency through a fair presentation of useful information (full disclosure) for decision-making purposes

ATTRIBUTES OF USEFUL INFORMATION

Existing framework	**Alternative views**
• Relevance	• Relevance
• Reliability	• Predictive value
• Comparability	• Faithful representation
• Understandability	• Free from bias
Constraints	• Verifiable
• Timeliness	
• Benefit versus cost	
• Balancing the qualitative characteristics	

UNDERLYING ASSUMPTIONS
Accrual basis   Going concern

14.4 Disclosure in the Financial Statements of Banks

Disclosure requirements related to financial statements have traditionally been a pillar of sound regulation. Disclosure is an effective mechanism to expose banks to market discipline. Although a bank is normally subject to supervision and provides regulatory authorities with information, this information is often confidential or market sensitive and is not always available to all categories of users. Disclosure in financial statements should therefore be sufficiently comprehensive to meet the needs of other users within the constraints of what can reasonably be required. Improved transparency through better disclosure may (but not necessarily) reduce the chances of a systemic banking crisis or the effects of contagion, as creditors and other market participants will be better able to distinguish between the financial circumstances that face different institutions and countries.

Users of financial statements need information to assist them in evaluating a bank's financial position and performance and in making economic decisions. Of key importance are a realistic valuation of assets, including sensitivities to future events and adverse developments, and the proper recognition of income and expenses. Equally important is the evaluation of a bank's entire risk profile, including on- and off-balance-sheet items, capital adequacy, the capacity to withstand short-term problems, and the ability to generate additional capital. Users may also need information to better understand the special characteristics of a bank's operations, in particular solvency, liquidity, and the relative degree of risk involved in various dimensions of the banking business.

The issuance of IFRS has followed developments in international financial markets. Over time, the coverage of IFRS has been broadened to both include new topics (for example, disclosure and presentation related to new financial instruments) and enhance the existing international standards.

Historically, Generally Accepted Accounting Practices (GAAP) did not place heavy burdens on banks to disclose their financial risk management practices. This situation changed in the 1990s with the introduction of International Accounting Standard (IAS) 30 (subsequently scrapped with introduction of IFRS 7) and IAS 32 (whose disclosure requirements were transferred to IFRS 7). IAS 32, which is now largely superseded by IFRS 7, resulted in many financial regulators requiring a "full disclosure" approach.

IAS 30 encouraged management to comment on financial statements describing the way liquidity, solvency, and other risks associated with the operations of a bank were managed and controlled. Although some banking risks may be reflected in financial statements, a commentary can help users to understand their management. That provision is now embodied in IFRS 7, which is applicable to all banks, meaning all financial institutions that take deposits and borrow from the general public with the objective of lending and investing and that fall within the scope of banking-related or similar legislation.

IAS 39 establishes principles for recognizing, measuring, and disclosing information about financial instruments in the financial statements. The standard significantly increases the use of fair value accounting for financial instruments, particularly on the assets side of the balance sheet. Despite the introduction of IAS 39, leading accounting standard setters are still deliberating the advantages and disadvantages of introducing fair market value accounting for financial assets and liabilities as well as for the corresponding risks. This process should foster a consistent, market-based approach to measuring the risk related to various financial instruments. However, without prudent and balanced standards for estimating fair value, the use of a fair-value model could reduce the reliability of financial statements and increase the volatility of earnings and equity measurements. This is particularly true when active markets do not exist, as is often the case for loans, which frequently account for the lion's share of a bank's assets.

IAS 39 distinguishes between four classes of financial assets: assets held at fair value through profit and loss (for example, trading and other elected securities); assets available for sale; assets held to maturity; and loans and receivables. In addition, IAS 39 identifies two classes of financial liabilities: those at fair value, and liabilities shown at amortized cost. The standard outlines the accounting approach in each case (see table 14.1). It also categorizes and sets out the accounting treatment for three types of hedging: (a) fair value, (b) cash flow, and (c) net investment in a foreign subsidiary.

Table 14.1 Measurement of Financial Assets and Liabilities under IAS 39

Category	Measurement	Financial Assets Classes	Financial Liabilities Classes	Comments
1	Fair value through profit and loss	Trading securities	Trading liabilities	Short sales or issued debt with intention to repurchase shortly
		Derivatives	Derivatives	Unless designated as qualifying hedging instruments
		Other elected assets	Other elected liabilities	Fair value option (elected)— inconsistencies reduced where part of a documented group risk management strategy, or liabilities contain embedded derivatives
2	Amortized cost	Held-to-maturity securities	Accounts payable Issued debt securities Deposits from customers	
3	Amortized cost	Loans and receivables	N/A	
4	Fair value through equity	Available-for-sale securities	N/A	

The only potentially controversial portion of IAS 39 relates to the treatment of impairments of financial instruments, which states that an asset is impaired if there is objective evidence (including observable data) as a result of one or more events that have already occurred after the initial recognition of the asset. Objective evidence includes significant financial difficulty of a debt issuer or obligor, a breach of contract such as a default or delinquency in interest or principal payments, or granting the borrower a concession that the lender would not otherwise consider.

IAS 39 requires that when performing a collective assessment of impairment, assets must be grouped according to similar credit risk characteristics, indicative of the debtors' ability to pay all amounts due according to the contractual terms. Loss events must have an impact on future cash flows that can be reliably estimated.

Losses expected as a result of future events, no matter how likely, are not recognized. (This conditionality appears to create a conflict with bank supervisory approaches that require a general percentage provision for loan losses, based on empirical evidence that such losses have actually occurred somewhere in the portfolio. The differences in approach need not be insurmountable if one considers historical realities related to loan portfolios.)

IAS 32 and IFRS 7 supplement other international financial reporting standards that apply equally to nonbank and banking entities. The disclosure requirements, as well as other accounting standards specific to banks, are derived from the IFRS framework. The standard entitled "Presentation of Financial Statements" gives general guidance on the basic principles, structure, and content of financial statements.

Although separate IFRS standards were issued (IAS 32, IAS 39, and IFRS 7), they are applied in practice as a unit because they deal with exactly the same accounting phenomenon. IAS 39, which deals with the recognition and measurement of financial instruments, also contains supplementary disclosures to those required by IAS 32.

IFRS 7 aims to rectify some of the remaining gaps in financial risk disclosure by adding to the existing accounting standards the requirements described in table 14.2.

Table 14.2 Financial Risk Disclosure Requirements under IFRS 7v

Measurement	Instruments	Nature & Extent of Risks	Significance	Statement of Financial Position	Statement of Comprehensive Income	Hedging
Assets						
Fair value through P&L	Trading securities			Carrying values	Net gains & losses	Description
	Designated fair value assets			Reclassification	Net gains & losses – separate disclosure of movements through equity – AFS assets	Gains & Losses
	Derivatives	Each type of risk from assets & liabilities: qualitative & quantitative	Value of financial instruments must be stated on Statement of Financial Position	Derecognition	Total interest income & expense (using effective interest rate method)	Effectiveness
		Credit risk – per class of asset	or	Collateral – for assets pledged		Ineffective portions transferred from equity – where applicable
Fair value through equity	Available-for-sale securities	Liquidity risk – all financial liabilities	Related amounts shown on Statement of Comprehensive Income	Impairments – by class		
Amortized securities	Held-to-maturity securities (HTM)	Market risk by type – all assets & liabilities				
Amortized assets – other	Loans & receivables					
Liabilities						
Fair value through P&L	Trading securities			Embedded equity derivatives		
	Designated fair value assets					
	Derivatives			Defaults & breaches (loans payable)		
Amortized liabilities	Other liabilities					

351

Current international financial reporting standards provide a solid and transparent basis for the development of national disclosure requirements. These standards already require banks to disclose extensive information on all of the categories of risk that have been addressed here, adding transparency to the presentation of financial statements.

The Basel Committee on Banking Supervision has stated its belief that the fair-value approach is appropriate in situations where it is workable—for example, when financial instruments are being held for trading purposes.

14.5 Application of Accounting Standards

For several years, but especially in the wake of the East Asian financial crises of the late 1990s, there has been criticism regarding deficiencies in bank accounting that have resulted in the incomplete and inadequate presentation of financial information in annual financial reports. Market participants perceive the opacity of financial information not only as official oversight but also as the Achilles' heel of effective corporate governance and market discipline. Market participants need a wide range of economic and financial information for decision-making purposes and therefore react negatively to poor disclosure.

There seems to be a perception among market participants and the general public that the lack of adequate information about a bank's financial position, results, and cash flow are the consequence of insufficient accounting standards. This misperception seems to stem from general ignorance of the sound accounting standards that already exist.

Contrary to popular belief among nonaccountants, the predominant problem is not always a lack of sound and adequate accounting standards, but rather that regulatory and accounting authorities do not enforce the principles underlying existing standards. In fact, the establishment of disclosure requirements is not sufficient in and of itself. Disclosure requirements have to be accompanied by active regulatory enforcement—and perhaps even fraud laws—to ensure that the information disclosed is complete, timely, and not deliberately misleading. Regulatory institutions need to have adequate enforcement capacities.

Both banks and their external auditors may lack proper incentives to disclose more than the regulatory authorities and market discipline demand of them. Market participants, as well as rating agencies, could therefore make a valuable contribution to improving the level of transparency in financial reporting by demanding comprehensive, full disclosure. They could also demonstrate a direct link between investor confidence and transparent disclosure. In addition, disclosure could be improved by peer pressure. A bank's competitors could demonstrate that disclosure is advantageous to an institution because investors and depositors are more likely to provide capital and deposits at lower prices to transparent entities than to nontransparent ones.

Disclosure Practices

A frequent problem with disclosure, especially that which involves a new system, is the hesitancy of a bank's management and supervisors, as well as market participants, to disclose highly negative information. Such information, which has the strongest potential to trigger a market reaction, typically is disclosed at the last possible moment and is often incomplete. Even professional members of the public, such as rating agencies, may be slow to react to and disclose potential problems. The Basel Committee for Banking Supervision has been monitoring bank disclosure practices for several years. In a May 2002 report on the results of the 2000 disclosure survey, the Basel Committee made the following observations:

- Most basic information relating to capital structure and ratios, accounting and presentation policies, credit risk, and market risk was well disclosed.

- Information about credit risk modeling, credit derivatives, and securitization was disclosed by fewer than half of the banks.

- The most notable increases in disclosure involved questions about complex capital instruments, policies and procedures for setting credit risk allowances, securitization, and operational and legal risks—although securitization disclosures still was not very frequent.

- Most banks continued to release fundamental quantitative data pertinent to their capital structure, as would be required under the Pillar 3 working paper. Although they were less forthcoming about their holdings of innovative and complex capital instruments, the rate of disclosure in this area has generally been improving.

- The risk-based capital ratio was almost always disclosed, but fewer than half of the banks provided information on the credit and market risks against which the capital serves as a buffer.

■ Most banks appeared to make fairly extensive disclosures about their internal models for market risk. The main opportunity for future improvement involves the results of stress testing.

■ Just over half of the banks described fully their process for assessing credit exposures, and only a few more provided summary information on the use of internal ratings. Fewer than half provided basic information about their credit risk models. These disclosure areas take increased importance under the proposed revision of the Basel Capital Accord, as disclosure of key information regarding the use of internal ratings will be necessary for banks to qualify for the internal ratings–based approach in the new accord. In this regard, the large improvement in the disclosure of the internal risk rating process since the 1999 survey is encouraging. In the area of asset securitization, less than one half of banks provided even the most basic disclosure of the amount and types of assets securitized and the associated accounting treatment.

■ Most banks disclosed key quantitative information concerning credit risk, another area with required disclosures under the Pillar 3 working paper. Disclosures of provisioning policies and procedures are improving. About one-half of the banks discussed the techniques they use to manage impaired assets. However, only a small number of banks disclosed the effect of their use of credit risk mitigants.

■ Approximately three-fourths of banks discussed their objectives for derivatives and their strategies for hedging risk. The proportion of banks making quantitative disclosures was lower, and trends here are mixed.

■ Approximately two-fifths of banks that use credit derivatives disclosed their strategy and objectives for the use of these instruments, as well as the amount outstanding. However, more detailed information was not often provided.

■ While approximately four-fifths of banks provided breakdowns of their trading activities by instrument type, somewhat fewer provided information about the diversification of their credit risks. Fewer than one-half supplied a categorical breakdown of problem credits.

■ There was a dramatic increase in the rate of disclosures of operational and legal risks since the first survey, although the level is still not as high as that for the more basic market and credit risk information.

■ Basic accounting policies and practices were generally well disclosed.

The results of the Basel Committee 2001 survey was published in May 2003 and a portion of the results are summarized in table 14.3.

Table 14.3 Public Disclosures by Banks

Accounting and Presentation Policies	1999	2000	2001
Total number of banks	57	55	54
Qualitative disclosures:			
Disclosed the basis of measurement for assets at initial recognition and subsequent periods, e.g., fair value or historical cost	98%	100%	100%
Described the accounting policies and method of income recognition used for trading activities (using both cash instruments and derivatives) and non-trading activities	91%	89%	93%
Described the treatment of hedging relationships affecting the measurement of assets	80%	85%	85%
Disclosed the basis for determining when assets are considered past-due and/or impaired for accounting and disclosure purposes (number of days where appropriate)	77%	80%	83%
Quantitative disclosures:			
Disclosed income and expense information grouped by nature or function within the bank	89%	98%	98%
Provided summary information about how trading activities affect earnings, based on internal measurement and accounting systems	88%	85%	83%
Distinguished between trading assets and trading liabilities	50%	48%	47%
All disclosures	**82%**	**84%**	**84%**

Source: *2001 Disclosure Survey,* Basel Committee on Banking Supervision, May 2003.

15

A Risk-Based Approach to Bank Supervision

Key Messages

- The analyst or supervisor should determine what happened, why it happened, the impact of events, and a credible future strategy to rectify unacceptable trends.

- The supervisory process of off- and on-site supervision is similar to the financial analysis of information, which has to be tested through verification of preliminary conclusions. On-site examination is essential, but could be performed by supervisors, analysts, or external auditors.

- Regulators and supervisors should ensure that all financial institutions are supervised using a consistent philosophy, to ensure a level playing field for financial intermediaries.

- Properly used, banking analysis can enhance the institutional development of the banks concerned.

- Supervisory review, recognized as Pillar 2, has become a key ingredient of the capital adequacy framework under the Basel II Accord.

15.1 Introduction: The Bank Supervisory Process

Banking supervision, based on the ongoing analytical review of banks, serves the public good as one of the important factors in maintaining stability and confidence in the financial system. It represents Pillar 2 of the Basel II Accord and has become the key ingredient of the capital adequacy framework. This chapter discusses the key principles of supervisory reviews and the relationship between banking risk analysis and the supervision process. From the methodological perspective, an analytical review of banks by supervisors is similar to that used by private sector analysts, external auditors, or a bank's own risk managers, except for the focus and ultimate purpose of the analysis.

Bank supervision, which normally includes off-site surveillance and on-site examinations, is an integral part of a much broader and continuous process, as summarized in figure 15.1. This process includes the establishment of a legal framework for the banking sector, the designation of regulatory and supervisory authorities, the definition of licensing conditions and criteria, and the enactment of regulations that limit the level of risk that banks are allowed to take. Other necessary steps include the establishment of a framework for prudential reporting and off-site surveillance and the execution of these activities, followed by on-site supervision. The results of on-site examinations provide inputs for the institutional development process of relevant banks and for the improvement of the regulatory and supervisory environment.

With growing integration and interdependence of international financial markets, banking supervision has become an increasingly important means to strengthen both national systems and the global financial system. In 1997, the Basel Committee on Banking Supervision (BCBS) published a set of principles, known as the Basel Core Principles (BCP), that provide a framework of minimum standards for sound supervisory practices and are considered universally applicable. The BCP are neutral about different approaches to supervision. Since their inception, the BCP have become a de facto standard for sound prudential regulation and supervision of banks. The updated 2005 version of the BCP is provided in appendix C.

In addition to effective supervision, other factors necessary for the stability of banking and financial systems and markets include sound and sustainable macroeconomic policies, a well-developed financial sector infrastructure, effective market discipline, and an adequate banking sector safety net (see chapter 2).

Figure 15.1 The Context of Bank Supervision

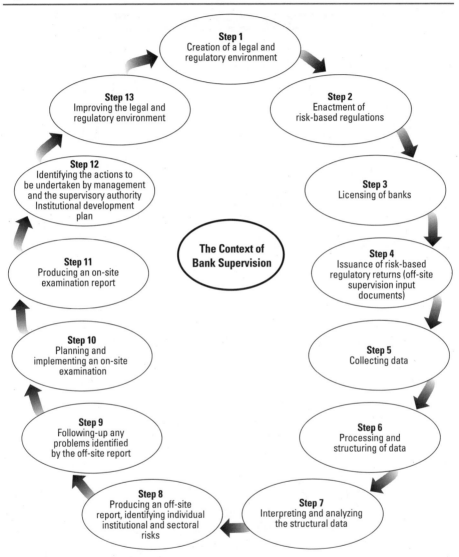

A risk-based supervisory analysis of banks follows a number of stages; the results of one stage serve as inputs to the next. The ultimate objective of this process is a set of recommendations that, if properly implemented, result in a safe, sound, and properly functioning financial intermediary. Table 15.1 summarizes the stages of the analytical review process.

Table 15.1 Stages of the Analytical Review Process

Analytical Phase	Source/Tools Available	Output
Structuring and collection of input data	Questionnaire, financial statements, other financial data	Completed input data, questionnaires, and financial data tables
Processing of data	Completed input data (questionnaires and financial data tables)	Processed output data
Analysis/interpretation of processed/structured output data	Data converted into information	Analytical results
Development of an off-site analysis report of the bank's risks	Analytical results and previous on-site examination reports	Off-site examination report and/or terms of reference for on-site examination
Follow-up through on-site examination, audit, or analytical review	Off-site examination report and terms of reference for on-site examination	On-site examination report and institutional development plan or a memorandum of understanding
Institutional strengthening	On-site examination report and memorandum of understanding for institutional development	Well-functioning financial intermediary
Repeat the process building on the previous reports and regulatory deficiencies identified	Repeat the process . . .	Repeat the process . . .

Pillar 1 of the Basel II Accord sets a buffer for uncertainties that affect the banking population as a whole. The buffer aims to provide reasonable assurance that a bank with good internal systems and well-managed controls, a "standard" business profile, and a well-diversified risk profile will meet the minimum goals for soundness, as embodied in Pillar 1. Bank-specific uncertainties are expected to be assessed and addressed under Pillar 2. Supervisors should therefore regularly review and evaluate banks' internal processes and systems, especially related to risk management and capital adequacy assessment, as well as their ability to monitor and ensure their compliance with regulatory capital ratios and other prudential norms (Pillar 2, Principle 2). In this context, supervisory processes should ensure that various instruments that can reduce Pillar 1 capital requirements are well understood and used as part of a sound, tested, and properly documented risk management process. If not, supervisors should require (or encourage) banks to operate with a capital buffer that is over and above the Pillar 1 standard (Pillar 2, Principle 3).

An analytical review normally comprises a review of the bank's financial conditions, its internal processes and systems, and specific issues related to risk exposure and risk management. In addition to verifying the conclusions reached during off-site reviews, on-site reviews cover a much larger number of topics and are more concerned with qualitative aspects, including the availability and quality of management information. The questions asked during all phases of the analytic review process should focus on

- what happened,

- why it happened,

- the impact of the event or trend,

- the actions or response of the bank's management, and

- the systems and tools that the bank had at its disposal to deal with the issue and whether it effectively utilized them.

The details that an analyst should look for during an analytical review related to risk management have been discussed in chapters 4 through 13. Analytical tools provided in this publication were discussed in section 1.5, including tables and graphs based on processed input data that relate to balance sheet structure, profitability, capital adequacy, credit and market risk, liquidity, and currency risk. Taken together, they make up a complete set of a bank's financial ratios that are normally subject to off-site surveillance. The tables enable analysts to judge the effectiveness of the risk management process and to measure performance. Combined with the qualitative information obtained from the questionnaire (see appendix 1), these statistical tables make up the raw material on which the analysis contained in off-site reports is based. Graphs provide a visual representation of results and are in essence a snapshot of the current situation in a bank. The graphs illustrated in the publication may also be used during the process of off-site surveillance as a starting point for on-site examination.

15.2 Banking Risks and the Accountability of Regulatory/Supervisory Authorities

During the course of their operations, banks are subject to a wide array of risks, as summarized in table 15.2. In general, banking risks fall into the following three categories:

- **Financial risks,** as discussed in chapters 7 through 12.

- **Operational risks** related to a bank's overall business strategy and the functioning of its internal systems, including computer systems and technology, compliance with policies and procedures, and the possibility of mismanagement and fraud (chapter 13).

- **Environmental risks,** including all types of exogenous risks that, if they were to materialize, could jeopardize a bank's operations or undermine its financial condition and capital adequacy. Such risks include political events (for example, the fall of a government), poor financial infrastructure, natural contagion resulting from the failure of a major bank or a market crash, banking crises, natural disasters, and civil wars. Event risks are, in most cases, unexpected until immediately before the event occurs. Therefore, banks may not be able to adequately prepare for such risks other than by maintaining a capital cushion. The dividing line between the end of an event risk and the beginning of systemic risk is often blurred.

Table 15.2 Banking Risk Exposures

Financial Risks	Operational Risks	Environmental Risks
Balance sheet structure	Internal fraud	Country & political risk
Earnings & income statement structure	External fraud	Macroeconomic policy
Capital adequacy	Employment practices and workplace safety	Financial infrastructure
Credit	Clients, products and business services	Legal infrastructure
Liquidity	Damage to physical assets	Banking crisis & contagion
Market	Business disruption and system failures (technology risk)	
Interest rate	Execution, delivery and process management	
Currency		

Risk that is inherent in banking should be recognized, monitored, and controlled. Some financial risks are regulated through prudential guidelines for a particular type of banking risk exposure. The effectiveness of a bank's management of financial risk, monitoring of risk exposure, and compliance with prudential guidelines by bank supervision form the backbone of the bank supervision process, both off- and on-site. Regulations, however, can be costly for a bank. The manner in which regulators perform their functions determines the specific impact of regulations on the market, as well as the *cost of compliance* for the bank. Costs include provision of information to regulators; maintenance of an institution's internal systems that measure risk and ensure compliance with regulations; and restrictions that may influence certain business decisions, effectively reducing a bank's profitability. In addition to the direct cost of regulation, hidden costs also exist, such as a bank's compromised ability to innovate or quickly adjust to changing market conditions, which might in turn prevent it from capitalizing on its comparative advantages or competitive position.

With regard to operational risks (with the exception of business strategy risk), regulators typically establish guidelines that banks are expected to follow. Adherence to the guidelines is subject to supervision, typically as part of an on-site examination. A bank's business strategy is also given attention. As part of the initial licensing process, the authorities review and implicitly endorse a bank's business strategy. The strategy and its risk implications are always discussed during the process of an on-site examination and possibly also in the context of off-site surveillance. In many countries, senior management is obliged to conduct quarterly discussions on a bank's business strategy with supervisory authorities, especially in the case of large banks upon which market stability may depend.

The category of risks related to a business environment may or may not fall within the scope of supervisory authorities. Banking system regulatory authorities (including the central bank) are usually closely related to many key aspects of a bank's business environment, however. Entry and licensing regulations effectively determine a banking system's structure and the level and nature of competition. The criteria for issuing licenses must therefore be consistent with those applied in ongoing supervision. If the supervisory authority is different from the licensing authority, the former should have a legal right to have its views considered by the latter.

Monetary authorities also play a critical role in determining a business environment. The choice, design, and use of monetary policy measures and instruments are inextricably related to banking system conditions, the nature of bank competition, and the capacity of the banking system to innovate. In the choice and use of policy instruments, pragmatic considerations (which imply a connection to supervisory authorities) are of prime importance. It is essential to look not only at specific policies or measures, but also at the context in which they are applied. Similar policies may be transmitted but work in different ways, depending on the structure, financial conditions, and dynamics of the banking system and markets. Supervisory authorities are not involved with other aspects of business environments that have risk implications, such as macroeconomic policies, which often determine supply and demand conditions in markets and are a major component of country risk. In addition, authorities are not usually directly concerned with the tax environment (which directly affects a bank's bottom line), the legal framework, or the financial sector infrastructure (including the payment system and registries), but they may be very influential in proposing changes and improvements in these areas.

Supervisory authorities play a critical role in event risks. Although these risks may not be foreseen and often cannot be prevented, the authorities evaluate the impact of such events on the status and condition of the banking system and of the markets. They also ensure that proper arrangements are put in place to minimize the impact and extent of disruption, to mobilize other authorities to effectively deal with the consequences of certain events, and, ultimately, to oversee the orderly exit of failed institutions.

15.3 The Supervisory Process

All banking systems have at least one regulatory and supervisory authority. However, the locus, structure, regulatory and enforcement powers, and specific responsibilities of each authority are different. This variation is usually a consequence of traditions and of the legal and economic environment of a particular country. Decisions on regulatory and supervisory authorities are sometimes politically motivated. In most countries, the regulatory and supervisory authority for the banking sector is assigned to the central bank, but the current trend is for the consolidation of all financial supervision in a separate entity, outside the central bank. The responsibilities of bank supervision usually include the following:

- Issuance and withdrawal of banking licenses on an exclusive basis

- Issuance and enforcement of prudential regulations and standards

- Authority to prescribe and obtain periodic reports (that is, establish prudential reporting as a precondition for off-site surveillance) and to perform on-site inspections

- Assessment of fines and penalties and the initiation of emergency actions, including cease and desist orders, management removal and suspension orders, and the imposition of conservatorship

- Closure and/or liquidation of banks

Supervisory review should specifically assess the following material risks faced by the bank:

■ Credit risk review involves internal risk rating systems, portfolio analysis and aggregation, securitization and use of complex credit derivatives, exposure to risk, and risk concentration.

■ Operational risk review involves assessing the bank's tolerance for operational risk and its approach to identifying, assessing, monitoring, controlling, and mitigating the risk.

■ Market risk review involves the methodologies used to assess and manage this risk by individual staff members, business units, and bankwide. For more sophisticated banks, the assessment of internal capital adequacy for market risk should be based, at a minimum, on value-at-risk modeling and stress testing, including risk concentration and illiquidity under stressful market scenarios. For all banks, supervisory review should include stress testing appropriate for the individual bank's trading activity.

■ Interest rate risk assessment should review assumptions, techniques, and management practices for all material interest rate positions, including relevant repricing and maturity data.

In addition, the supervisory review should examine the bank's management information reporting and systems, the manner in which business risks and activities are aggregated, and management's record in responding to emerging or changing risks. Close attention should be given to the bank's internal control structures—their coverage and their effectiveness.

The supervisory review process under Pillar 2 of the Basel II Accord grants initial approval and validation of banks' capacity to use "advanced" methods for capital assessment under Pillar 1, in particular the internal rating-based framework for credit risk and the advanced measurement approaches for operational risk. The review must verify compliance, on a continuing basis, with the minimum standards and disclosure requirements related to the use of advanced methods in Pillar 1. The review must assess risks that are not fully captured by the Pillar 1 process (for example, credit concentration risk) and factors not taken into account by the Pillar 1 process (for example, interest rate, business, and strategic risk). The impact of factors external to the bank (for example, business cycle effects) must be considered. The supervisory review process under Pillar 2 is intended not only to ensure that banks understand and have adequate risk management processes and capital to support all the risks in their business, but also to encourage banks to develop and use better risk management techniques in monitoring and managing their risks.

To be effective, a supervisory authority must have appropriate enforcement power and an adequate degree of autonomy. Enforcement and autonomy are necessary if the authority is to resist undue pressures from the government, banks and their shareholders, depositors and creditors, borrowers, and other people who use financial services. Supervisory authorities should command the respect of the banks they oversee.

The Basel Committee on Bank Supervision has identified certain preconditions and set certain standards for effective banking supervision (appendix C). These standards require that a supervisory authority has a clear, achievable, and consistent framework of responsibilities and objectives, as well as the ability to achieve them. If more than one supervisory authority exists, all must operate within a consistent and coordinated framework to avoid regulatory and supervisory arbitrage. Where distinctions between banking business and other deposit-taking entities are not clear, the latter could be allowed to operate as quasi-banks, with less regulation. Supervisory authorities should have adequate resources, including the staffing, funding, and technology needed to meet established objectives, provided on terms that do not undermine the autonomy, integrity, and independence of the supervisory agencies. Supervisors must be protected from personal and institutional liability for actions taken in good faith while performing their duties. Supervisory agencies should be obliged to cooperate and share relevant information, both domestically and abroad. This cooperation should be supported by arrangements for protecting the confidentiality of information.

Supervisory authorities, however, cannot guarantee that banks will not fail. The potential for bank failure is an integral part of risk taking. Supervisors have a role to play, but there is a difference between their role in the day-to-day supervision of solvent institutions and their handling of problem institutions to prevent contagion and systemic crisis. Supervisors should seek to intervene at an early stage to prevent capital from falling below the minimum levels required to support the risk characteristics of a particular bank and should require rapid remedial action if capital is not maintained or restored (Pillar 2, Principle 4 of the Basel II Accord). These actions may include intensifying the monitoring of the bank, restricting the payment of dividends, requiring the bank to prepare and implement a satisfactory capital adequacy restoration plan, and requiring the bank to raise additional capital immediately. Supervisors should have the discretion to use the tools best suited to the circumstances of the bank and its operating environment (see figure 15.2).

When approaching systemic issues, the key concern of supervisory authorities is to address threats to confidence in the financial system and of contagion to otherwise sound banks. The supervisor's responsibility is to make adequate arrangements that could facilitate the exit of problem banks with minimum disruption to the system. At the same time, the methods applied should minimize distortions to market signals and discipline. Individual bank failure, on the other hand, is an issue for shareholders and management. In some cases, a bank failure may become a political issue—especially in the case of large banks—and involve decisions whether, to what extent, and in what form public funds should be committed to turning the situation around.

Figure 15.2 Supervisory Tools

Supervisory Tools			
Tools	Area of application	Advantages	Disadvantages
Rules	Pillar I: Capital requirements	Certainty Simplicity Direct	Static Inflexible Limited
Incentives	Pillar I: Approaches	Behavioral impact	Sensitivity
Discretion	Pillar II: Supervisory review	Adaptable	Uncertainty Not comparable
Market discipline (Disclosure)	Pillar III	Market-based	Overshoots

Off-site Surveillance versus On-site Examination

An effective banking supervision system comprises some form of both off-site surveillance and on-site examination. Table 15.3 summarizes the different focuses of these two processes. Off-site surveillance is, in essence, an early-warning device that is based on the analysis of financial data supplied by banks. On-site examination builds upon and supplements off-site surveillance and enables supervisory authorities to examine details and to judge a bank's future viability. The extent of on-site work and the method by which it is carried out depend on a variety of factors. In addition to differences in supervisory approaches and techniques, the key determinant of the objectives and scope of supervision is whether they aim only to safeguard banking system stability or if they are also expected to protect the interest of depositors. In some countries, a mixed system of on-site examination exists that is based on collaboration between supervisors and external auditors.

Table 15.3 Off-site Surveillance versus On-site Examination

Off-Site Surveillance	On-Site Examination
Objectives	
Monitor the financial condition of both individual banks and the banking system	Monitor the financial condition, performance, and future viability of individual banks
Provide peer statistics and the means for comparison with a peer group	Assess reasons for deviations from peer group
Provide early identification of problems and noncompliance	Provide a detailed diagnosis of problems and noncompliance
Give priorities for the use of supervisory resources	Provide recommendations to management
Guide scheduling of on-site examinations	Initiate punitive actions as needed
Methodology	
Analytical, risk-based	Analytical, risk-based
Descriptive	Evaluative, tests descriptions
Uses questionnaires and prescribed reporting formats	Uses interrogation of and discussions with bank management and responsible staff
Based on financial data reporting	Based on on-site visits and examination of actual records
Uses	
Most effective in assessing trends in earnings and capital and comparing performance against peers	Most effective in determining the quality of management, the appropriateness of asset/liabilities and financial risk management, and the effectiveness of policies, procedures, systems, and controls
Input to sensitivity analysis, modeling, and forecasting	Input to institutional strengthening or development programs
Depends on the timeliness, accuracy, and completeness of financial information reported by banks	Allows verification to determine accuracy of financial information and adherence to sound accounting standards and principles
Provides comparative data in a standard format for supervisory authorities, financial analysts, and bank management	Uses comparative data and off-site prudential reports
Could be used to monitor selected types of financial institutions and the banking sector	
Input to economic and monetary policy makers	

Off-site surveillance. The central objective of off-site surveillance is to monitor the condition of individual banks, peer groups, and the banking system. The principles described in this publication provide the tools for a comprehensive off-site analysis of banks. Based on this assessment, the performance of a bank is then compared with its peer group and the banking sector overall to detect significant deviations from the peer group or sectoral norms and benchmarks. This process provides an early indication of an individual bank's problems as well as systemic problems; it also assists in the prioritization of the use of scarce supervisory resources in areas or activities under the greatest risk. Off-site monitoring systems rely on financial reporting in a prescribed format that is supplied by banks according to previously determined reporting schedules. Reporting formats and details vary among countries, although most supervisory authorities systematically collect and analyze data concerning liquidity, capital adequacy, credit risk, asset quality, concentration of and large exposures, interest rate, currency and market risks, earnings and profitability, and balance sheet structure. Supporting schedules may also be requested to provide greater detail of a bank's exposure to different types of risk and its capacity to bear that risk. Schedules are determined by the type and subject of related reports. For example, supervisory authorities may require liquidity to be reported on a weekly or even a daily basis, large exposures on a monthly basis, financial statements quarterly, and asset classification and provisions semiannually.

The sophistication and exact purpose of analytical reviews also vary from country to country. Most supervisory authorities use some form of ratio analysis. The current financial ratios of each bank are analyzed and compared to historical trends and to the performance of their peers to assess financial condition and compliance with prudential regulations. This process may also identify existing or forthcoming problems. Individual bank reports are aggregated to attain group (or peer) statistics for banks of a particular size, business profile, or geographical area. These aggregated reports can then be used as a diagnostic tool or in research and monetary policy analysis.

Off-site surveillance is less costly in terms of supervisory resources. Banks provide the information needed for supervisors to form a view of a bank's exposure to the various categories of financial risk. Supervisory authorities then manipulate and interpret the data. Although off-site surveillance allows supervisors to systematically monitor developments concerning a bank's financial condition and risk exposures, it has the following limitations:

■ The usefulness of reports depends on the quality of a bank's internal information systems and on the accuracy of reporting.

■ Reports have a standard format that may not adequately capture new types of risks or the particular activities of individual banks.

■ Reports are not able to sufficiently convey all factors affecting risk management, such as the quality of a bank's management personnel, policies, procedures, and internal systems.

On-site examinations enable supervisors to validate the information provided by a bank during the prudential reporting process, to establish the diagnosis and the exact cause of a bank's problems with an adequate level of detail, and to assess a bank's future viability or possible problem areas. More specifically, on-site examinations should help supervisors assess the accuracy of a bank's reports, overall operations and condition, the quality and competence of management, and the adequacy of risk management systems and internal control procedures. Other aspects that should be evaluated include the quality of the loan portfolio, adequacy of loan loss provisions and reserves, accounting and management information systems, the issues identified in off-site or previous on-site supervisory processes, adherence to laws and regulations, and the terms stipulated in the banking license. On-site examination is very demanding in terms of supervisory resources and usually can address only some of a bank's activities.

On-site examinations can take different forms depending on a bank's size and structure; available resources; and the sophistication, knowledge, and experience of supervisors. Supervisory authorities should establish clear internal guidelines on the objectives, frequency, and scope of on-site examinations. Policies and procedures should ensure that examinations are systematic and conducted in a thorough and consistent manner. In less-developed supervisory systems, the examination process often provides only a snapshot of a bank's condition, without assessing potential risks or the availability and quality of systems used by management to identify and manage them. On-site supervision begins with business transactions and proceeds from the bottom up. Examination results from the successive stages of supervision are compiled and eventually consolidated to arrive at final conclusions regarding a bank's overall financial condition and performance. This approach is characteristic of countries in which management information is unreliable and bank policies and procedures are not well articulated.

In well-developed banking systems, supervisors typically use a top-down approach that focuses on assessing how banks identify, measure, manage, and control risk. Supervisors are expected to diagnose the causes of a bank's problems and to ensure that they are addressed by preventive actions that can reduce the likelihood of recurrence. The starting point of an on-site examination is an assessment of objectives and policies related to risk management; the directions provided by the board and senior managers; and the coverage, quality, and effectiveness of systems used to monitor, quantify, and control risks. The completeness and effectiveness of a bank's written policies and procedures are then considered, as well as planning and budgeting, internal controls and audit procedures, and management information systems. Examination at the business-transaction level is required only if weaknesses exist in systems for identifying, measuring, and controlling risks. In many countries, external auditors examine systems and processes at this level.

Early-warning systems. In the 1990s, supervisory authorities started to refine their early-warning systems—aimed at supervisory risk assessments and identification of potential future problems in the financial system and individual banks. The systems generally combine qualitative and quantitative elements. Just as approaches to banking regulation and supervision differ from country to country, the designs of such early-warning systems also vary, but four generic types can be distinguished:

- **Supervisory bank rating systems.** The most well known of these is C-A-M-E-L-S (Capital adequacy, Asset quality, Management quality, Earning, Liquidity and Sensitivity to market risk). A composite rate is assigned to a bank typically as a result of an on-site examination.

- **Financial ratio and peer group analysis systems** (normatives). These are based on a set of financial variables (typically including capital adequacy, asset quality, profitability, and liquidity) that generate a warning if certain ratios exceed a predetermined critical level, fall within a predetermined interval, or are outliers with regard to the past performance of a bank.

- **Comprehensive bank risk assessment systems.** A comprehensive assessment of the risk profile of a bank is made by disaggregating a bank (or a banking group) into significant business units and assessing each separate business unit for all business risks. Scores are assigned for previously specified criteria, and assessment results are aggregated to arrive at the final score for the whole bank or banking group.

- **Statistical models.** These attempt to detect those risks most likely to lead to adverse future conditions in a bank. In contrast with the other three systems, the ultimate focus of statistical models is the prediction of the probability of future developments rather than a summary rating of the current condition of a bank. Statistical models are based on various indicators of future performance. For example, there are models that estimate a probability of a rating downgrade for an individual bank (for example, the probability that the most recent CAMEL rating will be downgraded based on financial data supplied in prudential reporting). Failure-of-survival prediction models are constructed on a sample of failed or distressed banks; the models aim to identify banks whose ratios or indicators (or changes thereof) are correlated to that of already failed or distressed banks. Expected-loss models are used in countries where the statistical basis of failed or distressed banks is not large enough to be able to link changes in specific financial variables to probabilities of failure. These models are based on failure probabilities derived from banks' exposure to credit risk and other data, such as the capacity of existing shareholders to supply additional capital. Some regulators have constructed statistical models based on other variables. For example, high assets growth that has not been adequately matched with strengthened management and institutional capacity has often been the culprit for bank failure. Therefore, a model tracing a high rate of asset growth combined with measures of institutional capacity could be used as an early-warning system.

Table 15.4 summarizes generic features of the most frequently used types of early-warning systems. In many cases, supervisory authorities use more then one early-warning system. The major issues with early-warning systems is the proper choice of variables upon which the prediction is based, the availability of reliable input data, and the limitations related to quantification of qualitative factors that are critically related to banks' performance (for example, management quality, institutional culture, integrity of internal controls).

Table 15.4 Generic Features of Early Warning Systems

	Assessment of Current financial Condition	Forecasting Future Fin. Condition	Use of Quantitative Analysis and Statistics	Use of Qualitative Assessments	Focus on Formal Risk Categories	Link with Formal Supervisory Actions
Supervisory Ratings						
on-site	***	*	*	***	*	***
off-site	***	*	**	*	**	*
Financial Ratio and Peer Group Analysis	***	*	***	*	**	*
Comprehensive Risk Assessment Systems	***	**	**	**	***	***
Statistical Models	**	***	***	*	**	*

*not significant; **significant; ***very significant

Source: BIS Paper on Supervisory Risk Assessment and Early Warning Systems, December 2000

The use of early-warning systems in a country provides an important head start for implementation of the Basel II Accord. Under the Basel II Accord, supervisory authorities are expected to evaluate the quality of external ratings and decide what would be a reasonable set of risk-weights to use in their jurisdiction for capital adequacy calculation. Peer group analysis, risk assessment systems, and statistical models provide a solid basis for rational decisions on such key parameters.

15.4 Consolidated Supervision

The institutional classification under which a financial intermediary operates has traditionally been assigned based on predominant financial instruments or services offered by the intermediary. The institutional classification designates regulatory and supervisory authorities for particular institutions and the corresponding regulatory treatment—for example, regarding minimum capital levels, capital adequacy, and other prudential requirements such as liquidity and cash reserves. Increasing financial market integration blurs the difference between various types of financial institutions and increases opportunities for regulatory or supervisory arbitrage, which ultimately increases systemic risk. Although perfect neutrality may not be possible or even necessary, authorities should strive to level the playing field for specific markets and to reduce the scope for regulatory arbitrage. In other words, when different financial institutions compete in the same market for identical purposes, their respective regulations must ensure competitive equality. The regulatory environments that potentially allow for regulatory (or supervisory) arbitrage display at least one of the following features:

- Inconsistent or conflicting regulatory philosophies for different types of financial institutions

- Deficiencies or inconsistencies in defining risks and prudential requirements for different types of financial institutions

- Differences in the cost of compliance for respective financial institutions

- Lack of coordination between regulatory and supervisory authorities in the financial sector

Supervision of Cross-Border Operations

The international expansion of banks increases the efficiency of both global and national markets, but it may create difficulties during the supervision process. For example, cross-border transactions may conceal a bank's problems from its home-country supervisors. Certain practices by subsidiaries in less-regulated environments are also hidden from home-country supervisors and may ultimately create losses that can impair the bank's capital. Internationalization could potentially be used as a vehicle to escape regulation and supervision in situations when problem assets are transferred to less-stringent regulatory environments or to areas with less effective supervision. Internationally active banks therefore present a challenge to supervisory authorities.

Cooperative efforts are needed to ensure that all aspects of international banking are subject to effective supervision and that remedial actions are well coordinated. The failure of a number of large, internationally active banks spurred the issuance of minimum standards for the supervision of such groups by the Basel Committee on Banking Supervision. The Basel concordat is based on the following principles:

- A capable home-country authority should supervise internationally active banks and banking groups on a consolidated basis.

- The creation of a cross-border banking establishment should receive the prior consent of both home- and host-country supervisory authorities. Such bilateral supervisory arrangements should be specified in a memorandum of understanding signed by both authorities.

- Home-country supervisory authorities should possess the right to collect information concerning the cross-border establishment of the banks and banking groups that they supervise. The collection by and exchange of information between authorities should be guided by principles of reciprocity and confidentiality. Confidential information should be safeguarded against disclosure to unauthorized parties.

- If a host-country supervisory authority determines that the home-country supervisory arrangements do not meet minimum standards, it can prohibit cross-border operations or impose restrictive measures that satisfy its standards.

- Home-country supervisory authorities should inform host-country authorities of changes in supervisory measures that have a significant bearing on the relevant bank's foreign operations.

One of the primary reasons why consolidated supervision is critical is the risk of a damaging loss of confidence and of contagion that extends beyond legal liability. Supervisory arrangements and techniques differ because of legal, institutional, historical, and other factors, so no single set of criteria exists to conclusively establish whether consolidated supervision is effective or not. In principle, consolidated supervision should assess and take into account all risks run by a banking group wherever they occur, including branches and subsidiaries, nonbank companies, and financial affiliates. More specifically, consolidated supervision is expected to support the principle that no banking operation, wherever located, should escape supervision. It also serves to prevent the double leveraging of capital and to ensure that all risks incurred by a banking group (no matter where it is booked) are evaluated and controlled on a global basis.

Consolidated supervision should extend beyond the mere consolidation of accounts. Supervisory authorities should consider the exact nature of the risks involved and design an appropriate approach to assessing them. Consolidated accounting may even be inappropriate when the nature of risk varies, for example, when market risk differs from market to market. The offsetting of market risks during the process of accounting consolidation may result in an inaccurate risk exposure position. Liquidity risk should be considered primarily on a market-by-market or currency-by-currency basis.

The Basel II Accord significantly extends the scope of multiple approvals. Consequently, the Accord recognizes the need to develop effective cross-border understandings on the application of capital standards to international banking groups, and effective cooperation and coordination between home- and host-country supervisors is an essential element of its successful implementation. Where a banking group has operations in at least one country other than its home country, implementation of the new Basel II Accord may require it to obtain approval for its use of certain advanced approaches (for example, internal ratings–based approach for credit risk or advanced measurement approach for operational risk) from relevant host-country supervisors on an individual or subconsolidated basis. In addition, the banking group may need approval from its home-country supervisor with respect to consolidated supervision under Basel II. The degree and nature of cooperation between supervisors may differ across these different supervisory responsibilities. Whatever arrangements are employed, banks would also have an important role to play in assisting the effective and efficient cross-border implementation efforts of supervisors.

Supervision of Conglomerates

Supervisory arrangements involving conglomerates are even more complex. An international financial group active in banking, securities, fund management, and insurance may be subject to a number of regulatory regimes and supervised by authorities in a number of countries. Problems related to a conglomerate's information, coordination, and compliance with prudential regulations—which are complex enough in a single-country environment—are compounded at the international level, particularly when operations involve emerging-market economies.

Financial conglomerates may have different shapes and structural features, reflecting varying laws and traditions. Key aspects to be considered in the supervision of conglomerates are the overall approach to supervision, the transparency of group structures, the assessment of capital adequacy, and the prevention of double gearing. In addition, contagion, the effect of intragroup exposures, and the consolidated treatment of large exposures play a role because of strong differences in exposure rules in banking, securities, and insurance.

The problem of consolidated supervision has been addressed internationally by a tripartite group consisting of representatives of the Basel Committee on Banking Supervision and interest groups involved in both the securities and insurance sectors. (The Joint Forum on Financial Conglomerates succeeded the informal tripartite group in 1996.) Their joint statement on the supervision of conglomerates specifies the following:

- All banks, securities firms, and other financial institutions should be subject to effective supervision, including that related to capital.

- Geographically and functionally diversified financial groups require consolidated supervision and special supervisory arrangements. Cooperation and information flow among supervisory authorities should be adequate and free from both national and international impediments.

- The transparency and integrity of markets and supervision rely on adequate reporting and disclosure of information.

The tripartite group recommended accounting-based consolidation as an appropriate technique to assess capital adequacy in homogeneous conglomerates. This process allows for the straight-forward comparison, using a single set of valuation principles, of total consolidated assets and liabilities, as well as the application at the parent level of capital adequacy rules to consolidated figures. With regard to heterogeneous conglomerates, the group recommended a combination of three techniques: the building-block prudential approach (whereby consolidation is performed following solo supervision by respective supervisory authorities), risk-based aggregation, and risk-based deduction.

The scope of application of the Basel II Accord provides specific requirements related to consolidation and supervision of financial conglomerates. The best approach to supervision and the assessment of capital adequacy continue to receive close international attention. The Basel Committee on Banking Supervision encourages the home and host supervisors of the major international financial and banking groups to continue discussions among themselves and with the institutions that they supervise. It is important that these group efforts continue to make progress and that home and host authorities build on the working relationships that are being developed to create effective cooperative mechanisms to implement the Basel II Accord.

15.5 Supervisory Cooperation with Internal and External Auditors

Internal auditing has been defined by the Institute of Internal Auditors as "an independent, objective activity that ... helps an organization to accomplish its objectives by bringing a systematic, disciplined approach to evaluate and improve the effectiveness of risk management, control and governance processes."

The Role of Internal Auditors

Although the importance of the internal audit function of a bank has been discussed in chapter 3, it is worth repeating that the function should cover all of a bank's activities in all its associated entities. It should be permanent, impartial, and technically competent, operating independently and reporting to a bank's board or to the chief executive officer.

Supervisory authorities normally issue regulatory requirements for banks' internal control systems, aiming to establish some basic principles for the system and quality of controls applied by banks. Although the extent of regulations varies, internal audit/control regulations normally cover policies and procedures for management of credit risk and other core banking risks, such as liquidity management, foreign exchange and interest rate risks, and risk management of derivatives and computer and telecommunication systems. On-site supervision normally includes an evaluation of internal controls in a bank and of the quality of the internal audit function. If satisfied with the quality of internal audit, supervisors can use the reports of internal auditors as a primary mechanism to identify control or management problems in the bank.

Use of External Auditors

External auditors and bank supervisors cover similar ground but focus on different aspects in their work. Auditors are primarily concerned with fair presentation in the annual financial statements and other reports supplied to shareholders and the general public. They are expected to express an opinion on whether financial statements and other prudential returns (when applicable) fairly present the condition and results of a bank's operations. To express such an opinion, auditors must also be satisfied with a bank's accounting policies and principles and the consistency of their application, and auditors must be sure that the bank's key functional systems are coherent, timely, and complete.

Because supervisory resources are scarce, to avoid duplication of examination efforts, supervisory authorities have come to increasingly rely on external auditors to assist in the on-site supervision process. Potential reliance on assessments and judgments of external auditors implies that supervisors have an interest in ensuring high bank auditing standards and that auditors meet certain quality criteria. In many countries, banking regulations require that the banks' external audits be carried out by auditors who have adequate professional expertise available in their firms and meet certain quality standards.

Auditors are often expected to report to the supervisory authorities any failures by banks to fulfill the requirements related to their banking license and other material breaches of laws and regulations—especially where the interests of depositors are jeopardized. In some countries the external auditors are asked to perform additional tasks of interest to the supervisors, such as to assess the adequacy of organizational and internal control systems, as well as the consistency of methods and databases used for the preparation of prudential reports, financial statements, and management's own internal reports.

A supervisor's request to an external auditor to assist in specific supervision-related tasks should be made in the context of a well-defined framework. This process demands, at a minimum, adherence to international accounting and auditing standards.

An important prerequisite for cooperation between the supervisory authorities and external auditors is a continuing dialogue between the supervisory authorities and the national professional accounting and auditing bodies. Such discussions should routinely cover all areas of mutual concern, including generally accepted accounting practices and auditing standards applicable to banks, as well as specific accounting problems, such as appropriate accounting techniques to be introduced for specific financial innovations.

Appendix A

Questionnaire: Analytical Review of Banks

The following questionnaire is intended primarily for use by consultants performing diagnostics of banks.

Name of bank:	Telephone number:
Address:	
Date completed:	Fax number:
Person(s) responsible for completion:	E-mail address:

1. Executive summary and recommendations

What are the biggest challenges facing your bank in the next few years?

What are your strategies to overcome those challenges?

What are your bank's greatest strengths?

What risks do lenders/investors face in lending money to your organization:

-external to your bank

-internal to your bank?

Why would money lent to your banks be a good investment for lenders/investors?

How would your bank use money lent by lenders/investors to develop financial markets or specific sectors in your country?

2. Institutional development needs

What are your bank's greatest development needs as identified in the conclusions and recommendations section (section 15) at the end of this report?

Which areas will you focus on in the coming year?

What role can lenders/investors play in assisting you with the development of your institution?

What active plans do you have to ensure that reforms are sustained?

Who would be the primary contact person in your organization to take responsibility for the institutional development plan and coordinate with lenders/investors if a loan is granted?

3. Overview of the financial sector and regulation – Tables A.1 and A.2

3.1 Status of financial infrastructure (disclosure, payment systems, securities clearing systems, and so forth)

3.2 Banking and the financial system: the status of financial market regulation

3.3 Banking regulation

3.4 Accounting regulation: Must financial statements be prepared in compliance with International Financial Reporting Standards?

Which are the key laws affecting the banking system in your country?

When were the banking laws and regulations last changed?

Description of any areas where current national legal practices cause difficulty for banks (for example, bankruptcy and foreclosure procedures).

Describe the supervisory approach and philosophy (of the regulators): the scope of the oversight activity, the frequency of visits by central bank officials, and reports or information that must be submitted on a regular basis. Please provide a copy of the most recent submission of each such report.

What is the minimum capital requirement and how do your capital adequacy guidelines differ from the BIS guidelines?

Describe any cash reserve and liquid asset requirements of the central bank.

Are prudential regulations strictly enforced?

Please describe any anticipated changes to the regulatory requirements (including provisioning requirements) that are planned (or rumored) for the future.

Please describe relationship with regulators and significant disputes, if any.

Please describe the results of the most recent review of your bank by the supervisory authorities. Please attach a copy of the supervisory review letter.

What was the method of grading, and what was the score your bank achieved?

4. Overview of the bank and its risk management culture

4.1 Historical background and general information – Table A.2

Provide a brief history of the bank, detailing incorporation dates, earlier names, mergers, major events, and so forth.

What is your ranking in the banking system:

By capital?

By assets?

What is the bank's main business focus and what are its main product areas? Also please identify key changes and milestones.

Describe special initiatives being undertaken for development of commercial/small business lending activities (including segment-specific delivery channels, product development, etc.) Please describe ways in which such focus is supported (relevant strengths, market data, competitive positioning, and so forth).

What is your bank's mission statement?

What is the bank's strategy relative to

- present and expected economic environment;
- sources of competitive strength;
- main elements of business strategy (lending, fee-based services, equity participation, and other areas of diversification or expansion, for example, geographic or product lines);
- strengths of principal competitors in main business areas (foreign/local/joint-venture banks);
- major business risks perceived and strategies to minimize such risks.

4.2 Group and bank organization structure – Tables A.3–A.6

Provide a group organization chart, table A.3, showing holding companies, ultimate controlling entities, associates, and subsidiaries (identifying major assets, shareholding, and management relationships).

Identify other financial institutions in the group.

Provide an organization chart of the bank under review (include as table A.4).

How many staff members does the bank have (table A.5)?

How many departments and divisions does the bank have? Name them and provide an organization chart describing the key departments and divisions as well as the number of staff in each.

How many branches does the bank have (table A.6)? Describe their geographic spread and size.

How many staff members have a post–high school education? Provide details about technical institute and university graduates.

Identify how the development of human resources complements the risk focus of the bank. (This is done to ensure that the right caliber staff is recruited and trained to enable compliance and maintenance of the risk management procedures established.)

To what extent are staff paid competitive market-based salaries to enhance retention of them?

To what extent are bonuses paid to staff?

What training is offered to staff?

How does the organizational structure encourage good risk management? (Also see risk management culture, section 4.5.)

4.3 Accounting systems, management information, and internal control

Provide audited annual financial statements for the past three years, together with copies of the auditors' management letters.

Provide unaudited accounts for each quarter this year-to-date.

Provide copies of any international prospectuses issued in the past five years.

Describe the status of the bank's accounting systems and records.

How much reliance can be placed on the financial reporting and information systems?

Describe IFRS implementation issues and difficulties in the bank.

Have there been any changes in the bank's accounting policies over the past four years? If so, please describe.

Describe accounting policies used in the bank, and provide a description of the key differences from IFRS. Elaborate on

- Income recognition/accrual
- Securities marking to market (IAS 39)
- Fixed asset revaluations

4.4 Information technology – Table A.7

Describe the computer systems in operation (both hardware and software), including microcomputers (whether used as terminals or stand-alone units).

What back-up and recovery systems are available?

How is security in the EDP area controlled?

4.5 Risk management culture and decision-making process – Table A.11

What major risks (stemming from either its products or the environment) does the bank face?	Risk supervision and management: How are current and proposed operations managed?
Planning and defining risk tolerance levels: Have the board and executive management delineated the level of risk they are willing to assume for each area and overall?	Risk monitoring: Evaluate the effectiveness of control implementation.
Risk identification: How is the risk in current operations identified?	How effectively are board-approved risk tolerance levels communicated in the organization?
	Evaluate the manner in which risk is being assumed, measured, limited, controlled, and reported.

5. Corporate governance

5.1 Shareholders/ownership – Table A.8

Describe major changes in shareholding and operations, including the dates of the changes, since foundation (mergers, acquisitions, divestments, and so forth).	Are there any provisions allowing shareholders voting rights that are not in proportion to their shareholding?
When was the last shareholders' meeting of the bank and how many shareholders were present? What percentage of the total shares did they represent?	Describe any options or other rights given to persons to acquire more share capital.
What is the main business of the key shareholders, and who controls those shareholders?	Do any resolutions require more than a simple majority to be accepted? If so, name such provisions.
	What direct involvement, if any, do the shareholders have with the bank, the board of directors, and the management board?

5.2 Board of directors – Table A.9 and A.11

For how long is the board of directors elected? What are the board's main objectives and responsibilities? Describe the board of directors' involvement with bank policy setting, especially in risk management. To what extent does the board of directors review financial information during the year and at year-end?	Is the board of directors committed to the active use of risk-based management information? These "ideal" management accounts should be the driving force in identifying where the bank wishes to see itself in terms of ideal critical management information. This goal should determine what other systems development and training should take place, and how.

5.3 Executive management – Tables A.10 and A.11

Who appoints the chief executive officer? Elaborate on the interaction between bank management and the bank's policy-setting board, the responsibility for the determination of bank policy and objectives, delegation of authority and responsibility, internal systems and procedures for performance reviews, and checks on accountability. Discuss the interaction between bank management and employees in carrying out the bank's objectives. Do senior management and the board receive and require risk-based management information on a regular basis?	Is risk-based management information used to ensure that procedures are in place to safeguard assets and depositors as well as ensure the integrity of data? Which management accounts should be developed to identify critical risk management issues for top management? (Distinguish between information needed on a daily basis, and information to be presented on a monthly or less frequent basis for management and directors' meetings.) Identify the risk management systems and procedures that must be designed to support the information needs of management, to ensure that the desire for proper risk management drives all systems development.

5.4 Internal audit/audit committee of the board – Table A.11

Describe the key objectives, role, and strategy of the internal audit department.	How many of the internal auditors have a formal audit or accounting qualification?
How many persons work in the internal audit department? Describe their experience, qualifications, and location by head office and branches.	How many of the internal auditors are specialized in • treasury audits • information technology audits
Do those who carry out the internal audit function report to a subcommittee of the board of directors? If not, to whom do they report and how frequently?	• other (describe) What is the frequency of branch and departmental internal audits?
Do the members of the board of directors receive and review the internal audit reports?	• Regular
Do internal audit reports discuss deviations from policies? What else is discussed in those reports?	• Irregular (surprise)
What is the average length of service (years) in internal audit of	Describe key areas receiving attention during an internal audit visit.
• head of internal audit	Summarize key audit comments, by category, in the latest internal audit.
• other auditors	Has evidence of fraud ever been found in examinations of your bank? If so, please describe.
	Describe the bank's anti-money-laundering procedures/control/internal audit processes.

5.5 External auditors

Are International Financial Reporting Standards (IFRS) and International Standards of Auditing (ISA) followed?	What audit and consulting fees have been paid to the auditors during the past two years?
Who are the external auditors of the bank and how long have they been auditing the financial statements? If they were appointed recently, name their predecessors and the reason for the change.	To what extent do the auditors evaluate the bank's risk management procedures?
Identify the major items reported on by the auditors during the past three years.	Discuss the involvement of and relationship between the external auditors and management.
Supply copies of the latest two management reports from the auditors.	How often do the regulators require that banks change their audit firm?

FINANCIAL RISK MANAGEMENT

6. Balance sheet structure and the changes therein – Tables A.12 and A.13

6.1 Composition of the balance sheet
   Asset structure: growth and changes
   Liabilities structure: growth and changes

6.2 Overall on- and off-balance-sheet growth

6.3 Low-earning and nonearning assets

Analyze the bank's balance sheet structure over time and describe

- what has happened

- why it happened

- the impact of the trend or observation

- the planned response to the situation

- alternative recommendations regarding the situation observed

Provide past financial statements and annual reports for your bank, and discuss recent financial performance.

Describe the structure of your balance sheet and any planned changes.

Describe (and quantify) the nature, volume, and anticipated use of credit commitments, contingent liabilities, guarantees, and other off-balance-sheet items.

7. Income statement structure and the changes therein (profitability/earnings) – Table A.14

7.1 Sources of income: changes in the structure and trends of income

7.2 Structure of assets compared with structure of income

7.3 Margins earned on intermediation business

7.4 Operating income and operating expenses breakdown

7.5 Return on assets and shareholders' funds

Analyze the bank's profitability over time and describe

- what has happened

- why it happened

- the impact of the trend or observation

- the planned response to the situation

- alternative recommendations regarding the situation observed

Describe the major sources of income and most profitable business areas.

Describe the bank's dividend payout policy.

Describe the extent to which accrued but uncollected interest is taken into income—especially if such interest income relates to loans that you or the bank place in risk categories of substandard or worse.

Describe the extent to which collateral values (rather than operating cash flows) are the basis for decisions to capitalize interest or to roll over extensions of credit.

List any income or expenditure recognition policies that might affect (or distort) earnings.

Describe the effect of material intergroup transactions, especially those relating to the transfer of earnings and asset/liability valuations.

Are there any revenue and expense items that may be significantly overstated or understated?

Describe areas and the manner in which greater efficiencies can be achieved.

8. Capital adequacy

8.1 Capital retention policies

8.2 Compliance with capital adequacy requirements

8.3 Potential future capital requirements

8.4 Structure of shareholders' funds

8.5 Risk profile of balance sheet assets

Analyze the bank's capital adequacy over time and describe

- what has happened
- why it happened
- the impact of the trend or observation
- the planned response to the situation
- alternative recommendations regarding the situation observed

What plans does the bank have for the maintenance of minimum regulatory capital, given your past growth and future plans for expansion?

What access does the bank have to capital and financial assistance?

What are the bank's growth experiences, plans, and prospects for the future?

Is capital growth funded by internal cash generation or capital contributions?

To what extent have reserves been generated by revaluations of fixed assets and investments, or from the capitalization of interest on classified loans?

In the case of capital contributions, were they in cash or in kind

(fixed assets)?

In the case of contributions in kind (fixed assets), state the proportion that such contributions (see table 5.3A) constitute as a percentage of total capital and describe the process used to obtain a reliable third-party valuation.

9. Credit risk management

9.1 Credit risk management policies, systems, and procedures

Use the structure of section 4.5 (risk management culture) to discuss the following questions.

How is credit risk managed in the bank? Include a description of the lending organization, concerned departments, management levels, and staffing.

Provide the profile and lending skills of your chief lending officers, credit managers and officers, and all relevant staff.

Describe the key risks that you face and control in this area.

What are your strengths as far as this risk area is concerned?

What are the most pressing development needs for your bank as far as this risk area is concerned?

Describe the top-level information prepared for the most senior management in the bank.

What information is asked for during the loan application request?

Describe the contents of loan files. How do you use this information to monitor the quality of loans?

Describe the standard loan process from the client's initial inquiry, or the bank's marketing efforts, to the final lending decision, and provide a description of the credit decision process.

What are the criteria used for granting loans? Also describe any specific limits, ratios, and so forth used by you in the evaluation process.

Describe any specific lending procedures and techniques for project appraisal, approvals, and legal finalization of projects, procurement and disbursement, as well as follow-up and supervision of such projects.

Describe any formalized credit policies, procedures, and underwriting criteria for the identification of target markets.

Discuss the procedures for management of problem loans, describing specialized workout departments or intensive care units and detailing their scope, skill, resources, and efficiency.

What instruments or remedies are available to ensure that borrowers repay their loans to the bank? Describe also the mechanisms that exist for legal recovery, foreclosure and repossession of collateral, and transmission of legal rights.

Describe the taxation deductions allowed for loan loss provisioning as well as the influence that taxation has on your bank's provisioning policy.

At what point do you suspend interest and how do you control the overall amounts owed by a client in such a case?

What is the total number of corporate and retail loans?

Has your bank made any loans on other than normal credit terms (pricing or directed)?

To what extent have you accepted equity in clients as payment for loans?

What percentage of loans have been rescheduled once?

What percentage of loans have been rescheduled more than once?

For what percentage of loans do you act as a fiscal agent?

9. Credit risk management (continued)

9.2 Profile of borrowers	Describe the major loan products offered by the bank.
9.3 Maturity of loans	Describe your bank's current policies, practices, and procedures to identify common ownership, control, and reliance on common cash flows. You should also, if appropriate, suggest new guidelines and new procedures by which concentrations should be identified and tracked in the bank.
9.4 Loan products	
9.5 Sectoral analysis of loans	
9.6 Large exposures to individuals and connected parties	
9.7 Loan and other asset classification and provisioning	Are all assets (in addition to the loan portfolio) with a credit risk in fact classified as to quality and provided against, when needed?
9.8 Analysis of loans in arrears	
9.9 Connected lending (to related parties)	
Analyze the bank's loan portfolios over time and describe	Describe your methodology for the determination of the level of reserves required.
• what has happened	To what extent do you rely on collateral for establishing the recommended reserves? Specify the methodology used to establish the value of the collateral. What types of collateral do you regard as acceptable?
• why it happened	
• the impact of the trend or observation	
• the planned response to the situation	Under what circumstances do you use specific reserves and when are general reserves used?
• alternative recommendations regarding the situation observed	

10. Organization of the treasury function – Table A.15

10.1 Organization of the treasury function	What hedging techniques and products are used to protect against mismatches?
10.2 Policy-setting environment: asset allocation, benchmarks, use of external managers	• Interest rate sensitivity
10.3 Market operations: funding, investing, and trading	• Exchange rate sensitivity
10.4 Risk analytics and compliance	Maturity profile sensitivity
10.5 Treasury operations (administration)	How does the bank consolidate and track exposures arising from lending, money market, FX settlement, trade-related transactions, and securities transactions to the same customer?
Describe the arrangements for disaster recovery/back-up/hot sites.	
How many persons work in the treasury?	How are overlimit trades and exception trades reported?
How are treasury counterparty limits approved and monitored? How often are limits reviewed?	How does the bank undertake treasury risk management/revaluation of positions?
Does your bank treasury use a telephone recording machine?	Describe the compliance officer's duties, experience, and qualifications.
Describe your process for treasury deal confirmations and reconciliation.	

11. Securities portfolio management (stable liquidity portfolio) – Tables A.16–A.19

Describe:

- what happened
- why it happened
- the impact of the trend or observation
- the planned response to the situation
- alternative recommendations regarding the situation observed

Describe the decision-making process for taking trading positions.

Explain the treatment of losses when liquidating securities investment positions when market value is less than cost.

Please describe the bank's policy of classifying securities into trading or investment categories and if this policy has changed recently.

12. Proprietary trading and market risk management – Tables A.16–A.19

12.2 Securities classification policies

12.3 Structure of the securities portfolios

12.4 Net effective open positions and potential capital exposures

12.5 Market risk attached to off-balance-sheet activities and derivatives

Describe

- what happened
- why it happened
- the impact of the trend or observation
- the planned response to the situation
- alternative recommendations regarding the situation observed

How is market risk managed in the bank?

Describe the key risks that you face and control in this area.

Describe the top-level information prepared for the most senior management in the bank.

What are your strengths as far as this risk area is concerned?

What are the most pressing development needs for your bank as far as this risk area is concerned?

Describe the Board's policies with regard to risk tolerance of derivatives exposures—onshore/offshore, exchange/OTC.

Describe the reports used to track derivatives exposure and risk management.

Describe settlement procedures for securities and their derivatives.

Are derivatives booked in all trading desks or traded separately?

Does the bank write options? If yes, which?

Are there unhedged options?

Describe the control of derivative credit risk.

Describe what computer systems are employed to monitor derivatives positions.

13. Asset-liability management (ALCO): interest rate risk management

Use the structure of section 4.5 (risk management culture) to discuss the following questions. Describe: • what happened • why it happened • the impact of the trend or observation • the planned response to the situation • alternative recommendations regarding the situation observed 13.1 Interest rate risk management policies, systems, and procedures 13.2 Forecasting interest rates 13.3 Measures to determine the potential impact of exogenous rate movements on the bank's capital	How is interest rate risk managed in the bank? Describe the key risks that you face and control in this area? How often does ALCO meet? What reports are presented to ALCO? Are ALCO minutes written and circulated? How does the bank determine its target gap structure, given the most likely interest rate scenarios? How are analyses performed to set strategies to achieve optimal target gap structure? Name the person or group who is assigned to ensure strategies are correctly implemented. What are your strengths as far as this risk area is concerned? What are the most pressing development needs for your bank as far as this risk area is concerned? Does the bank have an ALCO support unit? To whom does it report? What are its responsibilities?

14. Asset-liability management (ALCO): liquidity risk management

14.1 Liquidity risk management policies, systems, and procedures

14.2 Compliance with regulatory requirements

14.4 Sources of deposits—profile of depositors

14.3 Maturity structure of deposits

14.5 Large depositors and volatility of funding

14.6 Maturity mismatches of assets and liabilities

14.7 Liquidity risk measures

Describe

- what happened

- why it happened

- the impact of the trend or observation

- the planned response to the situation

- alternative recommendations regarding the situation observed

Use the structure of section 4.5 (risk management culture) to discuss the following questions.

How is liquidity risk managed in the bank?

Describe the key risks that you face and control in this area.

Describe the top-level information prepared for the most senior management in the bank.

What are your strengths as far as this risk area is concerned?

What are the most pressing development needs for your bank as far as this risk area is concerned?

How strong is the interbank market? What is your participation in that market?

Do you have adequate access to money markets or other ready sources of cash? If so, please describe these sources.

What reliance does your bank place on interest-sensitive funds?

To what extent do you make use of central bank credit? Report how many times you used central bank credit in the last 12 months, describing the different types of access used and the maximum amount involved.

What ability do you have to readily convert assets into cash?

Describe your capacity to meet unexpected deposit withdrawals and other demands for payment.

What other sources of funding do you have available in case of a shortage of liquidity.

How many depositors does the bank have in total?

15. Asset-liability management (ALCO): currency risk management

15.1 Currency risk management policies, systems, and procedures

15.2 Currency structure of assets and liabilities

15.3 Currency structure of off-balance-sheet activities

15.4 Maturity structure of foreign currency liabilities

15.5 Currency structure of loans and deposits

15.6 Net effective open position and capital exposed

Describe

- what happened

- why it happened

- the impact of the trend or observation

- the planned response to the situation

- alternative recommendations regarding the situation observed

Use the structure of section 4.5 (risk management culture) to discuss the following questions.

How does the bank manage its currency risks?

Describe the key risks that you face and control in this area?

Describe the top-level information prepared for the most senior management in the bank.

What are your strengths as far as this risk area is concerned?

What are the most pressing development needs for your bank as far as this risk area is concerned?

16. Operational Risk – Table A.20

16.1 Fraud experience—internal and external

16.2 Employment practices and workplace safety

16.3 Use of information technology to enhance operational risk management

16.4 Effectiveness of internal control processes

16.5 Use of management information for operational management purposes

17. Conclusions and Recommendations

Discuss the following.

17.1 The changes that appear necessary within the bank's culture and managerial practices, given the nature and relative complexity of its operations, including (as applicable)

• the need for full sponsorship by the board and executive management;

• the necessary enabling culture in which every manager is expected to consider risk (that is, to identify, measure, and report on risk exposure);

• the changes that appear necessary after the assessment of evaluation, monitoring, and reporting systems that cover critical risk functions;

• the convenience of adopting appropriate risk objectives for each function and for the bank as a whole;

• the need to institute a formal process for the general manager or CEO of the bank and the board to review and evaluate all expected and unexpected risks and all risk-taking activities; and

• the convenience of designating a member of senior executive management for overseeing all risk management, with authority to act on risk problems and ensure risk control.

17.2 The implications of the problems identified and for instituting a bankwide risk management function, the process and phases required for such action, and the role and function within the organization of the risk management senior official.

17.3 The manner in which risk management functions could be instituted in the bank.

17.4 The feasibility of installing effective, comprehensive, bankwide risk management and the implications for the bank.

Table A.1 Financial Regulation and Compliance

Category	Description of regulation	Bank's actual position (date)	Expected position after coming transaction
Shareholding			
Capital			
Minimum Equity			
Capital/Risk Weighted Assets			
Other Capital Ratios (Specify)			
Assets			
Single Borrower Limit (and connected lending)			
Group Borrower Limit (and connected lending/ loan concentrations)			
Aggregate Large Exposures Limit			
Investments (quoted)			
Investments (unquoted)			
Related Party Lending			
Industry Sector Limit			
Other Asset Ratios (specify)			
Loan classification guidelines *			
Normal Loans – General Provision (upper limit)			
Precautionary/Watch			
Substandard			
Doubtful			
Loss			
Liquidity			
Liquid Assets/Liabilities			
Loans/Deposits			
Other Liquidity Ratios (specify)			
Funding			
Reserves/Deposits			
Deposit/Capital Limit			
Funding Maturity Mismatch Limit			
Open FX Position			
Other Funding Ratios			
Other			
Market Risk Capital Requirements (value at risk)			
Derivatives			
Currency risk			
Investment Limits			
• for equity investments			
• for property and other fixed assets			
Suspension and Reversal of Interest			
Deposit Insurance			

* Loan classification guidelines: How are restructured/renegotiated loans treated for asset classification purposes? (Differentiate clearly between rules based on period that loan is past due and guidelines based on expected cash flow and recoverability of loan.) Is the provision required based on the total exposure to the client? Are these provisions calculated before or after allowance for the collateral? How much of the loan loss provision is tax deductible?

Table A.2 Market Share and Profile of Banking System

Market Share as a % of total market (estimate):	Foreign Banks %	Banking Groups %	Specialized Financial Institutions %	Your Key Competitor %	Other Domestic Banks %	Your Bank			
						Current Year %	Prior Year %	Prior Year -1 %	Prior Year-2 %
Total Corporate Loans – FX									
Total Corporate Loans – TL									
Total Deposits – FX									
Total Deposits – TL									
Leasing									
Trade Finance Letters of Credit									
Letters of Guarantee									
Residential Housing Mortgages									
FX Trading									
Retail/Consumer Lending									
Credit Cards									
Number of Bank Branches									
ATMs									
Asset Management									
Investment Banking (Advisory)									
Broking									
Securities Trading									
Other (Please Specify)									

Table A.5 Total Number of Employees*

	Year-to-Date	Current Year	Prior Year
Senior Management			
Corporate Lending			
Commercial Lending			
Small Business Lending			
Retail/Consumer Lending			
Leasing			
Trade Finance			
Off-Shore Banking			
Asset Management			
Investment Banking (Advisory)			
Brokering			
Investments			
Treasury			
Operations			
Internal Audit			
Other Categories (identify)			
Total			

* Show employee numbers per product group, including products sold through subsidiaries.

Table A.6 Branch Statistics

	Year-to-Date	Current Year	Prior Year
Total number of branches:			
• Metropolitan/Large Cities			
• Country areas			
• International			
Number of ATMs			
Average Staff Number			
Average Deposits			
Average Loan Assets			
Average Operating Expenses*			
Average Operating Income			

* Excluding interest cost and provisioning. Please provide breakdown of occupancy, depreciation, communication, business development and marketing, and other expenses.

Table A.7 Information Systems

Describe the computer technology used in the bank.

Function	Software Name/Vendor	Platform (for example, mainframe, PC)
Accounting		
Loans		
Foreign exchange processing		
Risk management		
Retail banking/branches		
MIS		
Credit cards		
Electronic mail		
Others (describe)		
Communications network		
Describe any ongoing communications problems experienced.		
Attach a diagram of the main IT configuration.		
Functionality: Does the IT system allow		
• Allocation of revenues and expenses by profit center or branch/line of business?		
• Accurate calculation of product profitability?		
IT Staff Analysis		
• System maintenance		
• Development		
• Other (describe)		
Budget: Describe the EDP budget for the current year:		
• Software		
• Hardware		
• Communications		
Budget: Describe the planned budget for		
• Software		
• Hardware		
• Communications		
Disaster Recovery: Describe the hot-site (back-up system).		
• Who operates it?		
• Where is it?		
• Hardware?		

Table A.8 Shareholding

Shareholders (as of _____)	Number of Shareholders	Shares Held		Percentage of Shares
		Number	Unit Size	
Private companies*				
Private individuals*				
Subtotal: private sector shareholders				
Public sector and government companies (less than 51 percent private) **				
Total shareholding				
List of shareholders who own more than 5 percent of the bank's shares	Name	Shares Held		Percentage of Shares
		Number	Unit Size	
List of shareholders and companies that effectively or indirectly own more than 5 percent of the bank's shares through their control over shareholders of the bank				

* The ultimate (and real) owner of the shares determines whether the shareholder is from the private or the public sector.

** If shares are held as nominees, indicate who the ultimate owner is.

Table A.9 Board of Directors

Name	Where Employed	Shareholders/ Entity Represented	Private Sector-Owned (Y/N)	Qualifications	Experience	Responsibility*

* Responsibility examples: administration, corporate banking, international division, domestic treasury, retail banking, internal control, finance and accounting, information systems, branch management.

Table A.10 Executive Management

Name	Qualifications	Experience	Responsibility *

* Responsibility examples: administration, corporate banking, international division, domestic treasury, retail banking, internal control, finance and accounting, information systems, branch management.

Table A.11 Key Risk Committee Memberships

Name	Qualifications	Experience	Responsibility *
Audit Committee of the Board			
ALCO			
Credit Committee			
Investment Committee			
Operational and Other Risk Committees			

* Responsibility examples: administration, corporate banking, international division, domestic treasury, retail banking, internal control, finance and accounting, information systems, branch management

Table A.12 Balance Sheet Assets

Assets	Prior Period-2	Prior Period-1	Prior Period	Current Period
Cash and cash balances with central banks				
Financial assets held for trading				
Derivatives held for trading				
Equity instruments				
Debt instruments				
Financial assets *designated* at fair value through profit or loss				
Available-for-sale financial assets				
Equity instruments				
Debt instruments				
Loans and receivables				
Held-to-maturity investments				
Debt instruments				
Loans and advances				
Derivatives – Hedge accounting purposes				
Tangible assets				
Property, Plant and Equipment				
Investment property				
Intangible assets				
Goodwill				
Other intangible assets				
Investments in associates, subsidiaries and joint ventures				
Tax assets				
Current tax assets				
Deferred tax assets				
Other assets				
Non-current assets and disposal groups classified as held for sale				
TOTAL ASSETS	100%	100%	100%	100%

Table A.13 Balance Sheet Liabilities

Liabilities	Prior Period-2	Prior Period-1	Prior Period	Current Period
Deposits from central banks				
Financial liabilities held for trading				
Derivatives held for trading				
Short positions				
Deposits from banks and other credit institutions				
Deposits from customers				
Debt certificates (including bonds intended for repurchase in short term)				
Other financial liabilities held for trading				
Financial liabilities designated at fair value through profit or loss				
Deposits from banks and other credit institutions				
Deposits from customers				
Debt certificates (including bonds)				
Subordinated liabilities				
Other financial liabilities designated at fair value through profit or loss				
Financial liabilities measured at amortized cost				
Deposits from banks and other credit institutions				
Deposits from customers				
Debt certificates (including bonds) – own securities issued				
Subordinated liabilities				
Financial liabilities associated with transferred financial assets				
Derivatives - Hedge accounting purposes				
Fair value hedges				
Cash flow hedges				
Hedge of a net investment in a foreign operation				
Fair value hedge of interest rate risk				
Cash flow hedge interest rate risk				
Fair value changes of the hedged items in portfolio hedge of interest rate risk				
Provisions				
Restructuring				
Pending legal issues and tax litigation				
Pensions and other post retirement benefit obligations				
Credit commitments and guarantees				
Onerous contracts				
Other provisions				
Tax liabilities				
Other liabilities				
Share capital repayable on demand (e.g. cooperative shares)				
Liabilities included in disposal groups classified as held for sale				
TOTAL LIABILITIES	100%	100%	100%	100%

Table A.14 Income Statement

Financial & Operating Income and Expenses	Prior Period -2	Prior Period -1	Prior Period	Current Period
Interest income				
Cash & cash balances with central banks				
Financial assets held for trading (if accounted for separately)				
Financial assets designated at fair value through profit or loss (if accounted for separately)				
Available-for-sale financial assets				
Loans and receivables (including finance leases)				
Held-to-maturity investments				
Derivatives – Hedge accounting, interest rate risk				
Other assets				
(Interest expenses)				
Deposits from central banks				
Financial liabilities held for trading (if accounted for separately)				
Financial liabilities designated at fair value through profit or loss (if accounted for separately)				
Financial liabilities measured at amortised cost				
Derivatives – Hedge accounting, interest rate risk				
Other liabilities				
Expenses on share capital repayable on demand				
Dividend income				
Financial assets held for trading (if accounted for separately)				
Financial assets designated at fair value through profit or loss (if accounted for separately)				
Available-for-sale financial assets				
Fee and commission income				
(Fee and commission expenses)				
Realised gains (losses) on financial assets & liabilities not measured at fair value through profit or loss, net				
Available-for-sale financial assets				
Loans and receivables (including finance leases)				
Held-to-maturity investments				
Financial liabilities measured at amortised cost				
Other				
Gains (losses) on financial assets and liabilities held for trading, net				
Equity instruments and related derivatives				
Interest rate instruments and related derivatives				
Foreign exchange trading				
Credit risk instruments and related derivatives				
Commodities and related derivatives				
Other (including hybrid derivatives)				
Gains (losses) on financial assets and liabilities designated at fair value through profit or loss, net				
Gains (losses) from hedge accounting, net				
Exchange differences, net				

Table A.14 Income Statement (continued)

Financial & Operating Income and Expenses	Prior Period -2	Prior Period -1	Prior Period	Current Period
Gains (losses) on derecognition of assets other than held for sale, net				
Other operating income				
Other operating expenses				
Administration costs				
Staff expenses				
General and administrative expenses				
Depreciation				
Property, Plant and Equipment				
Investment Properties				
Intangible assets (other than goodwill)				
Provisions				
Impairment				
Impairment on financial assets not measured at fair value through profit or loss				
Financial assets measured at cost (unquoted equity)				
Available-for-sale financial assets				
Loans and receivables (including finance leases)				
Held to maturity investments				
Impairment on non-financial assets				
Property, plant and equipment				
Investment properties				
Goodwill				
Intangible assets (other than goodwill)				
Investments in associates and joint ventures accounted for using the equity method				
Other				
Negative goodwill immediately recognised in profit or loss				
Share of the profit or loss of associates and joint ventures accounted for using the equity method				
Profit or loss from non-current assets and disposal groups classified as held for sale not qualifying as discontinued operations				
TOTAL PROFIT OR LOSS BEFORE TAX FROM CONTINUING OPERATIONS				
Tax expense (income) related to profit or loss from continuing operations				
TOTAL PROFIT OR LOSS AFTER TAX FROM CONTINUING OPERATIONS				
Profit or loss after tax from discontinued operations				
TOTAL PROFIT OR LOSS AFTER TAX AND DISCONTINUED OPERATIONS				
Profit or loss attributable to minority interest				
PROFIT OR LOSS ATTRIBUTABLE TO EQUITY HOLDERS OF THE PARENT	100%	100%	100%	100%

Table A.15 Organization of the Treasury Environment

Example: Activities per Functional Area

Policy Framework Income Earned from Securities	Market Operations	Risk Analytics & Compliance	Treasury Operations
Investment guidelines	Retail funding – local and foreign	Risk measurement (liquidity, credit and market and currency risk)	Cash management
Strategic asset allocation and benchmarks	Wholesale funding – local and foreign	Pricing, portfolio performance analytics, and reporting	Settlements
Asset-liability management: Managing the market exposures in the bank's balance sheet	Structured loans or funding	Governance, compliance, and operational risk	Accounting
Managing and use of external managers	Investment portfolio management (fixed income, money markets, asset and mortgage-backed securities, swaps, futures and options, equities)	Quantitative strategies and risk research (strategic asset allocation, benchmark construction, benchmark management, and modeling)	Information services – IT (could also be outside the treasury)
Model validation – independent from model development	Proprietary trading (instruments as above)		

Table A.16 Securities Trading Income

	Income Earned from Securities									Volumes Securities Traded					
	Trading Portfolio Income	Investment Portfolio (stable liquidity) Income	Total Income from Securities Portfolios	Current -4	Current -3	Current -2	Prior Period	Current Period	Current Budget	Current -4	Current -3	Current -2	Prior Period	Current Period	Current Budget
Public sector (central government and agencies) bonds															
Corporate bonds															
Structured products															
Asset-backed securities															
Mortgage-backed securities															
Asset swaps															
Money market instruments (LIBOR spread products)															
Certificates of deposit															
Time deposits															
Repurchase agreements															
Resale agreements															
Derivatives *															
Currency swaps															
Interest-rate swaps															
Futures and Options															
Currency forward contracts															
Quoted equities															
Unquoted equities															

* Purpose: Hedging / % is on behalf of clients (with underlying transaction) / Position-taking

Table A.17 Trading Controls

	Amount per balance sheet $	Counterparties Public sector	Counterparties Private sector	Average yield to maturity	Average maturity	VAR $	Trading limits Treasurer	Trading limits Managers	Trading limits Traders	Stop-loss limits Daily	Stop-loss limits Monthly	Stress tests
Public sector (central government and agencies) bonds												
Corporate bonds												
Structured products												
Asset-backed securities												
Mortgage-backed securities												
Asset swaps												
Money market instruments (LIBOR spread products)												
Certificates of deposit												
Time deposits												
Repurchase agreements												
Resale agreements												
Derivatives												
Currency swaps												
Interest-rate swaps												
Futures and options												
Currency forward contracts												
Quoted equities												
Unquoted equities												
TOTAL												

Table A.18 Potential Risk Analytics Reports

Risk Area	Title	Reference	Potential Reports – Details	Frequency			
				Daily	Weekly	Monthly	Periodic
Counterparty risk							
Market risk							
Liquidity risk							
Currency risk							
Performance measurement and analysis							

Table A.19 Example of Daily/Monthly Checklist of Portfolio Compliance Issues

Date and Reviewer:							
Rule	Reference	Short Description	Investment Management Agreement Language	Calculation of Guideline	Reporting Tool	Interpretation of Measure	Portfolio Reviewed
1. Laws							
2. Regulations							
3. Institutional Policies							
3.1 Risk limits							
4. Institutional Guidelines							
4.1 Investment Restrictions							
4.2 Allowable Duration Range							
4.3 Limit to Duration Range							
4.4 Eligible Instruments							
4.5 Issuer's Credit Rating							
4.6 Eligible Currency							
5. Operational Guidelines							
5.1 Issuer Concentration							

Table A.20 Treasury Operations: Reporting (Funding & Investing)

Reporting Area	Title	Reference	Sub-Report Types	Frequency			
				Daily	Weekly	Monthly	Periodic
A. Accounting Reports							
Financial reports			Trial Balance / Balance Sheet / Income Statement / Trade details / Settlement entries				
Holdings reports			Inventory / Asset allocations / Performance (return on investments) reports				
B. Control Reports							
Internal reconciliations			Systems-to-systems / Control accounts (suspense accounts)				
External reconciliations			Custodian reconciliations / cash account maintained by internal treasury function				
Cash			Control accounts with external banks / cash accounts with internal clients				
C. Pricing Reports							
Source reports			Reuters / Bloomberg / Brokers / Other pricing services				
Exception (Diagnostic) reports			Unusual fluctuations / New instruments				
Valuation reports			Fair value accounting (IAS 39)				
Analysis reports			Trends				
D. Operational Reports							
Transactional reports			Cash flows / Resets / Deal volumes / Call volumes / Settlement reports				
Operational risk			Analysis of trend impacts				
E. Regulatory Reports							
Security commissioners							
Central Bank							

Appendix B

Summary of Core Principles Evaluation

Core Principle by Principle Assessment

Name of country:		Telephone number:	
Address of supervisory authority:			
Date completed:		Fax number:	
Person(s) responsible for completion:		E-mail address:	
EVALUATION			

ASSESSMENT RATINGS

1	Compliant
2a	Largely compliant and efforts to achieve compliance are underway
2b	Largely compliant and efforts to achieve compliance are **not** underway
3a	Materially noncompliant and efforts to achieve compliance are underway
3b	Materially noncompliant and efforts to achieve compliance are **not** underway
4a	Noncompliant and efforts to achieve compliance are underway
4b	Noncompliant and efforts to achieve compliance are **not** underway

#	Summarized Description of Core Principles	Assessment				
		1	2	3	4	n/a
1	Framework for supervisory authority:					
1(1)	Clear responsibilities and **objectives** for each agency					
1(2)	Each such agency should possess operational **independence** and adequate resources					
1(3)	Suitable **legal framework**, including provisions relating to authorization of banking					
1(4)	**Enforcement powers** to address compliance with laws as well as safety and soundness concerns					
1(5)	**Legal protection** for supervisors					
1(6)	Arrangements for confidential **information sharing** between supervisors					
2	**Permissible activities** must be clearly defined, and control of the use of the word "bank"					
3	Right to set **licensing criteria** re governance and business plan and reject applications—prior consent of home country supervisor					
4	Authority to review and reject proposals to transfer significant **ownership** or controlling interests					
5	Establish and review major acquisitions/ **investment criteria** by a bank and resulting structures re risks or hindering of effective supervision					
6	Set minimum **capital adequacy** requirements/components of capital (Basel minimums for internationals)					
7	Ensuring that banks have a comprehensive **risk management** strategy in place					
8	Independent evaluation of **credit policies**, practices, and procedures related to granting of loans/investments					
9	Satisfied re practices and procedures for **loan evaluation**—the quality of assets/ loan loss provisions and reserves					
10	Satisfied with information systems and limits to restrict **large exposures** to single or related borrowers					
11	**Connected lending** to related companies and individuals on an arm's-length basis, effectively monitored, mitigate risks					
12	Identifying, monitoring, and controlling **country risk** and for maintaining reserves against such risks					
13	Accurately measure, monitor, and control **market risks**—specific limits and/or a capital charge					
14	Satisfied that banks have in place a **liquidity management strategy**					
15	Identify, assess, and monitor **operational risk**					
16	Effective systems identify, assess, and monitor **interest rate risk**					
17	**Internal controls** in place with regard to complexity of business—independent **external audit**					
18	Banks have adequate policies/ "know-your-customer" rules that promote high ethical and professional standards in the financial sector—to prevent **money laundering**					
19	Develop understanding. Independent **validation of** supervisory **information through on-site examinations** or use of external auditors					
20	Regular contact with **bank management** and a thorough understanding of the institution's operations					
21	Means of **off-site** analyzing prudential reports and statistical returns from banks on a solo and consolidated basis					
22	Banks maintain and publish financial statements that fairly reflect their condition using consistent **accounting** policies and practices providing a true and fair view of their financial condition on a regular basis					
23	Ability for timely **remedial measures** when banks commit prudential or regulatory violations, or where depositors are threatened in any other way, including ability to revoke the banking license					
24	Ability to supervise the banking group on a **consolidated supervision** basis. Global **consolidation** and supervision over internationally active banking ventures					
25	Contact/information exchange with other supervisory authorities to ensure effective **host country supervision. Supervision of foreign establishments** must require the same high standards as are required of domestic institutions and must have powers to share information needed by the home country supervisors					

Example: Core Principle 1 (1): An effective system of banking supervision will have clear responsibilities and objectives for each agency involved in the supervision of banks.

Essential criteria	Additional criteria
1. Laws are in place for banking, and for (each of) the agency (agencies) involved in banking supervision. The responsibilities and objectives of each of the agencies are clearly defined.	6. The supervisory agency sets out objectives and is subject to regular review of its performance against its responsibilities and objectives through a transparent reporting and assessment process.
2. The laws and/or supporting regulations provide a framework of minimum prudential standards that banks must meet.	7. The supervisory agency ensures that information on the financial strength and performance of the industry under its jurisdiction is publicly available.
3. There is a defined mechanism for coordinating actions between agencies responsible for banking supervision and evidence that it is used in practice.	
4. The supervisor participates in deciding when and how to effect the orderly resolution of a problem bank situation (which could include closure, assisting in restructuring, or merger with a stronger institution).	
5. Banking laws are updated as necessary to ensure that they remain effective and relevant to changing industry and regulatory practices.	

Discussion

Assessment

The country is largely compliant with Core Principle 1 (1). Efforts to achieve compliance are not underway.

Appendix C

Basel Core Principles for Effective Banking Supervision October 2006

The Basel Core Principles define 25 principles that are needed for a supervisory system to be effective. Those principles are broadly categorized into seven groups:

1. The objectives, independence, powers, transparency, and cooperation (Principle 1)

2. Licensing and structure (Principles 2 to 5)

3. Prudential regulation and requirements (Principles 6 to 18)

4. Methods of ongoing banking supervision (Principles 19 to 21)

5. Accounting and disclosure (Principle 22)

6. Corrective and remedial powers of supervisors (Principle 23)

7. Consolidated and cross-border banking supervision (Principles 24 and 25)

Objectives, Independence, Powers, Transparency, and Cooperation

Principle 1 – Objectives, independence, powers, transparency, and cooperation. An effective system of banking supervision will have clear responsibilities and **objectives** for each authority involved in the supervision of banks. Each such authority should possess operational **independence**, transparent processes, sound governance, and adequate resources, and be accountable for the discharge of its duties. A suitable **legal framework** for banking supervision is also necessary, including provisions relating to authorization of banking establishments and their ongoing supervision, **powers to address compliance** with laws as well as safety and soundness concerns, and **legal protection** for supervisors. Arrangements for **sharing information** between supervisors and protecting the confidentiality of such information should be in place.

Licensing and Structure

Principle 2 – Permissible activities: The permissible activities of institutions that are licensed and subject to supervision as banks must be clearly defined, and the use of the word "bank" in names should be controlled as far as possible.

Principle 3 – Licensing criteria: The licensing authority must have the power to set criteria and reject applications for establishments that do not meet the standards set. The licensing process, at a minimum, should consist of an assessment of the ownership structure and governance of the bank and its wider group, including the fitness and propriety of board members and senior management; its strategic and operating plan; internal controls and risk management; and its projected financial condition, including its capital base. Where the proposed owner or parent organization is a foreign bank, the prior consent of its home country supervisor should be obtained.

Principle 4 – Transfer of significant ownership: The supervisor has the power to review and reject any proposals to transfer significant ownership or controlling interests held directly or indirectly in existing banks to other parties.

Principle 5 – Major acquisitions: The supervisor has the power to review major acquisitions or investments by a bank, against prescribed criteria, including the establishment of cross-border operations, and confirming that corporate affiliations or structures do not expose the bank to undue risks or hinder effective supervision.

Prudential Regulation and Requirements

Principle 6 – Capital adequacy: Supervisors must set prudent and appropriate minimum capital adequacy requirements for banks that reflect the risks that the bank undertakes, and must define the components of capital, bearing in mind its ability to absorb losses. At least for internationally active banks, these requirements must not be less than those established in the applicable Basel requirement.

Principle 7 – Risk management process: Supervisors must be satisfied that banks and banking groups have in place a comprehensive risk management process (including board and senior management oversight) to identify, evaluate, monitor, and control or mitigate all material risks and to assess their overall capital adequacy in relation to their risk profile. These processes should be commensurate with the size and complexity of the institution.

Principle 8 – Credit risk: Supervisors must be satisfied that banks have a credit risk management process that takes into account the risk profile of the institution, with prudent policies and processes to identify, measure, monitor, and control credit risk (including counterparty risk). This would include the granting of loans and making of investments, the evaluation of the quality of such loans and investments, and the ongoing management of the loan and investment portfolios.

Principle 9 – Problem assets, provisions, and reserves: Supervisors must be satisfied that banks establish and adhere to adequate policies and processes for managing problem assets and evaluating the adequacy of provisions and reserves.

Principle 10 – Large exposure limits: Supervisors must be satisfied that banks have policies and processes that enable management to identify and manage concentrations within the portfolio, and supervisors must set prudential limits to restrict bank exposures to single counterparties or groups of connected counterparties.

Principle 11 – Exposures to related parties: To prevent abuses arising from exposures (both on balance sheet and off balance sheet) to related parties and to address conflict of interest, supervisors must have in place requirements that banks extend exposures to related companies and individuals on an arm's-length basis; these exposures are effectively monitored; appropriate steps are taken to control or mitigate the risks; and write-offs of such exposures are made according to standard policies and processes.

Principle 12 – Country and transfer risks: Supervisors must be satisfied that banks have adequate policies and processes for identifying, measuring, monitoring, and controlling country risk and transfer risk in their international lending and investment activities, and for maintaining adequate provisions and reserves against such risks.

Principle 13 – Market risks: Supervisors must be satisfied that banks have in place policies and processes that accurately identify, measure, monitor, and control market risks; supervisors should have powers to impose specific limits and/or a specific capital charge on market risk exposures, if warranted.

Principle 14 – Liquidity risk: Supervisors must be satisfied that banks have a liquidity management strategy that takes into account the risk profile of the institution, with prudent policies and processes to identify, measure, monitor, and control liquidity risk, and to manage liquidity on a day-to-day basis. Supervisors require banks to have contingency plans for handling liquidity problems.

Principle 15 – Operational risk: Supervisors must be satisfied that banks have in place risk management policies and processes to identify, assess, monitor, and control and mitigate operational risk. These policies and processes should be commensurate with the size and complexity of the bank.

Principle 16 – Interest rate risk in the banking book: Supervisors must be satisfied that banks have effective systems in place to identify, measure, monitor, and control interest rate risk in the banking book, including a well-defined strategy that has been approved by the board and implemented by senior management; these should be appropriate to the size and complexity of such risk.

Principle 17 – Internal control and audit: Supervisors must be satisfied that banks have in place internal controls that are adequate for the size and complexity of their business. These should include clear arrangements for delegating authority and responsibility; separation of the functions that involve committing the bank, paying away its funds, and accounting for its assets and liabilities; reconciliation of these processes; safeguarding the bank's assets; and appropriate independent internal audit and compliance functions to test adherence to these controls as well as applicable laws and regulations.

Principle 18 – Abuse of financial services: Supervisors must be satisfied that banks have adequate policies and processes in place, including strict "know-your-customer" rules, that promote high ethical and professional standards in the financial sector and prevent the bank from being used, intentionally or unintentionally, for criminal activities.

Methods of Ongoing Banking Supervision

Principle 19 – Supervisory approach: An effective banking supervisory system requires that supervisors develop and maintain a thorough understanding of the operations of individual banks and banking groups, and also of the banking system as a whole, focusing on safety and soundness and the stability of the banking system.

Principle 20 – Supervisory techniques: An effective banking supervisory system should consist of on-site and off-site supervision and regular contacts with bank management.

Principle 21 – Supervisory reporting: Supervisors must have a means of collecting, reviewing, and analyzing prudential reports and statistical returns from banks on both a solo and a consolidated basis, and a means of independent verification of these reports, through either on-site examinations or use of external experts.

Accounting and Disclosure

Principle 22 – Accounting and disclosure: Supervisors must be satisfied that each bank maintains adequate records drawn up in accordance with accounting policies and practices that are widely accepted internationally, and publishes, on a regular basis, information that fairly reflects its financial condition and profitability.

Corrective and Remedial Powers of Supervisors

Principle 23 – Corrective and remedial powers of supervisors: Supervisors must have at their disposal an adequate range of supervisory tools to bring about timely corrective actions. This includes the ability, where appropriate, to revoke the banking license or to recommend its revocation.

Consolidated and Cross-Border Banking Supervision

Principle 24 – Consolidated supervision: An essential element of banking supervision is that supervisors supervise the banking group on a consolidated basis, adequately monitoring and, as appropriate, applying prudential norms to all aspects of the business conducted by the group worldwide.

Principle 25 – Home-host relationships: Cross-border consolidated supervision requires cooperation and information exchange between home supervisors and the various other supervisors involved, primarily host banking supervisors. Banking supervisors must require the local operations of foreign banks to be conducted to the same standards as those required of domestic institutions.

Basel Committee on Banking Supervision
October 2006